WOMEN'S STUDIES QUARTERLY
VOLUME 52 NUMBERS 1 & 2 SPRING/SUMMER 2024
An educational project of the Feminist Press at the City University of New York and York College, City University of New York, with support from the Center for the Study of Women and Society and the Center for the Humanities at the Graduate Center, City University of New York

EDITORS
Shereen Inayatulla, York College, City University of New York
Andie Silva, York College, City University of New York

EDITORIAL DIRECTORS
Dána-Ain Davis and Kendra Sullivan

GUEST EDITORS
Tracey Jean Boisseau, Purdue University
Adrianna L. Ernstberger, Marian University

POETRY EDITORS
Cheryl Clarke
JP Howard
Julie R. Enszer

CREATIVE PROSE EDITORS
Keisha-Gaye Anderson
Lauren Cherelle
Vi Khi Nao

VISUAL ARTS EDITORS
Jah Elyse Sayers
Maya von Ziegesar

EDITORIAL ASSISTANTS
Jah Elyse Sayers
Maya von Ziegesar

EDITORIAL INTERN
Isabella Puentes

SOCIAL MEDIA & EVENTS MANAGER
Juwon Jun

EDITORS EMERITAE
Red Washburn 2020–2023 ▪ Brianne Waychoff 2020–2022 ▪ Natalie Havlin 2017–2020
Jillian M. Báez 2017–2020 ▪ Matt Brim 2014–2017 ▪ Cynthia Chris 2014–2017
Amy Herzog 2011–2014 ▪ Joe Rollins 2011–2014 ▪ Victoria Pitts-Taylor 2008–2011
Talia Schaffer 2008–2011 ▪ Cindi Katz 2004–2008 ▪ Nancy K. Miller 2004–2008
Diane Hope 2000–2004 ▪ Janet Zandy 1995–2000 ▪ Nancy Porter 1982–1992
Florence Howe 1972–1982; 1993–1994

The Feminist Press at the City University of New York

EXECUTIVE DIRECTOR & PUBLISHER
Margot Atwell

ART DIRECTOR
Drew Stevens

DEVELOPMENT COORDINATOR & MANAGING EDITOR
Rachel Page

WSQ: Women's Studies Quarterly, a peer-reviewed, theme-based journal, is published by the Feminist Press at the City University of New York.

COVER ART
FaceTime Series by Anna Berghuis

WEBSITE
feministpress.org/wsq
womensstudiesquarterly.com

EDITORIAL CORRESPONDENCE
WSQ: Women's Studies Quarterly, The Feminist Press at the City University of New York, The Graduate Center, 365 Fifth Avenue, Suite 5406, New York, NY 10016; wsqeditorial@gmail.com and wsqeditors@gmail.com.

PRINT SUBSCRIPTIONS
Subscribers in the United States: Individuals—$70 for 1 year; $175 for 3 years. Institutions—$99 for 1 year; $249 for 3 years. Subscribers outside the United States: Add $40 per year for delivery. To subscribe or change an address, contact *WSQ* Customer Service, The Feminist Press at the City University of New York, The Graduate Center, 365 Fifth Avenue, Suite 5406, New York, NY 10016; 212-817-7915; info@feministpress.org.

FORTHCOMING ISSUES
WSQ Unbearable Being(s), Debarati Biswas, New College of Florida, Laura Westengard, New York City College of Technology
WSQ No estamos a la intemperie: An open call, Kendra Sullivan, The Graduate Center, City University of New York, Ángeles Donoso Macaya, Borough of Manhattan Community College and The Graduate Center, City University of New York

RIGHTS & PERMISSIONS
Fred Courtright, The Permissions Company, 570-839-7477; permdude@eclipse.net.

SUBMISSION INFORMATION
For the most up-to-date guidelines, calls for papers, and information concerning forthcoming issues, write to wsqeditors@gmail.com or visit feministpress.org/wsq or womensstudiesquarterly.com.

ADVERTISING
For information on display-ad sizes, rates, exchanges, and schedules, please write to *WSQ* Marketing, The Feminist Press at the City University of New York, The Graduate Center, 365 Fifth Avenue, Suite 5406, New York, NY 10016; 212-817-7918; sales@feministpress.org.

ELECTRONIC ACCESS AND SUBSCRIPTIONS
Access to electronic databases containing backlist issues of *WSQ* may be purchased through JSTOR at www.jstor.org. Access to electronic databases containing current issues of *WSQ* may be purchased through Project MUSE at muse.jhu.edu, muse@muse.jhu.edu; and ProQuest at www.il.proquest.com, info@il.proquest.com. Individual electronic subscriptions for *WSQ* may also be purchased through Project MUSE.

Compilation copyright © 2024 by the Feminist Press at the City University of New York. Unless otherwise noted, copyright in the individual essays is held in the name of their authors.

ISSN: 0732-1562   ISBN: 978-1-55861-315-7 $30.00

EDITORIAL BOARD

Allia Abdullah-Matta, LaGuardia Community College
Linda Martín Alcoff, Hunter College and The Graduate Center, CUNY
Maria Rice Bellamy, College of Staten Island, CUNY
TJ Boisseau, Purdue University
Margot Bouman, The New School
Justin Brown, The Graduate Center, CUNY
Colette Cann, University of San Francisco
Sarah Chinn, Hunter College
Alyson Cole, The Graduate Center, CUNY
Tara L. Conley, Montclair State University
Paisley Currah, Brooklyn College
Dána-Ain Davis, Queens College and The Graduate Center, CUNY
Shelly Eversley, Baruch College CUNY
Jerilyn Fisher, Hostos Community College
Namulundah Florence, Brooklyn College
JV Fuqua, Queens College
Claudia Sofia Garriga-López, California State University
Katie Gentile, John Jay College
Gayatri Gopinath, New York University
Terri Gordon-Zolov, The New School
Christina Hanhardt, University of Maryland
Mobina Hashmi, Brooklyn College
Amy Herzog, Queens College
Heather Hewett, SUNY New Paltz
Jackie Hidalgo, Williams College
Gabrielle Hosein, University of the West Indies
Hsiao-Lan Hu, University of Detroit Mercy
Jade C. Huell, California State University, Northridge
Ren-yo Hwang, Mount Holyoke College
Crystal (Jack) Jackson, Arizona State University
Cristina Khan, SUNY Stony Brook University
Kyoo Lee, John Jay College and The Graduate Center, CUNY
Lore/tta LeMaster, Arizona State University
Heather Love, University of Pennsylvania
Karmen MacKendrick, Le Moyne College
Roopali Mukherjee, Queens College
Soniya Munshi, Borough of Manhattan Community College
Amber Jamilla Musser, The Graduate Center, CUNY
Premilla Nadasen, Barnard College
Sarah Soanirina Ohmer, Lehman College
Jackie Orr, The Maxwell School of Syracuse University
Rupal Oza, Hunter College and The Graduate Center, CUNY
Mary Phillips, Lehman College
Heather Rellihan, Anne Arundel Community College
Matt Richardson, UC Santa Barbara
Jennifer Rudolph, Connecticut College
Carolina Rupprecht, The Graduate Center, CUNY

L. Ayu Saraswati, University of Hawaiʻi
Gunja SenGupta, Brooklyn College
Barbara Shaw, Allegheny College
Lili Shi, Kingsborough Community College
Robyn Spencer, Lehman College
Saadia Toor, College of Staten Island
Laura Westengard, New York City College of Technology, CUNY
Kimberly Williams, Mount Royal University
Kimberly Williams Brown, Vassar College

INCOMING EDITORIAL BOARD (SPRING 2024)
Debarati Biswas, New York City College of Technology, CUNY
Simone Chess, Wayne State University
Ángeles Donoso Macaya, Borough of Manhattan Community College, CUNY
Emily Drabinski, Queens College, CUNY
Maria Rita Drumond Viana, Universidade Federal de Ouro Preto
Javiela Evangelista, New York City College of Technology, CUNY
Tanisha Ford, The Graduate Center, CUNY
Sean Grattan, Quincy University
Kate Haffey, University of Mary Washington
Allison Hammer, Southern Illinois University
Rashida Harrison, Michigan State University
Vani Kannan, Emory University
Sawyer Kemp, Queens College, CUNY
Jina B. Kim, Smith College
Shana MacDonald, University of Waterloo
Carolina Martins Vieira, HC-Universidade Federal de Minas Gerais
Kate Ozment, Cal Poly Pomona
Meredith Powers, York College, CUNY
Aneil Rallin, Independent Scholar
Roopika Risam, Dartmouth College
Katina L. Rogers, Inkcap Consulting
Sherita V. Roundtree, Towson University
LaToya Lydia Sawyer, St. John's University
Nina Sharma, Barnard College
Ravynn K. Stringfield, University of Richmond
Michael T. MacDonald, University of Michigan–Dearborn
Mariahadessa Tallie, Brown University
Cindy Tekobbe, University of Illinois Chicago
Stephanie Troutman Robbins, University of Arizona
Michelle Wright, Emory University
Anna Zeemont, Buffalo State University

Contents

10 **On the Cover**

13 **Editors' Note**
    Andie Silva and Shereen Inayatulla

17 **Introduction**
    Tracey Jean Boisseau and Adrianna L. Ernstberger

30 *WE WILL GET THRU THIS*
    Tracey Jean Boisseau

SECTION I. **CONVERSATIONS**

34 *Really? Really.*
    Kelle Louaillier

37 **What makes you hopeful for gender studies in Hungary, in the world?**
    Andrea Pető

49 **What happened to you in Brazil?**
    Judith Butler

67 **How did an anti-gender movement develop in Brazil?**
    James N. Green

77 **How are gender studies scholars feeling in Brazil?**
    Cristina Scheibe Wolff

85 **How should feminist studies in the United States mobilize for action?**
    Karsonya Wise Whitehead

93 **Will gender studies in Florida survive the United States' turn to the right?**
Diane Price Herndl

101 **How is anti-democratic repression affecting women's and gender studies in Turkey?**
Nurseli Yeşim Sünbüloğlu

107 **What are the challenges facing Africanist and African women's and gender studies scholars?**
Gabeba Baderoon, Maha Marouan, and Alicia Decker

117 **How are gender studies scholars resisting anti-gender politics in the United Kingdom?**
Clare Hemmings and Sumi Madhok

123 **Where are feminism and gender studies in Asia headed?**
Trimita Chakma

SECTION II. **MANIFESTOS**

130 *Exit*; *My Way Is Best*; *Shut Up*; *Are You Talking to Me?*
Cynthia Marsh

135 **Igniting Solidarities across Borders: South Feminist Futures (SFF) and the Promise of the South Feminist Manifesto**
Trimita Chakma

145 **Co-creating Inclusive Intersectional Democratic Spaces across Europe (CCINDLE): Counteracting Anti-gender through Feminist Knowledge**
Emanuela Lombardo and Paloma Caravantes

157 **SFNDHE: Feminist Scholars Demand Higher Education for All**
Eileen Boris, Aimee Loiselle, and Jennifer Mittelstadt

SECTION III. ESSAYS

168 *Bound*
Kyra Gregory

171 **Resisting the Epistemic Straight Gaze in the Anti-gender Era: Italian LGBTIQ+ Studies and Scholars, 2013–2023**
Massimo Prearo

189 **Making Gender and Sexuality Studies Illegal: Heteronationalism, Anti-gender Mobilization, and the Neoliberal "Utopian" Gaze in Bulgaria, 2018–2023**
Shaban Darakchi

209 **From the Courts, to the Streets, to the University: Fighting to Save Gender Studies in Pakistan, 2018–2023**
Rabbia Aslam

231 **Contesting Post-truth Chaos through Interdisciplinary Heterotopias**
Jeanette McVicker

251 **(Re)purposing, not "Rightsizing": Responding to Recent Attacks on Gender, Women's, and Sexuality Studies in the U.S. Academy**
Judy Rohrer

269 **Rage-ography: Rigor, Anti-wokeness, and Technoviolence**
Amy E. Slaton and Donna Riley

SECTION IV. BOOK REVIEWS

292 *Leaving*; *Suitcase Showcase—On the Move*
Jennifer Pinck

295 **Review of *Voices That Matter* by Marlene Schäfers**
Özgün Basmaz

301 **Review of *Flowers of Fire* by Hawon Jung**
Haeseong Park

305 **Review of *Fix the System, Not the Women* by Laura Bates**
Georgie Malone

309 **Review of *Feminism in Coalition* by Liza Taylor and *Healing Justice Lineages* by Cara Page and Erica Woodland**
Kimberly Williams Brown

317 **Review of *Sexual Misconduct in Academia*, edited by Erin Pritchard and Delyth Edwards**
Samantha Seybold

321 **Review of *Global Feminist Autoethnographies during COVID-19*, edited by Melanie Heath, Akosua K. Darkwah, Josephine Beoku-Betts, and Bandana Purkayastha, and *Strange and Difficult Times* by Nanjala Nyabola**
Anurekha Chari Wagh

329 **Review of *The Gendered Face of COVID-19 in the Global South* by Jean Grugel, Matt Barlow, Tallulah Lines, Maria Eugenia Giraudo, and Jessica Omukuti**
Melissa J. Buehler

333 **Review of *Rising Up, Living On* by Catherine E. Walsh**
Omi Salas-SantaCruz

339 **Review of *Public Feminisms*, edited by Carrie N. Baker and Aviva Dove-Viebahn**
Anna Hotter

SECTION V. **CREATIVE PROSE AND POETRY**

346 *isolation*
Sim Gill

349 **That Garden of Hope**
Bhavika Sicka

351 **Crazy Quilt Activism**
Elizabeth Gackstetter Nichols

357 **Pandemonium**
Debjani Chakravarty

359 **Rorschach**
Karen Morris

361 **Disposable Subjects**
Trung M. Nguyen

365 **On Pandemonium's Many Pressures**
Jennifer Schneider

367 *If You Know, You Know*; *Sunset Trip*
Jennifer Pinck

SECTION VI. **ALERTS & PROVOCATIONS**

371 **Disaster Capitalism Feeds Where Care Abandons:
A Provocation on the Case of U.S. Higher Education after COVID**
Tressie McMillan Cottom

Anna Berghuis. *FaceTime Series*, 2020. Oil on canvas, 16˝ × 20˝ each.

On the Cover

This project represents an experiment with and exploration of digital connection at a time of deepening social distancing due to the COVID-19 pandemic. Subjects sat for their portraits over FaceTime video calls that took place primarily between March and May of 2020. Amplifying the series as a snapshot in time, individual paintings are named by the date of the video call and placed in chronological order. *FaceTime Series* reveals the contradictory emotions arising during this unusual time and grapples with the idea of the highly curated and often idealized digital self.

Anna Berghuis (b. 1996) is a New York–based visual artist. Her work reckons with authenticity and performance of personality in a time of prolific image-making and sharing online. Distortion and the unreal play a large role in her figurative paintings. She received her AB in art history and studio arts from Princeton University. She has exhibited nationally in New York, Los Angeles, Miami, and Boston, and served as an inaugural resident at Long Meadow Art Residency, a four-month solo residency in the Berkshires. Her work is included in multiple private collections across the country. She can be reached at annaberghuisart.com.

Editors' Note

Andie Silva and Shereen Inayatulla

We want to begin this note by acknowledging that we live and work as immigrant settlers on Lenapehoking and to express our solidarity with Indigenous efforts to end oppression locally and globally. We understand that material action should always culminate in land back, and our acknowledgment therefore serves as a reminder to keep the struggle for collective liberation at the forefront of our daily lives.

It is worthy of mention that we are writing this land acknowledgment and editors' note in the early days of 2024, and we wish to emphasize that it has now been several months since the contributions in this issue were completed. This lapse in time feels significant. At present, we find ourselves navigating profoundly mixed emotions related to a sustainable sociopolitical future. Yet, we hold dearly to visions of a world in which social and environmental justice are centered as tenets within the tireless collective pursuit of liberation. This vision is propelled by the revolutionary work of feminist thinkers—those included in this special issue and beyond—whose capacity for transforming hostile living conditions toward an equitable future is indomitable.

This special issue, *Pandemonium*, reflects upon the ever-increasing attacks on women's, gender, and sexuality studies (WGS) programs and scholars on both micro and macro scales. The feminist labor, scholarship, and art encompassed in the pages ahead reflect a broad range of interventional activism, showcasing the myriad strategies employed to resist erasure and fight for social justice. As guest editors Tracey Jean Boisseau and Adrianna L. Ernstberger so poignantly describe in their introduction, while we must face the deeply damaging and long-lasting effects of recent far-right attacks, we may also find hope in the extent to which these attacks have galvanized feminist movements and prompted the formation of stalwart global coalitions. This issue is poised to serve as a valuable resource for readers invested in documenting and joining efforts to not just secure but reimagine the future of WGS within and beyond academic spaces.

In particular, we appreciate this issue's framing of feminist praxis as a conversation both literally, as we see in the first section, and figuratively, through the manifestos, reviews, and artwork that follow. *Pandemonium* demonstrates the immeasurable value of placing affect, human experience, and ethnographic memory at the center of feminist struggles. We are moved by the personal reflections that guide the issue, exemplified so powerfully in Dr. Tressie McMillan Cottom's concluding essay, which highlights care and wellness as forms of feminist labor that are too often downplayed or ignored.

The title of this special issue reminds us that we are still in the midst of an unprecedented health crisis, which disproportionately burdens the global majority that is BIPOC, disabled, and poor populations. It is impossible to gloss over the lives being robbed by the pandemic and the relentless grief rooted in such loss. These irreversible tragedies are the markings of a virus taking hold under already oppressive conditions. The very fact that *Pandemonium* emerges from this horrifying shared reality reaffirms feminist-led efforts for equity and justice, reminding us also to resist universalizing approaches to our labor and activism. While it is crucial that we remain engaged in social coalition at the local level, we cannot survive and thrive without finding ways to center and amplify global knowledges, aspirations, and care networks. This issue demonstrates that the path to building a safe, equitable future must be anchored in what Trimita Chakma's manifesto beautifully describes as "solidarities across borders."

We would like to express our gratitude to the guest editors of *Pandemonium*, Tracey Jean Boisseau and Adrianna L. Ernstberger, for materializing their brilliant vision in the pages of this issue. The labor they poured into planning, synthesizing, and editing this issue is truly commendable. Thank you to each and every contributor for sharing their work with *WSQ* audiences and to all of the reviewers of the pieces included here. We are continually grateful to the team at Feminist Press for their attention to detail at the level of production and distribution. In particular, we wish to thank editorial director Lauren Rosemary Hook, executive director Margot Atwell, and development coordinator/managing editor Rachel Page. Thank you also to director of community engagement Lucia Brown for ensuring each *WSQ* issue reaches a wide audience through social media promotion.

As always, we are incredibly grateful to the *WSQ* editorial assistants, Maya von Ziegesar, Googie Karrass, and Jah Elyse Sayers, for their steadfast labor, patience, and agility in balancing countless demands at once. A million thanks to the editorial directors, Kendra Sullivan (Center for the Humanities) and Dána-Ain Davis (Center for the Study of Women and Society), for offering continued support and strategies that help us navigate institutional intricacies on an ongoing basis. Thank you to the *WSQ* editorial board, whose intersectional, multidisciplinary perspectives help shape the journal, to the poetry, creative prose, and visual arts editors for providing thoughtful insights, and to Juwon Jun and Samson Starkweather for their expertise on planning issue launches in the absence of a budget. Lastly, we are grateful to our home institution, York College, CUNY, for exhibiting enthusiastic support, and to our ever-inspiring students, whose creative brilliance shapes the revolutionary and lasting future of our dreams.

Shereen Inayatulla
Professor of English
York College
City University of New York

Andie Silva
Associate Professor of English
York College
City University of New York

Introduction

Tracey Jean Boisseau and Adrianna L. Ernstberger

"Women Studies Departments in Indian Universities Face Threat of Closure," *Policy Studies* (blog), July 24, 2017.[1]
"For Scholars of Women's Studies, It's Been a Dangerous Year," *The Chronicle*, February 11, 2018.[2]
"From Kabul to Budapest, You Can Ban Gender Studies but You Can't Silence Us," *Euronews*, October 10, 2018.[3]
"Hungary's PM Bans Gender Study at Colleges Saying 'People Are Born Either Male or Female,'" *CNN*, October 19, 2018.[4]
"Global Attack on Gender Studies," *Inside Higher Ed*, December 4, 2018.[5]
"Academic Feminists Beware: Bolsonaro Is Out to Crush Brazil's 'Gender Ideology,'" *The Loop*, October 16, 2020.[6]
"How Covid-19 Is Devastating Women's Studies Programs across the U.S.," *Ms. Magazine*, December 3, 2020.[7]
"Women Studies Scholars Worry Their Programs Are at Risk for Being Cut amid Tightening Budgets," *Diverse Issues in Higher Education*, March 4, 2021.[8]
"Did 'Gender Studies' Lose Afghanistan?," *The Spectator*, August 19, 2021.[9]
"First, the Book-Banners Came for CRT and LGBTQ. Now They're Censoring Women's History: Wyoming Moves to Ban Gender Studies, Further Bringing GOP in Line with Russia's and Hungary's Authoritarian Crackdown," *Salon*, March 1, 2022.[10]
"Parents Are Going on Offensive to Fight Indoctrination in Education," Heritage Foundation, April 27, 2022.[11]
"Political Attacks on Women's Studies at Kuwait University Increase Scholars' Resolve," *Al-Fanar Media*, May 7, 2022.[12]

"Turkey Funds Women's Groups to Counter 'Feminist Threat': Government-Operated Women's Organizations Are Drowning Out Genuine Feminist Voices in Turkey," *openDemocracy*, May 20, 2022.[13]

"How an LGBTQ Court Ruling Sent Kenya into a Moral Panic," *Al Jazeera*, March 15, 2023.[14]

"Florida Legislation Threatens Gender Studies and Intersectionality: What Does It Mean?," *USA Today*, April 19, 2023.[15]

"Professor, Two Students Stabbed in Gender Studies Class at Canadian University," *Los Angeles Times*, June 29, 2023.[16]

"'Gender' Is at the Core of Attacks on Democracy in the U.S. and Abroad," *Ms. Magazine*, July 18, 2023.[17]

The cacophony of media and news is so loud we only hear their buzzing nonsense.

There's so much noise we can't hear ourselves think or speak.

So many trees we can't see the forest or a path we might take out of it.

WSQ: Pandemonium cuts a swath through the clamorous forest of news media to locate a clearing in its midst for generative contemplation regarding the state of our field. Here, we stage a festival of our own making. Leading the way is a parade of academic feminist voices documenting and reflecting on the tumultuous upheaval we are experiencing and pointing us in a collective direction. Rather than simply denying the confusion of our moment or plugging our ears to the noise produced by those who seek to diminish, demonize, or dismantle us, *Pandemonium* offers a forum for us to air our concerns and hear one another's stories. Included within are as many tales of triumph as tribulation. This is a party, not a wake.

Pandemonium returns *Women's Studies Quarterly* to its roots dug half a century ago, when, as its golden jubilee anniversary issue (*WSQ: 50!*) attests, it started as a newsletter for women's studies practitioners, scholars, educators, and readers. The goal was not merely to serve as an organ for the dissemination of our research. The original purpose animating the creators of the newsletter was to knit our discipline into being by giving us the tools and opportunity to talk to each other about what was happening in our own monodisciplines, in our institutions, with our research and teaching, in our careers, and in solidarity with our students at the interface between the academy and the "real" world of feminist struggle, radicalism, and activism. Our right-wing "anti-woke" and "anti-gender" adversaries are correct in one way at least: self-consciously intentional and self-reflective from the outset in the 1970s, the discipline of women's studies was never merely about creating yet another area of research and abstruse academic knowledge to add to the traditional fields represented in the university of old. Changing the academy to include women, "adding women" to traditional scholarship and "stirring" it up, was only the first step. We were always committed to changing the world and using the academy as foothold, harbor, and refueling station for ourselves as individual feminist changemakers; as incubator, crèche, and farmland for our community to germinate and grow that change. In the 1980s we organized ourselves into a politicized collective of feminist academics. In the 1990s our field redefined gender as a formation of power and broadened the scope of our commitment to women as traditionally defined to center and celebrate nonnormative genders and sexual identities. Since 2000 we have revolutionized the field's theorization of scholarship as intersectional, transnational, and anti-colonial feminist praxis. With *Pandemonium*, in this time of unprecedented poly-crisis, we have put these accumulated strengths and enlarged set of skills to work on the task of stitching ourselves as a community back together after three years of pandemic and mayhem, gathering ourselves once more into a self-consciously political collective, and turning our faces toward the political storms raging all around us. We invite readers to face head-on the pandemonium taking place outside and inside the academy and at the perforated boundary line between the two—turbulence that threatens our discipline and the half century of gendered revolution it has helped give birth to. However, and despite those ominous headlines above, we promise the news we have to report is anything but all bad—not by a mile.

Though this issue is not without order, rhyme, or rhythm, the forms the contents take are unorthodox. Unlike most academic journal issues, *Pandemonium* does not consist primarily of a collection of articles, each conveying research conducted over many years on a set of discrete topics centered within a particular established subfield of our discipline. There's limited opportunity to research what we are experiencing, or even to develop the methodologies we would need to study these experiences. How many of us put contemporary analysis of our own discipline at the center of our research or teaching? From a purely formalist perspective, one would say very few of us are scholarly experts on even the *history* of our field; virtually no one is an expert on what is happening to it in real time, everywhere. Looked at another way, from an autoethnographic and experientialist perspective, we are *all* experts—at least experts on the respective corners of the world of gender studies that we respectively inhabit—and only need to combine our perspectives and collectivize our voices to gain an appreciation of the whole. The special issue editors have taken the latter approach, putting our contributors in dialogue with one another and offering their work to readers as not so much secondary as primary sources that, if read collectively and through one another, produce a discernible snapshot of the state of the field at this moment in time—a moment we suspect represents a genuine watershed.

While most academic journal issues are designed with the expectation that readers will seek out an individual article based on their particular scholarly field of expertise, topic of interest, or teaching subject, we encourage a holistic reading of the issue by arranging it as a flow of discussion. Indeed, many of the issue's major contributions take the form of conversations the special issue editors conducted with leaders, scholars, activists, and practitioners of our discipline located around the world in hot spots of controversy or directly embroiled in political, ideological, and intellectual struggles over nonconformist, white supremacist, neocolonial, and patriarchal ideas about race, gender, and sexuality. The contribution these individuals made to those conversations supply immediate insight into the discipline's struggle for existence in places where neoliberal austerity excuses, amplified by the COVID-19 pandemic and in combination with the rise of authoritarianism, have generated serious threats taking the form of both legal and extralegal direct attacks. *Pandemonium* proudly refuses to sideline the spontaneity of insight afforded by freewheeling expression or dispense with the immediacy and urgency of personal experience. Though a deep engagement with long-standing historiographies and scholarly literatures informs the insights proffered by both interviewees and authors, admittedly readers will find more testimony than test results, more discernment than data analysis, more recounting and reconnoitering than referencing.

The first person whom readers will hear from in Section I: Conversations is Hungarian historian of European political extremism and the Holocaust, as well as fearless gender studies advocate, Andrea Pető. We interviewed her in June of 2023 from her new academic home in Central European University. "What makes you hopeful about gender studies in Hungary, in the world?" supplies critical historical perspective on the history of gender studies as a radical and revolutionary project, only dimmed—as Pető sees it—by its overly comfortable sequestration in a hopelessly illiberal and corporatized academy. Her vision of a more vibrant, relevant, politically engaged, and thriving discipline, following from its decertification by the Hungarian state and expulsion from universities elsewhere, exemplifies the vision and inspiration it will take to grow and revolutionize our field.

Judith Butler, widely recognized as among the most influential thinkers in our discipline, in "What happened to you in Brazil?" reflects on their experience at a prodemocracy academic conference held in Brazil in 2017 when the right wing whipped up an extremist populist protest against them. In their recounting of being physically menaced at the airport and seeing their effigy burned and raped in the streets, Butler explains how they became, in that moment, the face of "gender ideology" as targeted by the anti-gender movement in Brazil. They further elaborate more generally on the ways that anti-LGBTQIA+ hysteria has become a part of a larger form of extremist antidemocratic nationalism and authoritarianism sweeping across much of our world today.

Bringing our discussion back to Brazil and helping us to understand the specific complexities of Brazilian politics and history that produced such extremism directed against sexual and gender minorities, James N. Green, foremost historian of Brazil and longtime activist and organizer for gay rights, contextualizes the 2017 incident with Judith Butler. In "How did an anti-gender movement develop in Brazil?," Green takes us through the historical emergence of LGBT rights and the rise of an anti-gender movement targeting individuals and dovetailing with a long history of anti-leftist campaigns in Brazil and Latin America as a whole. Following Green, Cristina Scheibe Wolff, professor of history at Federal University in Santa Catarina in Brazil, gives us a view from inside the Brazilian academy of how feminist work continues to be done in support of gay, trans, and women's movements. She describes the status of gender studies as a discipline in today's Brazil and since the end of the Bolsonaro presidency. In response to our question "How are gender studies scholars feeling in Brazil?," Wolff evaluates the effects of the past ten years of the anti-gender movement. Like Pető, Wolff views political repression as having a paradoxical effect on women's, gender, and sexuality studies in Brazil—at once destabilizing and invigorating the field beyond both her most dire *and* sanguine of expectations.

From Brazil, we move north to try to understand the controversies and conflicts bedeviling women's, gender, and sexuality studies in the United States. Karsonya Wise Whitehead, former president of the National Women's Studies Association and founding director of the Karson Institute for Race, Peace, and Social Justice, responds to our question "How should feminist studies in the United States mobilize for action?" with a fervent call for feminist scholars to "lean into" political engagement not only on their campuses and at the national level but also in local contexts, particularly prekindergarten through twelfth-grade public education. In response to our question "Will gender studies in Florida survive the United States' turn to the right?," Diane Price Herndl, chair of the Department of Women's, Gender, and Sexuality Studies at the University of South Florida, walks us through resistance strategies and evasive tactics she employs to navigate the vicious racist and anti-feminist attacks on gender and critical race studies in a state that one might say sits at the eye of the storm that is "anti-wokeism" in the U.S.

Next the conversation leaps eastward across the Atlantic to engage Nurseli Yeşim Sünbüloğlu, professor of sociology and director of the Women and Family Studies Research Center at Kadir Has University in Istanbul, Turkey. In response to our question "How is antidemocratic repression affecting women's and gender studies in Turkey?," Sünbüloğlu starts with an explanation of her center's recent name change from the Gender and Women's Research Center to the Women and Family Studies Research Center—a change made at the behest of the Higher Education Council in Turkey this past year. After unpacking the politics involved in that name change, she ends by sharing with us the robust resistance and strategies Turkish intellectuals and feminist scholars have developed over a long history of top-down repression.

Moving south to Africa and radiating outward from the African continent to encompass the diaspora of African scholars and feminist academics located throughout the world, we learned about a new collective of academics—the African Feminist Initiative (AFI)—seeking to forge connections and collaborations through the creation of a new virtual platform. We spoke with AFI's leadership and founding members, Maha Marouan, Gabeba Baderoon, and Alicia Decker, about the particular issues and challenges facing African and Africanist feminist scholars on the continent and around the world both during the pandemic and since. A similar collaboration—the Transnational "Anti-gender" Movements and Resistance network—has recently formed by way of a series of international conferences organized by Clare Hemmings and Sumi Madhok, both based in the United Kingdom. They provide an overview of how anti-gender public narratives and legislation is attempting to hem in the discipline of gender studies in the U.K.

feminist, women's and gender, LGBT and queer, postcolonial, critical race and intersectional studies. It will only be through collective organizing and solidarity with others within and beyond our campuses that we salvage our discipline from the wreckage wrought by the neoliberal, illiberal, white supremacist, neocolonial, and neofascist forces that seek to hollow out or poison the twenty-first-century academy, alongside other public institutions and much of our physical world. This issue provides a glimpse of the organizing that is happening within and at the interface between our discipline and governing bodies all over the globe, and in its most transnational spaces. Though in no way comprehensive, *Pandemonium* gathers together some of the wisdom that our field's most influential leaders, committed advocates, and resolved activists have to share. By showcasing their visionary ideas, tactics of resistance, and collectivizing strategies, we intend to help protect and strengthen a discipline that serves as our "foothold, harbor, and refueling station" in the academy as well as an intellectual "incubator, crèche, and farmland" able to grow into being the just world we wish to live in. Our hope is that this issue contributes even a small bit of scaffolding to support the ongoing collective feminist project that is our discipline.

If there's one single message that animates this issue, it is that old saw we see at the end of so many of our signatures these days: we are the leaders that we've been looking for. We thank the many champions of our field who have contributed their voices and visions to *Pandemonium*; the senior editors of *WSQ* and Feminist Press staff, especially Maya von Ziegesar, for shepherding the issue into existence; and most of all our readers for linking arms with us to forge a way forward.

Tracey Jean Boisseau is a historian and associate professor as well as former director of women's, gender, and sexuality studies at Purdue University. Coeditor of *Feminist Legal History*, *Gendering the Fair*, and a special issue of the *NWSA Journal*, Boisseau is also author of *White Queen* (Indiana University Press, 2004) and more than two dozen interdisciplinary articles and chapters on the historical and transnational production of feminist identity. She can be reached at tjboisseau@purdue.edu.

Adrianna L. Ernstberger is assistant professor of history and chair of the Department of History and Global Studies at Marian University in Indianapolis, Indiana. She received her doctoral degree in global history from Purdue in 2017. She researches the social, political, and institutional history of transnational women's movements, with special focus on the Global South and the history of the development of women's and gender studies. She can be reached at aernstberger@marian.edu.

Notes

1. Geentanjali Ganjoli, "Women Studies Departments in Indian Universities Face Threat of Closure," *Policy Studies* (blog), July 24, 2017, https://policystudies.blogs.bristol.ac.uk/2017/07/24/women-studies-departments-in-indian-universities-face-threat-of-closure/.
2. Emma Kerr, "For Scholars of Women's Studies, It's Been a Dangerous Year," *The Chronicle*, February 11, 2018, https://www.chronicle.com/article/for-scholars-of-womens-studies-its-been-a-dangerous-year/.
3. Sahar Fetrat, "From Kabul to Budapest, You Can Ban Gender Studies but You Can't Silence Us," *Euronews*, October 10, 2018, https://www.euronews.com/2018/10/25/from-kabul-to-budapest-you-can-ban-gender-studies-but-you-can-t-silence-us-view.
4. Lauren Kent and Samantha Tapfumaneyi, "Hungary's PM Bans Gender Study at Colleges Saying 'People Are Born Either Male or Female,'" *CNN*, October 19, 2018, https://www.cnn.com/2018/10/19/europe/hungary-bans-gender-study-at-colleges-trnd/index.html.
5. Elizabeth Redden, "Global Attack on Gender Studies," *Inside Higher Ed*, December 4, 2018, https://www.insidehighered.com/news/2018/12/05/gender-studies-scholars-say-field-coming-under-attack-many-countries-around-globe.
6. Fernanda Barasuol, "Academic Feminists Beware: Bolsonaro Is Out to Crush Brazil's 'Gender Ideology,'" *The Loop*, October 16, 2020, https://theloop.ecpr.eu/academic-feminists-beware-bolsonaro-is-out-to-crush-brazils-gender-ideology/.
7. Jennifer Ash, "How Covid-19 Is Devastating Women's Studies Programs across the U.S.," *Ms. Magazine*, December 3, 2020, https://msmagazine.com/2020/12/03/how-covid-19-is-devastating-womens-studies-programs-across-the-u-s/.
8. Sara Weissman, "Women Studies Scholars Worry Their Programs Are at Risk for Being Cut amid Tightening Budgets," *Diverse Issues in Higher Education*, March 4, 2021, https://www.diverseeducation.com/demographics/women/article/15108728/women-studies-scholars-worry-their-programs-are-at-risk-for-being-cut-amid-tightening-budgets.
9. Cockburn, "Did 'Gender Studies' Lose Afghanistan?," *The Spectator*, August 19, 2021, https://thespectator.com/topic/did-gender-studies-lose-afghanistan/.
10. Amanda Marcotte, "First, the Book-Banners Came for CRT and LGBTQ. Now They're Censoring Women's History: Wyoming Moves to Ban Gender Studies, Further Bringing GOP in Line with Russia's and Hungary's Authoritarian Crackdown," *Salon*, March 1, 2022, https://www.salon.

com/2022/03/01/first-the-book-banners-came-for-crt-and-lgbtq-now-theyre-censoring-womens-history/.
11. John Schoof, "Parents Are Going on Offensive to Fight Indoctrination in Education," Heritage Foundation, April 27, 2022, https://www.heritage.org/education/commentary/parents-are-going-offensive-fight-indoctrination-education.
12. Amr EL-Tohamy, "Political Attacks on Women's Studies at Kuwait University Increase Scholars' Resolve," Al-Fanar Media, May 7, 2022, https://www.al-fanarmedia.org/2022/05/political-attacks-on-womens-studies-at-kuwait-university/.
13. Anna Ehrhart, "Turkey Funds Women's Groups to Counter 'Feminist Threat': Government-Operated Women's Organizations Are Drowning Out Genuine Feminist Voices in Turkey," *openDemocracy*, May 20, 2022, https://www.opendemocracy.net/en/5050/turkey-women-gongos-attack-feminists/.
14. "How an LGBTQ Court Ruling Sent Kenya into a Moral Panic," *Al Jazeera*, March 15, 2023, https://www.aljazeera.com/opinions/2023/3/15/how-an-lgbtq-court-ruling-sent-kenya-into-a-moral-panic.
15. Stephany Matat, "Florida Legislation Threatens Gender Studies and Intersectionality: What Does It Mean?," *USA Today*, April 19, 2023, https://www.usatoday.com/story/news/education/2023/04/19/desantis-gop-attacks-on-woke-gender-studies-rattles-professors-students/11690683002/.
16. Associated Press, "Professor, Two Students Stabbed in Gender Studies Class at Canadian University," *Los Angeles Times*, June 29, 2023, https://www.latimes.com/world-nation/story/2023-06-29/professor-students-stabbed-gender-studies-class-canada-university.
17. Alexandria Wilson-McDonald, "'Gender' Is at the Core of Attacks on Democracy in the U.S. and Abroad," *Ms. Magazine*, July 18, 2023, https://msmagazine.com/2023/07/18/gender-florida-lgbtq-abortion-women-czech-republic-slovakia-poland/.

Tracey Jean Boisseau is a historian of feminism and associate professor of women's, gender, and sexuality studies at Purdue University. She lives in Damariscotta—a coastal village in mid-coast Maine—where she took the photo *WE WILL GET THRU THIS* during the first month of the pandemic soon after all businesses in the village shut down, including the local community theater directly across the street from her home that had added this hopeful sign in lieu of the usual list of coming attractions. She can be reached at tjboisseau@purdue.edu.

Tracey Jean Boisseau. *WE WILL GET THRU THIS*, 2020. Photograph.

SECTION I. **CONVERSATIONS**

Kelle Louaillier is president emeritus of the progressive NGO Corporate Accountability. She currently provides strategic and process consulting and coaching to organizations, consortiums, leaders, and on key issues. Now residing on Cape Ann in Massachusetts, she is also a mixed media artist. She can be reached at kelle.lou@gmail.com or on Instagram @kl_undertaking.

Kelle Louaillier, *Really? Really.* 2023. Mixed media on wood panel, 14˝ x 16˝.

I woke up today. I saw myself. I asked, "Really?" and answered, "Really."

Or maybe it was you I was looking at?

My artistic practice is simply to create every day, using that which moves, sparks, speaks to, challenges, or entices me.

What makes you hopeful for gender studies in Hungary, in the world?
A conversation with Andrea Pető

Andrea Pető is a historian and professor in the Department of Gender Studies at Central European University in Vienna, Austria. She is also a research affiliate of the CEU Democracy Institute in Budapest, Hungary, and a doctor of science of the Hungarian Academy of Sciences. Her publications on gender, politics, the Holocaust, and war have been translated into twenty-three languages. In 2018 she was awarded the All European Academies (ALLEA) Madame de Staël Prize for Cultural Values, and in 2022 the University of Oslo Human Rights Award. She is doctor honoris causa of Södertörn University, Stockholm, Sweden. Recent publications include *The Women of the Arrow Cross Party: Invisible Hungarian Perpetrators in the Second World War* (2020) and *The Forgotten Massacre: Budapest in 1944* (2021). She can be reached at petoa@ceu.edu.

Editors of Pandemonium *spoke with Andrea Pető on June 12, 2023.*

What is unique in the Hungarian situation is that, in 2017, when the attack started on gender studies, it was not clear how this would end. But there's a fantastic Russian saying: when you think you are at the bottom, somebody's already knocking from below.

Things can always get worse.

What is unique in the Hungarian context is that our two-year MA program had just been accredited by the Central European University in 2004—and that was the first acknowledgment, really, of gender studies as a real discipline. For over ten years it was taught in English at a private American university where the students were getting fellowships. The next real game changer came in 2017 when, after several years, one of the public universities in Hungary submitted a request to initiate a teaching program in gender studies, to be conducted in Hungarian, in the public university system, asking for recognition that the faculty and the resources exist to teach it as part of a consortium of faculties in Hungary. This use of taxpayers' money and the blackmailing potential that comes with it, especially by a state captured by illiberals, was when the whole calamity started. A year later, without any explanation or any kind of dialogue, the whole program was canceled, and we were back to zero, deleted from the accredited study list. This is an important story because it shows how a field of study can be so easily delegitimized.

Probably you have seen that, more recently, in Romania there was also an attempt to delete gender studies, but the Parliament decided not to ratify that proposed legislation. So, in a sense, the Hungarian case is symptomatic because you have got the whole spectrum, the whole spectrum of attacks on gender studies.

It starts with attacking individuals who are more visible and active in public life, those who are publishing and giving interviews. Among others, I was one of those who had been attacked and put on the cover of the national newspapers as an enemy of the nation.

After this public attack, there was a kind of legal counterrevolution, which I don't need to explain to you in the U.S. They were using all possible legal methods to eliminate gender studies, and then came the moment when gender studies headed back to the point where it was before its institutionalization. So, turning time back, like, twenty years.

But the situation is much better than twenty years ago because these twenty years haven't been lost. Those twenty years earned certain achievements, and not only that, but several colleagues also now have degrees in our field. Luckily, none of the colleagues who have been teaching in those gender studies programs have been imprisoned, killed, or fired, as they have been in Russia, Turkey, and other places. So these colleagues are teaching, often, the same courses as they were teaching in the program that was accredited, only now they are doing so without the accreditation, even if now these courses count towards different degrees. Of course, university administrators are extremely conscientious about deleting possible references from gender studies from the visible descriptions of these courses.

Probably you have read the article "Disputing 'Gender' in Academia" in *Politics and Governance* I published with Yasmine Ergas, Jazgul Kochkorova, and Natalia Trujillo (2022). We identified four strategies of the ways illiberal governments have attacked gender studies in recent years. One is breaking.

That's what you see in Hungary. There is also a ban, which is using existing strategies. For example, you know, it accidentally turns out that you don't get funding or whatever resources you need, but it's not done outside the existing legal framework. And then there is the forging of laws—this is when they are creating new legal frameworks to make sure that gender studies is not able to function. And the last one is the most interesting. In Hungary, you don't find gender studies anymore, right? But what you can find is "family studies" or "women's studies" because of the de-specification. The third strategy to kill gender studies comes in two parts: One is the self-censorship applied by professionals as a survival strategy. So, you know, some gender studies faculty are simply not mentioning gender in their applications for funding or employment, but they are doing the same work they would have done before the de-specification. And now colleagues in Hungary have lots of state money going to support the so-called discipline of family studies. Some gender studies scholars have simply rebranded themselves to become "family studies" scholars. This is a strategy that colleagues in Russia, in Serbia, and in Turkey are applying to survive, and this produces very valuable scholarship.

Illiberal politics may be instrumentalizing the same concepts, but they are also emptying them of genuine political meaning and they are handpicking certain academics who are ready to play the role of the killer of these ideas. Luckily, in Hungary we don't see this particular strategy as much, this sort of "discourse capture," but that's probably because there are very few academics who are ready at the moment to play along with this game plan of the illiberal government.

Indeed, in Hungary, as far as the numbers are concerned, gender studies has never been so popular as it is now. The different programs have never had so many applicants as now. Gender studies has become cool! The best example is the Hungarian Sociological Association, which since 1998 has had a section called the "Feminist Section." I was the president of this section starting in 1998. But, you see, at this time and in this era, the left-liberal wing of the association was disinterested in gender studies. They did not want to be branded as "feminists"—feminists were not perceived as true leftists. But now it turns out that the young generation has reinvigorated this section of the Hungarian Sociological Association, and more than forty people are paying the hefty membership fee to participate in the Feminist Section. Probably because they already gave up the idea of making a career and, now, it does not matter if they are labeled "feminists" or not—not anymore. Before the illiberal take-over, being branded as a feminist was a problem, it was not at all a good ticket in the labor market.

So, yes, if you ask me how gender studies is doing in Hungary, the short answer is "bad," but the longer answer is that it's actually doing very well! And that's why I think we have a really *good* story to tell right now.

Not that we are not being targeted—of course we are. And to establish a program, well, yes, you must have accreditation, and then you must have an accreditation protocol to be able to teach in an accredited program. So when they deleted the *accredited* teaching program, they deleted the foundation of the program essentially. So that's why nobody is getting a degree in gender studies in Hungary right now. There is a *certificate* program in gender studies in the case of secondary teacher education, which is for teachers of foreign languages like English, but that's it. There is also a gender studies research center at Corvinus University, which is related to the subject of gender and work. But, as far as accredited gender studies, that's all we've got left.

No, I don't see, in the future, a new accreditation process being resurrected under this illiberal regime, because the Hungarian Accreditation Committees are just morally corrupt. I wrote a peer-reviewed academic article in English to be published in the *Berichte zur Wissenschaftsgeschichte* about academic authorization in illiberal states and then I was expected to withdraw the article following an order of the president of the Hungarian Accreditation Committee. So then I had to resign as I was not assisting with censorship.

But even with our de-specification, I would say that gender studies in Hungary is doing very well because of the professoriate, the scholarly faculty, that now exists and works in Hungary. That certainly did not exist twenty-five years ago. And because of how "cool" we have become. We are at the pressure point of politics in Hungary, and not only the young but the left no longer sees us as a silly, unimportant political group.

Honestly, I don't think the attacks by illiberal governments matter, because we don't need an *accredited* gender studies program, and anyway, there are no jobs in academia or public administration because, of course, the Hungarian government is not complying with any European requirements or guidelines concerning equity and justice requirements, at least as far as gender equality is concerned. I mean, the Hungarian government produces alibi documents about gender equality to qualify for European Union funding, which is, of course, tied to gender equality policies, but those gender equality policies are just not being implemented in Hungary anyway. It is all empty proxy gender policy, which also means that there is no need for academics like us to be employed in government to help make or carry out real policies aimed at achieving gender equity.

So, I mean, what is the purpose of gender studies in higher education in Hungary? What is the purpose of higher education itself? That's a big question, but in the case of gender studies, you know, are you aiming to produce more academics who are teaching more academics? Or are you aiming to train those who are going into policymaking, government jobs, and also NGO activists, meaning those people who are making changes in society? That's what you have now in Hungary because the two other avenues are closed, therefore you see lots of activists and lots of academics who don't have the chance to get a position in gender studies in the academy.

Now they are studying these courses and they are researching this—why? Because they think it's important! And, now, that's the only reason why they are doing so. And, I mean, that's the basis. That's the energy. That's what makes gender studies interesting and thriving. The reason to study and teach is that there is a social need for teaching and for research. Now the field is rooted in wide-ranging interest and popular support for gender studies.

It is clear to me that we gender studies professionals are getting important now *because* we are being attacked. *Because* we are getting attacked, suddenly we get respect from our so-called political allies. For example, again, the leadership of the Hungarian Sociological Association, which was working in the 1990s and 2002 and even in 2010, were all saying, "Oh sure, yeah, of course, let the women have their separate section. But, c'mon, let's talk about important issues." They were our allies in principle, but they became our allies in practice only when the attacks started, and they realized that gender studies is the site of the New Cold War.

This is elite failure and sleepwalking into a new age! They haven't seen or did not want to see that what was happening with gender studies was the litmus test of academic freedom and free scientific inquiry. Now, of course, it's too late to support us, to prevent us from being canceled from the university. It is truly funny that the illiberal politics that is supposedly protecting freedom of speech uses canceling so very efficiently against progressive academics.

But on the other hand, there is this new and increasing interest from the students too. Students are coming in saying, "I want to study gender!" Here in Hungary, gender studies has become a really popular science. Everybody has heard about gender studies now, right? That wasn't true even ten years ago. So the mainstreaming of gender studies happened *because* of the attacks on liberal values and because gender studies was at the forefront of that attack.

This kind of "paradoxical recognition," to use Éric Fassin's term, is extremely useful—extremely so. It is, in fact, a fantastic political opportunity for us. But that depends on us gender studies professors. We need to ask: how can we use this opportunity?

There are several differences between Hungary and the United States which come into play here. First of all, no matter if you are teaching in a community college or a research university, the living standard and the job security of gender studies faculty in the U.S. is much, much higher than in Eastern Europe. Of course, I have no illusions about precarity, but at least there are jobs there in the field as of today. So, in a sense, of course, you know, if you are earning a six-digit salary, you are going to be more concerned about your job and you don't see alternatives where you can earn such a salary. And that's just true. So salary is going to be the first thing you are worried about. You must be, certainly.

But in Central Europe and especially in Hungary, there was a very strong anti-communist democratic tradition, and there was always an alternative to the dominant hegemonic educational system, not only during communism but also in the years after. There were always several initiatives—a kind of "people's colleges" to help the poor but talented youngsters from the provinces. Or, during communist times, there were "flying universities," which were conducted in apartments of those who were not allowed to teach in state universities because of political reasons. You earn your living somewhere and them you think about important issues somewhere else. And, of course, I'm one of the products of this flying university, because I'm that old. There we were, you know, in kitchens, drinking enormous amounts of tea and discussing very important texts, and nobody was interested in the number of student credit hours, the "deliverables," or the teaching "outcomes." This managerial higher-educational language has taken over state-run universities, so I would say that this is the time for us to look for alternative spaces again. And to find resources to create alternative institutions.

I'm not sure that this neoliberalized higher education is a salvageable institutional format. There are more administrators than teachers or students, and stressed or extremely stressed students, and our university has maybe eleven full-time psychologists for twelve hundred students. Sure, the psychology counseling department is bigger than many other departments, because they want to keep these stressed students functioning, but the question remains, I mean, *why do we want to keep these students functioning?* Why attract all these students at all? I mean, they are facing unrealistic expectations about jobs that are out there, that they think they are being trained for. Meanwhile, they are not even enjoying the intellectual life of a university, even. When you lose the joy of doing intellectual work, you become a zombie. We are surrounded by zombies who look like humans, but they are not; they look like intellectuals, but they are not; they look like professionals, but they are just, you know, craftspersons—at best. They turned something intellectual and real into vocational training—even when there was no vocation at the other end. This kind of downward spiraling of neoliberal higher education is one of the main problems, and that also explains why *illiberal* higher education is so popular because the *illiberal* higher education is based on the mistakes and the cracks of *neoliberal* higher education.

Really, if you look at what is being established in the wake of all this—there is this new alternative institution in Budapest, for example, the Mathias Corvinus College. If you look at the design of the programs of these universities, they are personalized; they have small classes, direct access to the professors who are teaching things that matter, like human rights, international relations, and social work. Topics that are directly channeled to practical life. And they are training secondary school teachers who are bringing this knowledge to the people.

So, in a sense, of course, a tenured academic in New York would never imagine that there are other such institutions or could imagine giving up the holy grail of a tenured position for something so uncertain. But, in the part of the world I'm coming from, this holy grail had always been a kind of mixed blessing, because it was shameful during communism if you had tenure. Believe me, you had to pay a serious personal and political price for that position! And now here we are again in illiberal times when the state has been captured by illiberal forces, and you have to pay a serious price for having a salary that pays your utility bill.

The 1968 movement in the U.S. had some educational initiatives, but it did not really add up to a *structural* change in higher education, though it did seem to many people that the university was the source of, or could become a home for, radicalism. Very unlike Central Europe, where all the interesting ideas have always come from *outside* the system. Just looking at the important names from this region, they were all outside the established educational system . . . starting with Sigmund Freud!

It's never *all* outside the system, okay, that's true too, but still, there is this independent space that you can operate in. And, well, you might think, "Hey, I'm not rich and I'm never going to be rich, but I'm okay, I'm still doing okay. I can live." But in the U.S., well, if you are not rich then you are miserable *and* you are not taken seriously either.

In those very *il*liberal spaces of the U.S., well, it's pretty obvious where the funding comes from, like in the case of Steve Bannon and his planned mercenary school, which has long been financed, at least in part, by Polish taxpayers because the state is captured by the neoliberals and now the illiberals too. Like Opus Dei. Opus Dei is providing financing to and has a very strong cooperation with Harvard University, because of course, you know, these are elite institutions. And they are collaborating because they want to form a new elite, right? That elite very badly wants the universities—they don't want to just leave the universities up to the leftists like they don't matter. And yes, this is happening in Europe. The Hungarian government institution bought an Austrian private university as they are richer now than Oxford—so where's all that money coming from, and what is it that they are paying the university to do for it? The point is that these institutions are either products of the state captured by illiberal regimes financed by the taxpayers or by international transnational organizations like Opus Dei or other fundamentalist organizations, or they are financed by the Catholic Church. These are the illiberal institutions. The university as an institution now has been co-opted and conceptualized wrongly—as something that is expensive and that nobody wants to fund or even to go to. That is the result of the delegitimization coming from illiberal forces. The university is presented as a kind of dinosaur, which is extremely difficult to feed and which nobody knows what to do with.

So we've turned to creating alternative institutions. Probably you have seen that I'm one of the founding members of a new university: the University of New Europe. Everybody's asking who is funding it. That's all I hear: "Who is funding it?" The problem is not the funding as it is much more important to find new *ideas*, because, yeah, the funding is there—I mean, we are all pretty well-established senior academics, and we can always pull fifteen or fifty thousand dollars from different institutions. But the bigger question is, what is the funding for? What's that money going to do? And what is the message? What is new here? The University of New Europe is not a building with copy machines in the corridor and pale administrators working on their computers and sending you horrible messages about what you should be doing to make sure that they have a job! Instead, this is a space for common thinking and a university where the members are equal and they are thinking together, and the joy of thinking is there, and we are not worrying about the "credits" or the "deliverables" or the "seed money"—you know, all that money you are attracting for mediocre research that nobody reads.

Academic feminism and academic feminists have always been a part of the transnational feminist movement. The question is the relationship between academic feminists and their involvement in direct political action. Now, because of these anti-gender attacks, several colleagues are afraid of being labeled as "activists." Therefore, they want to rebrand gender studies as just another discipline with no political agenda. I think this is an important and noble attempt, maybe to save gender studies to fight another battle another day. But I'm not sure that this is possible or, really, that what we are salvaging is worth salvaging.

We are all different, but my best experience was when I was allowed to give a speech in a stadium in front of about five thousand people in Rome in the PES Congress. There are people, lots of academics and scholars, who really don't enjoy talking to five thousand people in a stadium. So, in a sense, each of us may have very different professional trajectories. And some colleagues do fantastic scholarly work, right? But they don't really want to do things outside the library or archive or their offices or classrooms, and not because they want to undermine the feminist cause, but because they just don't have the stamina, or the skills, or they don't know how to do this kind of work.

That sort of parallel development between activists and academic feminists has always been there, at the start, from the end of the nineteenth century onwards. It rarely happens that academic gender studies and feminist activism intersect. But they are now. When Joan Scott, for instance, was in Budapest, that was a time when there were strikes organized by university students supporting gender studies, and so she was invited to one of these teach-ins in front of the Parliament. I saw how much she enjoyed the discussion there in the tent. It was minus twenty degrees Celsius, horribly cold, and I don't know how she managed that, but there were all these youngsters looking at her, just waiting for her to speak, and she was giving a fantastic talk in this huge, cold tent, and, I mean, it had an impact, because if you are spending some hours in minus twenty in front of the Parliament, in a tent, then that message sticks. It changes the way you think, it changes how you act. Especially when you have got Joan Scott speaking about what feminist politics can do in Budapest, well, that's a different experience from the usual university lectures.

In the long run, if I can use my example when I published an article about the rapes committed by the Red Army in Hungary during the Second World War, well... who would have read it before all these attacks on gender studies? Now it has been read by more than two or three hundred thousand people even though it's got all these footnotes [*chuckle*]. And, sure, you can call this article an academic product, because, of course, it was a result of me being a privileged academic who has time, space, and training, and who can write peer-reviewed articles, and can give interviews like this one. But, on the other hand, the impact was much more than what an academic article usually has, and that's really because of all the attention our work can now draw. So I think this kind of, you know, the distinction between academia and activism is, as I said in my personal story, it might be present and still operating, but the distinction is not set in stone and we have an opportunity to bridge that gap like never before. And this is thanks to the attacks on us!

You ask what gives me hope? I am very, very hopeful even though we are living in a very gloomy world, in a period of the poly-crisis that we are experiencing, including the climate crisis, the financial crisis, the care crisis, the migration crisis, and now we have war in Ukraine. This is a very tense and crisis-ridden historical period. But what we need are *ideas*—ideas on how to move forward! And such ideas will not come from the old, narrow, illiberal universities or even the newer neoliberal universities. They will come from unexpected places; such places do not need bureaucratic project proposals, learning outcomes, Excel sheets, and credit transfers! These unexpected places can be your kitchen. Unexpected places can be a conference or a dinner party! There are so many places where new ideas can come from. If you just think about your career and make a list of the most inspiring people you have met, well, I'm not sure the people on that list were connected to the neoliberal universities.

Paradoxically, gender studies is living on, and has more political opportunities even, because we are now taken much more seriously. Previously, gender studies professionals were working in the cellar or the basement of the university or in an attic with lots of posters on the wall. Of course, this is where gender studies thrived, but also where it hid itself from historical challenges. And now, well, I mean, everybody speaks about gender studies now! The key is that we need to see that this is a fantastic opportunity, and not be blind to it.

So, in a sense, I'm extremely hopeful, because gender studies has been always on the margins; therefore, it has much more resilience than disciplines that have been used to being at the center. We are much more able to network, collaborate, work with very little resources, and mobilize different networks than, let's say, mathematicians, for example. So gender studies has always been rooted in the real problems of the world. Now what we have are a whole lot of very real problems and not so many possible solutions—and this has opened a window of opportunity for us. Gender studies has always been fantastic at building different alliances, and that's what we need now. We need to be setting up alliances, building dialogues, and thinking together.

I am sure this will happen. This will happen with or without us, but I hope gender studies scholars will be an important part of the solutions going forward. It is true that gender studies might miss this opportunity, especially if it is too inward-looking and too worried about itself and its institutional support and safety. Or if gender studies is too theory-focused. If it's too elitist, then it might be, it might become, totally marginalized and irrelevant. But the problems that needed solutions when gender studies was first developed . . . those problems are still there; in fact, they are among the burning issues of our moment.

So don't let yourself despair! Every moment you are spending in despair is a victory for the people who believe only what money buys and a victory for the illiberals who want us all to just give up and think we are already defeated. We aren't, and we just won't let it happen.

Our greatest strength lies in how much they underestimate us.

What happened to you in Brazil?
A conversation with Judith Butler

Judith Butler is distinguished professor in the Graduate School and former Maxine Elliot Professor in the Department of Comparative Literature and the Program of Critical Theory at the University of California, Berkeley. Their book *Who's Afraid of Gender?* will be published by Farrar, Strauss, and Giroux in 2024. They can be reached at jpbutler@berkeley.edu.

Editors of Pandemonium *spoke with Judith Butler on June 27, 2023.*

It was 2017.

I was in São Paulo for a conference, The Ends of Democracy, on the future of democracy and concerns about the emergence of authoritarianism sponsored by the International Consortium of Critical Theory Programs, an organization that has been really wonderful in bringing people together and keeping the perspectives really global and also putting race at the center rather than outside of the issues at stake. I took part in this conference as an organizer, not a speaker. Gender was not the principal focus, and I did not expect to be the center of the attention at that conference. This was, in fact, before Bolsonaro was elected as president of Brazil.

I was told in advance that there was a Twitter storm raging, a social media campaign had been organized against me—me personally—demanding that I should not be let into the country, that I should not be allowed to speak.

I understood that the protest was quite large, although it was not clear to me whether the group CitizenGO (an ultraconservative digital-activism group in Spain organized in 2013 by the ultra-Catholic far-right HazteOir) had produced bots to make it seem as if hundreds of thousands of people opposed me or whether there really were hundreds of thousands of people opposing me. I had no way of knowing. I'm still not sure.

But I arrived there in the midst of all that, and even before I disembarked from the plane, I was told the government of the city had provided security for me. I was whisked off the plane and taken to an area beneath the airport where some kind of government vehicle was waiting for me. And yes, that all felt rather frightening. I was also oddly grateful to the moderate-left city government at the time for providing those security services to protect me.

It wasn't until I arrived at the venue—SESC Pompéia—that I understood what they were telling me. I saw the crowds outside and they appeared large, at least to me. They were calling me the devil and they were waving pictures of me as a demonic figure. The picture was distorted, and my eyes were all red and in one picture I even had horns. And so my first thought was, "Ohhhh, that's antisemitism. And I know what that's about, that's old Nazi propaganda against Jews." So I felt, at first, like, "Oh, I'm being attacked as a Jew." And then it was like, um . . . no? Or, yes, maybe still yes. But also, no, you're being attacked because of what you stand for, which is something called "gender." But what idea of gender did they have?

I had then to ask, well, what does "gender" mean when these people are attacking me as "representing gender"? First of all, what is their ignorance about—of the history of feminism and gender studies—such that they would make the claim that *I* originated the concept of gender, which we all know is simply untrue. This idea that I made up this term, "gender," is quite funny, you know. But it is also deadly serious. They credit me with coining the term, when really of course there were many people working on gender and the idea of gender as something different from sex. Wow, what is erased and misunderstood are all those anthropologists working on gender, all that theory coming out of socialist feminism—all long before me! I was reading Rayna Rapp, Gayle Rubin, Juliet Mitchell, and *This Bridge Called My Back* back then. All that was published or in the works before I wrote *Gender Trouble* in the late 1980s. But these folks didn't really care about all that. They had found a person to embody and receive their fear and hatred, but also their ignorance.

At first, I wanted to respond: "Oh, hey, you know, you got your history wrong. Let me tell you about the history of gender and gender studies." But then it became clear that they were not interested in that history and they were deeply suspicious of the academic field. They wanted the academic field destroyed, but especially the concept of gender, and all the progressive

Anti-gender ideology protesters vie with counterprotesters in a series of demonstrations staged in front of SESC Pompéia, in the city of São Paulo, where the U.S. philosopher Judith Butler addressed a 2017 scholarly conference on threats to democracy. Butler is renowned for their philosophical writings on gender, especially their 1990 book *Gender Trouble*. Photos by Fábio Vieira/FotoRua, November 7, 2017. Photos and permissions provided by Getty Images.

legislation and movements that they associate with it. They didn't really care who they were destroying, or maybe even what they were destroying, exactly. In fact, they pictured me as a source of destruction, assisted by evangelical and right-wing Catholic propaganda, and so their call to destroy me seemed justified. Paradoxical and interesting, though, that they had to become a destructive force to drive out what they considered to be destructive. One should obviously ask, who is really destructive in this scene? Where do we find the truly destructive force?

And, I might mention, in another instance, there was another smaller campaign or a demonstration outside of an honorary-degree ceremony I participated in 2014 in Switzerland, where a woman had come up to me and said that she was praying for me. I replied, "There's no reason to pray for me." And she said, "Yes, there is, because you don't read the Bible, so you don't understand that God created male and female." I said, "Well, actually the Bible is sort of complex, there are different kinds of relationships to be found in the Bible." But she insisted, "No! Male and female—that is the natural order. You are against nature!" I said, "Well, actually, nature admits of great diversity." And then she looked at me like I was crazy, of course. I asked, "Well, did you ever read anything I wrote?" And she said, "No! I would never touch such a book." It was then I realized that to touch my book, to open its pages, to allow those words to enter her, would subject her to the Devil, allow the Devil to enter, or open her up to some kind of horrific *contamination*. So, no, her opposition to me was based on no reading. Her opposition to me was also an opposition to reading.

So, yeah, no academic field or academic history can actually reach these people, since they have a sense that, if they even read my words, they'd be mesmerized, they'd be transformed, they'd fall under the sway of the Devil and the Devil would win. A powerful fantasy!

So there I was, in the flesh, as someone real they could attack—literally as well as figuratively *attack*. This person, me, had been construed as making the claim that gender is completely made up, fabricated. They imagined me as saying: you're free to choose your gender, to become whoever you want to be, and in doing so, you can transcend culture, history, and nature. They see me as saying that anyone can embody that ideal of radical self-creation, though in fact this is not my view. Or maybe they saw me as saying that gender is a construct, that it's all artificial, and there is no "nature" that plays a role in gender. That, too, is not my view. The problem for them is that self-creation contests creationism, which means that it's not

God who created man and woman. For them, that implies that I'm *against* God's creation, against creatio*nism*, and whatever idea of freedom I have is one that threatens to supplant or counter the creative action taken by God. For them, God created men and women. The human being can only be understood in terms of that duality, those two categories. So for them, and for their God, there are no intersex people and no other ways of being gendered. There is a natural order and a natural family, created by God. All the people outside that framework, those "other" people, are apparently not "God-given," they are not *given* or created by God. And if they are working against creationism, then their work is the work of the Devil. I don't know what they believed exactly was "of" the Devil about me, but it was all very overwhelming, and I was frightened.

What also became clear is that they thought that if the taboo against gay and lesbian sexuality was lifted, or if trans people could secure a legal change of status, then all other taboos would also be negated. Hence, they accused me of pedophilia, or, rather, they understood pedophilia to follow from "gender." They should have looked first at the Catholic Church, whose record of violating children is the real one.

I had confronted vicious crowds before, but usually it was on the subject of Palestine, because I support Palestinian self-determination and object to the pervasive destruction of Palestinian life and culture by the state of Israel. I have been called a self-hating Jew by Zionists, even though my passion for justice was in part derived from Jewish ethics. I was used to that kind of protest, but in Brazil, I encountered a vicious protest which, at first, I did not quite understand.

And, yes, they did burn me in effigy. There was a particular image of me, a horrific image, with a distorted face, and on my torso I was wearing a red bikini top, with sequins or laminated. The message in this image was confusing to me. In some ways it struck me as funny, since if I were to wear a bikini top, well, that would be absurd, right? I am gendered in such a way that bikini tops are not in the picture, right? [*Laughter.*] One might conclude that they were placing a bikini on someone who would never wear one, but I think something else was going on. If the bikini is absurd, that assumes that I really am masculine, a masculine figure who would look ridiculous in a bikini. They were not saying, you are really a girl and should be wearing such a swimsuit. The bikini is only absurd if they accept my masculinity. That might be very nice of them, but that is not at all the way it went. The image was paradoxical, though, since their whole point is that if someone is assigned female at birth, then they are supposed to be, and to look, feminine. So it was almost like they gave me a trans identity that certainly, at that point, I had not given myself (I consider myself nonbinary). The bikini was, in their minds perhaps, what trans women wear, and they consider that absurd, given their view about the natural order. Were they imagining me as a trans woman? Attributed to my body, it was almost a kind of recognition of my masculinity. Should I stay in masculine swimwear? Without that assumption, the insult would not work. I mean, I was abused in that scene, demeaned by the image but also threatened with physical harm. Oddly though, I was also imbued with a certain power, and that power would become for me a kind of defiance once I started to go public in my opposition to the anti-gender ideology movement.

I still do think they were drawing on antisemitism to make their point, even though that point was about gender. We see that's what's happened in France, where one right-wing public figure has said, "Look, all this gender stuff comes from the Jewish Americans—Gayle Rubin, Joan Scott, Judith Butler." He claimed the Jews made all this up, so the anti-Christian aspects of this have been at work in many of these contexts, which brings us back to antisemitism again and again, at least as framing. But it was also drawing on the tradition of witch burning, and the public press in Brazil at the time identified and condemned it as such.

I had to stay inside the conference venue, the hotel, and I couldn't walk in the streets by myself. I couldn't walk by the protest, but I could hear it, and follow it online. I had a bodyguard the whole time—a lovely person in the arts who had never been a bodyguard before, but that was okay, we worked it out.

And though I was certainly frightened, I wasn't going to let it stop me from speaking. Though I wasn't even speaking about gender, which was the oddest thing ever, I suppose! I spoke about democracy, and the threats against it, and pointed to the crowds outside as one such threat.

That said, there was a supportive crowd that also appeared, and that crowd defended my right to speak and defended *me*—my person and the representations of me in some cases. The existence of that counterdemonstration was very important to me. Everybody in the conference gave me great support, as well as the city government. So I was not all that frightened for my life at the time the protest was happening. That only came later, at the airport.

When my partner, Wendy Brown, and I arrived back at the São Paulo airport to leave, we were accosted in the airport, and that's when I did see clearly that they were willing to do physical harm to me—to me personally, not just my image—and to Wendy. In fact, they came at me with large luggage carriers, metal conveyors with which they were going to attack and injure me, maybe even kill me, because I was apparently the Devil, and, as they said, the Devil needed to be expunged not only from Brazil but from the Earth as well. So I did feel fear for my life. I thought about Martin Luther King Jr.'s ethics of nonviolence and tried to walk calmly away toward the security gate at the departures area.

My partner, Wendy Brown, stood firm, however, and screamed at them. I encouraged her to move on with me, ignoring them. I wanted to move, and there she was, fearlessly telling them off. It was terrible, but I decided, okay, I'm not going run from these horrific people. I will keep my dignity in a slow and deliberate movement toward the gate.

But then they started screaming at me that I was a *pederast*. That allegation or fantasy always takes me by surprise. And yet, it had happened once earlier, when I was giving a paper on Martin Buber and Edward Said in another city, during the same trip to Brazil. A woman from the back of the room got up and screamed that I was a pedophile or a pederast. And I thought, "Where does this come from?"

So it turns out that if you're in favor of having sex outside of marriage or engage in sexuality other than heterosexuality (it could be gay, lesbian, bisexual), then that apparently means there are no constraints on you, and that means you would also permit humans to have sex with animals, or with children. In other words, the assumption is that you have lost all moral self-restriction around sex. Departing from "the natural order" means departing from all morality, losing a moral compass when it comes to sex. So, for them, there is a kind of "Pandora's box" view of sexuality that says, if you are not having sex within what they call the "natural" family, meaning heteronormative and married, if you are operating outside that frame, you are operating without any moral compass, so *anything* could happen. And yet that "anything" becomes a site of intense fantasy for them, including bestiality, incest, and the exploitation of children. Of course, this is all a false form of reasoning, and gay and lesbian people are among those who have thought most ethically about how to separate sexuality from harm. The moral compass is different, but never absent.

The anti-gender fanatics, and others like them in the U.K. or U.S., imagine that because we (by "we" I mean gender studies scholars) teach about homosexuality or masturbation, that we are teaching kids *how* to become homosexuals or *how* to masturbate, or *how* to become a lesbian, *how* to become trans. They imagine an ideological indoctrination that turns out to be a feature of their own imagination and to have little bearing on what happens in gender studies classrooms or in sex education courses for young people. Developing knowledge about sexuality and gender is not the same as prescribing how to have sex or what gender to become.

Of course, we're now seeing this in the case of Florida under the leadership of Governor DeSantis, but it has been clearly at work in Brazil for much longer, and it's now clearly at work in places like Italy, where Prime Minister Giorgia Meloni's discourse has been really quite nefarious. She is, as you may know, opposing gay parenting rights in Italy, and all legal recognition of trans identity. For her, you can only remain the sex you are assigned at birth. She follows many Christian nationalists in this view.

In any case, I did see that my life was at stake and that I had come to embody some anti-Christian, anti-nationalist, terribly frightening, demonic force that was sometimes figured as the "urban elite" from the Global North. A Global North intellectual who could, and would maybe, take apart Christianity at a moment's notice. In this sense, I felt myself also cast as Jewish.

I could not recognize myself in this portrayal of me, but I understood that I had become demonic in their eyes, perhaps also monstrous, that is, outside the human form. The idea of the monstrous has a long political and cultural history in Brazil. And many queer and trans activists have embraced the monstrous as an affirmative category. But even when it is owned and affirmed, it remains a kind of stigma that has been assigned to them for some time and which has to be negotiated with.

The upshot is that I was frightened and traumatized by it all. And now I have to decide where I can travel and what risks I am willing to take. Sadly, I won't be returning to Brazil. I can't travel to certain countries without security in place. That feels like a compromise, since I don't like security at all, and I don't want to live that way. But even recently, when I spoke in Denmark, they asked me before the event: "Do you want us to set up security? Including checkpoints to make sure nobody brings a gun into the event?" Oh, no, I don't want to live that way, so I said no. And I am taking risks of that sort. I mean, the Denmark right wing is not overwhelming, but it is nasty. And, certainly, now there are certain places I obviously can't go at all. Even going to Poland or Hungary at this point doesn't feel comfortable to me. And even though there are folks there doing great work exposing and resisting the anti-gender movement (which is almost always anti-migrant as well), they know how to live there, while I have no way of knowing whether I would be exposed to harm in ways that are not acceptable to me. Of course, we all know feminists and queer people, people trying to secure access to abortion clinics in the U.S., who are braced and doing good work, living their lives publicly yet with some degree of fear of violence and with the stigmatization and potential criminalization that comes with that stigma. The situation in Uganda is perhaps the worst, but throughout Europe, the U.S., and Latin America, there is organized rage against "gender" or "homosexuality" that often participates in eliminationist rhetoric.

Because I am overdetermined now, because I represent this nefarious thing, I am at risk. And I have to be careful now where I go, and I have to know where I cannot go.

There's a big misconception about academic life that is happening in Florida, but also in many states throughout the world, namely, that it's been overwhelmed by leftists or feminists or gay, lesbian, queer, and trans people, and that we're engaged in indoctrination that is ruining the minds of the young. Of course, by stoking that fear, DeSantis in Florida produces an alibi for the enhancement or augmentation of his own power. We see this when we see that people who are suspected of "woke-ism" are denied tenure, as happened at New College. You replace people on the board of trustees with those who are like-minded, right? You do if you are that kind of anti-democratic authoritarian.

Something very similar has happened in Turkey after the attempted coup a few years ago. Erdoğan basically decided to fill Boğaziçi University, which is arguably the most highly admired intellectual center in Turkey, with political appointees who would do his bidding and quell protest. And, yes, many there are, or were, leftist or left-oriented, but certainly they are primarily prodemocracy more than anything else. And Erdoğan sought to break that ethos, to break the whole Turkish university system of faculty governance, and to a large extent has succeeded, so that the remaining Turkish faculty cannot, or dare not, speak out in criticism of him, or even teach about democracy or Kurdish history.

The accusations against what's happening in the university, whether American or Turkish or Hungarian, or wherever this is happening, are very anti-intellectual, even more than anti-leftist or anti–anything else in particular.

The thing is, they don't actually understand how our classrooms work or how much disagreement there is in a gender studies classroom! I mean, come on, it's not like people or students are just like sitting around nodding, like, yeah, I agree, I agree, I agree ... oh my gosh, no, we all know, that's just not what happens in our classrooms!

Indeed, *everything* in a gender studies class is called into question. We have to go over it again, and again, like, why did you put *that* on the syllabus? Why are we reading *that*? Why don't we read this *other* work? Oh my God. Am I right? [*Laughter.*] I mean, we in gender studies live in this perpetual state of contestation and we're always trying to work it out with our students, and with each other.

Okay, so how do we handle conflict, and how do we stay connected without breaking apart? That is the main question for alliances that now need to come together to fight the anti-gender ideology movement.

And sometimes in alliances you do have to break, and what follows from that? And, you know, this is what feminism has been about for a long time, at least for all the decades that I've been part of it.

I think I came out as a feminist at age thirteen or fourteen (if not before). It's been a long set of very intense and meaningful disagreements ever since. Feminism and gender studies is a highly contested field, with many paradigms that are always clashing or blending in some interesting and creative ways. So while the field is caricatured by the right, and by trans-exclusionary feminists, as a totalitarian exercise, as a situation where you walk into the class and you have to agree with the teacher and recite certain kinds of dogma as if you're in a totalitarian government school or you're part of a fundamentalist religion. But actually what they fear are the very questions we raise.

It is the *questions* that terrify them.

The young people come home from college or university and say: Um, you know what? Maybe I'm going to change my gender. Or they want to talk about what they've been reading and the ideas they've encountered at school ... like maybe racism has been with the U.S. since its founding or with the founding of the Americas itself, with the first slave ship, and maybe those histories are deeply interlinked with the annihilation of Indigenous peoples? But, you don't want, you don't want to hear this from the youth, right? You don't want to have them *questioning* established narratives, and you certainly don't want them questioning much at all if you're evangelical Christian, I mean if you're a right-wing fundamentalist of some kind. You don't want them questioning the form of the normative family or the "natural" head of the family. You want all that to seem as if it's timeless and true, and it's the only way that people can or ever have lived. What you don't want is everything being called into question.

It's our questions that frighten them, even more than our answers; it's the questions we encourage our students to start asking.

Those questions are deeply disturbing to them, and yet they come back at us with this accusation of totalitarianism as if we have a single dogma we are imposing, as if we are the ones ruling out the questions. But they've never been in our classroom, and they don't read our books, and they're so deeply, *deeply* anti-intellectual that they don't even want to know what it is we are really doing or saying in those classrooms.

I have two responses to all this fear and anti-intellectual attacks on us and our field.

One is to say: It is true that gender and women's and sexuality studies does rely on critical thinking, on open critical inquiry. And in that way, it belongs, hopefully, to the idea of the university as a space of open inquiry, right? So we need to remind people that what we do in this field is also what we expect a university to do. And any university that doesn't operate in this way, centering open inquiry, is no longer operating really as a university at all.

At the same time, we're not just throwing everything into question and denying received truths randomly. We're actually trying to make a better world, right?

So it's important to acknowledge that we do have normative aspirations. We all care about equality, for instance. We may differ on how we define it or how best to achieve it. But we all care about equality, we all want a more equal world.

We all care about freedom, and we may argue about what kind of freedom or how to shift from ideas of personal liberty to collective freedom or how to think about freedom in terms of a critique of capitalism. We might think about embodied forms of freedom that don't belong to traditional political philosophy and that are distinctly feminist.

And we all also care about justice. And what justice looks like.

So the three pillars of democracy, we might say, are equality, freedom, and justice, and that's been true for a very long time, right? When we talk about equal rights, you know, one view is that everybody's equal because everyone is human. But some humans are more equal than others, and why is that the case? And what do we need to do to make freedom *substantive* rather than *abstract*? Or, how does freedom change once we understand what *women's* freedom is, or what *trans* freedom would look like? I mean, how do we reconceptualize those ideas in light of new social movements and the legitimate demands they are making?

So we are actually trying to rethink how we oppose inequality, how we oppose injustice. We affirm freedom, but we also acknowledge that each of those central concepts look and work differently in different histories.

And we need to know that history to know where we are and where we're going, and we need to understand the global range of discourses and practices of freedom and justice, and injustices. For that, we also need practices of translation.

So I think as much as we need to defend critical inquiry as part of women's, gender, and sexuality studies and the university itself, we also need to make clear to a larger public what we're really about, what world we're trying to imagine. And that we don't always agree with one another! We're having ongoing discussions about it all. That's part of what we're doing, and we need to translate this somehow out of our academic domains into more public ones to make people understand that when we talk about trans lives, we are saying that a trans life should be able to be lived freely.

People should be able to breathe and live openly without fear of violence and without pathologization. I mean, it's really not that complex, is it?

But let me add just one, just one other point:

It is important to see that the right has found a way to appropriate left arguments. Steve Bannon is the U.S. example of this, but he's collaborating and continues to collaborate throughout Europe with new fascists. And the Vatican does this, as well, claiming for instance that gender is a form of colonization, that it is imposed upon the poor people of the Global South, that it belongs properly only to urban elite institutions in the Global North. That argument fails to acknowledge the queer, travesti, and trans communities throughout Latin America or the complex vocabularies for gender outside the binary frame in Africa. The Vatican's critique of gender as colonial is not the same as the feminist critique that points out that the heteronormative binary was *imposed by* colonial powers. According to the feminist critique, the Vatican is intensifying that colonial imposition in the name of "decolonization." A shrewd strategy, but fundamentally false.

There is a history of understanding gender in relation to colonization, within feminism and the history of sexuality, and there's some great decolonial work, but for the most part, the feminists who are working within the decolonial framework are saying the gender binary was brought by colonizers, not the other way around. (The work of Argentine feminist philosopher María Lugones is a good example of this sort of insightful analysis). So opening that binary up to question is actually part of decolonization. The right says that we on the left are totalitarian or colonizing (depending on the context), but that allegation puts them on the side of resistance and decolonization. By confusing the terms in this way, they gain more power, exciting the public and fanning fascist sentiments that support their own form of authoritarianism, and that's a really tricky thing. By claiming that we indoctrinate students, or young people more generally, they position themselves as the open mind fighting against the dogma of the "woke."

So how did *they* get freedom on *their* side? And what would it mean for us to take freedom back? *To be the freedom fighters we believe* we *are?* They have managed to confuse the issues to such an extent that many people are confused by the debates on gender and race, not knowing what side to take.

Perhaps this is a chance or opportunity for us in the field of gender studies to move out into the world, to make publicly accessible what we do and why we do it and to give the rationales and the justification for our programs in public ways. I think that could be enormously important.

Such a project won't fully answer the question of whether we can stand up to the metrics that are being used to prioritize the STEM fields, but we should be arguing that other values are at stake in the university, wholly apart from the metrics that valorize the STEM fields, right? That's an internal battle that has to be conducted through a broad alliance of the humanities and the interpretive social sciences. Women's, gender, and sexuality studies obviously belongs in that matrix, although it also has strong connections to science studies now, and, you know, there's a lot of really important feminist work that's being done across those domains as well. We are hardly against science, but we do object to the selective appropriation of science, or the use of illegitimate science, to shore up their ideological agenda.

I do think that the first thing we have to do is refuse to let our internecine struggles take us down when we're facing these terrible attacks. It does worry me that the gender-critical movement *within* feminism has attacked gender studies in ways that parallel if not mimic the right-wing attack on gender. I am not sure they fully understand the alliances they have made, the right-wing agenda they are promoting.

Now, most of those folks would say that they're not right-wing, but they are feminists, and they, well, they think gender is a dangerous category and has imported a number of terrible errors into the study of women's, gender, and sexuality studies. But, in fact, their arguments are very often the same as the right's, which is why Putin could so easily align with J. K. Rowling. Of course, she was very right to refuse that alliance. I applaud her for that, but she should perhaps, along with her allies, rethink the kinds of arguments that they're putting out into the world, because, in fact, I don't think they are arguments; they are, instead, phantasms, which are also distorted and very fearful, and function much the same way that these fears and fearful phantasms function for the right wing.

It's really hard to argue with a phantasm! But I do think that gender-critical feminism is undermining the field. What they're saying needs to be transformed into a set of questions that we can think about and debate, like: Is it really the case that gender denies the materiality of sex? What do we mean by the "materiality of sex"? How do we approach that? And which concept of gender is better than what other concept? Is there only one concept of gender? Or are there many? If so, how do we judge among them?

What have we done when we accept a kind of caricature of gender as the enemy without actually doing the reading and thinking and researching to see, you know, how gender works in public life and economics, for example? How does it work when we talk about the "gender division of labor" or the gendering of the public sphere? We are not talking about gender identity, but gender as a relation of power that has a history and a future. Surely we are not, in such instances, talking about something fake. We are examining realities that have come into being in time and space, thus social realities or economic realities. None of this is fakery. If somebody needs to, for existential reasons, change the legal status of their sex, why does that threaten feminism? It does not. They are not faking something, but transforming themselves, and that transformation is a reality. They are not stealing anything, but laying claim to a category that no one owns. The idea that a trans woman is "really" a man masquerading as a woman relies on a questionable account of reality and a questionable form of judgment. Who are we to say that? Who are any of us to say there aren't more complex psychodynamics and complex existential matters at play than the binary gender so valued by Christian nationalism and hateful fascists?

I don't think we tell other people whether or not they should have children. We don't tell other people whether or not they should be heterosexual. And we don't tell other people whether or not they should be trans, either. We neither prohibit (as some TERFs do) nor prescribe (as the right thinks we do), for neither is in keeping with the kind of spirit of openness, generosity, and multiplicity that has been the best part of feminism, right?

Historians know the category of women has changed. What does it mean to be a woman if to be a woman changes through time and across location? How do we account for changes across cultures and languages? We're interested in that change, right? We're not interested in *stopping* that change. We're not saying, no, we now know what it—a woman—is, and we need this one definition in this language to serve as the basis of all thought and action going forward. Oh no, I don't think we do that, and there are good reasons we don't do that: because we don't have all the knowledge there is to have from our specific location and from within our language either.

I just find the gender-critical attacks to be really painful and really destructive, and that internecine fighting has to be resolved somehow.

But maybe we should be thinking how that infighting could become a useful antagonism. Can it? Or do we just have to win the debate? *Are* we winning that debate? Are we going to give all our time to fighting that fight with each other, or are we going to see that this fight between ourselves is serving the right-wing forces that are making the same arguments?

I think we need to be very critical about those feminists who ally with right-wing forces that would undermine *all* of our freedoms, because those folks are also attacking reproductive rights and they're also attacking laws protecting women from violence and sexual harassment, and gender and sexual minorities from violence and harassment and pathologization.

We need the larger picture in order to understand where we have to go.

You know, we went from worrying about the pandemic to worrying about whether drag queens should be reading stories to young children or whether trans rights are legitimate or whether abortion (or reproductive justice more broadly speaking) is something that the left should even care about. My sense is that the pandemic did alert people to the state of the world we live in. Climate catastrophe has also alerted people to the fragility of their lives. I think the anti-gender movement preys upon people's fear of destruction, their fear of the destruction of everyday life.

Yet most of that destruction is, as we know, actually coming from authoritarian, patriarchal states and fascist movements and capitalism and extractivism—especially in the Global South. And yet gender becomes a focus for many of these regimes and right-wing movements. They make the claim that gender, or what they call "gender," is what is threatening civilization with destruction.

Our feeling that our ways of life and our sense of the world are being destroyed or imperiled from many things, including war, is very handy, really very convenient, for those right-wing politicians and authoritarians (whether emerging or accomplished). They see that fear and then point at gay and lesbian rights, gay and lesbian parenting, single parenting, reproductive justice, or trans rights, drag queens and their cultural performances, and all of that suddenly becomes the focus of attack.

On the one hand, we could say, it's a massive displacement from the real sources of destruction that are at work in this world, which are mainly patriarchal and heteronormative and pervasively white. And it is that, for sure, but it's also a way of condensing all the different anxieties people have and stoking their fear and making them desire the kind of authoritarian rule that is on offer from the anti-gender powers.

So many of our basic coordinates in this world have been upended. I think we're in a kind of strange cycle where the fear of destruction is kind of what prompts this politics but also is what gets displaced and condensed and attributed to feminism or LGBTQIA+ rights, or reproductive freedom, or gay parenting, or . . . all of those things and more.

I think it's also important to see that the "anti-gender ideology movement," as they call it in Hungary and throughout Latin America (and is a term even used by DeSantis when he is not blasting "woke" everything) . . . it's the "anti-gender ideology" movement or network that has been rallying right-wing causes and opposing gay marriage, and opposing the Istanbul Convention, which as you know protects women against violence, both domestic and nondomestic violence. These folks have been at work for a long time connecting various regions of the world, mainly through the World Congress of Families and their digital allies. I think it's enormously important that we see that it has actually come to the United States in this form belatedly, even though our evangelical churches, the right-wing ones, were actively producing and exporting the framework for the global anti-gender movement for quite some time.

Most importantly, I think that instead of looking for the individuals who are fighting the fight, although there are many, I think we need to look for the *alliances* that are possible and that we probably need to shift and ask ourselves: What alliance do we need to be part of, do we want to create? What alliance is making this happen?

Throughout Eastern Europe, for instance, Andrea Pető in Hungary is one person and Agnieszka Graff in Poland is another, but, in fact, there's an enormous alliance of interconnected feminists that range from Serbia, connected to others in Eastern and Western Europe, as well of course in Latin America (I'm thinking especially of LasTesis, the Chilean collective). I've met people in Honduras, in all different parts of the world, in South Africa, and I've been online with gender studies scholars and activists at Makerere University in Uganda who are hard at work.

So we have to ask ourselves, who are "we"? Where and what's the local struggle, and how does this connect to the global level, and how do we move between the two in ways that are very effective?

After what happened in Brazil in 2017, I did become part of these alliances, and now I am less alone in the world and less frightened, because I am part of these larger alliances.

None of us wins a political battle alone, but only by finding, intensifying, and expanding our alliances. It can be painful to be in them, but we have to keep in mind where destruction is happening so we can enhance our ability to fight it.

So that, along the way, we do not make the mistake of destroying one another.

How did an anti-gender movement develop in Brazil?
A conversation with James N. Green

James N. Green is Carlos Manuel de Céspedes Chair of Latin American History at Brown University and professor of Brazilian history and culture. He is author of eleven books and edited collections on Brazil and Latin America, including *Beyond Carnival: Male Homosexuality in Twentieth-Century Brazil* ([1999] 2020); *We Cannot Remain Silent: Opposition to the Brazilian Dictatorship in the United States* ([2009] 2010); *Exile within Exiles: Herbert Daniel, Gay Brazilian Revolutionary* (2018); and *Brazil: Five Centuries of Change*, 3rd ed. (2018). He was president of the Brazilian Studies Association, BRASA (2002–4), and the BRASA Executive Director (2016–20). He is the national co-coordinator of the U.S. Network for Democracy in Brazil, and the president of the board of directors of the Washington Brazil Office. He can be reached at james_green@brown.edu.

Editors *of* Pandemonium *spoke with James N. Green on June 20, 2023.*

Brazil was under a dictatorship from 1964 until 1985. It had been in the process of a sort of slow-motion return to democracy, which started in 1974 when new social movements joining with the more traditional left emerged to fight against the dictatorship.

I was one of the founders of the LGBT movement, which was at the time called the "homosexual movement." It was started mostly by men. Then women joined, and they developed their own autonomy, and formed their own separatist lesbian groups and feminist women's groups. I became a feminist in 1969, and I came out as gay in 1973 and was very much involved in the anti-war movement and in the New Left in the United States, even before I lived in Brazil (between 1976 and 1981). The feminist movement was very important to the gay rights movement, even though, in Brazil, in the 1980s, there was a bit of a downturn in terms of feminism and its ability to take

WSQ: Women's Studies Quarterly 52: 1 & 2 (Spring/Summer 2024) © 2024 by James N. Green and Tracey Jean Boisseau. All rights reserved.

hold in the institutions, which had to do with Brazilian dictatorship. And when that was overthrown, then there was a real flowering and resurgence in the movement in the 1990s. And, as a result of this resurgence, we saw a slow but steadily growing number of women's studies centers founded at several important universities, and more and more feminist historians and scholars in the social sciences and the humanities were hired and became prominent voices in the academy.

The most important universities in Brazil are publicly funded and have free admissions, and it was at these institutions that women's studies and those pushing for LGBT studies took hold. At first, scholarship was mostly shared and aired at national conferences that were held annually or maybe biannually, and eventually, in the early 2000s, more vigorous possibilities came about for people to be able to study LGBTQIA+ subjects.

So centers were formed for women's studies and gender studies, and then there were some formal articulations of LGBT studies in different programs. All this really began to happen only in the 1990s, when Brazil really began opening up. New MA, and then PhD, programs formed in the early 2000s too. And by then, trans women and men were becoming more visible and at that point started to find space within the academy for themselves and began to teach LGBT studies and gender studies.

So that's part of the historical background of how women's and gender studies emerged in Brazil. But you need to understand what's happened in the last few years in Brazil to understand where things stand today.

A far-right politician, a former army officer named Jair Bolsonaro was elected in 2018, someone much along the lines of Donald Trump, and so I think if we understand Donald Trump, we can understand by analogy what's happened in Brazil. Like Trump, Bolsonaro built a far-right coalition of anti-communists, anti-leftists, evangelical Christians pushing neoliberal economic policies. Under Bolsonaro, there was a really sharp attack on every democratic gain that had been achieved in Brazil for almost thirty years in the process of democratization and consolidating democracy after 1988, when a new constitution replaced the autocratic 1967 constitution forged under military dictatorship, to establish the Nova República (New Republic).

For certain, one of the biggest ways in which the academic world was most affected by the rise of Bolsonaro and his far-right coalition was the pressure and attention that was suddenly given to what is called "gender ideology" and to the teaching of gender studies.

By "gender" the right means (allegedly) promoting ideas about gender identity as constructed and as "performance," which is perceived as critical and negative about the patriarchal family, Brazilian society, and evangelical Christian values. We're very familiar in the United States with these ideas, but this attack from the far-right on academic gender studies was being instrumentalized in Brazil in a much stronger way than Trump was doing in the United States. In his presidency, Trump didn't attack LGBT people and address gender issues all that explicitly, although his supporters certainly did. But, in Brazil, one of the most important sites where these confrontations took place was in the university. Bolsonaro launched a frontal attack aimed directly at the universities. In Brazil, gender studies, even more than race, was at the center point of that attack.

One example of this that is very important—not in terms of its size or budget, but in terms of its symbolic importance—is what happened at the Ministry of Human Rights, which really had, in the years before Bolsonaro, raised many important questions about violence against women and LGBTQIA+ people. But, under Bolsonaro, that ministry was transformed into the Ministry of Women, the Family, and Human Rights and was handed over to an evangelical female Christian pastor named Damares Alves—a woman who very famously said "boys wear blue, girls wear pink." This became her signature phrase that she would chant in speeches and rallies, where she committed herself to ending the "abuse" of the ideological "indoctrination" of children. She talked a lot about the abuse she suffered as a child, and she linked that abuse to what she sees as "gender ideology," viewing it as a kind of sexual abuse of children. She really moved the ministry to the very far right and to the religious fringes. One of her main political promises was to eradicate "gender ideology"—which really means homosexuality and feminism but also and especially trans people, who are seen as a threat to the youth of Brazil.

The other element of Bolsonaro's attack, besides this specific critique of "gender ideology" supposedly being promoted in the classroom, was a notion of fighting to have what in Latin America is called "Schools without Political Parties" (known in Portuguese as "Escola sem Partido" or EsP) and the creation, under Bolsonaro, of "civilian-military" high schools meant to counter leftist teachings and root out Marxists, socialists, and communists from the teaching profession. Now, there's been a long tradition of leftist and Marxist resistance to the dictatorship that ruled Brazil between 1964 and 1985. So, actually, the right is correct in saying that universities are, or have been, "bastions" of leftist thinking in Brazil. Not entirely, of course, but in general, especially the social sciences and humanities—which have always been left-leaning. Bolsonaro tried to wipe this out. This meant, for instance, students taping teachers in class (illegally, because, in Brazil, it's not allowed without permission from the professor), and then posting this on the internet and denouncing professors to get them pushed out of their jobs or forcing them to spend time and money to fight lawsuits and making it really difficult to exist in the academy at all. It was also a real silencing factor, and there are many people throughout the country—not just at the universities, but in any school—who were affected. Let's say you had gone to the university, you had a teaching certificate, and you were teaching, maybe you were teaching ideas about gender. Suddenly, you could have a legal case brought against you, and you would have to hire a lawyer. That is extremely expensive and difficult, and very scary for most people.

The other thing Bolsonaro did or tried to do was to defund or underfund the public university system, and he created a lot of difficulties that way. He couldn't defund everything or gut all the programs he wanted to destroy, because it's a big bureaucracy that has existed for years and there was a lot of resistance or inertia to overcome. In fact, throughout the period when Bolsanaro was president, academic production on LGBTQIA+ continued, certainly. I was on, probably, ten masters' and doctoral dissertation committees in Brazil on such topics in that period. So, while the four years under Bolsonaro became a real fight for academic freedom generally, on top of three painful years of COVID, his climate and vaccine denialism (which we are also familiar with in the United States), the fact is that people continued to produce scholarship and teach. It's not as if everyone was afraid and they couldn't do anything and just stopped. In fact, the universities as a whole were, and are still, a place of very strong resistance.

It's also true that, over the last ten years since affirmative action programs in federal universities were implemented, there's a whole new socioeconomic group of people attending universities, mostly Black people, Indigenous people, trans people. This fact alone has produced an increased sentiment of resistance to far-right policies within universities.

So, yes, we saw this start to play out even before Bolsonaro became president. For instance, when Judith Butler was invited to speak in Brazil in 2017—recall that was the year *before* Bolsonaro's election—they were attacked and denounced publicly and then harassed in person at the airport because they had become so high-profile. Organized right-wing groups promoting their "anti-gender ideology" used Butler's visit to whip up all these protests, and then the protests were widely reported in regular media, and from there it just snowballed.

It was a really big deal that a foreigner, a very important feminist in the United States, came to Brazil, and they got all this visibility in the media. This is why people recognized them in the airport, and why they were trying to attack Butler even as they were leaving the country. It's not that they were famous in Brazil *before* the protests. The only people who really even knew about Judith Butler were a small number of people in academia—such as people in the social sciences who knew them. But they aren't Angela Davis. Angela Davis has become a massive global phenomenon, especially among those in the Black movement in Brazil. Butler isn't a popular figure—not someone most people in Brazil would have heard of. So, what's important here to note is that Judith Butler only became famous, in a popular sense, in Brazil, because of the media campaign and digital protests mounted against them.

And, sure, part of that was that they were coming from the Global North. It should be said that academia in Brazil *has* been colonized by foreign influences. The elites in the nineteenth century looked to France as a kind of intellectual vanguard. Well into the twentieth century, there's been a notion of Brazil being behind, you know, a little behind the rest of the world. There's a lag time in getting information as well as ideas from other parts of the world, and many Brazilian intellectuals look to the Global North as kind of intellectual referent. Many of the theoretical contributions of feminism and gender theory and even ideas about race that were produced in the Global North have come to Brazil in recent decades, many times after these ideas were already digested in the United States. The fact is, however, that Brazilian universities have really changed in the last twenty years, and in important ways that bears on this question of gender studies and Marxism, in particular.

Let me explain. When left-leaning President Luiz Inácio Lula da Silva (popularly known as Lula) was elected the first time in 2002, he expanded the number of public universities as well as the number of slots for undergraduates to be able to attend these (tuition-free) institutions. More importantly, even, I would say, is that, over time, universities implemented a quota system based on race.

In Brazil, although public universities are free, you have to pass an entrance exam to get in. And who was going to be able to pass that? Mostly the kids from upper middle and elite classes who had attended good, mostly private, high schools. And those people have been mostly white, or at least not Black. But due to popular pressure brought by the Black movement and others, a very effective quota system was established, which entirely transformed public universities in Brazil. So half of all the slots for admission into federal universities now have quotas for Black people, Indigenous people, and other categories. This has meant, in the last ten years, that Brazilian public universities, which are considered the best in the country (and among the best in Latin America) have been *radically* transformed in terms of the composition of the student body. And, of course, who's there determines who will be trained to become teachers, and on and on. It used to be that you would mostly have just upper-middle-class white students at the university, along with a few very highly talented non-whites, but really only a very small handful of very talented people from lower socioeconomic sectors of the society would make it to university. And that makes a big difference, doesn't it? That has radically changed, and the number of people of color at public universities in Brazil has transformed these institutions. For them, Angela Davis has become a really important symbol as a radical Black feminist woman academic. There's even a collective of women called the Angela Davis Collective. She's been an inspirational figure on a whole different political level.

The controversy stirred up about Judith Butler—that was different and maybe in an opposite way. Butler was just someone invited to give some talks. No one outside of academia would have known or cared about these talks. But then people on the right realized: "Oh, this is a person we could attack," even though they never had read anything by or about them and didn't really know anything other than what they might have found on a Wikipedia page. The right wing used this as a way to kind of set an example. This was at one of the worst moments in recent Brazilian history.

You see, the year before all this happened, the left-wing president at the time, Dilma Rousseff, had been impeached and removed from office. Her vice president, Michel Temer, who had been part of a broad coalition government, stabbed her in the back, supported her impeachment, and then assumed the presidency himself for the rest of her term, August 2016 to December 2018. So it was during this period, his coming to power, when there was a shift from the left to the right. This transition, which was both political and cultural, was taking place when Judith Butler was in the country, and this was exactly at the same time that right-wing forces were starting to mobilize very strongly. They were looking for a good target to gather their forces and provide a focal point for their movement.

But, you know, this also became an opportunity for the left and progressive forces too. They used the incident and the extremism of the public protests against Judith Butler to show what the right was capable of and to expose how radical it was becoming by then, especially how threatening the attacks against the university, and particularly how vicious the attacks against feminist, gender, and queer studies in particular, had become. For some, this has been a way to consolidate resistance, and it has strengthened people's determination to defend gender studies, women's studies, LGBT studies.

So I think it did serve to silence people *and* to generate resistance at the same time. Both things happened.

At some point, there was really very effective government pressure against teaching material on gender or LGBT studies in a classroom. You couldn't use even the *word* "gender." You couldn't teach or pose questions about gender or sexuality in the classroom, based on directives coming from the Ministry of Education. Of course, those directives were difficult to enforce. Still, there were parents who would get their kids to maybe film a teacher saying something, post it on the internet, then complain about it and mount a whole campaign over it.

In general, the far-right discourse against the concept of "gender" creates a climate that makes it hard, or harder, to debate and teach these questions and ideas. Professors, unlike teachers at lower levels of education, are generally protected by being at university, but not entirely, and so there are cases throughout the country of individual professors being targeted, and everybody sees that and no one wants to be targeted. So, I would say, there have been multiple kinds of responses. Some people organized resistance and mobilized because they were really determined to defend gender studies. Other people, who withdrew, were fearful or concerned about what this might mean in terms of their own career and the legal jeopardy this would place them in.

I think it's really important to understand that what we have been seeing in Brazil and Eastern Europe, and more recently in the United States, is really global. These antidemocratic attacks are a worldwide phenomenon. If Marine Le Pen wins the next presidential election in France, that will energize the far right in Latin America and in Brazil, because the right wing here will be buoyed by that, at least temporarily buoyed, for sure. But it's also important to note the national differences. Brazil is definitely much better for queer people than certain places in Africa, where in some countries it has gotten very dangerous to be queer. That dovetails with antidemocratic authoritarianism, doesn't it? In that regard, Israel is particularly interesting, because it's the place in the world where there's been the most consistent organized resistance to these kinds of antidemocratic attacks. For twenty weeks in a row, people went out in the streets of Tel Aviv and other cities, protesting what is clearly an attack on democracy there (as of this week, the protests are ongoing). And that's what it is going to take—permanent mobilization. Elections won't—can't—solve problems within societies that are totally polarized and particularly if the divide is almost fifty-fifty. And where is this sort of divide *not* happening?

Bolsonaro was, of course, defeated in 2022 in a very close race by the former president of Brazil, Luiz Inácio Lula da Silva, who had first been elected president in 2002 and was reelected in 2006. He won a third term after spending 580 days in prison on corruption charges which were subsequently dismissed, but clearly, the country—just like the United States in 2016 and 2020—was extremely divided over the election. And it is still divided. The right is still attacking and using the Congress as their principal means to attack, because they have a strong following in the Congress and they have a majority in both houses, and that will make it very difficult for Lula to govern.

Lula has been in power for only six months, after suffering a mob attack not unlike our January 6 attack on the U.S. Capitol. On January 8, just a week after Lula was inaugurated in Brasilia, several thousand people invaded the Congress, the seat of the Supreme Court, and the Presidential Palace and destroyed property. It was an attempt to carry out a coup to overturn the election of Lula. Fortunately, the armed forces were divided, in part because of international pressure. I helped to organize some of that international pressure through an organization called the Washington Brazil Office, which sought to make sure that the Biden administration supported the electoral process and accepted the results. And he did. He did so immediately, which was really important at that moment. U.S. congressional statements, letters, and declarations were also essential in this regard. The Brazilian military knew it was not going to get U.S. support; it was not getting the green light to do anything like a coup. And so, even though the military, too, was divided, the attempted coup was unsuccessful, because the military, as a whole, did not back a coup attempt.

Currently in Brazil we see a process of rebuilding in all levels of society.

The new Lula government has appointed some amazing people to certain ministries. I mean really quite fabulous people. There's visibility for trans people, for example, in the Ministry of Human Rights. Symmy Larrat, Brazil's National Secretary for the promotion of LGBTQIA+ rights, is a trans woman. She currently occupies the most important and highest position in the government dealing with LGBTQ rights, and she is a very politicized trans woman. She had been the president of the Brazilian LGBT Association (ABGLT) prior to taking on this role.

Brazil is a very contradictory country. Even when it was under a dictatorship, it was very different from the dictatorships found in other countries. I think that the tradition of thirty years, forty years fighting for democracy has been one of the reasons why there has been such strong resistance to the right's agenda.

But that's not to say the country isn't *extremely* polarized. Again, much like the United States, there's a hard-core 30 percent of the electorate which supports Bolsonaro and will continue to do so, no matter what. Even though there was an attempt to purge his supporters within the bureaucracy of the government, that hasn't been entirely effective either. There remains a lot of people who are occupying spaces and are doing things to undercut the current government. Additionally, there is an extremely conservative Congress and, therefore, it's very hard to get a lot of good social measures approved and implemented into law. In Brazil, presidents can make executive decrees, and these decrees are valid for a certain amount of time, but then they have to be ratified by the Congress. It has been very difficult to get some of Lula's legislative agenda approved. Just like Trump in the United States, Bolsonaro might be declared ineligible in the next couple weeks to run for the presidency again, for some of the things he did while he was president.[1]

Regardless of what happens with Bolsonaro, the movement that he represents has not gone away just because Lula got just a tiny bit larger fraction of the vote. The right is going to reorganize and go on the offensive again. And with a society this incredibly polarized, you can't tell what's going to happen.

But I have to say, now there's a new generation of younger people coming up, like in the United States, in Europe, and in other parts of the world, who have opportunities for self-determination and self-expression that were just not there for me when I was young. That is really quite powerful and not so easily suppressed. I think, in terms of feminism, a large number of people of color at Brazilian universities have been appropriating many ideas of feminism, and in different ways that strengthen feminism. Women in the Black movement are really the clear leaders now. Black feminist discourse is becoming stronger and stronger, not just in theory but in practice, and in terms of people understanding the importance of Black women in leadership roles in politics and in social movements. This has really been revolutionary, and that's not so easy to bottle up again.

Besides, you know, heterosexuals are amazingly proficient at producing children who are queer, aren't they? Queerness doesn't just go away because you think it should.

And, for this reason, I think the feminist and LGBTQIA+ movements and their supporters in academia will be able to resist ongoing assaults in Brazil. Look at the LGBTQIA+ parade in São Paulo we just had! Organizers claimed that about three million people participated in this annual event. Even if that's an exaggeration, *at least a million people were in that parade*. And that's a *really huge* number of people. It's the largest LGBT parade in the world, so you have a really dynamic movement in Brazil that is very strong and highly visible. That visibility has all the effects on the culture that you would expect it to have, including on universities.

Yes, I would say there's *growing* support for queer and for gender studies in Brazil, and for developing multiple ways of understanding these questions and issues within and outside of universities, even if the far right isn't just going to suddenly fade away because of one election.

The fact is that we aren't going away either.

Note

1. In June 2023, the Brazilian Superior Electoral Court, which oversees elections, ruled that Bolsonaro was ineligible to run for office until 2030.

How are gender studies scholars feeling in Brazil?
A conversation with Cristina Scheibe Wolff

Cristina Scheibe Wolff, a historian of women's and gender history, is full professor in the History Department of the Federal University of Santa Catarina in Brazil (UFSC). She coordinates LEGH—Gender and History Studies Laboratory (https://legh.cfh.ufsc.br). She is a member of the editorial board of *Revista Estudos Feministas* (https://www.scielo.br/j/ref/). Her current research, "The Internet as a Field of Disputes for Gender Equality," is supported by FAPESC and CNPq. Among her primary publications are *Mulheres da floresta: uma história*, or *Women of the Forest: A History, 1890–1945* (1999). Newer works include "The Electromagnetic Shape of Feminism: Weathering Brazil's Political Crisis" (*Journal of International Women's Studies*, 2019); *Mulheres de luta: Feminismo e esquerdas no Brasil* or *Women of Struggle: Feminism and the Left Wing in Brazil, 1964–1985* (2019), and *Políticas da emoção e do gênero no Cone Sul* or *Politics of Gender and Emotions in South America* (2021). She can be reached at cristina.wolff@ufsc.br.

Editors of Pandemonium *spoke with Cristina Scheibe Wolff on July 7, 2023.*

In Brazil, certainly in my university, it's a pretty good environment right now for women's and gender studies. We have a lot of people who work in gender and women's studies in the university. So we have a good deal of support and faculty resources. And, most importantly, we have the Instituto de Estudos de Gênero (Gender Studies Institute)[1] and there is also Laboratório de Estudos de Gênero e História (Laboratory of Gender and History Studies).[2] Those are interdisciplinary centers, but they do not function like a department. I'm in the History Department, each faculty has an appointment in a department, and the institute does not have faculty lines. But that also means we are independent of departments. We are employed by the federal government, for research we often obtain funding from other agencies, but the majority are governmental agencies like CAPES, CNPq, and FAPESC. But the institute is very important. It is very, very important to the study of gender in Brazil and, really, to all of Latin America.

We do three principal things at the institute:

We edit a journal, *Revista Estudos Feministas*.[3] This is maybe the most important, or recognized and referenced, gender studies journal in Latin America.

We also hold a really huge seminar or conference that's called Fazendo Gênero, or, in English, "Doing Gender."[4] That conference is held every three years. We are now organizing for the next one, which will be held in 2024. I think it's going to be a really important conference next year, because it will be the first in-person conference since before the pandemic. I expect this next conference will be the biggest one ever, perhaps.

Of course, we do other things, like research collaborations and publications, and we host some speaker series and events aimed at students and other events bringing gender studies scholars together. We have a concentration area in gender studies in the human sciences interdisciplinary PhD program for doctoral students to be credentialed in the field. And we have a social media presence, of course, which really makes our voices heard even more broadly.

So we have a lot of support and energy for gender studies here, but, for sure, we really started to feel the pressure, I would say, ten years ago, starting in 2013. That's when there was a very difficult discussion in Brazil about the National Education Plan for the next ten years. In this debate, it began to appear that the question of gender ideology was going to be the biggest issue. The Catholic Church in Brazil, and the evangelical churches, they kind of coalesced with right-wing forces into a movement that was called the "anti-gender ideology" movement. So I would say it really began then.

And very quickly, they began to launch attacks, some quite personal, against individual teachers, especially teachers in basic education, not as much university professors yet, this was at the basic levels of education in Brazil. But pretty quickly, the universities also were starting to be called too political, too ideological. They were speaking all the time in the Congress about this, and the outrage over it was constantly in the media and just exploded in social media networks.

There was a case brought against a professor in, not my university, but in the State University of Santa Catarina (UDESC). That professor was a member of our institute. And she had an MA student, someone with a lot of followers on Instagram, who was elected a state deputy in 2018 with a campaign largely based on her anti-feminism stance. The state deputy accused our colleague, Marlene de Fáveri, of "feminist indoctrination" combined with a sort of "Christian-phobia"—which means a kind of a hatred of, or discrimination against, Christianity. That deputy processed the professor, and this processing was important to her campaign, it got her known and elected.

Of course, all this was really quite staged. I mean, the deputy had entered the master's program, in the first place, with a totally false scholarly project she claimed to want to do about feminism and gender, but all the while she planned to accuse a feminist professor of indoctrination and go public with it, to drum up support for her candidacy. In the middle of this campaign against the professor, this state deputy linked to another movement that was very strong in Brazil and Latin America at the time, called "School without Politics" or "Escola sem Partido" (EsP). And, you know, it really is this simple idea that school should not be about politics, and anything that threatens or is critical of the church, the state, the economy, foreign relations, you know, really anything that's critical at all about anything can be called "politics," of course!

But this EsP became a huge movement in Latin America and in Brazil specifically. And, pretty suddenly, the focus—which originally was mostly about Marxists in academia, who criticize capitalism and class relations—suddenly was shifting to focus on those of us teaching about gender and sexual relationships and identity.

The leaders of the EsP movement tried to pass legislation in every state and municipality against what they called "gender ideology"—and they are still trying, even today, and even though the Supreme Court decided that was unconstitutional, they are still trying.

That term—"gender ideology"—you know, it's only a phrase that is meant to inspire panic and make teachers and professors fearful. But it worked: they put a lot of fear into the minds of teachers and professors, and, you know, in the History Department, we teach people who will become teachers, so now we see students coming to the university already very fearful about studying gender issues. This hasn't ended: teachers who are working in the schools now, who have been through this as university students, have and are suffering from attacks, even outright aggressions towards them. Only this week, there was a case about a teacher who was violently harassed by a parent of one of his students, a parent who was also a police officer—and this was just because the teacher spoke about gender in the classroom. It's still happening and still a huge part of what gender studies scholars and teachers are facing in Brazil.

But just because there are a lot of accusations and aggression expressed towards us, still, that doesn't mean we don't have a lot of support and aren't seeing a huge increase, actually, in student interest in gender studies. I have more students in my gender history class than ever before, and we have a lot more people in our conferences, coming to our speaking events—really, it's like never before. Even with the pandemic . . . in some ways, that only amplified the interest in our work and our ability to reach people. I don't know how many talks I gave during the pandemic, over the internet, and you know, you reach even more people that way than we could have ever imagined back when I started teaching as a professor. Even just this year, since January, I have given maybe four or five talks over the internet—that's basically every month. And we are doing this now normally, even apart from the need for remote instruction that was created by the pandemic. Since that need passed, we find we've all just gotten used to it and the internet technologies have just made it so much easier to reach so many people and for us to communicate with each other. Even if the way the internet is public and our talks can be recorded and used against us, well, yes, that puts some fear in people, but at the same time it creates the conditions for a movement that is stronger and involves more people too.

Now, that's the good news. But that is not to say there hasn't been a whole lot of fear created—fear for our programs and our careers and maybe even our personal safety that was produced especially during the Bolsonaro years. At that time, we were afraid that they would either get rid of the interdisciplinary concentration or possibly even purge all feminists from the university.

In 2018, when Bolsonaro won the election, I, personally, had a lot of fear of this happening. In the end, you know, he didn't really accomplish anything like that. I think he wanted to, and he made public promises that he would, but maybe he didn't have the power to do it. And so, between 2018 and 2022, what he could do, he did: he cut funds for the university. The government support became very low, not only for gender studies but for all the humanities and social sciences and even for technological sciences. But I had already secured some funding for research projects that were ongoing and established long before he came along. The long and slow ways that academia functions really worked in our favor then—many of us managed to continue our own independent research for precisely this reason.

But the funding for the journal was pretty much gone. And that was very, very difficult, considering how important that publication is to all of gender studies as a field. We managed, somehow. JSTOR provided some funding for the journal, which was key, and those dollars, you know, they multiply a lot. And that way, if you can imagine, we were able to publish our three issues each year, every year, even during Bolsonaro and even all through the pandemic. Pulling funding was one thing, but he didn't manage to exert censorship over the journal. And, you know, to fire any one of us, well, that requires a process and takes a long time—just like anything else at the university!—and Bolsonaro did not have that long time or care enough to make that his priority, I guess. What he wanted, and what he used us for, was as a rhetorical target that would help get people very excited very quickly.

Speaking for myself, I have tenure, I'm a full professor, and I have many publications and do research, and I get grants and am on fellowships, so I'm very recognized in my field, and I, personally, never suffered any personal attack. In my own department, the History Department, I have the formal, you know, public support of my colleagues and the department administration. That doesn't mean there isn't tension. There are a lot of tensions in the department, because, you know, there is always this kind of tension in any department, and when the politics on the outside get bad, those tensions can get pretty bad too. But that's quite normal.

The problem is that lots of faculty in the regular departments and traditional disciplines like history, you know, they argue, they have argued for a long, long time, that gender is not important or, in my case, women's history is not the important history, these are not the important questions we should be studying. Women are more like, you know, *perfume* ... [*laughter*] ... it's nice to have, it smells nice, but you don't need it.

The controversy and the attacks, well, actually that made it a lot harder to say you don't need to study gender in history or women are not political subjects. You know, in the struggle between left and right in Latin America, it seems power is all about class and imperialism maybe, but not about gender. There were a lot of people, good left-wing people, who would say, ah, it's not important. They aren't saying that so much now, not with these attacks. Now, it seems clear that the question of gender and sexuality and women *is* very important and is *very* political and is really quite worth studying and being serious about.

So, because of all these attacks, I would say it has become more clear that feminists and feminist scholars belong to the left and not the right, even though of course a lot of women are right-wing, but *feminism* is not at all right-wing.

I want to say a little bit here about the incident with Judith Butler, who was attacked when they came to Brazil in 2017, and I know that got a lot of attention in the United States. The conference they came to speak at did not take place where I am, in Florianópolis, so I was not a part of those events. But we did hear about it, of course, and we were very appalled to hear about what was happening, it was quite terrible. But maybe it didn't stand out so much for us at that moment because there had also just been the coup against Dilma Rousseff in 2016. The coup was very misogynist. The discourse for taking Dilma down was very misogynist, in fact. So, at the time of Judith Butler's visit, we were all reeling still from many public expressions of misogyny. There was also, at this time, an attack on a museum that had a show with people who were naked and that came under vicious attack by the same movement—the MBL, or Movimento Brasil Livre (Free Brazil Movement). But of course, you know, we assign Judith Butler's work in our courses, and in our published texts, so seeing that incident explode on someone whose work we teach, that had an impact on us, of course. But it was a part of a bigger set of public incidents and so was not something that stood out as much for us as probably for them and for the media outside of Brazil to report on.

There was also a lot happening that year that was good too, that I was more focused on. Even with all these heinous incidents and misogyny, that same year, in July of 2017, just three months before Judith Butler came to Brazil, we held our Doing Gender conference, at the same time as the Women's World's Congress, and we had nine thousand people attending! It was on YouTube and transmitted online. What a huge event that was, and such an accomplishment. And we experienced no such attacks on those conferences.

Something like that happening now since Lula won the election, yeah, I think would be different, I think we would be more shocked. With Lula in the government, even here in Santa Catarina in South Brazil, the state where Bolsonaro and his followers had the highest voting rate, things feel very different than they did when Bolsonaro was in power. Although the right wing here continues to launch their attacks on "gender ideology" (and communism, of course), they are not able to get as much traction against us or so easily whip up as much public protest or panic as they did while Bolsonaro was pushing his agenda.

About the future?

What I think is going to be most difficult is the renewal of younger generations of feminist scholars and teachers. We leaders, the ones that built the Gender Institute, we are getting old now. We have some new professors coming up, new people beginning to enter the university, but not all of them want to work the way we have worked, the way that feminists have always had to work in the university, and women in general, which is often doing things for no money, doing things as volunteers. Because there is a lot of voluntary work involved in this kind of thing. Not just teaching but, for example, the journal; you know you don't get anything for the hours you spend on the journal. And that's being called into question by younger women. They don't want to be taken advantage of, they don't want to do all the things that women always do for free, you know. And, I understand, they have a point—we taught them that point! But the fact is, this is also work that you believe in, work that creates the world you want to live in, so you do it for free or it doesn't happen at all. You don't usually get paid to change the world.

For example, I think the only reason the journal is still surviving is because we have some professors who are retired and yet continue to work on the journal. That's the secret way of unpaid labor, right? Like the grandmothers who do the mothering because their daughters do the working. They have to do it for nothing, right?

Let me say though, even with all this worry, in this moment, I am optimistic, absolutely! If this were last year, perhaps I would not be. But at this moment, I really am very optimistic. It's not easy. It's not an easy path. It's hard work to keep growing, especially with all that is happening around us. But I see how people are very motivated. Maybe more motivated than ever. The young people, young students in master's programs, in PhD programs, and even in the undergraduate programs, they are very motivated about gender studies, and sexuality studies too, certainly. I think feminists' movements—in plural, because it's not one, it's multiple—are growing, exploding, really. Feminists, and digital feminists, and radical feminists, and trans feminists. You know, there is a lot of discussion and some disagreements, but that's good because it's growing, it's not stagnant, it's alive, and it is not weakening.

And certainly there is a strong relationship between these feminist movements and the university, because a lot of these feminists are or were our students! A lot of them who are in these feminist movements learned about the movements at the university. That's how we know we have had, and are still having, a huge impact on our society.

Feminism in Brazil, and at the university, is very alive.

As alive as ever, or more so.

Notes

1. See Instituto de Estudos de Gênero, n.d.
2. See Laboratório de Estudos de Gênero e História, n.d.
3. See Scientific Electronic Library Online, n.d.
4. See Fazendo Gênero 13, n.d.

Works Cited

Fazendo Gênero 13. n.d. "Welcome." Accessed January 10, 2024. https://www.fg2024.eventos.dype.com.br/.

Instituto de Estudos de Gênero. n.d. "Início." Accessed January 10, 2024. https://ieg.ufsc.br/.

Laboratório de Estudos de Gênero e História. n.d. "Início." Accessed January 10, 2024. https://legh.cfh.ufsc.br/.

Scientific Electronic Library Online. n.d. "Revista Estudos Feministas." Accessed January 10, 2024. https://www.scielo.br/j/ref/.

How should feminist studies in the United States mobilize for action?
A conversation with Karsonya Wise Whitehead

Karsonya Wise Whitehead is past president of the National Women's Studies Association, professor of communication and African and African American studies at Loyola University Maryland, and the founding executive director of the Karson Institute for Race, Peace & Social Justice. She can be reached at kewhitehead@loyola.edu.

Editors of Pandemonium *spoke with Karsonya Wise Whitehead on June 23, 2023.*

This is not a moment for us to be quiet.

This is a point where the NWSA [National Women's Studies Association] needs to stand in front of our members to support them. My role as president is to use our big, really huge, platform to speak up in this moment and be active. We're facing multiple battles at this point. It's not just women's and gender studies that is under attack, it's also African American history and LGBTQIA+ studies. So it is a multilayered challenge, and all of these issues are equally as important, but they're equally as taxing, and so, yes, the question definitely is: where do we go from here?

When I take a look at what is happening around the country and what has been building to the moment that we are in, I'd say we were not prepared for how vicious the attack was going to be, I don't think. We have been watching this build in support of what is happening in places like Florida and Texas. And maybe that did not surprise us so much—I mean seeing all this take place in Texas or North Carolina, South Carolina, Georgia, Indiana, even Ohio. But what is surprising is the way in which the conservative

WSQ: Women's Studies Quarterly 52: 1 & 2 (Spring/Summer 2024) © 2024 by Karsonya Wise Whitehead and Tracey Jean Boisseau. All rights reserved.

right has been able to organize on the local level. And that's giving me a lot of reason for concern. I think we have spent a lot of time watching the national level, watching those politicians, or watching what governors are doing, making sure that we are putting people in those offices, but we haven't been paying enough attention to the *local* organizing. So if you look at West Virginia and the fact that even though West Virginia positions itself as a blue state, we know it's purple, because on the local level you have conservative right-wing politicians who have been voted onto the school board, or the town council, and that's where the attacks are taking place, and the impact is really being felt.

Yes, I would say it's a twofold attack. I think sometimes people conflate the two levels of attack, and I'm not sure it is strategic for us to do so.

I think there's a very specific set of attacks on American education happening in the pre-kindergarten through twelfth-grade environment. And when you start talking about public and independent elementary and high schools, well, that is a different attack than what's happening in colleges and universities. Colleges and universities are places where you can really push and believe in and exercise free thought. That's where students are taking courses in women's and gender studies and sexuality studies. They can choose how they want to design their major. Professors in colleges can— well, if their departments are not being closed—still offer those types of courses, and students can participate in this sort of open and free debate and exchange. We can still invite speakers to be able to delve into these topics. And, even if our department has closed, even if we're being funneled to other departments, we can think about what the next step is going to be for ourselves as teachers and as scholars.

That's a different battle than what's taking place in pre-kindergarten through twelfth grade right now in the U.S. These people's livelihoods are at stake; they are at risk of losing their jobs, or in some states (if you think about Florida and Texas, specifically) you can possibly be arrested and charged with a crime. When you combine *that* with the book banning? And what's happening with libraries? Well, I think it's clear we have to respond to this in ways that go well beyond just what we see happening in colleges and universities.

My greatest concern is what's happening in pre-K through twelfth grade, and so the work around academic freedom for those teachers and educators and administrators is very important. We have to recognize that it's the online public harassment that is hitting hard. It's the ways in which teachers are being positioned in the middle of this intense political struggle. I am concerned about the future state of American education, because if you start to shift and change what's happening in pre-kindergarten, in first and second grade, then you will see this issue filtering up to the college level when the students finally reach that level, when they finally understand that what they've been taught is only a very circular and very narrow view of American history.

This is taking us backwards.

And, you know, it's particularly a very personal attack, too. When you think about women's and gender studies, how long it took us to introduce that, I mean the fight it took to even get that *on the table*. Even the fight to allow women to be a part of the university, to be *welcome* on a college campus. We finally had women being admitted in places in ... when? 1960? or 1970? In some cases, 1980? I'm on the Columbia University campus, and it was 1983 before women were finally able to be a part of this campus. And once women were on campus in real numbers, that's when we saw women's and gender studies growing naturally out of that, out of women's presence on campus. So, yes, this struggle is taking us back—way, way back—to a time when women, and people of color and working people, were not even welcome on campus.

And in the U.S., you know, it is not just the field of women's and gender studies, not just LGBTQIA+ studies. It is also African American history too. What we're seeing here is a total cultural war on all our fields and really any work that challenges the status quo. Teaching our fields is different than teaching philosophy or math, where you can uphold the white and male supremacist structure, the structure that's built simply on the words and the history and the lives of white men. If you want, you can uphold that because you're just teaching math, right? Or maybe you're talking about philosophy written by dead white men. Our work is completely situated in challenging the status quo, in upending the way in which things have always been done, and in shifting the way that women are seen in our society, and those who gender-identify as women or as something other than what they were assigned are seen. It's shifting gender norms and gendered understandings. Hey, we are challenging the way that people see themselves in this country, and that is not a comfortable position. That's never going to be comfortable.

If we look at what has been done historically, we can see every step that has been taken to lead us to this moment. There has always been an underlying attack on women's and gender studies. There's always been pushback against us, you know, treating our field as if we were not as important to the curriculum as the core that they've laid out as the primary course of study that students will take. Well, they'll say, you don't actually need a women's history course. You can just take "American" history and maybe—*maybe*—we'll just include some women and some Black people, okay, and maybe even some Latinos, and we'll cover everything through this lens, right? We'll do that in February. Or, we'll do that in March. But then we're really going to situate American history as pretty much a white, male story. That's why it's so challenging. That's why it's also so hard for people to understand, because we're talking about work that gets into the hearts and minds of people. It is not simply taking a test where you can add one plus one, and if you get two, then I know you've got it and I give you a grade.

We're talking about the kind of teaching that eventually leads to students marching out for Black Lives Matter. It leads to tenth-grade students marching out for gun control. It leads to eleventh-grade students challenging gender norms. They are going to expand their world. They are going to challenge what they have been taught is the norm, because they're being taught that there's something *different* that exists out there. This is the kind of hearts-and-minds work that we do, and if you want to stop that type of work from being done, well, you've got to stop the teaching, right? And that's exactly what they are trying to do. Because they don't want to change society, now, do they?

So if what we do was just confined to the campus, it would not be as concerning to people that are not in the academy. I often believe that those of us who live in the academy, sometimes we take the issues of moving commas around the page, and we accelerate the work we're doing to thinking, well, that's really the most important thing in the world. And, you know, we all know it's not, but then you realize that the attacks on our field are closely related to what is happening with the *Dobbs* decision, right? We see the connections between the sociopolitical and what's happening in the academy. That's what we *do*. And we can see it's a twofold attack, which is why we know what we are doing *is* really important, and *is* really relevant, otherwise we wouldn't even be considered a threat. They'd be just ignoring us, and starving us, like they always do, hoping we'll get tired and give up.

But this is exactly why we're *not* giving in, and this is why we can't give up.

They're not just trying to close women's and gender studies. They're not just outing professors in the newspaper and putting us in the middle of their cultural wars. They're not just talking about banning books and going after "critical race theory" when, really, they want to talk about culturally responsive teaching. Oh, they understand the difference, and they're making legal strides to displace the rights and freedoms that women and people of color have fought hard for in this country. That fight and that struggle is closely attached and aligned with the work we're doing in the classroom, and they know that.

There are multiple strategies we have to pursue. I think the lenses that you choose to use will help you find the strategy that's going to be most effective for you.

The idea of leaning in for my work as a president of the NWSA, the very specific lens I use as a Black radical feminist—how I see the world? I look to the work of Angela Davis or Kimberlé Crenshaw; I look to the work of radical Black feminists who have taught me, have shown me, have modeled for me that leaning in is the *only* option. It's leaning in or death, because if you don't directly oppose them, then they're going to take your silence as a form of being complicit and they're going to continue and then you're going to find yourself in positions that if you had just leaned in earlier, you could have avoided some of what's coming down the line. If you had just drawn the line in the sand earlier, then you would be very aware of when they cross it, and then you will know how to act, because if you don't draw the line, then the line keeps moving. They'll give you crumbs because they're convinced that you're just that hungry. And so you take the crumbs they give you rather than demanding what it is that you're really trying to get. And, well, that is a very deliberate, *intentional* strategy, that you're going to lean in.

That's what I talk about when I describe myself within the academy as an activist-academic—and be sure that the word *activist* comes before the word *academic*! You can be sure that, to me, the struggle is not just about writing papers, though that is important. But just as or more important is: Are you willing to show up in the spaces to do the work that needs to be done? To go into the classroom, to be on the ground, to be in person, challenging what is happening? Now, that's a full-time job, and not everyone can work on that type of strategic level.

The second strategy is to be a little bit more clandestine about it, right? Like, clandestine in terms of how you're going to operate, taking a look at the field, determining the best time to move, determining the best strategy for that moment. Sometimes it's a direct approach, sometimes it's an indirect approach, sometimes you want people to march, sometimes you want them to meet, but you have multiple approaches, and multiple strategies going on at the same time. That's the work that allows the movement to continue—that's really the sustainable work.

The activist work gets people's attention, gets them to focus on what you are doing and what you have to say. When NWSA participated in the African American Policy Forum's National Day of Action, our goals were to get people talking about the book banning, about what's happening with gender studies, LGBTQIA+ studies, what's happening in African American history, and what's happening in classrooms from pre-K all the way up to seniors in high school. That was to get people involved, and we told them how they could do something—even if it was in this low-hanging-fruit kind of way. Like, go buy a banned book, take a picture up with it, and then give it to a young person. Yes, some of that is, like, really low-hanging fruit, but that day of action was the activist work, and that work has to be done.

The more academic work is: How do you sustain the movement over the long haul? How do you build a long-term political strategy so that when it's time to vote, you get people to come out to the polls? How do you help them to understand that what we're seeing *now* is a result of their deciding to vote, or not vote, in elections that took place two years ago? And if we want to see something different, not today but three years from now, well, we've got to vote en masse two years from now. That's the kind of long-term type of work that a lot of people who become academics and scholars and teachers are just not comfortable with. But it's just what we have to do, it's the work that needs to get done, and we do that work so we can go back to the work that we trained for and we believe in.

People want to see change happen immediately. And I get that. I don't like to see injustice. I want change. I see you're attacking my field. I want you to stop. But I think we have to start looking at both of the strategies that I laid out, right? I mean, how do we use both? How do we use one kind of strategy to get people's attention? To cut through all the chaotic noises out there, from social media, to Fox News? How do we get the attention of politicians to show them that this is an important issue at this moment. Take their attention away from, say, the *Titan* rescue that's just going on, and say, you know what, while you're focused on that, look at all the other things that are happening.

Activists know that a march is not going to change a law, not immediately. A march is not going to change a bill or create legislation. That requires long-term work where you're showing up and you're voting people out of office. You're putting in the people who will support the right things. That takes long-term work, and I think that academics have to think really clearly about coming out of the Ivory Tower to do that work. Because the Ivory Tower is a very safe place to be when your department is valued, right? You get into the academy and, well, you can be there fifteen, twenty, thirty years. It's a very comfortable place to be *except* when they close your department, right? And then you look around and think: What have I been doing? How did I not notice that all this can go away if we aren't fighting for it all the time?

I'm aware there's a lot of despair among students, but also with our colleagues too, and we forget that these attacks and the constant undercutting, on top of the pandemic, has really affected teachers and our colleagues as well as our students. There's despair, there's fear, and there's anger. If you've been in a struggle for a little bit of time and you're watching how all the things you sacrificed to help programs and curricula get built are being easily torn down by those who have no sense of the work that's been put into it, by people who have no understanding that these are fields that are actually saving people's lives. It saves their lives because these students finally have a voice. They finally have a place that they can call their home. So many of our students are not just taking our courses out of curiosity, although intellectual curiosity is a good thing and a good reason to take our courses. But a lot find us, seek us out, because they need to find a way to think about themselves, they need a language, and a history that they can see themselves in. Our courses, unlike most college courses, save people's lives.

So the fact is, we can't just despair and give up. We have to practice self-care and find a way to support our colleagues to get them through the despair. Because we cannot help mobilize students if we're in a space where we feel we can't live and we can't move forward. I do think we need to talk about getting our colleagues out of the state of despair they are in, helping them to understand that this is not a time for hiding and hoping, this is a time for action.

We also need to understand what it takes to help to mobilize our students and help to move them beyond a place of despair. I mean, we're looking at the next generation of leaders. So how do we get them excited about their college career experience, but beyond that, help them to understand that they are very powerful because they're the next wave of voters? You don't need to go down to the White House to start to do this work. You can do this work on your own campus and then start to recognize that there are campuses around you that you can begin to connect with because there's power in numbers.

I call myself a pessimist with optimist leanings.

And what gives this pessimist the most hope is when I look at the new generation: Gen Z. They came of age during Black Lives Matter, during the pandemic. There was an energy happening on campuses and in high schools and middle schools, and they were actively involved in all that. This is also the generation that may have a memory of the presidency of Barack Obama, but they were deeply engaged with the presidency of Donald Trump too. They were politicized by the Trump presidency. They saw that democracy is fragile and belongs to the people. They came of age dealing with shootings in schools, and instead of just accepting it, they marched out. This is the generation that said, when it comes to climate change, they said that something *can* be done and they marched out for that too. They said enough is enough. And they learned early on that there's power in collective numbers. What we need to do is help this generation keep the hope and be the change we need to keep moving forward.

Because we are not going to go quietly into that good night, right?

This is our moment. We were waiting for it. We were preparing for it. And now it's here.

Will gender studies in Florida survive the United States' turn to the right?
A conversation with Diane Price Herndl

Diane Price Herndl is professor of women's, gender, and sexuality studies at the University of South Florida, where she was chair from 2013 to 2023. Before moving to USF in 2010, she taught at the UNC School of Medicine, the University of Vermont, New Mexico State University, and Iowa State University; she directed the Women's Studies programs at NMSU and ISU. Her research and teaching have focused on illness narratives and disability studies, especially the cultural discourses of breast cancer, but most recently she has been working on gender and science fiction as well as feminisms in higher education administration. She can be reached at priceherndl@usf.edu.

Editors of Pandemonium *spoke with Diane Price Herndl on June 20, 2023.*

That's a big question, but my gut says yes. We will survive this.

We just celebrated our fiftieth anniversary of the founding of the women's studies program, so it's not like women's and gender studies is a new thing for Florida. We're not, you know, one of those programs that just got off the ground and now we're suddenly recruiting and "grooming" and doing all the things that they seem to think we're doing. But, in fact, we are more than surviving; I'd say we're growing.

Even this year, even though we are in the eye of the storm, and through all that Governor DeSantis has put us through this year, the fact is the number of students taking our classes is through the roof. *Through. The. Roof!*

And it isn't just student interest; we are growing in other important ways too. We just added "sexuality" to our name; we did that this year, this year when you would think we might be trying to hide. But we're not. We're not hiding.

And we added "sexuality" to "women's and gender" studies, mostly with the support of the administration and the rest of the faculty. I mean, sure, there were a couple of people who said, "Are you sure you think this is a good time to be doing a thing like that?" But we were sure, yes, we were absolutely sure it's a good time to be doing this, adding sexuality to "women's" and "gender," partly because, you know, "sexuality" studies isn't actually under attack here in Florida. Their weakness is their ignorance. It's not like they've been taking our classes! So, you know, they really don't know what they're talking about, or what we're doing.

I also think I have a perspective on this because of my age and how long I've been in this field, and how long I've been chair.

I mean, I've been around for a really long time, so this is not my first rodeo. In fact, I was in graduate school during the very worst of the last time we were under this kind of focused, concerted political attack. That was the Reagan administration, in the 1980s. Forty years ago, they may actually have had some grounds to be anxious, because women's and gender studies was really new; it was about ten years old, as just a discipline even. There were a whole lot of programs being founded in the eighties, maybe the majority were founded in that decade, even in the decade when the rise of the conservative Reagan revolution was raining down on us.

So this feels really familiar in some ways. In other ways, it feels really new.

And part of what's new is how this relates to the pandemic, because I think it does. Your idea of starting with the pandemic and thinking about its relationship to the current political situation is right on the money. I actually think the pandemic has a lot to do with where we are right now. I see a lot of connection between the pandemic and this assault on gender studies.

Although it's kind of sideways.

I think the way this relates to what happened during the pandemic is that there was a lot of mobilization against the power of the state. Lots of people who never imagined themselves as oppressed by the government—except maybe by having to pay taxes—suddenly were thinking their government was taking away their freedoms, telling them what to do: you know, wear a mask and stay indoors and don't go to that wedding or that family holiday, and then take vaccinations. The right wing immediately realized that they could mobilize the kind of anger people felt at having to restrict their movements. And there was this divide, class divide, between people who could do their work remotely and those who couldn't, and we (university professors) were on one side of that divide, right? It wasn't how any of us really wanted to do our jobs, but we could do our jobs that way, and that isn't true if you're working in a factory, or in retail, or delivering packages, or doing care work, or you're the cable guy, you know, you couldn't work remotely and if you couldn't work, you weren't getting paid. I think that mobilized a lot of working-class people to feel like the traditional party that had supported workers against corporations, the Democrats, had just completely swung over to supporting the intellectual elites, you know, the college-educated elite, and that's partly why we became such a target. And we in gender studies and race studies, we became the focus. Not, you know, climate change, or war.

And then, you know, Fox News (and worse outlets) started pushing those emotional buttons: "Oh, you know, it's a bunch of liberal feminists and queers and trans who are trying to do this to you. They've taken over the schools, and all the teachers, and now they're saying America is bad and your kids are probably queer or will want to be a different gender," and "They think they know better than you, they think they're better than you."

The conservative news pundits who hate us try to make everyone hate us. They sort of merged us with teachers, or working people's memories of teachers, who wouldn't let you do all those things you wanted to do back in high school and you hated school and they made you feel bad about yourself, so therefore you hate all of them. And now they're teaching your kids and, you know, God help you if your kids are coming home saying, I don't know, mom, you know, I don't know that I think queers are such bad people. Well, some parents, hearing that from their kids, they're going to just lose it, you know. And so I do think there's a lot of connection, at least in the United States, certainly in Florida, between the pandemic and all this hostility against the universities and against those of us teaching women's and gender studies and critical race studies.

One of the things that we're dealing with here in Florida, and I think in most places around the country, are newly empowered parents and parent groups. And that sounds really great, right? I mean, we always wanted parents involved with the schools. You want parents involved with their kids' schooling. But then, these parents, they only got involved because they want their kind of narrow-minded ignorance to prevail at school. They don't want anyone teaching their kids that they are free, should be free, to express gender and sexuality any way they choose. And if they are white, they don't want anyone teaching their kids about race and racism and the history of slavery. They are still fighting the Civil War around here.

And the right-wing power elite are just using these parents and getting them even more riled up. The news reports here are covering these hostile and chaotic school board meetings and just making it worse. They have eight-hour meetings because it takes that long for everybody to get their minute in, and they're shouting matches, really.

Maybe the worst is what we have now, these Moms for Liberty. It's a woman-led movement, in fact a lot of the right-wing resistance in Florida is coming from right-wing mothers. I find them terrifying, because they are really powerful, they're organized, and they have, in many ways, learned all the lessons from feminist organizing. Now, they're just turning feminism on its head and even using the language of women's empowerment. It's very, very, very frightening.

A lot of what we're doing to sidestep all this is just doing all the same things that we have been doing, just now we are not trumpeting it as diversity education per se anymore. And we don't need to, anyway, we certainly don't need to impose diversity policies on a homogeneous student body. The diversity of Florida is amazing. The Latino population is enormous. The Black population is strong. The LGBTQ population is profound in Florida. I mean, we have long, long gay rights and gay culture history. So all we have to do is engage these communities in a real way. And that strategy, so far, is really working. I'll be honest, we just haven't had to change anything.

What we're trying to do is walk the letter of the law, and so all of us have become kind of armchair lawyers in trying to figure out what our comfort zone is with how far do we want to push things?

For instance, this new law, the new law that specifically affects the university system in Florida, applies only to what's called the gen ed or the common core curriculum. That's the curriculum that mandates the minimum combination of courses that every student has to have taken to graduate. So the state of Florida has already interfered a lot with what courses are in or out of the gen ed core. I've never worked anywhere that interferes as much as the state of Florida interferes with gen ed. So, just to explain, we have a common core curriculum that has to be taught at all of the state colleges and universities so that students can transfer between them and easily shift from one to the other. But the gen ed curriculum is not the majority of courses on offer, of course. All of what DeSantis is doing really only applies to those few common courses that are already a part of the state curriculum, and, well, big surprise ... WGS has never had a course in that common curriculum! So this whole brouhaha doesn't really touch us, does it? I mean, where it really hurts is Introduction to American History and African American History, and that can't, what? even mention race anymore? Yes, that is a huge problem. But since they had already marginalized women's and gender studies, they can't really touch us directly now the way they can get at history.

So then we have to go back to last year's law HB7, which specified the whole list of things that we can and can't teach. Now that's under an injunction right now. You know, even the judge actually said this law is "positively dystopian." Which says a lot. And it's true. It specifies as one of its pillars that you cannot teach that there is systemic racism and sexism in the United States of America. It's like you can't admit the sky is blue.

But you're asking how we navigate all that. Well, between the time that the law went into effect and the time it went under injunction, I wrote a bunch of guidelines for my department, trying to help them interpret the law and the University General Counsel who sent out a memo outlining what you can and can't do and their take on what you can teach in your classroom, a lot of which boiled down to "you cannot force students to agree with a particular political viewpoint."

And we were all like, "Well, hello! Welcome to higher education!" That's not how it actually works, you know? I mean, my students are pretty clear on the concept that I'm a feminist and they have some ideas about what that means, but they also know that I'm never going to make them write a paper that makes them say: "I hereby solemnly swear . . ." *anything*. We don't do that! That's not what critical thinking or critical inquiry looks like.

It's probably worth noting that during the seven months after the law had been signed, but before it went under injunction, there were twelve complaints [in the whole state] brought against faculty who were supposedly in violation of the law. Four of them were completely groundless. They were by people who were not even students at the universities, they had just seen a course description online maybe. And then several more of them were submitted by parents of students. And all of these violations were looked into, all were found to be nonissues, they were misunderstandings at best, complaints about things that were not even really going on.

Most of us had already put right into our syllabus or our course descriptions that students are not expected to agree with . . . well, with anything. Of course, some students are always going to think that's why they didn't do well in the course. But no, inevitably the fact is, you didn't get graded down because you disagreed with me. You just didn't do the reading, or you didn't understand what you read, or you didn't write the assignment, even.

So we were all in the habit of making that clear to students, but now we put together a workshop for faculty on how to do their job while conforming with the law. Which really wasn't that hard, because none of us are doing the kind of indoctrination that they are accusing us of anyway! I mean, when we are grading them, what we're measuring, we're not measuring whether we've turned them into good feminists or not, because that's not our job. Our job is to help them understand new ideas and learn how to think critically, and express themselves accurately, and that's all, really.

The one thing that could have been a little sticky is that the law forbids us from "teaching activism." And, of course, we had some components of activism in our curriculum—what women's and gender studies program doesn't? So what we're doing is, we're now calling that "community engagement." And "community engagement" is a stated goal and value of the university, so that's okay. So we also learned better how to articulate how the community engagement is connected to the material of the class. Now, that can get a little tricky, because students will try to, like, claim that getting more parking spots on campus is "community engagement" and try to get credit for something entirely unrelated to gender studies, so we had to be clear that it's not just *any* community engagement but engagement that illustrates the ideas of the course. And you have to walk a fine line between the ideas of the course and "activism." That gets a little tricky.

So this is all new—I mean, the new guidelines and the law really goes into effect on July 1. Just yesterday, our syllabi for the summer session were due, and we still don't have any kind of guidance coming from the University Counsel. We are only ten days away now! So I wrote some guidelines myself and just sent it out to my faculty. Yes, just this week!

Meanwhile, we are swamped with student interest like never before. We've had to hire a bunch of full-time visiting people just to cover the demand for our courses. We've got this really quite *enormous* demand. I mean, literally, right now summer session starts next Monday and I've got one course that has one seat left unfilled. I mean, we're practically fully enrolled for the fall, and we've opened section after section after section ... As soon as we open a section, the section fills. Because our students are dying for this stuff, right?

If nothing else, the good side of DeSantis's assault is that it has activated our students, and they are much more savvy about all this and much more engaged and much more concerned about it than at any time I've ever seen in my long career. A lot of our students are taking our courses, calling themselves "stealth majors" because they either can't tell their parents what they are majoring in or they can't navigate the university system of majors to fit us in officially. I mean, that's not good for them because they don't graduate with the credential. And it's not good for our bottom line, because we can't claim them as majors, so it looks like, from the dean's metrics, that we don't have a lot of students. But that makes no sense either, if you look at our student credit production numbers, which is doing nothing but growing, as I said.

Of course, the same kids who are "stealth majors," who can't tell their parents they are taking our courses, are often the very same kids who are not out to their parents either. And their parents have no idea, or try to pretend not to see it. We are a lifeline for those kids.

I'm confident that we will survive and continue, and even thrive, because I remember the 1970s and I remember the 1960s, I remember how bad it was for women and how it was worse for women of color and so much worse for the LGBTQ community back then, when I was young. I remember all of those really bad days. I remember when people on TV thought it was okay to say: "We don't need to treat AIDS. It's just god's punishment for being gay. We should just let them all die." That wasn't that long ago.

But that wasn't the end of the story, was it?

There was a time in the eighties when I was convinced it wouldn't survive, that we wouldn't have feminist studies into the twenty-first century. That they'll just kill us with a thousand cuts. But we did, we survived, somehow, and it actually got stronger and it got better and the tent got bigger, and I think the same thing is going to happen with this, I think. We'll get through this, because if there's anything that our communities have proven, it is that we're resilient.

We will survive. Yes, we will, despite this roller coaster of a year.

But then you ask me if I'm hopeful? And, well, I wouldn't say *hopeful* exactly, it isn't the right word. I would rather say I'm *confident*. Because I'm confident that we'll keep fighting and that's a little bit different from the idea that we can just hope our way forward, and everything's going to be fine, isn't it? And that's my leadership style too.

What's my leadership style? It goes something like this:

So they just dumped a huge smoking pile of shit in our backyard . . . I say, let's figure out how we can compost that and grow our garden . . . *bigger than ever.*

How is anti-democratic repression affecting women's and gender studies in Turkey?

A conversation with Nurseli Yeşim Sünbüloğlu

Nurseli Yeşim Sünbüloğlu is a visiting faculty and director of the Women and Family Studies Research Center at Kadir Has University located in Istanbul, Turkey. Her research focuses on masculinities, disability, militarism, nationalism, and anti-gender backlash. Her most recent publication has appeared in *NORMA: International Journal for Masculinity Studies* (2022). She edited a volume in Turkish on militarism, nationalism, and men and masculinities in Turkey (2013). She is a member of the Initiative for Critical Studies of Masculinities. She has coordinated two gender projects, "Non-Violent Masculinities Workshops Manual" (2020–2021) and "e-Gen (Equality Generation) Module for Young Men at High Schools" (2022–2023), and has been a researcher in other projects focusing on gender-based violence, gender backlash, and institutionalization of gender equality. She can be reached at yesim.sunbuloglu@khas.edu.tr.

Editors of Pandemonium *spoke with Nurseli Yeşim Sünbüloğlu on July 25, 2023.*

So, it makes sense to start with the recent changing of our name—from the Gender and Women's Research Center to the Women and Family Studies Research Center.

This change is quite recent, just six months ago, in fact. This came about probably because of a study—an annual survey has been going on for three or four years, the product of a collaboration with a local NGO called Kaos GL (short for Kaos Gay and Lesbian Cultural Research and Solidarity), which supports and promotes human rights for LGBTQAI+ people in Turkey. My university has collaborated annually with this NGO to provide research support for their study of discrimination against LGBTI+ employees in public and private sectors in Turkey. This time, this collaboration put us on the radar of certain conservative government agencies. They took notice of us because there was a press release to promote that year's (2021) study that came out last year (2022). We had to remove all kinds of references to the study on our website as well as references to the rights of sexual minorities in general. We also had to change the name of the research center from "gender and women's" to "women and family."

This kind of attention and pressure from political authorities is not unique to us or to our university. They've been doing this kind of thing to quite a lot of state universities. A majority of women's studies centers in Turkey have gone through the same name change. In fact, I would say all universities in Turkey are feeling this pressure. All universities are under some kind of control, but their authority over some of the private universities might be less, depending on the situation. Depending on exactly where the private universities get their research funding from, they may have more room to maneuver around politically contentious issues, not only issues of gender and sexuality but lots of other politically contentious issues as well. Whereas the state universities—my university is a private university—are under a lot more direct pressure, and so are their gender scholars.

So, you know, this sort of pressure and repression—it's been going on for quite some time. But the name change was, I would say, significant—a significant signal more than an actual change. At Kadir Has, we are actually one of the few universities in Turkey that still promotes feminist research and calls it "feminist" research in our mission statement right there on the website beneath that new name "women and family studies."

Of course, their insistence we take out "gender" and add "family" to our name reflects how very narrow their understanding of women's studies, or any discipline, really is. Their thinking is that women's studies is just about women and their domestic life in the family, or should be! And so, if we add "family" into the name, then these studies will naturally—I don't know, maybe automatically?—reflect this kind of thinking, that women are only important as they relate to family matters. Of course, studying the family can also be very political! And family studies is a critical scientific discipline on its own. But, you know, they think of "family studies" as just ideas that support a (conservative, traditional definition of a) family—a patriarchal idea of what a family is. So, yeah, stick the word "family" in and they think they have changed us. After the name change, we were joking that one of the first projects we might support would be to study how the conservative, patriarchal family in Turkey is changing! The point is we can do a lot under the auspices of that name change that aligns with our mission anyway.

But even though the name change does not, in itself, largely affect what we do or what our mission really is, the fact that they would pay such close attention to us and make us change our name—well, that was new and quite significant, we think. Obviously, it makes us more aware about what we say in public, or how we define ourselves, what kinds of projects we feel we can do without getting more attention, who we can collaborate with and for what purposes. So, yes, on the one hand it is a minor thing that maybe doesn't mean much, but on the other hand, I think it's actually affecting us a lot. And probably that was their intention after all.

I don't feel personally threatened, not about my job or my position. It's more of a fear that something will happen to the center itself because that's, you know, that's the real threat. But that would not mean I lose my job at the university, either. I am affiliated with the gender and women's studies PhD program, but I am a faculty of what's called the Core Program and my appointment would still be in the Core Program, teaching first-year students mainly. On the other hand, it would transform a lot of what I do here at the university, of course.

And of course, I mean, I would continue to publish. In fact, my recent forthcoming publication with a colleague is about gender backlash in Turkey. We have experienced no restrictions on topics in our publications. And certain gender research receives quite strong support, especially those studies that are funded internationally, and in particular those projects that are focused on gender equality. The Higher Education Council can't get around that funding; in fact, just three days ago, we got funding for a project on men's engagement in gender equality efforts by NGOs in Turkey, from the national funding body itself. And the reviewer report for our application even asked us to pay *more* attention to the sociopolitical atmosphere, the atmosphere of gender inequality and discrimination in Turkey, so that's also true. It's not black and white. One hand of the government doesn't always know what the other hand is doing.

We, as gender scholars, sometimes self-censor—as a strategy—in our work and academic events we organize. But, again, the strategy is to just remove the single buzzwords that get all the attention of the authorities, not change the substance really at all.

I do think we self-censor in our teaching, to some extent, not with the postgraduates, but the undergraduates whom you really don't know, it might be risky. Because there's this complaint mechanism where citizens can directly complain to the presidency office. That's a very direct, effective way to complain, not through the police or any other institution, but directly, you know, through your own initiative. There have definitely been incidences of these complaints leading to consequences such as a faculty member—at a different university—at risk of losing her position. Now, that gets a lot of attention—I think the most controversial one was even reported in the United States—and that has an effect on us too.

Of course, we've got students on both sides, you know, those who will complain that you are a feminist, but also those who are already aware of gender discrimination and are enthusiastic to discuss this topic in class. Some are more fervent in how they express themselves. Some students make it very explicit that they don't like to discuss gender equality. Some male students, and some female students too, are particularly and explicitly unhappy discussing gender equality, or feminism, but then when you start talking about intersectionality and we specifically focus on how, say, Black men are criminalized because of their gender and race at the same time . . . well, when we talk about that and give specific examples that show how men are hurt by the systems of power that are in place, well, then they're all ears! And they become very interested, you know, all of a sudden. In this way, it is still possible to catch their attention and create a learning environment where hopefully they can start thinking about examples of discrimination against women as well.

All students in our Core Program take the same set of courses, the same modules, and one of those modules is "gender and diversity." And that hasn't changed. And especially research on gender and equality goes on and is even supported—supported even by the state. The current landscape of research, research in general and feminist research included, is so closely tied to international funding bodies and other kinds of networks that I don't think it will be cut out completely, because to be able to apply to the EU for research funding, a university must have a gender equality plan in action, and this is still a requirement. So the Higher Education Council and national funding bodies want all the universities to have their own gender equality plans. That's the irony. I mean, of course, they don't care about whether the plans are being implemented effectively, or even at all, but all universities must have this plan in place, because it's a requirement.

So, on the one hand, all these gender projects are going on, and the universities have their gender equality plans . . . and on the other hand, there are all these, you know, pressures and this self-censorship happening.

Yes, there's increasing authoritarianism in Turkey, but the state bureaucracy is vast, there's all kinds of institutions and state-run programs with international collaborations as well as civil-society institutions. When you consider all of them, it's a complex web of networks and institutions. Regardless of how authoritarian a political party or just one person can be, his or his party's power cannot have absolute control over this complex web of institutions and networks. It's just not possible in Turkey, given its long history of strong institutions. Yet again, I cannot deny the atmosphere is pretty stifling at the moment.

Also, you must understand, Turkey has a very long history of being under authoritarian rule, to various extents, even under military rule, although the current one has particular features and power. Turkey has this very long history, over many decades, even going back to the Ottoman Empire, so ordinary people have developed strategies, various resistance strategies. And I think we are still benefiting from this, from the remnants of various democratic movements and traditions—significantly feminist movements.

So, yes, both things are true. The authoritarianism and the resistance. Both are a big part of Turkey's history.

The fact is, people really aren't sure how the authoritarian power trickles down to them... or not. Sometimes you don't feel it directly, but that might be when it is most powerful, when you have to guess at its power over you.

I was just sitting on a review panel for a project to be submitted to the national funding body. This was a PhD student's project, on gender in education. They have less experience, obviously; they're less secure than a lot of faculty, and they didn't know where to draw the line in their proposal when it comes to politics. We faculty all noticed there was not a single word to refer to the political context in Turkey. Not a single word! I mean, how can you possibly study gender equity in higher education and make zero reference to the larger political context of gender and gender inequality? You simply can't do that, right? And this is a PhD in gender and women's studies, too! They were so afraid to say the wrong thing, they were simply self-censoring—censoring themselves far beyond what was necessary, in fact.

That was an important lesson for me personally, to see that self-censorship can be more effective than the actual repression probably is even capable of being. That's probably going to be an important lesson for all of us to keep in mind. And not just in Turkey!

What are the challenges facing Africanist and African women's and gender studies scholars?
A conversation with Gabeba Baderoon, Maha Marouan, and Alicia Decker

---

Gabeba Baderoon is associate professor of women's, gender, and sexuality studies, African studies, and comparative literature at the Pennsylvania State University, where she codirects the African Feminist Initiative. She received a PhD in English from the University of Cape Town. Baderoon is the author of *Regarding Muslims: From Slavery to Post-Apartheid* (2014) and the poetry collections *The Dream in the Next Body* (2008), *A Hundred Silences* (2008), and *The History of Intimacy* (2021). She is also coeditor with Desiree Lewis of the award-winning collection of essays *Surfacing: On Being Black and Feminist in South Africa* (2021). With Alicia Decker, she coedited a special issue of *Meridians: Feminism, Race, Transnationalism*, "African Feminisms: Cartographies for the Twenty-First Century" (2018). She can be reached at gxb26@psu.edu.

Maha Marouan is an African feminist scholar, writer, and documentarian. She is associate professor of women's, gender, and sexuality studies, African American studies, and African studies at the Pennsylvania State University, where she codirects the African Feminist Initiative. Her published works include *Witches, Goddesses, and Angry Spirits: The Politics of Spiritual Liberation in African Diaspora Women's Fiction* (2013); a coedited volume, *Race and Displacement: Nation, Migration, and Identity in the Twenty-First Century* (2013); and a Women Make Movies documentary, *Voices of Muslim Women in the U.S. South* (2015). Marouan is currently coediting, with Zinhle ka'Nobuhlaluse and Alicia Decker, a special issue of *Feminist Formations*, "Writing African Feminist Subjectivities" (forthcoming in 2024). She can be reached at mzm24@psu.edu.

Alicia Decker is associate professor of women's, gender, and sexuality studies, African studies, and history at the Pennsylvania State University, where she serves as head of the Department of Women's, Gender, and Sexuality Studies and codirector of the African Feminist Initiative. She is the author of *In Idi Amin's Shadow: Women, Gender, and Militarism in Uganda* (2014); coauthor with Andrea L. Arrington of *Africanizing Democracies: 1980–Present* (2015);

and coeditor of "African Feminisms: Cartographies for the Twenty-First Century," a special issue of *Meridians: Feminism, Race, Transnationalism* (2018). Decker is currently coediting, with Maha Marouan and Zinhle ka'Nobuhlaluse, a special issue of *Feminist Formations*, "Writing African Feminist Subjectivities" (forthcoming in 2024). She can be reached at acd207@psu.edu.

Editors of Pandemonium *spoke with Gabeba Baderoon, Maha Marouan, and Alicia Decker on August 4 and 28, 2023.*

Alicia Decker: Out of our shared challenges came the idea to create an alternative space to engage in critical conversations and scholarly work on feminist issues in Africa and the African diaspora—dynamics that are not equitable all the time. The African Feminist Initiative (AFI) is a transnational virtual community that my colleague Gabeba Baderoon and I started at Penn State in 2015. Gabeba and I came together to create a space to think critically about African feminisms, a truly global transnational collective that is actively engaged in all levels of feminist activism, dialogue, and research both within and outside the academy. In 2018, Maha joined us as our third codirector, so the three of us function as equals . . . as a triumvirate. As of 2023, AFI has over five hundred members, many from Africa, but also from Europe, South America, Asia, and North America. We have held six international conferences and workshops and have become a hub for virtual transnational feminist movement across different kinds of borders. AFI serves as an example of a feminist community that's growing in the midst of backlash. Transnational feminisms are obviously not new, but it does seem like it is a space that is continuing to grow and thrive, consisting of actively politicized communities addressing some of the challenges the discipline is facing and ensuring there is space for conversations that are more challenging in certain institutional and national settings.

Gabeba Baderoon: I'm a South African, so a lot of my work tends to be on South Africa. I have strong connections with the universities there. Austerity has been the reality there, and in the U.S., of course, too. I'm so grateful to have this as my job. So how does something like women's and gender studies in Africa flourish? The story is sometimes a little surprising: sometimes outside of the classroom. But there are also positive developments to report on what is happening inside the classroom and inside the university. For instance, the development of the Department of Feminist Studies at the

University of Cape Town is just a magnificent arrival of something that has been in discussion among many of us for a long time, since the late 1990s.

Maha Marouan: I grew up in Morocco, that's my home, but I work at a U.S. institution, so when I do work in the continent, I am challenged differently. Some of the challenges for me are: How do you form feminist solidarities transnationally? How do you challenge global hierarchies? How do you forge feminist linkages without undermining feminist politics of resistance as forged in the specificity of one's history and locale? I get a sense at times that I am caught between two worlds, but most of the time, I feel deeply enriched by my positionality. The work that we do through AFI is to continue to find linkages and learn from one another. We do that through our monthly feminist dialogues, we do it through transnational collaborative projects that reflect the complexity of our commitment and positionality but without privileging one particular mode of knowledge. This does not mean this is a smooth-sailing process. In fact, I am constantly faced with challenges.

Identity politics play a part. For instance, Alicia's idea to work collaboratively with scholars from different parts of the continent to examine the state of women and gender studies in academia was an important initiative. But there was a lot of tension when all of us from different backgrounds and locales met. Because Alicia and I are academically situated in the Global North, we were perceived by many of our colleagues in the continent as reinforcing these global hierarchies by undertaking this project. My African belonging was also challenged. As a North African, I was perceived as "less authentically" African—despite the fact that I do not subscribe to the colonial division of North and sub-Saharan Africa as two separate entities. So collaborative work requires introspection, reflection, and the need to always explore what connects us even when we are hurt and frustrated.

Alicia Decker: The AFI membership is made up of scholars, or scholars-in-training, feminist nongovernmental organizations, individuals working in various local and national governments, and activists who use art as their primary medium for impacting social change. AFI provides space for all of us working on feminist issues to speak across these so-called boundaries and really challenge those of us in the academy to think about how we can have more real-world applications for the stuff that we're doing as scholars. We also bring people to Penn State for in-person workshops and conferences, but like many of us during the pandemic, we really expanded our virtual footprint. And now we're just doing it because we love being able to have people on the continent and in Europe come to our things, and it's really cool.

I'm super proud of what we've accomplished. I really am. It's cool and we've certainly pissed some people off, and we've made some mistakes, which we talk about in the introduction to a 2018 special issue of *Meridians*, "African Feminisms: Cartographies for the Twenty-First Century," that Gabeba and I coedited. We talk a little bit about the AFI and the challenges, the hiccups of doing transnational feminist organizing, especially when we're based in the North, but trying to use the power and the privilege to create more equity and opportunities. Many of the contributions came from activists working with NGOs on issues such as sex worker rights in South Africa, menstrual equity in Kenya, and working on the neighborhood scale to grow food on the African feminist principle of "sufficiency" in Eswatini. From the outset, we intentionally worked to cultivate a membership that reflected the vast array of approaches to feminist work.

Maha Marouan: I'm optimistic about the future of women's and gender studies, but one of the main challenges in the Moroccan academy, for instance, is how limited the educational system is. There is very little academic training in feminist research methodologies, despite the presence of a significant number of incredible feminist scholars in the universities, as well as a younger generation of students highly invested in feminism. But this is a systemic issue.

Gabeba Baderoon: That is a problem, especially for graduate students who are interested in African feminism but who may have nothing or little to turn to in their institution. They are really hungry and trying to take an interest in the kind of thing Maha was talking about. But, even in that area, there's new hope because of new transnational and trans-institutional collaborations we are trying to forge. For example, Maha just created an online version of one of her courses—that arena contains a lot of potential and power to change things for our field.

Alicia Decker: Just going to add on to that . . . I think the confluence of COVID and advancements of distance technologies—like the conversation we are having here, that we can have between us. That's relatively new.

And that all came about at once, and at a perfect time for us to expand our platform from primarily in-person engagements to digital spaces. And so a lot of the work that we're doing now is possible in ways that it hadn't been before Zoom and other distance technologies became something that we all knew about. That changes the game quite a bit, especially in terms of transnational collaborations and especially maybe North-South collaboration and South-to-South collaboration.

Gabeba Baderoon: Absolutely. I would say those changes and new collaborations permit us to develop a graduate-level African feminism course that we can offer online to scholars on the continent. We've just been contacted by another institute, not from either the continent or North America, looking to cooperate and create some type of module that will work across a lot of platforms and contexts. We're also cooperating with Stellenbosch University in South Africa about creating an African feminist methodology module. These types of more accessible forms of higher education are changing the landscape of gender and women's studies.

Maha Marouan: I've noticed that there is more attention being paid to gender studies in the continent compared to the U.S. In the case of northern and western parts of the continent where I work, gender critique is becoming increasingly important to academic research. I do not mean to be cynical, but the United Nations also often dictates what's important, and what's not, through the projects they fund. Gender mainstreaming has become a hot topic in many countries of the Global South. There are new organizations that have mushroomed in different parts of the continent in the last decade because of international funding. Generally, much of that funding is put to good use and towards feminist causes, as I see more and more young feminists who are invested in advocating for gender equality.

Gabeba Baderoon: Yeah, I think I can echo what Maha is saying, from a South African perspective. I mentioned the formation of the Department of African Feminist Studies at the University of Cape Town. In addition, there is a whole lot of attention to the issue of feminist protests—and the feminist analysis of nationwide student protests against austerity more generally. I think the absorption of feminists into technocratic positions during the formation of the South African Nation, after 1994, hurt feminist practices more broadly, but the consequences of that broader neglect, in terms of violence against women and our subjection and erasure from national narratives about liberation and in defining the state, have really come under critique from activists, scholars, artists, and politicians. Now it's actually a very prominent topic, and that attention is being reflected in the support, at least some support, being given to feminist studies at the university. Though that's not universally the case. There have been situations where centers of gender studies have been closed down.

At the same time, there are other very important initiatives like the South African National Research Chair in African Feminist Imagination held by Professor Pumla Dineo Gqola at Nelson Mandela University and the South African National Research Chair in Gender and Politics held by Professor Amanda Gouws at Stellenbosch University—such positions are nationally funded for seven years and they are honorary positions, which means they are giving national visibility to African feminism. As a reflection of the AFI's relation with such initiatives, both Professor Gqola and Professor Gouws will be visiting Penn State in 2024, both on AFI Feminist Residencies. Pumla also contributed an important and widely cited chapter to *Surfacing: On Being Black and Feminist in South Africa*, a book I coedited with the important South African feminist scholar Desiree Lewis and to which the AFI contributed some funding for its publication. So these examples from South Africa show that there is national funding and national recognition along with the development of gender studies centers at the University of Limpopo, Nelson Mandela University, and influential gatherings of feminists such as the annual AFEMS conference created by Sharlene Khan and Lynda Gichanda Spencer—all signs of the visibility and importance of feminist analysis and critique in the country.

Now, whether it is always reflected in the budgets of universities—well, that's a different question, isn't it? Yes, sometimes universities like to say they're feminist, when it just means they may have a feminist represented on that committee. She's been invited to that committee, so . . . that means feminists are often over-extended in service. Sometimes being there also advances the feminist agenda, but there's always room for more feminists and more commitment on the part of universities to really make feminist change happen.

Alicia Decker: I feel very disconnected from Uganda the last couple of years just because of the position I'm doing now as department head and all the travel restrictions, but certainly I see a growing backlash against some of the feminist issues that we thought we—here in the U.S. and on the continent—had already been accomplished. I talked to a Ugandan friend not too long ago about how things are going there since the passage of the latest antihomosexuality legislation, and she forwarded me emails from activists in various parts of the country, in rural areas, and said that it's bad. It's really bad. So, certainly, while Uganda has the only school of women's and gender studies on the continent with its own dean, I think gender mainstreaming and to some extent, gender studies, have become kind of a palatable way of talking about men's roles and women's roles without really engaging in serious feminist critique—and avoiding engaging in the kind of feminist re-envisioning we really need. So while that level of gender mainstreaming is acceptable to the masses or the nation-state in Uganda, more radical critiques are not, and you can get what we see happening with hate-filled legislation such as the Anti-Homosexuality Act. And, yeah, nobody really knows what to do with it now that it has passed, maybe because WGSS has been so depoliticized by "gender mainstreaming" in development and aid funding.[1]

This is not to suggest that people have not been fighting against this sort of legislation on the ground, because they certainly have been. But what I'm getting at is the contradiction: how can there be such strong vitriol against sexual pluralism and diversity in a place that has one of the most important, the only, school of women's and gender studies? What's that about? And I think the answer has got to be that gender mainstreaming has become so ... well, "mainstream" that it's just not political anymore.

Gabeba Baderoon: I think there's a really interesting debate in that comment, Alicia, a debate that we can have about the state and the role of the state in African contexts especially. As you know, 2024 will be the thirtieth anniversary of South Africa's Democratic elections. For me I'm hoping we can have some of these interesting discussions on women's relationship to the state. The debates around the state I see happening in the U.S. among scholars, that feels to me extremely distant, a shying away from wanting to engage the state. It's complicated. I mean, what happens in the post-colony when the state manifests all the legacies of the secular colonial state but is nonetheless a majority Black state, or an African state? How does one engage with that, and how might a feminist ... an African feminist ... engage?

Maha Marouan: I am optimistic about the future of WGSS in Africa and around the world. But, at the same time, my optimism goes hand-in-hand with recognizing the commodification of feminism that is taking place in many parts of the continent. In Morocco, the support from international NGOs, as well as the support from the state that goes into funding some women's organizations that do not necessarily have a feminist vision or are not particularly committed to a feminist agenda, does not help in advancing the cause. In fact, this can create a disconnect between some women's organizations and the community of grassroots feminist activists, researchers, and academics who are doing the critical work necessary to advancing gender equality.

Young people on the continent have a kind of political commitment that makes me very optimistic, though. There are very concrete issues that are being challenged at the moment in Morocco. Young feminists are following in the footsteps of their predecessors and continue to mobilize for further changes to the Moroccan Family Law, especially as it relates to women's rights within the institution of marriage, divorce law, the right to custody, and child support.[2] There is also mobilizing against domestic and sexual violence, advocating for girls' education, especially in rural areas—among a few other issues.

In the U.S., I continue to be inspired by many of my students. I teach graduate courses on transnational feminisms, and it is heartwarming to see my graduate students' commitment to a decolonial praxis, their investment in learning and developing strategies to help them challenge global systems of inequality, and their attentiveness to feminist ethics of research. And that is ultimately the value of the work we do as professors—exposing our students to new forms of knowledge and assisting them in being ethical researchers and activists.

Gabeba Baderoon: At the same time, I think, the spaces outside our classrooms are necessary too. When there was no women and gender studies programming, there were protest marches. There were study groups. There were the public centers in universities. Those continue to be there, and maybe some are growing, so maybe they need to become part of our thinking about how education happens again. So we will find spaces where we continue to survive and do the work, and I think we are in a particularly challenging space in the U.S. at the moment . . . but we're not only in the U.S., we're in the world as a whole! We can allow the U.S. to see itself and come to ask about places where, in fact, women's and gender studies may be growing, or people are speaking about patriarchy or the feminist analysis of the national budget. These debates are happening in other parts of the world, and those places can show the U.S. the alternatives that are out there. Personal activism, faculty activism, broader activism—this is all part of what it means to be a feminist academic.

Alicia Decker: One thing I would just say, too, it's not just that I'm hopeful about WGSS, but I also think it's imperative. I don't think we really have a choice, right? And so we're at this moment... like, I don't see an alternative other than sticking my head in the sand! We don't have the luxury of wondering whether we *can* be hopeful. I just don't think we have the luxury of that right now, there's too much at stake.

Gabeba Baderoon: You know... we've been writing about this power—the power of the teacher and the word—for thousands of years. It is one of our sources of power for all of humanity. So I think that to go on teaching and taking care of our students, that's what's important. Like how Maha is caring that her students' attention is focused on something that is necessary but may also be shortsighted. So we care about this, and the quality of the teaching will convey that caring and why it matters. So I am really, powerfully optimistic, not only from my own experience but also the thousands of years of human history saying the teachers are always going to have power.

You know, I was away from teaching for a semester, and I just came back, and I was just talking with a professor: his birthday was yesterday, he's in his sixties and has been teaching for decades. And I realized from both my experience of just a week of teaching and his experience of decades... there is something really powerful and magical that happens across those four months of a semester, and then across the four years that you have students in your courses.

And I will never forget that the power of a teacher in a classroom will linger for the rest of that person's life, and that is why we are under attack ... because there is power in what we do.

Notes

1. For the Ugandan legislation, see Republic of Uganda 2023. For more on the anticipated human rights consequences, see International Commission of Jurists 2023; for a Kenyan and AFI member's perspective, see Okech 2023; for a Ugandan queer activist perspective, see Kemigisa 2023.
2. For more on recent changes to the Moroccan Family Code, see Alami 2023.

Works Cited

Alami, Aida. 2023. "The Decades-Long Fight to Change Morocco's Family Law." *The Tahrir Institute for Middle East Policy*, August 10, 2023. https://timep.org/2023/08/10/the-decades-long-fight-to-change-moroccos-family-law/.

International Commission of Jurists. 2023. "Uganda: The Enactment of 'the Anti-Homosexuality Act, 2023' Will Foster Further Stigma, Discrimination and Violence against Lesbian, Gay, Bisexual, Transgender and Intersex Persons." *International Commission of Jurists*, June 13, 2023. https://www.icj.org/uganda-the-enactment-of-the-anti-homosexuality-act-2023-will-foster-further-stigma-discrimination-and-violence-against-lesbian-gay-bisexual-transgender-and-intersex-persons/.

Kemigisa, Jackline. 2023. "Why I've Joined the Court Challenge against Uganda's Anti-Gay Law." *Open Democracy*, June 2, 2023. https://www.opendemocracy.net/en/5050/uganda-anti-homosexuality-act-2023-petition-constitutional-court/.

Okech, Awino. 2023. "Uganda's Anti-Homosexuality Law Is a Patriarchal Backlash against Progress." *The Conversation*, May 31, 2023. https://theconversation.com/ugandas-anti-homosexuality-law-is-a-patriarchal-backlash-against-progress-206681.

Republic of Uganda. 2023. *Anti-Homosexuality Act, 2023*. https://www.parliament.go.ug/sites/default/files/The%20Anti-Homosexuality%20Act%2C%202023.pdf.

How are gender studies scholars resisting anti-gender politics in the United Kingdom?

A conversation with Clare Hemmings and Sumi Madhok

Clare Hemmings is professor of feminist theory in the Department of Gender Studies at the LSE. She is the author of *Why Stories Matter* (2011) and *Considering Emma Goldman* (2018), and the principal investigator for the Arts and Humanities Research Council Network Transnational "Anti-Gender" Movements and Resistance. Her recent article "'But I Thought We'd Already Won That Argument!' 'Anti-Gender' Mobilizations, Affect and Temporality," for *Feminist Studies,* addresses issues of temporality, affect, and anti-gender discourse. She can be reached at c.hemmings@lse.ac.uk.

Sumi Madhok is professor of political theory and gender studies in the Department of Gender Studies at the LSE. Her most recent book, *Vernacular Rights Cultures: The Politics of Origins, Human Rights and Gendered Struggles for Justice*, is the winner of the Susan Strange Best Book Prize and the 2022 Sussex International Theory Prize. It also received the International Studies Association's Lee Ann Fujii Book Prize Honorable Mention. She can be reached at s.madhok@lse.ac.uk.

Editors of Pandemonium *spoke with Clare Hemmings and Sumi Madhok on August 3, 2023.*

Clare Hemmings: Sumi and I were recently supported by an Arts and Humanities Research Council grant in Britain to build a network called Transnational "Anti-gender" Movements and Resistance: Narratives and Interventions.

Sumi Madhok: This network is something that was perhaps one of the first projects of its kind, particularly in the U.K. academy, to get funded, and frankly we were quite surprised given the political climate in the U.K. To see the research councils in the U.K. academy support this feminist transnational network of scholars who are researching these questions in different parts of the globe, has been very heartening.

Clare Hemmings: Our aim has been to bring scholars together to consider threats to gender and queer studies as fields as well as to feminism, LGBT communities—especially trans communities—migrants, refugees, and Black communities. These communities and the threats against them are all quite connected, of course. In the U.K. right now, the kinds of work that we do within these communities has become increasingly difficult—increasingly subjected to challenges and aggression. Even just being able to use the term "gender" as a critical intervention has been subject to attack, let alone when articulated as a racialized, classed, or sexual category related to social meanings. Hostility to universities from the U.K. government has been increasing generally—particularly towards the interdisciplinary humanities—and attacks on gender studies are underwritten by these "culture wars" that are anti-feminist and racist. And our department has been directly attacked for its work, precisely because we are visibly resisting these developments.

But this is not just about the U.K., of course. We very much wanted to put together a network that was transnational in scope to link that to other experiences of anti-feminist, anti trans, anti-migrant politics in different locations, let's say in India or Pakistan, in South Africa or Uganda, in Hungary, Poland, Brazil, and so on, as well as within the U.K. and across Europe generally. We wanted to open up a space where we could have frank conversations that are increasingly difficult to have in hostile environments.

Sumi Madhok: Yes, and of course there has also been a sort of "split within" that we wanted to address too—splits within women's rights or what sometimes is termed "gender equality" advocates. A split has opened up between intersectional feminists and groups that self-identify as "feminist"—sometimes—who are mobilizing against trans rights and disavow gender studies, which has a very particular kind of intellectual framework that's being challenged on both transnational and gender essentialist grounds.

I would say these attacks are not only a matter of the world outside being against gender studies or against universities; actually, there is also a challenge being mounted within universities and among feminists in the U.K. There are some feminists who take an anti-trans position, although we don't see that present as much within gender studies at the university. We don't see a split within the field certainly, but what we do see is a kind of passivity or silence on the question of trans or nonbinary rights, a default position maybe where . . . if you're not speaking up to make it very clear that the work you're doing is trans-inclusive, but you continue to use terms like *men* and *women* without further qualification or in ways that are inclusive of trans and nonbinary and other queer folk . . . well, that says something too, doesn't it?

Clare Hemmings: Yes, it says a lot in a context where we have powerful organizations and individuals who are pushing very similar kinds of campaigns as we see in France, claiming that, in education, particularly primary and secondary education but also in higher education, the question of binary sex needs to be retained and that anything other than that is, you know, meaningless or mindless or perverse or absurd. There's a kind of feminism that claims to be about the protection of women who are "born" women and this notion that "I, as a woman, have been continuously marginalized and so I am the person now who speaks from the place of having been marginal, and here I am being marginalized again."

In fact, there's been a series of very important court cases in the U.K. where gender-critical academics, who usually either have resigned or have been on temporary contracts, have made grievances (whether legal or internal) about being forced out of employment. And those cases went in favor of supporting gender-critical positions as needing protection against discrimination of a belief system. So "gender-critical" now exists as a protected belief system that cannot be cited as a reason to be fired from your job. This does not mean, however, that you can never say boo against this belief in gender as binary and rooted in biology either, though, right? It doesn't mean that gender-critical positions can therefore be expressed to the detriment of others without any challenge, or that challenging someone on their belief system is a problem or is illegal. It just means people can't lose their jobs because of it, which, I have to say, I agree with. I don't think people should lose their jobs for particular *beliefs*, unless of course they're engaging in hate speech or discriminatory behavior. That's why the line between freedom of speech and hate speech is so contested, of course.

One of the things that's happening in the U.K. is the split that also exists with the LGBT community. Some of the organizations that are the most openly trans-hostile are LGB organizations, because they see their own agendas and terrain being eroded. So they are articulating lesbian, gay, or bisexual rights as sex-specific rights. There's really quite a bit at stake, and that split is really wide and is growing, I think. And both splits—within feminism, within LGBT communities—trade on the Conservative Party's absolutely disingenuous claiming of lesbian and gay equality agendas. They're not really interested in safeguarding gay or lesbian or bisexual rights, but the strategy is to split them off and rely on the accepted body of rights law that has been established, to hold the line against trans and nonbinary, gender-nonconforming people and ideas about gender, constructing these communities as the primary threat to sexual equality.

Gender studies, as a field in the U.K., was already decimated in the 1990s. There is no undergraduate program in gender in the U.K., and while teaching at the graduate level is vibrant, ours is the only gender studies *department* in the U.K. And now we are a highly visible target. The ways in which right-wing and also some left-wing forces align within populism has produced a kind of global politics that ultimately relies on anti-gender and racist arguments and practices in order to consolidate its power. It all feels quite relentless.

Sumi Madhok: I also think it is important to remember this has a half century of global political and economic consensus behind it, and one which has been building steadily. Maybe the greatest success of neoliberalism has been that none of this is seen as surprising to us anymore, even when it takes a real turn to the ultra-right. For the vast majority of people, this has just become the way things are, and that's why the news of shutting down gender studies departments is not even picked up in the media, and it's not even a big question in the U.K. academy that all the gender studies departments (except one) in the U.K. have gone away. It's always only the same people at universities who notice or care or are talking about it. This normalization, fatalism, and lack of pushback against the relentless onslaught on research and teaching of gender and critical race scholarship counts among the successes of the whole neoliberal turn in the academy.

An important site where gender studies and critical race studies is currently being debated is in the U.K. Parliament. Recently, it passed a "free speech" bill, which is basically aimed at research and the universities, and crudely conflates strongly held and carefully crafted principles of academic freedom with those of free speech, imagined as "anything goes." Academic freedom is not the unfettered right to never be challenged. It was never that, not at all. And this idea of free speech is not about protecting academic speech either. It is aimed at discouraging research in the universities precisely because universities are popularly perceived as somehow not aligned with right-wing conservative politics.

Clare Hemmings: But, for the most part, the curriculum itself in U.K. universities has yet to be tampered with directly by the state. There are too many institutionalized levels of decision-making for that to work, for the moment at least. The number of people making those decisions is already quite vast, and so far, that's not been an area where there's a possibility really to intervene or challenge us, not directly.

Sumi Madhok: Right, and that's a source of hope. At the moment, we aren't being told by the state what to think or say or research about or teach or write. But, really, I'm very hopeful about the future for much more than just that reason. I'm hopeful on three counts.

One reason for hope is that the backlash itself demonstrates how transformative women's and gender studies and critical race theory teaching and research have been. The fact that you see this kind of backlash is because of the transformation, and you see the transformation, of course, across all spheres of life, right? We see this all around us, certainly. And if the transformation *is* fragile, it is fragile precisely because it is such a revolutionary transformation that has forced the hegemonic, the dominant, the oppressor to alter and rearrange itself—even if only temporarily, perhaps.

Second, I'm hopeful because of the student body and how the students are responding and pushing back against all this. There's only one gender studies department left in the U.K., but that department is large, it's the largest in Europe, it's the second largest, after Rutgers in the U.S., maybe in the world. And it continues to grow year after year, too. We aren't slowing down. Now there must be a reason for this, right? There's a reason students want what we teach and study, so in that sense we are standing tall against this backlash, and that's the reason there's a backlash in the first place.

Finally, the Transnational "Anti-Gender" Movements and Resistance Network we have begun to build, through three conferences (the last one is scheduled six months from now, in February 2024), gives me hope. The network has been brought about because of what we are facing, and the transnational solidarity it represents gives me hope—enormous hope, in fact!—for the future of our discipline and, more generally, for the work that we do in the world.

Clare Hemmings: Yeah, like Sumi, I'm hopeful too, and especially about new forms of collective resistance we are seeing. I think there's been new or renewed forms of solidarity that have come to the fore where relationships have been forged between movements and interest groups that did not see their connection to each other before.

Where are feminism and gender studies in Asia headed?
A conversation with Trimita Chakma

Trimita Chakma, a dedicated feminist researcher and activist, originally hails from the Indigenous Chakma hill tribe of Bangladesh. She recently completed her MA in Asian women's studies at Ewha Womans University in South Korea and holds an MSc in IT management from Carnegie Mellon University. Currently, Trimita is engaged in coordinating the development of the South Feminist Manifesto at South Feminist Futures, a cross-regional manifesto aiming to ignite new solidarities between feminist movements across the Global South. Drawing on over a decade of experience championing feminist social justice, Trimita brings her expertise in Feminist Participatory Action Research (FPAR) tools to address key issues like climate justice, labor rights, and land rights of marginalized communities. In 2022, she cofounded the FPAR Academy to promote education on feminist participatory methodologies. Through her work with Public Services International, Trimita also supports labor organizing campaigns in the Asia-Pacific region. She can be reached at trimita@fparacademy.com.

Editors of Pandemonium *spoke with Trimita Chakma on August 16, 2023.*

Hi, I'm originally an Indigenous woman from Bangladesh and I'm joining you from Seoul, South Korea, today. My key expertise lies in feminist participatory action research (FPAR). I recently cofounded an organization called Feminist Participatory Action Research Academy (FPAR Academy), which is an online learning platform for feminist education and activism. For us, FPAR is a political choice. It is a collective, bottom-up, intersectional feminist methodology. We support and empower marginalized groups to advocate for changes in their communities. FPAR challenges patriarchy, racism, heteronormativity, fascism, and other forms of social injustices. The aim of the FPAR Academy is to foster feminist education through deepening our understanding of how FPAR can contribute to building and strengthening movements to create long-lasting structural change. We are incorporated in Malaysia, but we are transnational in nature. I also currently work as an independent consultant with several feminist organizations. I graduated with my MA this year from Ewha Womans University and my topic of research was conceptualizing Asian women's studies. My goal was to understand women's studies in the Global South, in Asia in particular and from Asian perspectives, and I wanted to study it in an Asian context, so that is why I went to Ewha in South Korea.

My perspective is maybe not so scholarly, because I identify more as an activist, so maybe a lot of my views will come from that experience. But, I mean, for me, I don't see much difference between women's and gender studies and feminist activism. Because, you know, it's all intertwined. But maybe I can give you more perspectives on the attacks that have been launched against feminism in general in the parts of Asia I am most familiar with, and I think academic feminism has been a target of some of that, in part because academic feminism is sitting on that line between institutionalized feminism, state institutions, and civil society.

It's important to keep in mind that, in Asia, feminism and gender studies are seen as Western imports, in general, right? So feminist institutions are not as strong or deeply rooted as they are in the U.S., for example, especially in terms of academic institutionalization of feminism.

The other complexity in all this is Asian as an identity. Everyone wants to decenter the West, but at the same time, they [Ewha Womans University] are trying to create a center in East Asia, you know, even though there are all these other South Asian or Southeast Asian countries and the idea of being "Asian" is up for grabs. It was interesting to me to find that Koreans don't actually think of themselves as "Asian," and when they say "Asian women's studies," they mean women who I would say are Southeast Asian, but not necessarily Korean or Japanese, who are East Asians. Living in Korea has been an interesting experience in terms of understanding gender here. But I would say it's a bit messy in terms of what "Asian" women's studies is or whom it applies to or who is centered in all that. For me, I would say that there is no such thing as Asian women's studies, because we haven't been able to define what an Asian woman is. There is not enough understanding of that complexity, I think the theoretical foundations of that, and an overemphasis on local contexts, singular national contexts, has been a limitation for growing the field and connecting Asian scholars to each other and activist groups. Let's say it could be better.

So, just to give you a bit of understanding of South Korea: it also has one of the worst gender pay gaps, and when I came here in 2020, there was also the Nth Room digital sex crime case, so that was really exploding. Women in South Korea are not in executive positions—very few women, maybe 5 percent in large companies. It's better in the National Assembly, but still less than 20 percent. So there is a long-standing problem of gender inequality here anyways, but when the new president, Yoon Suk Yeol, came in last year, he came in with the support of young anti-feminist men who are really threatened by the feminist #MeToo movement in South Korea. Suk Yeol almost immediately tried to abolish the gender equality ministry, saying feminists treat men like sex criminals and there is no gender inequality in current society, and supporting women's rights means rights will be reduced for men. So, yes, for sure, gender equality and feminism are really central right now to South Korean politics. And this is the environment in which women's and gender studies programs have to operate.

Having said that, I think the feminist and gender studies scholars that I've come across, certainly the ones who have established this women's studies program at Ewha, have a lot of hope. There are a lot of progressive ideas backing this, and of course it is in part propelled by the United Nations' 1995 Beijing Platform for Action. That's the leading platform that compelled governments to commit to supporting gender equality. But that funding, and really everything that fuels the state's support of gender equality movements, depends on what sort of administration comes into power.

I mean, that's not different from the far right in North America, when those administrations and parties come into power and then attack the institutions that support the things that feminists have been fighting for, for so many decades.

When Modi came into power in India, he made it almost impossible for NGOs—even big, established, and not very political NGOs like Oxfam—to operate. He withdrew the registrations of something like over six hundred NGOs, which included the registrations of some of the organizations I work with. Now it's very difficult to even reach out to workers in India or the grassroots groups that we most want to support. And, of course, this has a huge impact on gender equality organizing, not just labor but gender also, right? Because they intersect, of course. We are all connected.

But the disconnect is there too. Disconnect between academic work on gender, and the labor and climate justice movements, which is really a huge problem. So, for example, I'd say the academics are at least a few years behind where the movements are. For my MA thesis, I've actually gone and looked at all the articles that were published in the last ten years in the *Asian Journal of Women's Studies*, and the theoretical and analytical work is way behind what's happening on the ground. I think that's probably just a function of the slow pace of academic work, but it really puts the field out of step with political reality.

Maybe the field just needs more time to grow a bit more. When I have spoken to the founders who established this Ewha program, they are real visionaries, and there's several hundreds of them in their network. And they have a congress. This does allow that sort of periphery-to-periphery knowledge exchange. But I think resourcing has been very limited, and there's lots of ups and downs with that, so this also prevents new and relevant scholarship from flourishing. I think the academic space, in general, is suffering because of a lack of resourcing and institutional support. For instance, I don't see it growing in Bangladesh anytime soon. It's just not a vibrant growing area. I'm not saying it's useless. It's just behind and really needs to be resourced.

If you look at feminist research in Asia, you find that a very small amount of the aid money or philanthropy flows into women-led organizations, and that's true for the academic gender studies programs as well. The budgets don't allow for much. There's also, of course, a lot of co-optation of Global South feminism. We've seen a huge rise of corporate feminism, with young women going and getting a degree in women's studies just to get a job with corporations or government organizations, and development industries. And, when you see that, you see the program becomes tailored to their placement in these jobs, and as it becomes more and more job oriented, the feminist analysis becomes more and more window dressing, and privatized, so gender studies just becomes another business, with a business model—just like anything else.

There's also a split I see between the younger feminists in South Korea (known as "Young Young Feminists"), of women in their twenties, where you'll find transphobic sentiments expressed. They seem to be still holding onto the idea of the "biological woman," which is an outdated essentialist idea. The feminist movement is sort of fragmenting over this issue of gender and how you define it. Back in Bangladesh, I used to work very closely with, let's say, more like second-wave feminists, and they are really, you know, well established. They have done amazing work, and I always tell people we are standing on their shoulders in Bangladesh. Because of their work, I had access to many things that they fought for, especially in the area of stopping violence against women. But now when I speak with them, they are having trouble connecting with the intergenerational feminist movement. Especially the newer gender, sexuality, and nonbinary discourses. They cannot talk about these topics; they cannot even have a conversation. So I'm kind of in the middle, right? The younger feminists are thinking I'm cool, and I get it. And the older feminists also feel comfortable, like they can talk to me without being canceled. For sure, the older feminists really want to work with the younger ones, but they don't know how to converse without getting canceled.

So I think we are seeing that fragmentation of generational feminists, and for me, that's definitely new. And here's where academic feminism comes in, maybe, in a powerful way. I think academic women's and gender studies is very important, because this is the space where we can all access the writings of these amazing feminists from different generations, from different contexts—like the work of African feminists, which can really move you, it can fundamentally shift your thinking.

There is a new organization that's called South Feminist Futures I'm working with to develop a South Feminist manifesto. The idea of this is to connect the Global South Feminists across the regions. Our manifesto will say what feminism is supposed to be like, guiding it strategically towards collective organizing. The fragmentations we are seeing . . . well, that's the challenge, isn't it?

So I've been part of a few movements. I'm an Indigenous woman, and there's a vibrant Indigenous Peoples' movement, and my history in Bangladesh is rooted in a post-colonial, post-conflict context. The austerity that we discuss now is something I understand. My mother and her generation lost their entire land under a dam. That was in the 1960s. We have been fighting for our Indigenous territorial politics for some time, but that struggle is still extremely patriarchal too. So that's a problem. My journey began in that movement first, but it was difficult because I tried to introduce feminism in that space and the men weren't happy. It's very male-dominated at the center. On the other hand, of course, the larger Indigenous Peoples' movement is very central to the current climate justice movement. So it's enormously important, but there's no space for feminists like me.

And then I got involved with the national feminist movement in

Bangladesh, but the problem with that movement is it is led by women who are middle class and upper class. I mean, they do very good theoretical work and organizing work and NGO-led work, a lot of development work that is very good. But somehow they rarely work with the labor movement, which is interesting because, in Bangladesh, women factory workers are central to the labor force, along with female domestic workers, of course, who are also being organized now. But this disconnect between the feminists and the labor movement is a serious weakness.

I don't think the feminist movement is big enough at the moment to change the world, not when it is so disconnected from the Indigenous movement and the labor movement. I think labor movements can change the world—I mean, for one thing, they have the numbers, right?—but not as long as they are seriously patriarchal. My position is that the labor movement needs to be more feminist and support Indigenous leadership. Feminists need to support labor organizing. And the labor movement needs feminists. They need each other.

I think all of these movements—feminist, Indigenous, and labor—can connect through the climate and environmental movements, because that affects all sections of society, all classes and all genders, and everybody is going to be hit by the climate crisis. How can we fight this huge fight when the movements are very small and fragmented? We are fighting a constantly evolving global capitalism.

We have to really get together if we are going to win the struggle.

SECTION II. **MANIFESTOS**

Cynthia Marsh was educated at Moore College of Art (BFA), Rochester Institute of Technology (MFA), and by the larger world that informs our ideas. Marsh was a founding member of the Women's Graphic Center @ the (historic) Woman's Building in Los Angeles. Following a distinguished academic career, Marsh has reignited her imprint, Studio One Eye Open. Her prints, artist books, and community portfolios reside in museums and university collections throughout the country. She can be reached at marshc@apsu.edu.

Cynthia Marsh, *Exit*, 1988. Four-color offset lithography, page from artist book *We Live the Good Life*.

Cynthia Marsh is a note-taker, a cultural reporter who juxtaposes words and images to document the visual noise that surrounds us.

hey you –

**MY WAY
IS BEST!**

Cynthia Marsh, *My Way Is Best*, 1986. Offset lithography,
limited edition artist book (cover).

shut up

Cynthia Marsh, *Shut Up*, 1988. Four-color offset lithography, page from artist book *We Live the Good Life*.

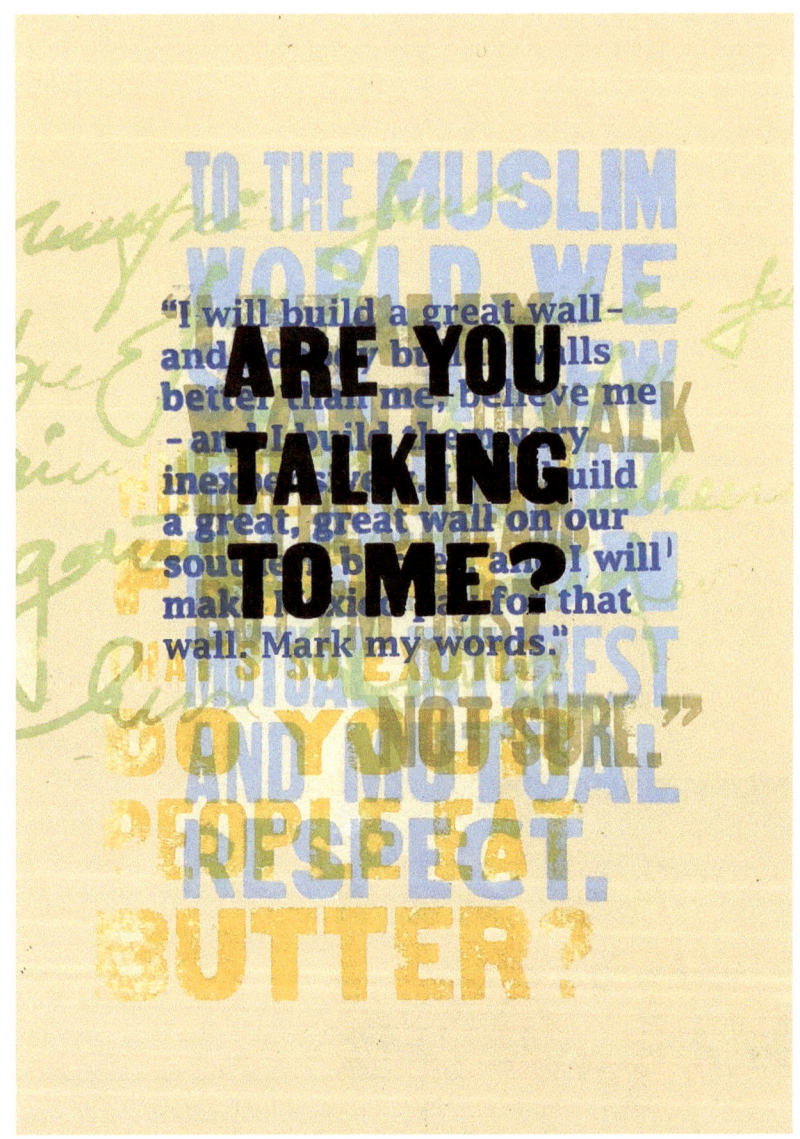

Cynthia Marsh, *Are You Talking to Me?*, 2018. Silkscreen and letterpress print.

Igniting Solidarities across Borders: South Feminist Futures (SFF) and the Promise of the South Feminist Manifesto

Trimita Chakma

Abstract: This article examines the forthcoming South Feminist Manifesto spearheaded by South Feminist Futures, a transnational network of feminists from the Global South. Through extensive cross-regional consultations, the manifesto initiative promises to build solidarity and advance decolonial, anti-capitalist feminism across the Global South. It aims to center plural Southern voices and contexts, integrating diverse critical frameworks from Third World feminism to queer theory. By foregrounding lived realities of Southern women and trans and nonbinary people, the manifesto promises to generate fresh insights and creative South-South solidarities. Drawing inspiration from the pioneering *Women's Manifesto for Ghana*, it strives to catalyze feminist consciousness raising, movement revival, and more caring, just futures across borders. The article analyzes the manifesto's transformative promises. **Keywords:** South feminisms, decolonial feminism, South-South cooperation, solidarity, manifestos, social movements

Introduction

As feminists across the Global South confront the colliding crises of climate breakdown, rising authoritarianism, and deepening global inequalities, the need to reinvigorate and strengthen solidarity and cooperation between feminist movements throughout the South has become an urgent necessity. While momentum exists in various progressive social justice movements, feminist movements often find their concerns and agendas neglected in mainstream South-South cooperation initiatives and global justice platforms. This is apparent in intergovernmental initiatives between Global

South nations, ranging from the 1955 Bandung Declaration to modern undertakings like BRICS (formed in 2009). For instance, despite vigorous women's organizing and activism that ran concurrent to these assemblies, the resultant cooperation agreements have often overlooked the unique challenges faced by women and other marginalized groups (Armstrong 2016; Ahmed 2017).[1] While these agreements might engage with broader themes of inequality, they seldom confront colonial gender norms or champion LGBTQ+ rights.

This oversight is not exclusive to the South; it's also evident in contemporary progressive agendas from the North. While addressing themes like environmentalism and economic justice, many often miss the intersectionality of these crises and sideline the essential role of women's leadership in realizing sustainable development. An exemplar is the "Eco-socialist Manifesto" (2001), which has been criticized for its scant emphasis on inclusivity and intersectional feminist standpoints (Kovel and Löwy 2001). Questions arise about the authenticity of its integration of marginalized voices, such as those of mothers and forest inhabitants, beyond mere symbolic inclusion (Salleh 2010). The recurrent absence of robust feminist perspectives in both South-South collaborations and global justice efforts underscores the pressing need for a specialized Southern feminist platform that directly challenges interconnected systems of oppression.

The proposed South Feminist Manifesto, set to launch in 2024 by South Feminist Futures, represents one pivotal effort to address this gap.[2] Through extensive consultations spanning the Global South, the cross-regional manifesto aims to place diverse Southern voices at the forefront, integrating varied critical frameworks, from decolonial to Third World feminism to queer theory, and generating visions for more just futures. The manifesto promises to fuse anti-imperialist, anti-colonial politics with core commitments to dismantling cis-heteropatriarchy, white supremacy, and exploitative capitalism.

Drawing Inspiration from the *Women's Manifesto for Ghana*

The pioneering case of the *Women's Manifesto for Ghana* demonstrates this promise in action. Developed through extensive grassroots consultations from 2003 to 2004, the manifesto strengthened women's organizing and consciousness across Ghanaian society. As Rose Mensah-Kutin of ABANTU for Development noted in her presentation to South Feminist Futures in August 2023, the manifesto consultation process created spaces for Ghanaian marginalized women to articulate their needs and reclaim authority over their lives. It inspired collective action by building solidarity across lines of ethnicity, religion, and geography. Over time, it has remained a living document enriching Ghanaian women's advocacy. As Mensah-Kutin stressed, the inclusive, movement-building spirit of the process was pivotal for its impact. She shared that universities in Ghana now use the manifesto as a key text on women's rights and gender equality. The manifesto has also become a central reference document that people point to as an agenda owned by Ghanaian women to further women's rights and gender equality within democratic governance.

By amplifying local women's priorities instead of outside expert opinions, the participatory methodology challenged knowledge hierarchies steeped in coloniality. The manifesto expanded consciousness around intersecting systems of oppression, and possible alternatives aligned with African realities. Its emphasis on care work, informal livelihoods, and maternal health underscored the connections between care and justice. The manifesto galvanized women to organize and demand change by providing a platform to voice shared concerns. The manifesto continues to inspire new generations of African feminist activism.

This case demonstrates how Southern feminist manifestos grounded in participatory, decolonial approaches can redefine development and foreign policy discourses long dominated by Northern framings. They can catalyze processes of unlearning internalized colonial mentalities around gender, race, and class. By recentering plural epistemologies and fostering solidarity across difference, Southern feminist movements can unlock women's collective power to resist oppression and shape liberatory futures.

The proposed South Feminist Manifesto process promises to extend this legacy, creating spaces for consciousness raising and movement revival. As economic, political, and ecological crises deepen, the need for bold visions and compassionate solidarity becomes more urgent. The manifesto initiative resonates with calls for participatory knowledge production, grassroots mobilization, and radical care ethics. Through its emphasis on anger, hope, action, joy, and mutual transformation, it aims to build a nurturing home for South feminist solidarity.

The Promise of the South Feminist Manifesto
Centering Southern Voices and Solidarities

As postcolonial scholars like Chandra Mohanty have emphasized, situating gender relations within the sociocultural legacies of colonialism and imperialism remains essential for impactful feminist praxis (1988, 2003). Generalized critiques of "women's oppression" that are devoid of nuanced analysis risk reinforcing colonialist tropes regarding a homogenized "backward" Third World woman (Mohanty 1988, 80). Instead, historically grounded, materialist analysis reveals the heterogeneity of women's lives across the South, while also uncovering shared experiences of colonial control over bodies, lands, and cultures (Mohanty, Russo, and Torres 1991).

Postcolonial feminist scholars urge Western feminists to avoid colonizing attitudes that posit an essentialized "Third World difference" and to foreground diverse voices and contexts across the South (Mohanty 2003, 519). For feminists situated in formerly colonized regions, balancing critiques of local patriarchal norms with resistance against ongoing Northern hegemony in knowledge production and global governance becomes imperative. As Mohanty (2003, 505) articulates, such situated, anti-imperialist struggles build "feminist solidarities across borders."

The proposed South Feminist Manifesto promises to advance this agenda of situated Southern knowledge creation. Its participatory methodology centers on the lived experiences and standpoints of Southern actors, through activities like multilingual focus groups with diverse communities. Extensive consultations with activists and organizations aim to ground the manifesto in grassroots discourse rather than external policy dictates. This foregrounding of plural Southern narratives, aligned with context-attentive analysis, provides potential to generate fresh insights and creative South-South solidarities.

Contesting Global Hierarchies of Knowledge

Legacies of coloniality continue to shape knowledge production processes and institutions, framing Southern epistemes as inherently subjective while positioning Northern thought as the authoritative wellspring of "universal" theory (Connell 2014). Feminist movements confront similar marginalization, with Northern liberal discourses and policy frames claiming a quasi-universal status often at odds with Southern contexts. The dominance of Western epistemes often leads to marginalizing alternative worldviews that challenge Eurocentric assumptions, rather than substantively engaging them. This "othering" of contesting knowledge claims demonstrates the West's continued epistemic privilege and hegemony globally (Santos, Nunes, and Meneses 2008).

Decolonial feminists like María Lugones (2010) interrogate these hierarchies by revealing the gendered logic of coloniality and affirming pluralistic knowledges derived from lived experience. Scholar-activist centers in the South like Articulación Feminista Marcosur advance decolonial feminism praxis through participatory research and movement-building engaging rural, urban, Indigenous, and Afro-descendent women across Latin America (Korol 2016).

The South Feminist Manifesto promises to extend this epistemic decolonization project. Its commitment to participatory development foregrounding Southern standpoints promises to generate insights beyond hegemonic framings. The regional anchoring provides proximity to lived contexts unavailable to Northern researchers, while cross-regional dialogue yields novel syntheses transcending single case studies. This fusion of situated immersion and macroperspectives on South feminisms promises to stretch knowledge frontiers, contesting global hierarchies.

Reclaiming South-South Solidarity on Feminist Terms

Early decolonization-era conferences like 1955 Bandung galvanized anti-colonial unity and cooperation between countries of the South, building solidarity around shared identities and experiences of subjugation by Western powers. However, ensuing South-South cooperation often adopted a state-centric framing, downplaying civil society and social movement engagement (Najam 2005). Gender concerns took a back seat, despite vigorous women's mobilizations parallel to these gatherings. The proposed South Feminist Manifesto promises to reclaim and transform this legacy by placing feminist internationalism at the center, integrating concerns of women, LGBTQ+ groups, and other marginalized communities. Instead of co-optation, feminist networks seek transformation and mutual accountability within South-South cooperation, underscoring intersectionality, bodily autonomy, and climate justice. The manifesto promises to center these priorities, creates space for excluded voices, and builds solidarities across differences to redefine South-South cooperation on feminist terms. It strives to move beyond state-led discourses to enable connections between trade unions, informal workers, Indigenous peoples, queer activists, and more based on shared objectives of dismantling interconnected systems of oppression linked to capitalism, authoritarianism, and cis-heteropatriarchy.

The manifesto foregrounds relationality and interdependence rather than rigid divisions along regional, ethnic, or linguistic lines. This re-embeds cooperation in an ethic of care while expanding possibilities for solidarity across borders. The rich legacy of Bandung can thereby be reclaimed and reinterpreted through a feminist lens attuned to structural critique, collective care, and more inclusive, liberatory visions for South-South cooperation.

Envisioning Care-Centered Futures

The COVID-19 pandemic and climate change effects necessitate urgent attention to care needs. Feminist scholars posit the concept of an "ethics of care" entailing mutually responsible relationships attentive to power imbalances and reliant on moral emotions like empathy (Held 2005). South feminisms expand this by underscoring care's grounded, relational practice interwoven with justice. The manifesto initiative promises to move beyond despair to propose care-centered solutions. It aligns with scholarship on feminist economics that challenges assumptions of selfish individualism and profit-focused paradigms within mainstream economics. It calls for centering collective well-being, social provisioning, and stewardship of nature.

The manifesto centers collective care praxis while challenging the exploitation of women's care labor. In conceptualizing development alternatives, the manifesto promises to foreground care work, livelihoods of informal workers, climate-resilient agriculture, and universal social protection while counteracting the exploitation of nature and human lives for capital accumulation.

Care framed as a collective obligation also connects South feminist visions to ecological stewardship and climate justice. It links struggles against extractive industries threatening Indigenous lands to resistance against racist border regimes dividing families. The manifesto promises to advance climate and migrant justice by care and solidarity against forces of capitalism and nativism that instrumentalize human lives and nature for profit-making. Its emphasis on collective solutions promises to yield fresh insights of value to both scholars and activists working to build caring, just economies attuned to oppressed groups' priorities.

The Time for Transformation Is Now

This historical moment, defined by converging social, economic, and ecological unraveling, demands bold visions accompanied by compassionate solidarity. A sense of collective purpose is needed—one that looks beyond returns to shareholders or national interests, to center historically marginalized communities' aspirations. The South Feminist Manifesto promises such a broad, coalitional platform. Through its embrace of radical care ethics and coalition-building, the manifesto initiative resonates with scholarship on feminist futurisms.

Most significantly, the manifesto promises to create a nurturing space amidst struggle—a space for joy, hope, and mutual transformation. This invokes bell hooks's characterization of Black women's activism as generating liberatory "homeplaces" for consciousness-raising, solidarity, and world changing ([1990] 2015, 42). As Jennifer Nash explained, Black feminist organizations from 1968 to 1987 served as intellectual, political, and emotional "homeplaces" where Black feminists developed shared critiques, activism, and canons (2011, 451). These nurturing spaces for growth and spiritual healing were antidotes to the wounds of racist domination, as hooks described. The manifesto similarly seeks to create a nurturing home for South feminist solidarity and revival.

Just as the Combahee River Collective catalyzed Black feminist organizing in the 1970s, the manifesto may ignite new solidarities advancing decolonial, anti-capitalist, intersectional praxis today to build more just and caring futures. The time has come to resuscitate South feminist solidarity. Supporting this collective effort promises to be every feminist's duty in our troubled yet profoundly promising times.

Trimita Chakma, a dedicated feminist researcher and activist, originally hails from the Indigenous Chakma hill tribe of Bangladesh. She recently completed her MA in Asian women's studies at Ewha Womans University in South Korea and holds an MSc in IT management from Carnegie Mellon University. Currently Trimita is engaged in coordinating the development of the South Feminist Manifesto at South Feminist Futures, a cross-regional manifesto aiming to ignite new solidarities between feminist movements across the Global South. Drawing on over a decade of experience championing feminist social justice, Trimita brings her expertise in Feminist Participatory Action Research (FPAR) tools to address key issues like climate justice, labor rights, and land rights of marginalized communities. In 2022 she cofounded the FPAR Academy to promote education on feminist participatory methodologies. Through her work with Public Services International, Trimita also supports labor organizing campaigns in the Asia-Pacific region. She can be reached at trimita@fparacademy.com.

Notes

1. See poster by Garima Karia, which provides an overview of four conferences related to women in Asia and Africa between 1947 and 1961: "Forgotten Femissaries: Women's Diplomacy in the Afro-Asian World (1945–1975)," Department of History and Classical Studies, McGill University, https://www.mcgill.ca/arts-internships/files/arts-internships/aria_final_poster_garima_karia.pdf.
2. South Feminist Futures is a transnational association of women, trans, and nonbinary people from the Global South and Black, Indigenous, and other people of color who are women, trans, and nonbinary in the Global North (South-in-North).

Works Cited

Ahmed, Aziza. 2017. "Bandung's Legacy: Solidarity and Contestation in Global Women's Rights." In *Bandung, Global History, and International Law*, edited by Luis Eslava, Michael Fakhri, and Vasuki Nesiah, 1st ed., 450–64. Cambridge, U.K.: Cambridge University Press. https://doi.org/10.1017/9781316414880.030.

Armstrong, Elisabeth. 2016. "Before Bandung: The Anti-Imperialist Women's Movement in Asia and the Women's International Democratic Federation." *Signs: Journal of Women in Culture and Society* 41 (2): 305–31. https://doi.org/10.1086/682921

Connell, Raewyn. 2014. "Rethinking Gender from the South." *Feminist Studies* 40 (3): 518–39.

Held, Virginia. 2005. *The Ethics of Care*. New York: Oxford University Press.

hooks, bell. 2015. *Yearning: Race, Gender, and Cultural Politics*. New York: Routledge.

Korol, Claudia. 2016. *Feminismos populares: Pedagogías y políticas*. Rio de Janeiro: El Colectivo.

Kovel, Joel, and Michael Löwy. 2001. "Eco-socialist Manifesto." *Capitalism Nature Socialism*. https://www.cnsjournal.org/about/an-ecosocialist-manifesto/.

Lugones, María. 2010. "Toward a Decolonial Feminism." *Hypatia* 25 (4): 742–59.

Mohanty, Chandra Talpade. 1988. "Under Western Eyes: Feminist Scholarship and Colonial Discourses." *Feminist Review* 30 (1): 61–88. https://doi.org/10.1057/fr.1988.42.

———. 2003. "'Under Western Eyes' Revisited: Feminist Solidarity through Anticapitalist Struggles." *Signs: Journal of Women in Culture and Society* 28 (2): 499–535. https://doi.org/10.1086/342914.

Mohanty, Chandra Talpade, Ann Russo, and Lourdes Torres, eds. 1991. *Third World Women and the Politics of Feminism*. Bloomington: Indiana University Press.

Najam, Adil. 2005. "Developing Countries and Global Environmental Governance: From Contestation to Participation to Engagement." *International Environmental Agreements: Politics, Law and Economics* 5 (3): 303–21. https://doi.org/10.1007/s10784-005-3807-6.

Nash, Jennifer C. 2011. "'Home Truths' on Intersectionality." *Yale Journal of Law and Feminism*, no. 23, 445–70.

Salleh, Ariel. 2010. "From Metabolic Rift to 'Metabolic Value': Reflections on Environmental Sociology and the Alternative Globalization Movement." *Organization & Environment* 23 (2): 205–19. https://doi.org/10.1177/1086026610372134.

Santos, Boaventura de Sousa, Joao Arriscado Nunes, and Maria Paula Meneses. 2008. "Introduction: Opening Up the Canon of Knowledge and Recognition of Difference." In *Another Knowledge Is Possible: Beyond Northern Epistemologies*, edited by Boaventura de Sousa Santos, xix–lxii. Reinventing Social Emancipation: Toward New Manifestos 3. London: Verso.

Co-creating Inclusive Intersectional Democratic Spaces across Europe (CCINDLE): Counteracting Anti-gender through Feminist Knowledge

Emanuela Lombardo and Paloma Caravantes

Abstract: The construction of feminist democratic societal projects relies on the production of feminist knowledge and ideas within social movements, as well as academic, professional, and institutional settings. In the context of a rising opposition against democracy and gender, race, and sexuality equality at a global level, the European Union has launched the call Feminisms for a New Age of Democracy with the purpose of supporting knowledge production about opposition to gender equality in Europe and feminist democratic responses. The CCINDLE (Co-creating Inclusive Intersectional Democratic Spaces across Europe) project is one of the funded research projects under this call. CCINDLE's objectives include analyzing not only anti-gender politics and the problems that they create for democracy in Europe but especially feminist movements' and institutional responses to anti-gender and anti-democratic forces. The project aims to co-create feminist knowledge with the actors that are already working to counter the antidemocratic project that anti-gender movements and far right parties are trying to construct, and to envision feminist futures building on theories and practices of intersectional justice, inclusion, and participation in European democracies. **Keywords:** feminist knowledge, democracy, anti-gender, democratic backsliding, gender equality, feminist politics, Europe

The rise of far-right anti-feminist, anti-queer and anti-trans, white supremacist discourses, movements, and politics is challenging equality and democracy at a global level. These actors threaten inclusionary dimensions of democracy while explicitly targeting marginalized collectives and positions within and beyond academia. A growing scholarship is working not only to study this phenomenon but also to generate knowledge and theorize responses to these attacks against democratic values of equality, inclusion, and participation.

In the European context, democratic backsliding and the backlash against gender equality and minority rights has progressively become one of the central concerns of social sciences production (Roggeband and Krizsan 2020). Scholars are elaborating collaborative scholarship to understand the similarities and dynamics across European countries. In 2021, one of the European Union's executive bodies, the European Commission, endorsed and promoted this scholarship, launching a funding call titled Feminisms for a New Age of Democracy (European Commission 2021) with the purpose of supporting knowledge production about opposition to gender equality in Europe and feminist democratic responses. Co-creating Inclusive Intersectional Democratic Spaces across Europe (CCINDLE), in which we both participate as researchers, was one of the awarded projects that researches the interdependent relationship between feminism and democracy and emphasizes the relevance of feminist movements and institutional responses to counter opposition against gender equality and democracy.

An Exclusionary Drift in European Democracies

Gender equality is a fundamental value of European democracies, and the adoption of gender equality policies, while certainly having room for improvement, has been at the core of European politics for decades. Yet, an oppositional climate has increased over the last two decades, with a "new" form of resistance against different equality policies that threatens the principle of equality and achievements in gender and sexuality equality in European democracies (Kuhar and Paternotte 2017; Lombardo et al. 2021; Verloo 2018).

Radical-right populist parties, anti-gender and anti–LGBTQI+ rights movements, and other far-right actors have grown in European political systems, actively opposing gender equality and LGBTQI+ and racialized groups' rights (Graff and Korolczuk 2021; Kuhar and Paternotte 2017). Combining nostalgia for a traditional gender order with nativist discourses that demonize "outsiders," these discourses and practices promote majoritarian interpretations of democratic governance and thwart key tenets of liberal democracy, such as women's and minorities' rights (Froio 2018; Köttig et al. 2017). Opposition against different forms of equality manifests through attacks and delegitimation of gender and LGBTQI+ equality policies and institutions, discrediting feminist knowledge, attacking and defunding feminist and LGBTQI+ organizations, and employing hateful misogynistic, homophobic, transphobic, and racist speech (Datta 2021; Denkovski et al. 2021; Paternotte and Kuhar 2018; Zacharenko 2020).

Attacks and discursive violence against women, LGBTQI+ and racialized people, and other marginalized groups are democratically problematic, because they intimidate them through vilification, shaming, and humiliation, sending a message about their supposed inferiority, even excluding them from humanity (Emejulu 2022), thus limiting their participation rights and expelling them from the public sphere (Krizsan and Roggeband 2021; Krook 2020). Beyond such visible contestations, equality policies are also being threatened by the dismantling of equality institutions and implementation arrangements, reorienting them towards the defense of the traditional patriarchal and heteronormative family, as well as by the undermining of existing directives and the erosion of accountability mechanisms (Krizsan and Roggeband 2018).

Increasing Role of Feminist Scholarship

The field of gender and politics has grown over the last decades through the efforts of political and social scientists who have put gender, sexuality, and intersectional perspectives at the center of analytical and methodological reflections of political institutions, processes, policies, and outcomes (Christoffersen 2021; Lombardo and Meier 2022). These efforts have strengthened the institutional position of scholarship on politics in relation to gender and sexuality—and more recently, intersectionality—within the academic fields of political science, sociology, and critical theory (Ahrens et al. 2021). The institutionalization of such efforts is reflected in the increasing membership of the Standing Group on Gender and Politics at the European Consortium for Political Research (ECPR), and the participation in the biennial European Conferences on Politics and Gender (ECPG), organized since 2009. While these academic spaces are not free from exclusionary dynamics, as the open letter from the anti-racist section of the ECPG 2022 shows,[1] they have contributed to open spaces for self-reflection in the discipline to advance gender-sensitive and intersectionally inclusionary approaches to research and teaching in political science.

In the context of growing challenges to gender, sexuality, and critical race studies opposed by anti-gender and far-right groups, the role of public institutions in supporting and funding feminist research is especially important. Responding to the rising attacks against gender equality—one of the European Union's fundamental values, enshrined in Article 2 of the Treaty of the European Union and the policy document titled Gender Equality Strategy 2020–2025[2]—the European Commission issued a funding call, "Feminisms for a New Age of Democracy," in 2021 (European Commission 2021). The call offered funding for projects "promoting gender equality theoretically and practically" and finding solutions in dialogue with civil society organizations and other stakeholders (European Commission 2021). Explicitly framing the quality of democratic governance as a matter of more inclusive European societies, it called for reflections to counter gender equality and anti-feminist strategies and policies promoted by "extreme populist discourses" (European Commission 2021). Resulting from this call, five international teams have received funding to develop projects, including CCINDLE, Co-creating Inclusive Intersectional Democratic Spaces across Europe;[3] FIERCE, Feminist Movements Revitalizing Democracy in Europe;[4] PushBackLash, a group focusing on anti-gender backlash and democratic pushback;[5] RESIST, Fostering Queer Feminist Intersectional Resistances against Transnational Anti-gender Politics;[6] and UNTWIST, a group that provides policy recommendations to regain marginalized feminists as mainstream voters.[7]

The CCINDLE project aims at producing academic work on the anti-gender, racist, LGBTQI+phobic opposition that attacks core values of democracy, intersectional inclusion, and equitable participation in political processes. CCINDLE strives not only to analyze these attacks but also to work on potential solutions. Co-creation of solutions to the crisis of democracy, with feminist, anti-racist, and LGBTQI+ movements, civil society, and institutional actors already working in this field, is a core goal of CCINDLE. A team of gender and politics researchers will develop CCINDLE's objectives, which include analyzing not only anti-gender and anti-feminist attacks and the problems of democracy in Europe that they create and reveal but also, especially, feminist activist and institutional responses to anti-gender and anti-democratic forces. The case studies are seven European countries with different social and political backgrounds, from the center, east, south, north, and west of Europe—Belgium, Hungary, Italy, Poland, Spain, Sweden, and the United Kingdom—as well as the supranational level of the European Union.

Feminist Politics as a Democratizing Force

CCINDLE understands democracy as a constant, contested, and unfinished process of democratization (Tilly 2007), where rights and freedoms are not achieved or lost once and for all but rather the object of ongoing struggles. Some social and political forces support democratization, while others oppose democratization, therefore contributing to democratic backsliding. Building on the attention to the relationship between democracy and equality (Verloo 2016), CCINDLE analyzes democratization and democratic backsliding as gendered processes, to better understand how the current backlash resonates with deeper exclusions and long-existing problems in the Western democratic model (CCINDLE 2021).

While CCINDLE departs from the idea that the recent rise of anti-gender, anti-LGBTQI+, and openly racist actors is the tip of the iceberg of deeply rooted exclusions in contemporary European societies that are problematic for democracy, it also considers feminist politics as one of the key forces that struggle for democratization (Verloo 2016). As a political project, feminism aims at transforming unequal gender and intersectional power hierarchies through "a vision of an alternative" and actions to redress injustice (Dean and Maiguashca 2018, 386). Feminist politics democratizes the state by questioning gender and intersectional inequalities in areas such as economy, gender-based violence, care, sexual and reproductive health, political representation, intimate citizenship rights, and knowledge. Feminist politics also democratizes the state by claiming new rights for formerly excluded subjects and issues (Verloo 2016), as is the case with activists' demand of public policies to address gender-based violence, reproductive justice, or LGBTQI+ rights (Ayoub and Paternotte 2014; Krizsan and Roggeband 2018; Luna 2020; Verloo 2016). In addition, feminist politics democratizes the public sphere by promoting inclusionary and participatory processes (Young 1990). Intersectional inclusion of marginalized groups' claims in policymaking counteracts privileges and exclusions that tend to be structured around gender intersecting with class, race, ethnicity, sexuality, age, citizenship status, and other inequalities (Crenshaw 1991; Fraser 1990; Hill Collins 1990). Participation in the making of decisions empowers citizens in the everyday practice of democracy (Pateman 1970).

Therefore, feminist politics is a democratizing force in that it experiments with future projects of society based on the centrality of the common good, political solidarity, care for the people and the planet, and intersectionality of gender, race, class, and other inequalities (CCINDLE 2021; Federici 2018; Hill Collins 1990; hooks 1986; Mellor 1998; Sander-Staudt 2011). As a result, feminist politics performs a critical function for democracy by scrutinizing power and holding the state accountable for gender equality commitments (Galligan 2015), as well as envisioning feminist future projects of society (Rawłuszko 2022). If feminist politics is a necessary ingredient for democratization, it needs democracy for performing these vital functions. Democracy and gender equality have an interdependent relationship, as Mieke Verloo (2016) claims: "The more democracy, the more chances for gender equality; the more gender equality there is, the more chances for democracy."

The interdependent relationship between democracy and gender equality is explicitly recognized in several scholarly works (Alonso and Lombardo 2018; Caravantes and Lombardo 2024; Lombardo et al. 2021; Verloo 2016; Walby 2009) that establish a link between democratization and attention to gender equality, broadly speaking. As Alonso and Lombardo (2018) argue, democracies show progress in women's status concerning health, education, economic participation, and political empowerment (Tripp 2013). Since democracies allow more freedom of organization and expression to civil society than autocracies, they offer greater opportunities for feminist, LGBTQI+, anti-racist, and human rights groups to influence the state (Htun and Weldon 2010). Citizens in democracies also tend to express more egalitarian public opinions (Inglehart and Norris 2003). A quality democracy is therefore needed for feminist politics to work towards deepening gender equality rights, and can contribute to a positive feedback loop, democratizing societies even deeper.

Coproduction of Knowledge as a Method, Goal, and Object of Study
The construction of feminist democratic societal projects relies on the production of feminist knowledge and ideas within social movements as well as academic, professional, and institutional contexts. Knowledge production plays a key role in the CCINDLE project. First, CCINDLE aims at co-creating knowledge with key actors that are already working on the ground to respond to anti-gender, racist, and LGBTQI+phobic campaigns and other antidemocratic forces. Through different initiatives such as Feminist Democracy Labs, and other networking and dissemination activities, CCINDLE seeks to collaborate with prodemocracy think tanks,

feminist donors, feminist associations, feminist media, and gender-related professional associations to increase the quality of democracy and make democracy across Europe more resilient and inclusive (CCINDLE 2021).

Second, CCINDLE seeks to intervene in mainstream disciplinary debates on democracy and politics that are taking place in political science, sociology, and other social sciences. The goal of these dialogues is threefold: (1) exposing the historical weaknesses of European democracies concerning gender, race, and sexuality equality that have been traditionally overlooked in mainstream scholarship; (2) giving relevance to the study of the phenomenon of anti-feminist opposition as a crucial factor in democratic backsliding; and (3) emphasizing the potential of feminist theories and practices for providing concrete approaches and tools to counter anti-gender and other antidemocratic forces more effectively.

Third, knowledge production is also a central object of study in the CCINDLE project. This is because knowledge has been one of the central mechanisms employed in campaigns by anti-gender actors to make their antidemocratic project hegemonic (see Paternotte and Verloo 2021; Verloo 2018). Anti-gender knowledge strategies work, for instance, through the discrediting of feminist knowledge as "gender ideology," the forging of alliances with other anti-gender and antidemocratic actors by using gender as a "symbolic glue" (Kováts and Põim 2015), thus creating an "opportunistic synergy" between anti-gender movements and far-right political parties (Graff and Korolczuk 2021, 24; Lavizzari and Prearo 2018). Anti-gender knowledge production—as materialized in the attacks against critical studies, such as critical race theory, feminist and gender studies, queer and LGBTQI+ studies within larger campaigns against academic freedom and critical thinking—is an important object of study of the project.

Since CCINDLE's focus is both on increasing our understanding of these campaigns and on generating solutions, the project also seeks to co-create feminist knowledge to resist and debunk the antidemocratic project that anti-gender movements and far-right parties are trying to construct. Envisioning and imagining feminist futures building on theories and practices of intersectional justice, inclusion, and participation in European democracies is therefore an important endeavor for the CCINDLE research team to challenge anti-gender and anti-feminist movements and policies, strengthen those actors already resisting these, and protect civic democratic culture in Europe.

Emanuela Lombardo is associate professor of political science at the Complutense University of Madrid (Spain). Her lines of research are gender equality policies, especially adoption and implementation, in the European Union and Spain, and feminism and democracy. She directs the Gender and Politics research group (GEYPO ref. 970799) with María Bustelo, and is principal investigator of a work package and of the UCM team in the Horizon Europe CCINDLE project on democracy and feminism (ref. 101061256, 2022–2026). Her latest monograph is *Gender and Political Analysis* (with Johanna Kantola, Palgrave, 2017). Recent articles have been published in *Policy & Politics*, *European Journal of Political Research*, *Journal of Common Market Studies*, *Social Politics*, *International Political Science Review*, and *Policy and Society*. She has edited the special issues "De-democratization and Opposition to Gender Equality Politics in Europe" (*Social Politics*, 2021, with Johanna Kantola and Ruth Rubio), "Populism and Feminist Politics" (*International Political Science Review*, 2020, with Johanna Kantola), "Care Policies in Practice" (*Policy and Society* 28, no. 4, 2019, with Rossella Ciccia) and "Policymaking from a Gender + Equality Perspective" (*Journal of Women, Politics and Policy* 38, no. 1, 2017, with Petra Meier and Mieke Verloo). She has been a coordinator for the evaluation of gender research projects in the social sciences panel of Spain's National Research Agency (2018–2021). She can be reached at elombard@ucm.es.

Paloma Caravantes is a Marie Skłodowska-Curie Actions postdoctoral researcher at the Department of Political Science and Administration of Complutense University of Madrid (Spain), with the project Local Democratic Governance towards Equality: Implementation of Gender+ Equality Policies in times of Anti-gender and Democratic Backsliding (LODGE, ref. 101067130). In 2019, she received her PhD in women's and gender studies at Rutgers University and is an elected member of the steering committee of the Standing Group on Gender and Politics at the European Consortium for Political Research (ECPR). She has published in *Policy & Politics*, *Politics & Gender*, *International Political Science Review*, *Men and Masculinities*, *Critical Discourse Studies*, and *Journal of Contemporary European Studies*, as well as coauthored a monograph on the implementation of intersectionality in local public policies. Her current research explores processes of feminist democratization at the local level and the implementation of intersectionality and gender equality approaches in public policies. She can be reached at pcaravan@ucm.es.

Notes

1. The letter is available as a Google doc at https://docs.google.com/document/d/12HDFEIjZGPsoc2WEHdSEwzZSqWourlvBzc45jAVyP0I/edit#heading=h.ppn5iy3ffjv.
2. To read the report, see European Commission 2020.
3. For more information, see CCINDLE 2021.
4. To read more about FIERCE, see FIERCE 2022.
5. For more information, see PushBackLash 2022.
6. For more information, see RESIST 2022.
7. For a description of the program, see UNTWIST 2022.

Acknowledgments

We wish to thank the European Research Executive Agency of the European Commission for funding the CCINDLE project (ref. 101061256, Co-creating Inclusive Intersectional Democratic Spaces across Europe), Mieke Verloo for serving as project coordinator and for her helpful feedback on a former draft, and our co-participants in the CCINDLE team who make this research possible.

Works Cited

Ahrens, Petra, Silvia Erzeel, Elizabeth Evans, Johanna Kantola, Roman Kuhar, and Emanuela Lombardo. 2021. "Gender and Politics Research in Europe: Towards a Consolidation of a Flourishing Political Science Subfield?" *European Political Science* 20 (1):105–22.

Alonso, Alba, and Emanuela Lombardo. 2018. "Gender Equality and De-democratization Processes: The Case of Spain." *Politics and Governance* 6 (3): 78–89.

Ayoub, Phillip M., and David Paternotte. 2014. *LGBT Activism and the Making of Europe: A Rainbow Europe?* Basingstoke: Palgrave Macmillan.

Caravantes, Paloma, and Emanuela Lombardo. 2024. "Feminist Democratic Innovations in Policy and Politics." *Policy & Politics*, 1–23.

CCINDLE. 2021. Co-creating Inclusive Intersectional Democratic Spaces across Europe. Proposal no. 101061256. Horizon Europe. Call: HORIZON-CL2-2021-DEMOCRACY-01 (Protecting and nurturing democracies). https://doi.org/10.3030/101061256.

Christoffersen, Ashlee. 2021. "The Politics of Intersectional Practice: Competing Concepts of Intersectionality." *Policy & Politics* 49 (4): 573–93.

Crenshaw, Kimberlé W. 1991. "Mapping the Margins: Intersectionality, Identity Politics, and Violence against Women of Color." *Stanford Law Review*, no. 43, 1241–99.

Datta, Neil. 2021. *Tip of the Iceberg: Religious Extremist Funders against Human Rights for Sexuality and Reproductive Health in Europe, 2009–2018*. European Parliamentary Forum for Sexual and Reproductive Rights. https://www.epfweb.org/sites/default/files/2021-08/Tip%20of%20the%20Iceberg%20August%202021%20Final.pdf.

Dean, Jonathan, and Bice Maiguashca. 2018. "Gender, Power, and Left Politics: From Feminization to 'Feministization.'" *Politics & Gender* 14 (3): 376–406.

Denkovski, Damjan, Nina Bernarding, and Kristina Lunz. 2021. *Power over Rights: Understanding and Countering the Transnational Anti-gender Movement*. Berlin: Center for Feminist Foreign Policy. https://

centreforfeministforeignpolicy.org/2022/11/15/power-over-rights-understanding-and-countering-the-anti-gender-campaigns/.

Emejulu, Akwugo. 2022. *Fugitive Feminism*. London: Silver Press.

European Commission. 2020. *A Union of Equality: Gender Equality Strategy 2020–2025*. Brussels: European Commission. https://eur-lex.europa.eu/legal-content/EN/TXT/PDF/?uri=CELEX:52020DC0152&from=EN.

European Commission. 2021. "Feminisms for a New Age of Democracy." HORIZON-CL2-2021 -DEMOCRACY-01-03. https://ec.europa.eu/info/funding-tenders/opportunities/portal/screen/opportunities/topic-details/horizon-cl2-2021-democracy-01-03.

Federici, Silvia. 2018. *Re-enchanting the World: Feminism and the Politics of the Commons*. Oakland: PM Press; Brooklyn: Kairos.

FIERCE. 2022. Feminist Movements Revitalizing Democracy in Europe. Proposal no. 101061748. Horizon Europe. Call: HORIZON-CL2-2021-DEMOCRACY-01. https://doi.org/10.3030/101061748.

Fraser, Nancy. 1990. "Rethinking the Public Sphere: A Contribution to the Critique of Actually Existing Democracy." *Social Text*, nos. 25–26, 56–80.

Froio, Caterina. 2018. "Race, Religion, or Culture? Framing Islam between Racism and Neo-racism in the Online Network of the French Far Right." *Perspectives on Politics* 16 (3): 696–709.

Galligan, Yvone. 2015. *States of Democracy: Gender and Politics in the European Union*. London: Routledge.

Graff, Agnieszka, and Elżbieta Korolczuk. 2021. *Anti-gender Politics in the Populist Moment*. Abingdon: Routledge.

Hill Collins, Patricia. 1990. "Black Feminist Thought in the Matrix of Domination." In *Black Feminist Thought: Knowledge, Consciousness, and the Politics of Empowerment*, 221–38. Boston, MA: Unwin Hyman.

hooks, bell. 1986. "Sisterhood: Political Solidarity between Women." *Feminist Review* 23 (1): 125–38.

Htun, Mala, and Laurel Weldon. 2010. "When Do Governments Promote Women's Rights? A Framework for the Comparative Analysis of Sex Equality Policy." *Perspectives on Politics* 8 (1): 207–16.

Inglehart, Ronald, and Pippa Norris. 2003. *Rising Tide: Gender Equality and Cultural Change around the World*. Cambridge: Cambridge University Press.

Köttig, Michaela, Renate Bitzan, and Andrea Pető, eds. 2017. *Gender and Far Right Politics in Europe*. Basingstoke: Palgrave Macmillan.

Kováts, Eszter, and Maari Põim, eds. 2015. "Gender as Symbolic Glue: The Position and Role of Conservative and Far Right Parties in the Anti-gender Mobilization in Europe." Foundation for European Progressive Studies. https://library.fes.de/pdf-files/bueros/budapest/11382.pdf.

Krizsan, Andrea, and Conny Roggeband. 2018. "Towards a Conceptual Framework for Struggles over Democracy in Backsliding States: Gender Equality Policy in Central Eastern Europe." *Politics & Governance* 6 (3): 90–100.

———. 2021. *Politicizing Gender and Democracy in the Context of the Istanbul Convention*. Basingstoke: Palgrave Macmillan.

Krook, Mona Lena. 2020. *Violence against Women in Politics*. Oxford: Oxford University Press.

Kuhar, Roman, and David Paternotte, eds. 2017. *Anti-gender Campaigns in Europe: Mobilizing against Equality*. London: Rowman & Littlefield.

Lavizzari, Anna, and Massimo Prearo. 2018. "The Anti-gender Movement in Italy: Catholic Participation between Electoral and Protest Politics." *European Societies* 21 (3): 422–42.

Lombardo, Emanuela, Johanna Kantola, and Ruth Rubio-Marin. 2021. "De-democratization and Opposition to Gender Equality Politics in Europe." *Social Politics* 28 (3): 521–31.

Lombardo, Emanuela, and Petra Meier. 2022. "Challenging Boundaries to Expand Frontiers in Gender and Policy Studies." *Policy & Politics*, no. 1, 99–115.

Luna, Zakiya. 2020. *Reproductive Rights as Human Rights: Women of Color and the Fight for Reproductive Justice*. New York: NYU Press.

Mellor, Mary. 1998. *Feminism and Ecology*. New York: NYU Press.

Pateman, Carole. 1970. *Participation and Democratic Theory*. Cambridge: Cambridge University Press.

Paternotte, David, and Roman Kuhar. 2018. "Disentangling and Locating the 'Global Right': Anti-gender Campaigns in Europe." *Politics and Governance* 6 (3): 6–19.

Paternotte, David, and Mieke Verloo. 2021. "De-democratization and the Politics of Knowledge: Unpacking the Cultural Marxism Narrative." *Social Politics* 28 (3): 556–78.

PushBackLash. 2022. Anti-gender Backlash and Democratic Pushback. Proposal no. 101061687. Horizon Europe. Call: HORIZON-CL2-2021-DEMOCRACY-01. https://doi.org/10.3030/101061687.

Rawłuszko, Marta. 2022. "Producing Solidarities in Practice." *European Journal of Politics and Gender* 5 (3): 382–98.

RESIST. 2022. Fostering Queer Feminist Intersectional Resistances against Transnational Anti-gender Politics. Proposal no. 101060749. Horizon Europe. Call: HORIZON-CL2-2021-DEMOCRACY-01 (Protecting and nurturing democracies). https://doi.org/10.3030/101060749.

Roggeband, Conny, and Andrea Krizsan. 2020. "Democratic Backsliding and the

Backlash against Women's Rights: Understanding the Current Challenges for Feminist Politics." Discussion Paper UN Women 35. https://www.unwomen.org/sites/default/files/Headquarters/Attachments/Sections/Library/Publications/2020/Discussion-paper-Democratic-backsliding-and-the-backlash-against-womens-rights-en.pdf.

Sander-Staudt, Maureen. 2011. "Care Ethics." In *Internet Encyclopedia of Philosophy*, edited by James Fieser and Bradley Dowden. https://iep.utm.edu/care-ethics/.

Tilly, Charles. 2007. *Democracy*. Cambridge: Cambridge University Press.

Tripp, Aili Mari. 2013. "Political Systems and Gender." In *The Oxford Handbook of Gender and Politics*, edited by Georgina Waylen, Karen Celis, Johanna Kantola, and Laurel Weldon. Oxford: Oxford University Press.

UNTWIST. 2022. UNTWIST: Policy Recommendations to Regain "Losers of Feminism" as Mainstream Voters. Proposal no. 101060836. Horizon Europe. Call: HORIZON-CL2-2021-DEMOCRACY-01 (Protecting and nurturing democracies). https://doi.org/10.3030/101060836.

Verloo, Mieke. 2016. "The Challenge of Gender Inequality in Chapter 14: Inequality as a Challenge to Democracy." International Panel on Social Progress, coordinated by Richard Bellamy and Wolfgang Merkel. https://comment.ipsp.org/chapter/chapter-14-inequality-challenge-democracy.

———. 2018. "Gender Knowledge, and Opposition to the Feminist Project: Extreme-Right Populist Parties in the Netherlands." *Politics and Governance* 6 (3): 20–30.

Walby, Sylvia. 2009. *Globalization and Inequalities: Complexity and Contested Modernity*. London: Sage.

Young, Iris Marion. 1990. *Justice and the Politics of Difference*. Princeton, NJ: Princeton University Press.

Zacharenko, Elena. 2020. "Anti-gender Mobilisations in Europe." *The Greens / EFA in the European Parliament*. https://heidihautala.fi/wp-content/uploads/2020/12/Anti-gender-Mobilisations-in-Europe_Nov25.pdf.

SFNDHE: Feminist Scholars Demand Higher Education for All

Eileen Boris, Aimee Loiselle, and Jennifer Mittelstadt

Abstract: Scholars for a New Deal for Higher Education (SFNDHE) emerged during the COVID-19 pandemic to facilitate and help drive a coordinated response across the country and its territories to the assaults on the funding of higher education, the precariousness of academic labor, and the burden on students. This essay describes its founding, programs, and ongoing fight to obtain federal support for free college combined with fair labor standards for staff, substituting secure jobs for contingent labor. **Keywords:** higher education, academic labor, College for All, contingent faculty, austerity, academic freedom

On May 15, 2023, during a sensational press event staged with Chris Rufo at the recently restructured New College of Florida in Sarasota, Governor Ron DeSantis signed three bills that attack academic freedom. The first bill prohibits intellectual pursuits related to "theories that systemic racism, sexism, oppression, and privilege are inherent in the institutions of the United States." DeSantis and his allies in the legislature deployed this language, with its incendiary effect on their supporters, as both justification and cover for additional assaults on learning, teaching, and research. The legislative package expands the hiring and firing powers of university boards and presidents, limits protections for tenured faculty members, and prohibits spending related to diversity, equity, and inclusion beyond what is required by accreditors—anticipating what is becoming another front in the fight over higher education. Nine days later, DeSantis announced that he was running for president.

Florida's right-wing Republicans are generating a model for asserting control of public higher education state by state. DeSantis and his legislative cronies are not alone. Across the globe, academic workers and academic freedom face multiplying modes of attack that have become increasingly coordinated: relentless tax cuts, restrictions on state allocations, dark private funding sources, institutional debt and consultant fees, outsourcing and contingent contracts, limits on teaching content and library collections, restrictions on use of research funds, loss of tenure lines by attrition, and outright dismantling of tenure (the last shrinking perimeter of financial and intellectual security). To address the broad and sustained attack on higher education as a whole, we must begin to imagine, and fight for, solutions that can address the damages which originated before but were then exacerbated by the COVID-19 pandemic.

The expanding web of legislation and regulations grew from six decades of critiques and reductions that targeted higher education, particularly public colleges and universities. Under neoliberal regimes, both Republican and Democrat, austerity measures cut taxes, depleted public allocations to education, and encouraged adjunctification of instruction as well as corporatization and financialization of our institutions. This juggernaut eroded the power of faculty and practices of shared governance while shifting resources toward financial gain and away from instruction and research (especially in the arts and humanities), shared production of knowledge, and education of students.

We previously understood the various assaults as distinct attacks—as a problem for scholars who study gender and sexuality, a concern for those who research the history of race, a conflict over "freedom of speech," a dilemma for adjunct faculty or librarians, or a challenge for students seeking access and affordability in their quest for a degree. Each urgent issue was fought campus by campus, with various professional associations making separate statements at different times. However, we've come to see such issues as connected parts of one tremendous problem, an intertwined right-wing and finance-capitalist co-optation of higher education. Piecemeal solutions will not do. A larger coordinated response is necessary, one in which instructors, researchers, and academic and service staff across categories rebuild their leverage together. We have to link the issues of academic freedom, teaching loads and research support, terms of employment, conditions of labor, and funding. We have to unite our campuses and professional associations.

Scholars for a New Deal for Higher Education (SFNDHE) emerged to facilitate and help drive this coordinated response across the country and its territories. To generate alternative pathways for the future, we hoped to spark a collective effort to transform the current discontent and distress into organized resistance. This group of scholars initially galvanized as a response to the COVID-19 pandemic and its jarring exposure of the layered crises at our colleges and universities—but it has launched from that foundation into a larger movement[1] for quality higher education[2] for all faculty, staff, students, and communities. We redirected our research and writing skills, honed through the study of race, gender, the welfare state, culture, and political economy, to bring our intersectional feminist analysis to bear on the crisis of higher education.

In late March 2020, members of Congress acknowledged but failed to stem the mounting fiscal crisis as campuses closed, students withdrew and demanded refunds, and state legislatures announced their inability to sustain budgets for higher education systems. The Coronavirus Aid, Relief, and Economic Security (CARES) Act provided $14 billion to colleges and universities, $10 billion less than it gave to the airline industry, which employs only one-sixth as many workers as are found in higher education.[3] Lacking substantial government support, college and university administrators unleashed a tidal wave of cuts and layoffs while maintaining tuition at unprecedented highs even as students and their households lost the ability to pay bills.

Jennifer Mittelstadt, a historian at Rutgers University, New Brunswick, invited several feminist colleagues from public and private universities across the country to meet on Zoom during April 2020 to discuss how they could address the accelerating crises. Coming together over the following months, we determined that while each college campus had its own distinct financial problems, the disaster was a general one, so the solutions—and our advocacy—required an immediate focus on the federal level.

Many of us were policy and social movement historians, and we turned to the past for understanding and inspiration. The magnitude of the collapse prompted us to consider previous times of overwhelming national disruption, and the potential for relief and reform. We landed on the Great Depression of the 1930s and the New Deal. New Dealers asked not only what had provoked the stock market crash and banking collapse but also what the financial implosion and rampant unemployment suggested about broader failures in the economic and social system. While their answers upheld the male breadwinner ideal, reinforced racial discrimination, and did not address the problems of all Americans, they stoked the beginnings of federal reform. We began to imagine what a New Deal for Higher Education—a truer, fairer New Deal—might look like. We began to ask questions about which problems facing higher education resulted from the onset of the pandemic and which ones reflected historic and systemic issues. And we asked whether *this* new deal might demand innovative means of funding, overseeing, and governing higher education to make it fairer for all.

SFNDHE grew from these discussions. We hoped to push the federal government to commit to higher education as a public good, with increased funding realigned to serve academic needs, stabilize public systems and small regional private colleges, and reduce student debt. We also sought to mobilize the American Association of University Professors (AAUP) and American Federation of Teachers (AFT) to rally members to fight back, and we reached out to colleagues across the country to inquire whether they would like to help craft a united approach, across regions and institutions and across different subsets of campus communities. The SFNDHE Executive Board expanded to include contingent faculty, postdoctoral fellows, and graduate students.

SFNDHE's initial goal for 2021 was to secure additional federal stimulus funding during the COVID-19 emergency and connect it to reforms related to student debt and prevention of campus layoffs. The organization's long-term goal initially was to help set the Biden presidency's higher education agenda, in which the federal government would commit to more direct funding and tie it to supporting the economic security of the academic labor force as well as justice, equity, and access. To make this effort more effective and collaborative, SFNDHE initiated a partnership with AAUP and AFT national leadership to launch New Deal for Higher Education,[4] a campaign to lobby the Biden White House and key congressional leadership to commit to this vision.

As our analysis proceeded, we recognized that all the dilemmas and cuts we had been fighting were connected as one large problem. Like previous feminist scholars, our arguments and actions both widened and deepened as we demystified the "interlocking systems" of exploitation and extraction (Combahee 1977). We launched working groups focused on legislative action, racial justice, fair labor, and budget and finance, and invited new contributing members to collaborate on a variety of projects and presentations.

In May 2021, SFNDHE members wrote a brief for Senator Bernie Sanders's office as his staff worked with Representative Pramila Jayapal's to write an updated College for All bill. Several of our suggested labor provisions, including a requirement for increased tenure lines and contingent pay and benefits equity, made it into the final bill, which competed with Biden's American Families Plan and Senator Tammy Baldwin's America's College Promise. The actual budget allocation in the heavily compromised Build Back Better package of legislation, which passed in November 2021, was not what SFNDHE had hoped for—but we had created a nationwide network and a new framework for confronting the crises in higher education.

During that year, energized by the urgency of the pandemic and inspired by the possibility of a Democratic-led federal government, SFNDHE had produced a "white paper" with the Roosevelt Institute (Kahn et al. 2020); submitted a detailed brief on College for All; guest-edited a spring 2021 special issue of AAUP's *Academe* about demanding a new deal for higher education (Boris and Orleck 2021); coordinated a series of webinars and panels about racial justice, debt, contingency, and tackling austerity;[5] organized an opening plenary on College for All with the Labor and Working-Class History Association (LAWCHA);[6] published several articles and op-eds;[7] and helped plan a labor summit that led to the formation of Higher Education Labor United (HELU), a nationwide coalition of unions. We had momentum, and our members came from all regions of the continental United States and had discovered a sense of purpose and camaraderie in resistance.

As feminist scholars, we know we must continue to work to change the public conversation, create new narratives and build partnerships that reframe the many issues in higher education as one big problem, and call for nationwide transformation. In fall 2022 we guest-edited another special issue of AAUP's *Academe* about revolutionizing budget and finance, and all the articles include action steps as well as analysis. The issue also provides a tool kit for budget and finance activism that's so loaded we call it a rucksack (Loiselle and Miller, eds. 2022). In November 2023, Lisa Levenstein organized our first solo virtual forum, Dispatches from the Crisis at West Virginia University, in which Karma Chávez facilitated a conversation with professors Lisa DiBartolomeo and Jessica Wilkerson. SFNDHE members have co-hosted additional webinars and coordinated roundtables at multiple conferences, including the National Women's Studies Association and the Berkshire Conference on the History of Women, Gender, and Sexuality.

We continue to publish articles and essays, and interested readers can find details in the "Our Work" section of the SFNDHE website (SFNDHE 2023).

SFNDHE carries on its efforts to change the horizon of what is possible and to imagine higher education as a true public good for all students, faculty, staff, and communities. This means more writing and speaking to build awareness; collaborating with diverse groups who care about higher education; offering ways for people to get involved through the use of SFNDHE tool kits for conference roundtables, op-eds, and faculty senate resolutions, hosting summits; working with professional organizations to educate and promote policy change; and partnering with labor unions and chapters, documented on our website (SFNDHE 2023). SFNDHE welcomes members who want to use the available tool kits, share projects, or write together. We want to foster collaboration for action and substantive change.

In this regard, we recently began a campaign to bring a resolution to academic societies such as the American Historical Association. This effort aims to build coordinated, interdisciplinary action to stem the crisis in higher education and demand federal monies that attach fair employment to institutional funding for both college affordability and stable academic jobs. After all, the very survival of the professional societies depends on a secure and decently compensated labor force of faculty for memberships, conference attendance, and peer review.

Contingent faculty and staff—the great majority of workers in higher education—and, increasingly, all scholars without endowed chairs are stretched to the limit after decades of austerity budgets, adjunctification, and resource-centered management. We face upper administrators who emphasize credit ratings, real estate development, endowments and rainy day funds, and athletics over intellectual pursuits. Feminist scholars are particularly vulnerable to attacks on their syllabi, teaching, research, and job security. Black women have inordinate student debt (Carrazana and Mithani 2023), while women in general are more likely to be contingent workers (Spitalniak 2023). The last hired are the first left behind. The resulting loss of shared governance and leverage on our campuses has eroded our options. Campus discussions and public awareness are not enough anymore. We must work together to demand changes that are tied to funding with shared governance over budgets. We want to see this funding dependent on labor provisions and limits on tuition hikes, with restrictions on its use for institutional debt servicing, commercial real estate, payment of management fees, or athletics.

Over the past six decades, right-wing politicians and neoliberal policymakers have taken control of state budgets with an ideology that dictates tax cuts and budget shell games during good times and bad, surpluses and deficits. Private donors, Wall Street firms, and finance analysts like Moody's have been effective at infiltrating campuses with so-called market-based decision-making that prioritizes return on investment and salaries for consultants over the educational mission and the stability of full-time academic workers. Ambitious politicians like DeSantis ally with agitators like Rufo to capitalize on this situation and attack academic freedom in all facets. The Supreme Court conservative majority's recent obstruction of race-based affirmative action and student debt cancellation has damaged access and equitable education, just as Texas, Florida, and other states legislate against even basic managerial versions of DEI (diversity, equity, and inclusion).

We have to counter this coordinated drive with our demands for "higher education for all" so we can establish job security, center learning and research, and sustain intellectual pursuits. The Higher Ed for All coalition in Massachusetts offers one model. It's building on the success of a multi-year campaign by the Fair Share coalition to amend the state constitution with a wealth tax that requires the revenue go toward public education and transportation. When we build such constructive links across funding, employment, and student conditions, we restructure all the pieces that allow scholarly teaching and learning, research, and publication to operate in any meaningful way. More and more scholars, editors, and directors of professional associations recognize this reality, and we continue to develop these alliances to fight for higher education as a public good. In all this activism, we should acknowledge that feminists have led the way.

Eileen Boris is the Hull Professor of Feminist Studies at the University of California, Santa Barbara. She writes on the home as a workplace and the racialized gendered state. Her current project is a microhistory of the 1947 slavery case *U.S. v. Ingalls* involving the confinement of a Black domestic worker by her white woman employer. She can be reached at eboris@ucsb.edu.

Aimee Loiselle is an assistant professor of history at Central Connecticut State University. She researches women workers in global supply chains entwined with U.S. imperialism and popular representations of labor and wealth. Her book, *Beyond Norma Rae: How Puerto Rican and Southern White Women Fought for a Place in the American*

Working Class, was recently published by the University of North Carolina Press. She can be reached at aimee.loiselle@uconn.edu.

Jennifer Mittelstadt is professor of history at Rutgers University, where she teaches and researches the history of the twentieth-century United States, with a focus on the state, politics and political movements, the military, and foreign affairs. She is currently working on a book about grassroots right-wing participation in U.S. foreign policy in the twentieth century. She can be reached at jen.mittelstadt@gmail.com.

Notes

1. For a press release by a supporting organization, see New York State United Teachers 2023.
2. For a discussion by a related organization, see Massachusetts Teachers Organization 2023.
3. See the U.S. Department of the Treasury's press release at U.S. Department of the Treasury 2020.
4. For a video of the official launch of the New Deal for Higher Education with AAUP and AFT, see AFTHQ 2021.
5. Updates can be read at A New Deal for Higher Education, n.d.
6. To view the plenary, see Labor and Working-Class History Association 2021.
7. For an example of such an op-ed, see Adair and Sesanker 2021.

Works Cited

Adair, Stephen, and Colena Sesanker. 2021. "Should Two- and Four-Year Degrees Be Free?" *New York Times*, May 13, 2021. https://www.nytimes.com/2021/05/13/opinion/community-college-student-debt-sanders.html.

AFTHQ. 2021. "A New Deal for Higher Education." YouTube, February 12, 2021. https://www.youtube.com/watch?v=vnOjeEdjSC0.

A New Deal for Higher Education. n.d. "Latest News." Accessed January 16, 2023. https://newdealforhighered.org/news-and-updates/.

Boris, Eileen, and Annelise Orleck, eds. 2021. "A New Deal for Higher Education." *Academe* 107 (2). https://www.aaup.org/issue/spring-2021-new-deal-higher-education.

Carrazana, Chabeli, and Jasmine Mithani. 2023. "How Student Loan Debt Has Fueled the Pay Gap for Black Women." *The 19th*, July 27, 2023. https://19thnews.org/2023/07/student-loan-debt-pay-gap-black-women/.

Combahee River Collective. 1977. "The Combahee River Collective Statement." *BlackPast*, November 16, 2012. https://www.blackpast.org/african-american-history/combahee-river-collective-statement-1977/.

Kahn, Suzanne, Jennifer Mittelstadt, and Lisa Levenstein. 2020. "A True New Deal for Higher Education: How a Stimulus for Higher Ed Can Advance Progressive Policy Goals." Roosevelt Institute, December 16, 2020. https://rooseveltinstitute.org/publications/true-new-deal-for-higher-education-stimulus-advance-progressive-policy-goals/.

Labor and Working-Class History Association. 2021. "Opening Plenary, LAWCHA Conference, May 20, 2021." YouTube. https://www.youtube.com/watch/v=fCsj9Jiit9U.

Loiselle, Aimee, and Jennifer M. Miller. 2022. "Budget and Finance Rucksack: Tools and Resources for Tackling Austerity." *Academe* 108 (4). https://www.aaup.org/article/budget-and-finance-rucksack.

Loiselle, Aimee, and Jennifer M. Miller, eds. 2022. "Revolutionizing Higher Education Budget and Finance." *Academe* 108 (4). https://www.aaup.org/issue/fall-2022-revolutionizing-higher-education-budget-and-finance.

Massachusetts Teachers Organization. 2023. "Higher Ed for All Coalition Calls for a Major Investment in Public Universities, Colleges and Students." *Massachusetts Teachers Association*, January 4, 2023. https://massteacher.org/news/2023/01/higher-ed-for-all-campaign.

New York State United Teachers. 2023. "NYSUT Activists Rally for New Deal for Higher Education, with Broad Support from Voters." March 9, 2023. https://www.nysut.org/news/2023/march/media-release-committee-of-100.

SFNDHE (Scholars for a New Deal for Higher Education). 2023. "Our Work and Our Resources." https://scholarsforanewdealforhighered.org.

Spitalniak, Laura. 2023. "Contingent Faculty Jobs Are Still the Standard, AAUP Report Finds." *Higher Ed Dive*, March 28, 2023. https://www.highereddive.com/news/contingent-faculty-jobs-are-still-the-new-standard-aaup/646094/.

U.S. Department of the Treasury. 2020. "Treasury Implementing CARES Act Programs for Aviation and National Security Industries." April 25, 2020. https://home.treasury.gov/news/press-releases/treasury-implementing-cares-act-programs-for-aviation-and-national-security-industries.

SECTION III. **ESSAYS**

Kyra Gregory (they/them) is a printmaker, painter, and collage artist born in Richmond, Virginia, and currently living and working in Queens, New York. They graduated from Princeton University in 2019 with a major in visual arts and a certificate in gender and sexuality studies. They can be reached at kmgregory16@gmail.com.

Kyra Gregory, *Bound*, 2022. Woodblock print on paper.

My work is rooted in an existential search for self and community, and driven by my personal experiences navigating queerness, mental illness, and spirituality in an emotionally complex and devastating world. *Bound* illustrates some of the somatic symptoms of major depression that I experience—emotional paralysis that spreads through the body. I create art as a coping mechanism and a call for solidarity.

Resisting the Epistemic Straight Gaze in the Anti-gender Era: Italian LGBTIQ+ Studies and Scholars, 2013–2023

Massimo Prearo

Abstract: This article discusses the challenges faced by scholars involved in gender and LGBTIQ+ studies and research, within a context of increased attacks by anti-gender coalitions of social movements and parties. It highlights the precarious and vulnerable position of gender and LGBTIQ+ scholars in an academic environment set by neoliberal agendas and anti-gender rhetoric. The contribution reflects on the role of academic institutions in reinforcing dominant power structures and the resistance efforts by LGBTIQ+ scholars against this backdrop. The study underscores the importance of understanding these dynamics for the future of LGBTIQ+ studies and the broader context of academic freedom and knowledge production in Italy and beyond. **Keywords:** LGBTIQ+ scholars, anti-gender movements, academic freedom, neoliberalism, Italy

In recent years, attacks on gender studies in Europe have been part of a broader trend of targeting gender politics as "symptoms" of the diffusion of the so-called gender ideology (Datta and Paternotte 2023; Graff and Korolczuk 2022; Kuhar and Paternotte 2017). Within academia, this criticism also extended to alleged radicalized and politicized scholars (Paternotte and Verloo 2021). In addition to the increase in attacks on gender studies, the populist and radical right wing sought to repress academic freedom, as in the Hungarian case (Lombardo, Kantola, and Rubio-Marin 2021; Grzebalska and Pető 2018; Pető 2020). Furthermore, the rise of a neoliberal agenda within academia and scientific research has significantly affected all European universities, especially since the Bologna Process started in 1999.

Within this historical and political framework, Italy represents an interesting case study for understanding the effects of intersecting factors: on the one hand, a significant presence of gender scholars combined with a lack of institutionalization of gender studies—as a recent report has shown (Barilà Ciocca et al. 2022)—and, on the other, a prevailing anti-gender context (Prearo 2024).

In Italian academia, gender studies and gender scholars have become the target of a wide range of political and social actors, including anti-gender movements, right-wing parties (although not limited to them), anti-progressive and conservative media, and even academics (Möser et al. 2022). Recently, groups of feminists identifying as gender-critical have joined the battle on this anti-gender front—although drawing on a different theoretical and political background (Prearo 2023; Biagini 2021).

This contribution is divided into three main sections. First, I describe how the anti-gender mobilization created a discursive and political set of opportunities for the attacks against gender and LGBTIQ+ studies and scholars. Then, I reflect on the experience of precariousness and vulnerability in the context of these mobilizations in Italian academia. Following up on that, I explore the role of academic institutions in maintaining a straight gaze that reinforces dominant power structures and, lastly, the condition of resistance to it from the perspective of an LGBTIQ+ scholar.

Anti-gender Mobilizations as Discursive and Political Opportunities

Anti-gender campaigns in Italy started in the summer of 2013 with the emergence of La Manif pour Tous Italia. However, radical Catholic and anti-choice activists had already begun disseminating and mobilizing tools against the "gender ideology." At the time, the Italian parliament debated three significant bills: one against LGBTIQ+ hate crimes, one on gender education in schools, and one on the legal recognition of same-sex couples (Donà 2021; Ozzano 2020). A conservative front was formed, initially bringing together anti-gender movements and right-wing parties, and mobilizing in the street and within institutions. A few years later, in 2021, this religious and right-wing front succeeded in stopping the anti–hate crimes bill (Bernini 2021; Feo 2022), partly due to the mobilization of a branch of Italian feminism opposed to non-sex-based gender-affirmative approaches to gender identity (Ashley 2023) and to the legitimation of surrogacy (Ammaturo 2020).

Thus, the mobilization of new Catholic movements in the public arena, which first positioned themselves as moral entrepreneurs of the anti-gender cause (Lavizzari and Prearo 2019), has benefited other and quite different actors, producing opportunities which are at once discursive and political (Edenborg 2021; Norocel and Szabó 2019). Firstly, they are discursive because the anti-gender rhetorical device at the center of the struggle against gender ideology (Garbagnoli 2016) has introduced a new conceptual framework and vocabulary to challenge gender and LGBTIQ+ studies and politics. The new language of opposition has a secularized form and substance that purports to be grounded in science, citing fields such as biology, medicine, or anthropology. Therefore, it moves beyond the confines of the Vatican and the Catholic Church, where it originated (Paternotte 2023), and becomes a discursive tool available in the public domain for institutional, political, and social actors, including the media (see the insightful work on this topic by Pető and Kováts 2017). These tools function as discursive "ready-mades": objects created to define—and contest—gender and LGBTIQ+ studies and policies as public threats. They are perceived as weapons used by international lobbies aiming to destroy humanity in favor of a new transhumanism, primarily targeting children and their identity (Righetti 2021).

Secondly, such opportunities are inherently political. Owning to their adaptability and powerful rhetorical nature, the anti-gender campaign has become a public and conflicting issue. It has given rise to a new agenda of opposition to gender and LGBTIQ+ studies and policies. This agenda has found support amongst conservative and populist radical right parties in Italy (Ozzano 2019; Pirro 2023; Trappolin 2022). These parties have used it to rekindle a political divide, presenting it as a conflict between, on the one hand, progressive stances promoted by supposedly radicalized minority groups and, on the other, conservative positions guided by a "common sense" that rejects the anti-naturalist proposal of gender and LGBTIQ+ studies (Norocel and Paternotte 2023). This is also why gender and LGBTIQ+ politics have become a central conflict between libertarian or democratic positions and traditionalist and authoritarian positions. Libertarian and democratic positions are inspired by the principles of freedom, equality, and justice and propose social transformation through legislative innovation, such as the recognition of the rights of same-sex couples and gender self-determination. On the other hand, traditionalist and authoritarian positions propose restrictive and repressive policies aimed at limiting sexual rights (Dietze and Roth 2020). This has become particularly evident in Italy with the rise of far-right leader Giorgia Meloni in 2022 (De Giorgi et al. 2023), whose government seeks to repress the emancipation and freedom of LGBTIQ+ lives—cause for concern, given Italy's low level of legal protection for gender and sexual minorities (Santos 2013).

This is the context in which we must situate gender and, even more specifically, LGBTIQ+ studies and scholars in Italy. The attacks and repression they face are not solely the result of a persistent heteropatriarchal configuration that feeds and sustains socially widespread representations and practices of sexism, homophobia, transphobia, or LGBTIQ+phobia. They are also the consequence of anti-gender and anti-LGBTIQ+ mobilizations.

Experiencing Precariousness and Vulnerability

In 2017, as I sought contracts that would enable my continued work in academia, I came across an opportunity to join a research project titled Subjects of the Law and Vulnerability as a postdoctoral researcher. Given my expertise in LGBTIQ+ activism in Italy, I pitched a project on and with LGBTIQ+ migrants to better understand the governance of LGBTIQ+ migration and LGBTIQ+ asylum seekers' requests in Italy. As part of this research, I conducted a political ethnography within LGBTIQ+ migrant support organizations (Prearo 2021). In 2018, in response to a need expressed by the associations I was working with, I proposed a one-day workshop of study and training activities on LGBTIQ+ asylum at the University of Verona's Department of Human Sciences where I had previously been and currently am employed. However, when the local radical right heard of the event, it triggered an intense dispute involving proponents of the workshop, its opponents, and the university's administration. I quote here the account that the director of the PoliTeSse Research Center at the University of Verona, co-organizer of the event, gives of the affair:

> In May 2018 "Forza Nuova" [a neofascist group] announced that it was ready to prevent "also by force" the holding of the conference titled "Richiedenti asilo: Orientamento sessuale e identità di genere" [Asylum seekers: Sexual orientation and gender identity], which [the research center] PoliTeSse had organised together with the Hannah Arendt Centre for Political Studies, the departments of Human Sciences and Legal Sciences of the University of Verona, and three associations supporting migrant and LGBTQI+ people, ASGI–Association for Legal Studies on Immigration, Association PINK and Arcigay Pianeta Milk–LGBT* Center. The rector of the University of Verona, Nicola Sartor, reacted by suspending the conference and releasing an equivocal note to the press, in which instead of simply condemning

the neo-fascist group's threats, he covertly scolded those who had organized the initiative, placing Forza Nuova on the same level as the advocacy groups involved. The note stated that the event, dedicated to "politically and ethically controversial issues," had "abandoned the scientific sphere to become a terrain of confrontation and, above all, of search for visibility for different activists from a range of positions." The rector's decision was quickly followed by a broad-based local, national, and international mobilization. A vigil was organized in Verona outside the Administration building to protest against the canceling of the conference. Many associations and university research centers from all over Italy released public statements. An open letter was published in the French newspaper *Liberation* and in the Italian newspaper *Il Manifesto*, which had very quickly gathered the signatures of more than 150 academics of international fame—among them, Etienne Balibar, Judith Butler, Lee Edelman, Christine Delphy, Éric Fassin, David M. Halperin, Paul B. Preciado, Chiara Saraceno, and Joan W. Scott. The rector, now obviously fearful of losing face, quickly announced that an initiative centered on the same issues would be planned for September. The associations instead organized the same conference, though smaller, without university funds and outside of it altogether, on the day initially established, 25 May. (Bernini 2021, 17)

This was not the first, nor the last, attack that we, researchers at the PoliTeSse Research Center at the University of Verona, have faced. As another example, Lorenzo Bernini was even the subject of a parliamentary question by Massimiliano Fedriga (former MP and now president of the Friuli Venezia Giulia region):

Fedriga pointed out that "Lorenzo Bernini," in addition to being "a researcher in political philosophy who writes about gender studies and queer theories (according to which there is no single way of being men and women, but a multiplicity of identities and experiences)," is also "a fixed presence at many gay prides." (Bernini 2021, 17)

In reflecting on the nature and impact of these events, I observe two dimensions characterizing them: the political moment and the context-defining conditions. On the one hand, there is the immediate situation marked by events, pressures (sometimes repression), and the resulting resistance. In response to this attack, the Research Center PoliTeSse called for an assembly aiming to bring together all the people inside and outside the Italian university working in the broad field of gender studies. Within a few weeks, we organized the first Congress of Gender and Sexuality Studies in Italy at the University of Verona in June 2018, attended by about 150 people from all over Italy. This congress was the first step in the process of collective construction that led in March 2019 to the establishment of the Italian Network of Gender, Intersex, Feminist, Transfeminist, and Sexuality Studies (GIFTS). At the same time, the international conference of ultraconservative forces, the World Congress of Families, was being held in Verona (Pavan 2020).

On the other hand, as LGBTIQ+ scholars focusing on LGBTIQ+ issues and working with people and communities, we are often represented and objectified as uncomfortable or unwanted subjects within the institution (Ayoub 2022). This occurs even before political forces, groups, and movements of various kinds single us out for attack. The stigma associated with LGBTIQ+ issues and people tarnishes our identity and professional standing. For us, the vulnerability generated by the physical and symbolic violence shaping the lives of LGBTIQ+ people is not simply an object or a variable to consider in research. Anti-LGBTIQ+ stigma is a factor that produces social positions subjugating individuals who find themselves living or inhabiting those positions at a given time in a given context. Although, as academics, we are in a position of social privilege, as LGBTIQ+ scholars, we share that vulnerability and stigma with those who participate in our research. We must also grapple with doubts regarding our scientific rigor because of our close identification with or proximity to our field of study—this only exacerbates the prevailing stigma. Conservative and anti-gender factions frequently leverage this argument to undermine research on same-sex families and in the realm of trans studies and issues.

Moments and conditions that generate vulnerable scholars in the specific field of gender and LGBTIQ+ studies are structured around another constitutive dimension: precariousness. As David Paternotte points out,

> it must be stated that, despite the existence of vibrant professional organizations such as Atgender (the European Association for Gender Research, Education, and Documentation), gender studies is poorly consolidated as a field of study in Europe. In many countries, such as Italy or Poland, there are no specific masters or other academic programs in gender studies, and where these do exist, most are fairly recent, as in Belgium or France. Moreover, few independent gender studies departments exist in the region, and almost no institution awards PhD degrees in the field. Therefore, the situation differs significantly from that in the United States: while European

gender scholars have been carrying out gender research for decades, they are still struggling to institutionalize their field of study. Attacks on gender studies in Europe target a precarious field of research. (Paternotte 2019)

As LGBTIQ+ precarious workers involved in LGBTIQ+ studies, we experience double vulnerability. In the Italian case, prolonged precariousness, short-term contracts, and unstable selection criteria and methods—subject to continuous reform—define incoming university careers. When I faced those attacks, I was in a condition of professional precarity—hired on a temporary contract that put me in a situation of integral subjection. Amongst the uncertainty surrounding one's future, and the conditionality of a possible contract renewal, resisting as a LGBTIQ+ scholar was a challenging condition.

In other words, the constitutive precariousness of the researcher's position in a neoliberal university system goes hand-in-hand with a permanent condition of risk related to the potential consequences of our desired or performed resistance. Although resistance is a necessary and empowering response to attacks and pressures, it must be enacted strategically. Resistance is undoubtedly a courageous act rooted in the long history of LGBTIQ+ struggles and mobilizations, but it can also be risky and comes with serious potential consequences (Ayoub and Stoeckl 2024). While not all LGBTIQ+ researchers may identify as activists, working on and with LGBTIQ+ issues, people, and communities implies a stigmatized and discriminated position within the academic space. Then the question is: how can one effectively defend oneself against such attacks while facing the challenges of vulnerability and precariousness as an LGBTIQ+ researcher?

Under the Straight Gaze of the University

My research focuses on the historical, political, and social aspects of LGBTIQ+ politics, studied from various perspectives, such as those of LGBTIQ+ mobilizations and movements, LGBTIQ+ migration, anti-gender and anti-LGBTIQ+ movements, and, more recently, LGBTIQ+ political careers. This scientific work is inherently coproduced in collaboration with LGBTIQ+ individuals involved in the research process, from data collection to analysis to dissemination and communication of results. As such, I consider myself as a researcher involved in the co-production of scientific knowledge that is not separate from the social context and the individuals participating in the research process. From this perspective, the research work and the reality it studies exist in a continuum, which can take on different forms depending on the situation; from an open communication space to one for exchange, sharing, and even conflict. But what lies on this continuum is not only the object of knowledge but also the social context of LGBTIQ+ scholars and lives, including their stigma and the intertwined state of risk, precariousness, and vulnerability they share. LGBTIQ+ scholars working on and with LGBTIQ+ issues, people, and communities grapple with potential hazards related to their stance within academia and the broader public domain. The development of LGBTIQ+ studies and their dissemination in both the scientific and public spheres involve a complex interplay of conflict, particularly in the current historical moment marked by an unprecedented assault that not only questions their scientific validity but also their legitimacy (Paternotte 2018). This assault has even gone as far as attempts to ban these studies from the university and school systems. As such, the intertwined logic of risk, precariousness, and vulnerability determines and hinders the agency of LGBTIQ+ scholars.

The options are either to surrender or quit, which unfortunately is the only possible path for many who face unsustainable precarity and vulnerability, or to defend oneself and resist. However, the latter requires individual and collective resources, including financial ones. It also entails taking on the risk of moving between the inside and outside of the university. In fact, the visibility of stigma can be generative of proud alliances and creative strategies as a "queer art of failure" (Halberstam 2012), but it also exposes the researcher to anti-LGBTIQ+ violence. To clarify the idea of a bodily state defined by the risk of violence, I would like to refer to a passage from Elsa Dorlin's book on the philosophy of violence:

> Enduring violence generates a negative cognitive and emotional attitude that determines the individuals who experience it as always on the lookout, paying close attention to the world and others. They live in a state of "radical anxiety," and it is exhausting to have to deny, minimize, defuse, endure, reduce, and avoid violence, to have to take shelter, protect yourself, defend oneself. This means developing a series of rationalizations in order to understand others and to make your own actions seem reasonable and normal, for instance movements, attitudes, and actions deployed to avoid irritating others or to not encourage or trigger their violence. It also means living with affects and emotions (which, although nearly imperceptible, are constant) and getting used to their violence, desensitizing yourself

and accepting it. "Concern for others" here has nothing to do with *doing* something to help, care for, comfort, reassure, or protect them; rather, we are concerned for others in order to anticipate what they want, will, or can *do to us*—which might devalue, exhaust, insult, isolate, injure, worry, deny, frighten, or de-realize us.

... Such attention could just as well be described as a long labor of denial, avoidance, and defusing; it is also a way of maintaining distance (maintaining safety), or fleeing, or even of preparing for conflict, for combat.... The kind of attention required of the dominated consists of always projecting yourself onto the intentions of others, melting into their representations as a way of defending yourself. This is a product of the dominated's knowledge—their incredibly in-depth knowledge—of the dominant group. (Dorlin 2018, 172–73)

Building knowledge on the dominating power object constantly casts LGBTIQ+ scholars in a light of precariousness and vulnerability. Dorlin describes this process as a specific form of technology of power that creates risk for the subject, who becomes a visible body of stigma. This body must forget, deny, conceal, omit, or suspend its situated subjectivity to navigate between the inside and outside of the university space. Not as a subject for itself, but rather as a bundle of knowledge radically oriented towards others. To anticipate their moves. The panopticon eye monitors every movement, every action, and even every desire of LGBTIQ+ scholars, measuring their deviation:

The subject's work in paying attention to their objects is exhausting: the level of attention must be high to gain the knowledge needed for self-defense. This intense focus occurs continuously and without interruption, or almost. The need to be on the alert nearly every instant leads to exhaustion and prevents subjects of knowledge from paying attention to themselves. Their own representations, impressions, desires, intentions, and emotions take the back seat, where they are treated as if they were doubtful, fantastic, false, trivial, insignificant.... Put differently, the ceaseless effort to know others as well as possible in an attempt to defend ourselves from what they might do to us is a technology of power that manifests through the production of ignorance—and not ignorance of ourselves but of our power of action, which we come to see as alien and alienated. Authentically modest, witnessing, submissive, drained, and docile, the dominated are assigned to a cognitive relationship and alienating gnoseological work. They develop a knowledge about the dominant, which constitutes an archive of the ways the dominant are phenomenally and ideologically all-powerful. (Dorlin 2018, 173–74)

This permanent state of attention applies to every aspect of a LGBTIQ+ scholar's body and subjectivity: when they speak within the institution, whether in an internal meeting, during a seminar or conference, or even in a friendly gathering of a standing group on gender and politics, where LGBTIQ+ scholars may be welcome but still somehow regarded as "strangers." It also applies to irritated reactions when they speak out at public events, present their work, or give interviews to the media. A simplistic view of the challenges faced by LGBTIQ+ scholars working with LGBTIQ+ issues, people, and communities would reduce it to mere exclusion or repression. However, in the context of the neoliberal governance of the university, the situation is much more complex and insidious. Sara Ahmed argues:

> I became co-director of the Institute for Women's Studies at Lancaster University in 2000. I began to attend faculty meetings. I was the only person of color at these meetings. It is important to note that I noticed this: whiteness tends to be visible to those who do not inhabit it (though not always, and not only). During the discussion of one item at a faculty meeting on equality, the dean said something like "race is too difficult to deal with." I remember wanting to challenge this. But the difficulty of speaking about racism as a person of color meant that I did not speak up during but after the meeting, and even then I wrote rather than spoke. Saying that race is "too difficult" is how racism gets reproduced, I put in an email to the dean. The belief that racism is inevitable is how racism becomes inevitable, I pointed out. (One of the favorite arguments made by senior management was that the university was "very white" because of geography—and that you can't do anything about geography.) Do something about it, he replies. It shouldn't be up to me, I answer.
> ... The dean spoke to the director of human resources. She got in contact with me, offering an invitation to become a member of the newly formed race equality team responsible for writing our university's race equality policy. There were two academics on the team, both people of color. There are problems and pitfalls in becoming a diversity person as a person of color. There is a script that stops anyone reading the situation as a becoming. You already embody diversity by providing an institution of whiteness with color. (Ahmed 2012, 3–4)

Ahmed's concern about being "stuck *in* institutions by being stuck *to* a category" (Ahmed 2012, 4) is something precarious researchers do not have the privilege to care about yet. Writing that letter for an LGBTIQ+ precarious scholar would be too risky. The point, however, is a different one. What does it mean to embody the stigma behind the straightness of the institution?

For a long time, my research on LGBTIQ+ politics has preceded my queerness; no need for me to come out, because my work outed, and continues to out, me constantly. Not because of the naive assumption that working on LGBTIQ+ issues requires being LGBTIQ+. But instead because of my epistemological and methodological choices, my stance towards the communities and people I work with, my way of addressing the LGBTIQ+ stigma and sharing it with research participants, and my primary interest in the circularity of knowledge between academia, social movements, and the public arena. Each of these factors puts me on the continuum of the LGBTIQ+ risk, which is much more than mere community membership, affective bonding, epistemological empathy, or programmatic or ideological convergence. It is a social and political field of care, struggle, and conflict that precedes both me and my work. It is the historical here and now that encompasses the reality of homo-lesbo-bi-transphobia; it is the political regime of heterosexuality (Wittig 1992). Thus, being constantly out in a closeted straight institution means being constantly stuck to a liminal position between inside and outside—not just of the category or my queerness, but of the institution itself.

Toward an Epistemic Resistance

In April 2023, the Italian newspaper *Il Manifesto* published an interview with me about the Italian anti-gender and pro-life movements, coinciding with the International Trans Day of Visibility. In the interview, I discussed my recent observations on the extent of anti-gender mobilization and the convergence of goals between ultrareligious movements, so-called radical feminism (or radfem groups), and a new form of anti-trans activism. I then mentioned organizations like GenSpect in the UK, Observatoire de la Petite Sirène or Ypomoni in France, and GenerAzioneD in Italy that have emerged in recent years. They perform a kind of "anti-gender" activism that does not share the religious genealogy of the anti-gender movements of the 2010s (such as La Manif pour Tous) and that is closer to the "gender-critical" claim of trans-hostile feminism. Scholars of anti-gender politics and mobilizations have observed and are studying this relatively new phenomenon, which emerged unexpectedly within the field of anti-gender campaigns (Cabral Grinspan et al. 2023).

Anti-trans, trans-hostile, and gender-critical groups intercepted my interview and used it to mobilize activists and trolls on social networks to discredit me. They portrayed me as a mere activist or an academic impostor who is "obsessed" with anti-gender issues or, more trivially, as an idiot. While I take comfort in saying, "Haters gonna hate," these campaigns and attacks do not simply aim to discredit me. Instead, they plan to undermine scholars perceived as "radical transactivists" or "transideologists," precisely like anti-gender (religious-based and right-wing) actors mobilized against scholars identified as "gender ideologists," "LGBT ideologists," or "woke" activists. Beyond the targeted scholars, these attacks seek to demolish a specific way of knowledge production that embodies the LGBTIQ+ stigma and positions itself in the LGBTIQ+ continuum. More than just a simple ethical or epistemological choice, I define this LGBTIQ+ continuum as a standpoint, an epistemic state that concerns the empirical construction of knowledge and thus the material condition of being an LGBTIQ+ scholar working on and with LGBTIQ+ issues, people, and communities (Browne et al. 2010).

To conclude, I would like to emphasize two points. Firstly, it is important to note that it is not just gender or LGBTIQ+ studies, or critical studies more generally, that are under attack and at risk. Rather, it is a specific mode of knowledge production and circulation enacted by LGBTIQ+ scholars adopting an *epistemic queer state*, making them vulnerable within straight institutions. This vulnerability is inherently related to stigma and discrimination that doubles queer researchers' precariousness and shapes their position as short-term, stigmatized, unexpected, and awkward and thus places them at risk. The epistemic queer state constitutes the spot where anti-gender and anti-trans actors and discourses converge in mobilizing and voicing an *epistemic straight claim* (see also, for a similar definition, Petrovic and Rosiek 2007). For anti-gender actors, this claim is the heterosexual and traditional defense of the natural order of the family rooted in the eternal "anthropological" truth of the sexual difference, while anti-trans actors refer to a theoretical matrix marked by a normative sex-based vision of gender. Both perspectives converge in their attempt to "naturalize" humanity, opposing social constructivist epistemologies.

The second point concerns the risk faced by LGBTIQ+ scholars working on and with LGBTIQ+ issues, people, and communities in a context "under siege," exhaustingly engaged in the labor of caring about what others could do to them. And thus, permanently worrying about the effects that these unpredictable "others" could have on their trajectory, career, or even life—as Elsa Dorlin notes. The in-depth knowledge this attention generates is also one of the forms of resistance against the epistemic straight gaze, which seeks to undermine the position of LGBTIQ+ scholars within the institution and discredit their voices in the public arena.

Far from any triumphalist rhetoric, it must be acknowledged that there is a profound *fatigue* related to this negative caring work, a fatigue of being permanently at risk, under attack. There is an unbearable, debilitating, overwhelming, and demoralizing fatigue of being constantly caught in the tension of mastering a dominant knowledge to strategically defend the minority knowledge we, as LGBTIQ+ scholars in an epistemic queer state, co-produce and embody (González 2020).

In my experience, I would never have been able to endure the weight of institutional precariousness and political vulnerability if I had not had the opportunity to work with an epistemic queer community to build academic networks of sharing, support, and positive care. These networks provided safe spaces within academic institutions and disciplinary areas. I would not have had the strength to resist the weight of stigma and the straight institutional and disciplinary gaze if the epistemic queer state of my research could not have found the caring attention of epistemic peers at specific and special conferences, seminars, and journals—and of course also within my own department and university. Unfortunately, LGBTIQ+ scholars working on and with LGBTIQ+ issues, people, and communities too often experience refusals and rejections that question the very premise of their research without bothering to go into detail. Too often they end up at academic events relegated to the limbo of indifference, because straight contexts can make it impossible to see the concrete reality, the saliency, or even the existence of LGBTIQ+ issues, people, and communities. Conversely, they may have been forced to play the role of the minority spokesperson to check the box of policy diversity-friendliness.

National and international networks of LGBTIQ+ studies and scholars, as well as national and international groups of LGBTIQ+ studies and scholars within professional associations, are crucial in creating conditions of resistance to the straightness of the academic institution. It is also important to have national and international scientific journals of LGBTIQ+

studies and scholars that are not merely embedded in the broader field of gender studies as a minority-plus. These networks, groups, and journals may provide spaces for LGBTIQ+ scholars working on and with LGBTIQ+ issues, people, and communities, to collectively assume the risk of being precarious and vulnerable within the straight institution and share the weight of the LGBTIQ+ stigma, to—eventually—resist.

Massimo Prearo is a political scientist and assistant professor at the Department of Human Science of the University of Verona, where he is also scientific coordinator of the Research Center PoliTeSse–Politics and Theories of Sexuality. His latest book is *Anti-gender Mobilizations, Religion and Politics: An Italian Case Study* (Routledge, 2024). He can be reached at massimo.prearo@univr.it.

Works Cited

Ahmed, Sara. 2012. *On Being Included: Racism and Diversity in Institutional Life*. Durham, NC: Duke University Press.

Ammaturo, Francesca Romana. 2020. "Framing and Shaming: LGBT Activism, Feminism and the Construction of 'Gestational Surrogacy' in Italy." *Social Movement Studies* 19 (4): 447–63.

Ashley, Florence. 2023. "Interrogating Gender-Exploratory Therapy." *Perspectives on Psychological Science* 18 (2): 472–81.

Ayoub, Phillip M. 2022. "Not That Niche: Making Room for the Study of LGBTIQ People in Political Science." *European Journal of Politics and Gender* 5 (2): 154–72.

Ayoub, Phillip M., and Katrin Stoeckl. 2024. *The Global Fight Against LGBTI Rights: How Transnational Conservative Networks Target Sexual and Gender Minorities*. New York: NYU Press.

Barilà Ciocca, Francesco, Beatrice Gusmano, Emanuele Iula, Aurora Perego, and Massimo Prearo, eds. 2022. *Rapporto-pilota sugli studi di genere, intersex, femministi, transfemministi e sulla sessualità*. Rete GIFTS, Report n.1. https://retegifts.wordpress.com/2022/10/05/rapporto-pilota-sugli-studi-di-genere-intersex-femministi-transfemministi-e-sulla-sessualita-in-italia-2022/.

Bernini, Lorenzo. 2021. "Much Ado about Nothing? DDL Zan, Eternal Fascism and the Ghosts of Sexuality." *Soft Power. Revista Euro-Americana de Teoría e Historia de la Política y del Derecho* 51 (1): 59–75.

Biagini, Elena. 2021. "'Sottosotto': Contraddizioni manifeste; La critica lesbofemminista al pensiero della differenza." *Diacronie: Studi di storia contemporanea: LGBTQIA+; Sessualità, soggettività, movimenti, linguaggi* 47 (3): 107–26.

Browne, Kath, Catherine J. Nash, and Kath Woodward, eds. 2010. *Queer Methods and Methodologies: Intersecting Queer Theories and Social Science Research.* Farnham: Ashgate.

Cabral Grinspan, Mauro, Ilana Eloit, David Paternotte, and Mieke Verloo. 2023. "Exploring TERFnesses." *DiGeSt: Journal of Diversity and Gender Studies* 10 (2): 1–13.

Datta, Neil, and David Paternotte. 2023. "'Gender Ideology' Battles in the European Bubble." In *The Christian Right in Europe: Movements, Networks and Denominations*, edited by Gabriele L. Mascolo, 37–56. London: Palgrave Macmillan.

De Giorgi, Elisabetta, Alice Cavalieri, and Francesca Feo. 2021. "From Opposition Leader to Prime Minister: Giorgia Meloni and Women's Issues in the Italian Radical Right." *Politics and Gender* 17 (1): 154–58.

Dietze, Gabriele, and Julia Roth, eds. 2020. *Right-Wing Populism and Gender: European Perspectives and Beyond.* Bielefeld: Transcript Verlag.

Donà, Alessia. 2021. "Somewhere over the Rainbow: Italy and the Regulation of Same-Sex Unions." *Modern Italy* 26 (3): 261–74. https://doi.org/10.1017/mit.2021.28.

Dorlin, Elsa. 2018. *Self-Defense: Feminism and the Politics of Violence.* London: Verso.

Edenborg, Emil. 2021. "Anti-gender Politics as Discourse Coalitions: Russia's Domestic and International Promotion of 'Traditional Values.'" *Problems of Post-communism* 68 (1): 1–10.

Feo, Francesca. 2022. "Legislative Reforms to Fight Discrimination and Violence against LGBTQ+: The Failure of the Zan Bill in Italy." *European Journal of Politics and Gender* 5 (1): 149–51.

Garbagnoli, Sara. 2016. "Against the Heresy of Immanence: Vatican's 'Gender' as a New Rhetorical Device against the Denaturalization of the Sexual Order." *Religion and Gender* 6 (2): 187–204.

González, Melissa M. 2020. "Queer Battle Fatigue, or How I Learned to Stop Worrying and Love the Imposter Inside Me." *GLQ: A Journal of Lesbian and Gay Studies* 26 (2): 236–38.

Graff, Agnieszka, and Elżbieta Korolczuk. 2022. *Anti-gender Politics in the Populist Moment.* Abingdon: Routledge.

Grzebalska, Weronika, and Andrea Pető. 2018. "The Gendered Modus Operandi of the Illiberal Transformation in Hungary and Poland." *Women's Studies International Forum*, no. 68, 164–72.

Halberstam, Jack. 2012. *The Queer Art of Failure.* Durham, NC: Duke University Press.

Kuhar, Roman, and David Paternotte, eds. 2017. *Anti-gender Campaigns in Europe: Mobilizing against Equality.* London: Rowman & Littlefield.

Lavizzari, Anna, and Massimo Prearo. 2019. "The Anti-gender Movement in Italy: Catholic Participation between Electoral and Protest Politics." *European Societies* 21 (3): 422–42.

Lombardo, Emanuela, Johanna Kantola, and Ruth Rubio-Marín. 2021. "Special Issue: De-democratization and Opposition to Gender Equality Politics in Europe." *Social Politics: International Studies in Gender, State and Society* 28 (3): 521–31.

Möser, Cornelia, Jennifer Ramme, and Judit Takacs, eds. 2022. *Paradoxical Right-Wing Sexual Politics in Europe*. Basingstoke: Palgrave Macmillan.

Norocel, Ov Cristian, and David Paternotte. 2023. "The Dis/articulation of Anti-gender Politics in Eastern Europe: Introduction." *Problems of Post-Communism* 70 (2): 123–29.

Norocel, Ov Cristian, and Gabriella Szabó. 2019. "Special Issue: Mapping the Discursive Opportunities for Radical-Right Populist Politics across Eastern Europe." *Problems of Post-communism* 66 (1): 1–7.

Ozzano, Luca. 2019. "Religion, Cleavages, and Right-Wing Populist Parties: The Italian Case." *Review of Faith and International Affairs* 17 (1): 65–77.

———. 2020. "Last but Not Least: How Italy Finally Legalized Same-Sex Unions." *Contemporary Italian Politics* 12 (1): 43–61.

Paternotte, David. 2018. "Coming Out of the Political Science Closet: The Study of LGBT Politics in Europe." *European Journal of Politics and Gender* 1 (1–2): 55–74.

———. 2019. "Gender Studies and the Dismantling of Critical Knowledge in Europe: Assaults on Gender Studies Are Part of an Attack on Democracy." *Academe* 105 (4). https://www.aaup.org/article/gender-studies-and-dismantling-critical-knowledge-europe.

———. 2023. "Victor Frankenstein and His Creature: The Many Lives of 'Gender Ideology.'" *International Review of Sociology* 33 (1): 80–104.

Paternotte, David, and Mieke Verloo. 2021. "De-democratization and the Politics of Knowledge: Unpacking the Cultural Marxism Narrative." *Social Politics: International Studies in Gender, State and Society* 28 (3): 556–78.

Pavan, Elena. 2020. "We Are Family: The Conflict between Conservative Movements and Feminists." *Contemporary Italian Politics* 12 (2): 243–57.

Pető, Andrea. 2020. "Academic Freedom and Gender Studies: An Alliance Forged in Fire." *Gender and Sexuality*, no. 15, 9–24.

Pető, Andrea, and Eszter Kováts. 2017. "Anti-gender Movements in Hungary. A Discourse without a Movement?" In *Anti-gender Campaigns in Europe: Mobilizing against Equality*, edited by Roman Kuhar and David Paternotte, 117–31. London: Rowman & Littlefield.

Petrovic, John, and Rosiek, Jerry. 2007. "From Teacher Knowledge to Queered Teacher Knowledge Research." In *Queering Straight Teachers: Discourse and*

Identity in Education, edited by N. Rodriguez and W. Pinar, 201–31. New York: Peter Lang.

Pirro, Andrea L. P. 2023. "Far Right: The Significance of an Umbrella Concept." *Nations and Nationalism* 29 (1): 101–12.

Prearo, Massimo. 2021. "The Moral Politics of LGBTI Asylum: How the State Deals with the SOGI Framework." *Journal of Refugee Studies* 34 (2): 1454–76.

———. 2023. "The Anti-gender and Gender-critical Roots of the Italian Anti-trans Parent Activism." *DiGeSt: Journal of Diversity and Gender Studies* 10 (2): 115–117.

———. 2024. *Anti-gender Mobilizations, Religion and Politics: An Italian Case Study*. London: Routledge.

Righetti, Nicola. 2021. "The Anti-gender Debate on Social Media: A Computational Communication Science Analysis of Networks, Activism, and Misinformation." *Comunicazione politica: Quadrimestrale dell'associazione italiana di comunicazione politica*, no. 2, 223–50.

Santos, Ana Cristina. 2013. *Social Movements and Sexual Citizenship in Southern Europe*. Basingstoke: Palgrave Macmillan.

Trappolin, Luca. 2022. "Right-Wing Sexual Politics and 'Anti-gender' Mobilization in Italy: Key Features and Latest Developments." In *Paradoxical Right-Wing Sexual Politics in Europe*, edited by Cornelia Möser, Jennifer Ramme, and Judit Takács, 119–43. Cham: Springer International Publishing.

Wittig, Monique. 1992. *The Straight Mind and Other Essays*. Boston, MA: Beacon Press.

Making Gender and Sexuality Studies Illegal: Heteronationalism, Anti-gender Mobilization, and the Neoliberal "Utopian" Gaze in Bulgaria, 2018–2023

Shaban Darakchi

Abstract: The past decade has witnessed an escalating, well-financed, and well-organized international mobilization against any study, policy, or discussion related to gender or LGBTQI+ issues in many parts of the world. The countries of Central and Eastern Europe have been disproportionately affected by this backlash, resulting in public threats and violence against scholars and representatives of the nongovernmental sector who work on gender and LGBTQI+ issues. The anti-gender mobilization has been extremely successful in Bulgaria, where there have been numerous threats against scholars, nongovernmental organizations, and public figures dealing with gender and sexuality issues. The Bulgarian Constitutional Court was the first court on a global level to pronounce the term "gender" anti-constitutional in response to a request submitted by the government regarding ratification of the so-called Istanbul Convention. Dealing with gender and LGBTQI+ studies in Bulgaria is believed to be "illegal" by many, based on the court's decision. As a result, any approaches to gender and sexuality that do not fit essentialist and religious beliefs have become dangerous and have endangered knowledge in many contexts. In this paper, I discuss the rapid development of the anti-gender mobilization within certain neoliberal discourses and values, and using the concept of a "neoliberal utopian gaze," I outline the challenges gender and sexuality studies have faced. Based on case studies, personal experiences, and public discourses, the paper explores how gender and sexuality studies have been affected by (1) institutional decisions, (2) manipulation of scientific information, (3) radical political populism, (4) transnational religious movements, and (5) the advancement of social media. Finally, the paper discusses possible solutions to this alarming trend, paying particular attention to academic solidarity, knowledge production, and institutionally coordinated policies. **Keywords:** anti-gender campaigns, LGBTQI+ studies, scholars at risk, academic freedom, populism, Eastern Europe

Introduction

One day in the spring of 2017, I was scrolling down my Facebook feed, and I noticed an event on the "anti-gender campaigns" organized in Brussels. It was an event devoted to a collective book edited by Roman Kuhar and David Paternotte (Kuhar and Paternotte 2017). Although I knew the works of both editors, I did not pay significant attention to the event. The wording of the book title, *Anti-gender Campaigns in Europe*, did not speak much to me, and neither did I read the description of the event in detail. Back then, I somehow disregarded the above-mentioned book event and continued working on the topics I was interested in.

In late December 2017, six months later, I noticed something very disturbing on my Facebook feed. There were mounting posts in different groups and discussions warning against the threat of the so-called Istanbul Convention. Created by the Council of Europe, this convention aims to fight gender-based violence among the member states of the council. Suddenly, this convention became a central topic in the public discussions. A central point of this rather sudden moral panic was the term "gender." According to those who were channeling this moral panic, the term "gender" means "transgenderism," "third gender," and "homosexual," to name a few definitions. An absurd translation of gender as "social sex" in many documents and some academic texts, in which sex is believed to be socially based, not gender based, contributed to this discourse.

The main message of this campaign was that the convention is an elitist tool to destroy the Bulgarian nation and to convert children into nonheterosexual and transgender people (Darakchi 2019). The term "gender" until then was used mainly in academia, and "the new meaning" of gender was widely promoted on social media within well-constructed and well-organized political and religious campaigns. Historically, the alt-right propaganda hidden behind the term "gender" has been the most successful populist strategy I have observed in the Bulgarian context. It is more powerful than other topics used to spread moral panic, such as the references to "invasive refugees" and "lazy Roma people" used previously by the alt-right actors, because it touches on the most sacred things for the majority—nationality and children; therefore, the danger is projected as "immediate" and "endangering" everyone. These events that I first witnessed on Facebook led to significant political mobilization, mounting hate speech, public threats, and online and institutional abuse of many professionals, and the anti-gender rhetoric remains a dominant populist strategy in Bulgaria up to today.

As a sociologist who knows the meaning and intent of "gender" as opposed to "sex," I felt I was living in some kind of distorted reality, or watching a hidden camera show, wherein many people who have filled in many forms stating their own gender pretend that they do not know the real meaning of this term—or, at least, I had assumed they knew the real meaning. It was an explosive and dangerous reality, and while some public figures fought this false discourse, most academics, including me, did not comment on it in the media, mainly due to our fear of backlash, humiliation, and threats. This was a hard way for many of us to learn that the real meaning of the term "gender" remains unknown among the majority of people, an effect of the neoliberal utopian gaze, which was fixated on the "proliferating future," promoting a misplaced belief that the majority of the population is now democratic and progressive. In this situation of mounting anxiety, I started exploring the topic in academic sources, and I initially recalled the book event I had disregarded a few months before. When I found the book and read it, I was able to recognize and explain many events, messages, and strategies I had observed previously. It all had a name: "anti-gender campaigns" and "anti-gender mobilizations."

The Neoliberal "Utopian" Gaze

Upon reflection, at the time when I first saw the book on "anti-gender" mobilization, I was a junior researcher in sociology working on topics of gender and sexuality at the Institute of Philosophy and Sociology at the Bulgarian Academy of Sciences (BAS), a position I still hold, and even I must have looked at this event with what I call in this text a "neoliberal utopian gaze." The critical perspective in this essay is based on my reflections as a "neoliberal subject" in academia (Archer 2008) in a process of reconsidering certain utopian ways of thinking and exploring the need for counteractions (Giroux 2003).

I did not recognize the anti-gender mobilization as an important topic at that time due to two main reasons. First of all, I grew up in a post-communist society guided by neoliberal principles protecting and guaranteeing academic freedom, freedom of expression, expanding human rights, and equality—"a promised land" to settle in, running away from the ghost of the communist past. Born into a Muslim community that underwent brutal name- and identity-change policies during the communist regime, I found this rhetoric all the more appealing. When I first encountered the topic of anti-gender mobilization, I had attended several conferences across the world. I had lived and worked with different fellowships in the U.S., Australia, and several European countries. Expanding my academic and personal networks, I surrounded myself professionally and personally with people who believed in the bright future of gender and sexuality studies. I was in a bubble! A bubble that echoed the rhetoric of European Union slogans emphasizing the progress achieved and the ongoing expansion of academic freedom. Being indulged in this otherwise pleasant bubble, I was completely invested in developing my postdoctoral project on the social construction of sexual minorities in Bulgaria, and I tended to consider any religious or alt-right antidemocratic activities either as populist campaigns or holdovers from the communist past, which I believed would disappear one day.

The second reason I did not recognize the unrest regarding gender politics as alarming is that I was working on gender and sexuality in an environment where almost nobody worked on these topics—I used to have a false feeling of freedom and openness regarding these topics within this environment, as I had not encountered any backlash from my colleagues. I was in yet another bubble, where we did not discuss gender and sexuality in an academic context. In other words, I was fixated on the positive "bright future" that was ahead of us, ignoring the processes outside of my bubble, looking through the neoliberal, promising, utopian gaze, which had become a dominant way to approach social reality even in my academic activities. At that point, I knew a small number of people from other Bulgarian institutions dealing with gender and sexuality; however, we did not meet on a regular basis, and we had no professional discussions or forums. If we had had such discussions, they might have included a discussion on any early signs of what followed in Bulgaria a few months later.

Referring metaphorically to my professional and personal background as seeing through a neoliberal utopian gaze, I criticize mainly my own reactions to experiences situated in a post-communist country. The anti-gender mobilizations have made it possible for me to reflect on myself as a "neoliberal subject in academia," although I do not identify myself exclusively as a left-leaning or liberal-leaning scholar. Due to my working-class background, I graduated from the least prestigious university in Bulgaria, where the sociological theories and approaches were extremely dated. I am still learning rhetoric and approaches, which some have had the privilege to learn at a younger age in prestigious institutions. On the other hand, the European Union's educational programs, and certain otherwise neoliberal academic specializations, have given a chance for many with a similar social background to mine to grow, improve their knowledge, and participate in the academic debate on an international level. This is an opportunity I would never have had during the communist regime in Bulgaria, given the resistance of my community to the regime. Criticizing neoliberal academia is possible independent of one's political beliefs, and hopefully the anti-scientific backlash will provoke the same reflection among those who use exclusively liberal and neoliberal approaches in their work and are trapped in a certain bubble.

The Neoliberal "Utopian" Gaze as an Approach and Methodology

In my case, the neoliberal utopian gaze is a product of (1) a specific political context of systematic anti-communism in Bulgaria and unquestionable engagement with neoliberal social and political discourses; (2) the European Union's discourse of political and social values, which pays attention mostly to the social progress and the advancing human rights complementing the economic progress and growth (Gregor and Grzebalska 2016) and ignores certain backlash forces and cultural differences (Rawłuszko 2021); (3) an underprivileged minority background that makes the former two desirable and empowering; (4) an educational environment that does not teach critical sociology; and (5) "exoticization" of my research subject as insignificant, and lack of proper attention to it on an institutional level. These components make the neoliberal gaze utopian, because it belittles any backlash and pictures an "unproblematic reality" and a bright future.

The various combinations of these components in different contexts allow us to identify distinctive groups of scholars that might ignore the anti-gender mobilization. That said, it takes only one of these components to create a utopian gaze; for example, a stable academic position in a conventional field in the social sciences might produce a bubble and reduce one's sensibility to anti-scientific discourses and populist movements. Not only is this an academic particularism that ignores the interconnectedness between anti-gender mobilization, the rest of the scientific fields, and academic freedom in general, but it is also a narrative that denigrates and further exoticizes gender studies as "unnecessary provocations" in "these uncertain times," as a colleague of mine mentioned recently. Such accounts often lack basic knowledge of the mechanisms of the anti-gender mobilization, their expanding approach, and the manipulation of science in general. This is the case of many scholars in social sciences, especially in Bulgaria, and of many professional associations that do not pay any attention to the anti-gender mobilization despite the alarming tendencies and the furious public debates. Therefore, I would argue that we can use the neoliberal utopian gaze as a methodological and epistemological tool for reflection and self-reflection in academia.

The "neoliberal utopian gaze" shall be understood as a strategy for self-reflection, self-care (Archer 2008), and resistance to and reassessment of neoliberal utopian regimes in academia (Giroux 2003), and include five main questions for consideration:

1. Do I work in an academic bubble?
2. Does my background define my academic bubble and academic approach?
3. Do I know well the movements working against science and basic human rights in my context?
4. How can these movements affect my work from a long-term perspective?
5. Do I care about the well-being of my fellow researchers?

The consideration of the neoliberal utopian gaze is a methodology of care, solidarity, and academic freedom. It's a tool for self-reflection and bears the potential to create a powerful narrative that can be inspiring and warning. This is extremely important in times when the anti-gender movements project "gender ideology" as a strategy by the elites against the working class (Graff 2021).

The anti-gender campaigns are well-structured and well-financed (Lovenduski 2022) transnational movements and mobilizations that aim to abolish women's and LGBTQI+ rights using similar strategies in different contexts, and there is a growing number of extensive studies investigating these processes (Graff 2021; Kuhar and Paternotte 2017; Korolczuk and Graff 2018). In the next few paragraphs, I will pay attention to several subtopics that explain the mechanism of the anti-gender campaigns and their effect on gender and sexuality studies in the Bulgarian context.

Political Context and the Production of Dangerous and Endangered Knowledge

The anti-gender discourse in Bulgaria was introduced by an organization called Society and Values. Although registered as a public body, this organization was founded by members of an evangelical church with close ties to evangelical churches in the U.S. (Darakchi 2019). In September 2017, a few months before the political use of gender moral panic, Society and Values published a petition against the ratification of the Istanbul Convention. The influence of the evangelical churches in Bulgaria during the Trump administration, paraphrasing Puar (2018), is a case of "heteronationalism" imported and maintained by actors who post pictures of Trump's administration on social media and praise his policies in books and forums. When the ruling government submitted the ratification to parliament, the rhetoric used by Society and Values was immediately translated into public discourse by the nationalist parties (partners in the ruling cabinet), many other entities and public figures, and most of the religious denominations.

Surprisingly, the leader of the Bulgarian Socialist Party (the successor of the Communist Party), Kornelia Ninova, also engaged in this rhetoric, although her party had held many events calling for the ratification of the Convention. The ruling party decided to submit the case to the Bulgarian Constitutional Court. At that time, I considered the case closed, because, looking through my neoliberal utopian glasses, I could not imagine there would be a judge who would not know what gender was; we are a member state of the European Union, after all! I was wrong, very wrong, again. In July 2018, eight members of the Constitutional Court decided that "gender" is an anti-constitutional term incompatible with Bulgarian Christian tradition and values. Four members of the court opposed that decision; however, they remained a minority. All five female judges ruled against the ratification of the convention. More recently, in March 2023, the anti-gender campaigners scored another "victory." The Supreme Court of Cassation rejected a case requesting gender transition, arguing that the law does not consider such cases. This disrupted a thirty-year-long practice during which individual cases were considered and some were given permission for gender transition based on medically achieved biological transition.

The development of anti-gender campaigns in Bulgaria is interesting for two main reasons. In many other countries, anti-gender campaigns were based on previous anti-abortion and anti-LGBTQI+ campaigns, while in Bulgaria, these events erupted suddenly. A second significant difference is that the Bulgarian Socialist Party is perhaps the only "socialist" party in the world that engages in anti-gender rhetoric. Moreover, the party leader ran an election campaign in March 2023 engaging mainly with anti-gender rhetoric and calling for a referendum against the inclusion of "gender ideology" in schools. This once again confirms the strategic use of the anti-gender campaigns in Bulgaria as a tool for electoral support. Furthermore, similar to other places, the anti-gender campaigns have established social media groups and leaders who are using these platforms to promote conspiracies about COVID-19, vaccines, and the war in Ukraine, to name a few. The anti-gender campaigns in Bulgaria created a platform for backlash against the global "elites" that "aim to destroy the working class."

These developments have undoubtedly framed gender and LGBTQI+ studies as dangerous knowledge. Using the decision of the Constitutional Court as an argument, many people writing in social media comments believe that studying gender and LGBTQI+ topics is an illegal activity, and some even believe that scholars dealing with these subjects need to be sentenced. Moreover, university teachers and scholars are targeted online, and their pictures are posted under shocking titles in right-wing media outlets with a large audience. Additionally, any organization or professional who deals with these topics is declared a national "traitor." While used strategically in the campaigns of different parties, the very words "gender" and "sexuality" are becoming endangered as well. To protect themselves, some organizations have excluded the word "gender" from their names. Some others have strategically replaced the word "gender" in project and university classes with generic terms such as "equality," "human rights," "women's studies," et cetera. Only a few people are working on gender and sexuality in Bulgaria, and these events will make the development of the field extremely difficult and endangered, keeping new initiatives and professionals away from this topic. Similar processes are taking place in Hungary (perhaps the most famous case), Poland, Slovakia, Croatia, and many other countries (Korolczuk and Graff 2018). Institutional support for scholars is very important in this context; however, in many settings, the institutions themselves also engage in anti-gender rhetoric.

Institutional Contexts

Doing gender and sexuality studies in neoliberal academia is a difficult task for many. In many cases, these topics are the first to be sacrificed when funding cuts are needed (Rohde and Takács 2022). Moreover, many scholars in the field are being "exoticized" by their colleagues and departments (LaSala et al. 2008). The development of anti-gender campaigns poses even greater challenges to the development of the field on an institutional level. During the turmoil of the anti-gender campaigns in Bulgaria in late May 2018, several colleagues called to tell me to check my inbox, as something important was going on within my institute. To cut a long story short, someone from the institute's scientific council unlawfully sent a project proposal to a right-wing public figure with close ties to Trump's administration at that time, who managed to provoke yet another wave of hateful comments. This document was a short abstract describing a research proposal for UNESCO research grants that aimed to identify teachers' gender stereotypes in different ethnic and religious settings in Bulgaria. I had agreed to participate in it, so my name was on it.

In the next few days, many colleagues from my institute exchanged emails on a common email list where they repeated the anti-gender rhetoric outlining the "dangers" it brings. Interestingly, all of them, without exception, were our colleagues in philosophy. A picture of me ended up in one of the biggest and oldest newspapers in Bulgaria, currently converted into a far-right tabloid-style news media outlet. The title they used was "Gender Agents from the Academy Bought with 24 Thousand Dollars." In the following days, a local newspaper in the region where I was born attached my religious-minority background, Muslim, to my identity as a "gender agent." During this stressful time, the board of the academy blocked any further actions related to this project, and it remains blocked to this day. Reflecting on these events, I realized there were dormant anti-gender signs in my institution that I had neglected. A few years earlier, I had received a comment in an internal evaluation for small grants that stated the topic of LGBTQI+ bullying in schools does not align with the Bulgarian Christian tradition. Furthermore, I remembered that one of the professors who discussed my PhD thesis stated with unhidden disgust on her face that she was "tired of that gender topic." These colleagues with anti-gender bias were predominantly women, another significant aspect of the anti-gender movements, which I will discuss in the next sections. I had ignored these signs, assuming that these were isolated cases of individuals still influenced by communism who would be retired soon.

The more recent events made me realize that my neoliberal utopian gaze had neglected to notice the anti-gender undercurrents around me, and that the environment I work in can be quite hostile toward the subject and the scholars dealing with gender topics. My belief that the Bulgarian Academy of Sciences was the most prestigious and, expectedly, the most progressive and informed scientific institution in Bulgaria fell apart. Currently, there are cases of microaggressions against me and my colleagues who work on the topic. Some occur at events; some are stated in the common email list using appropriate discussion to jump onto this topic. Two months ago, I received a reply in a discussion by a professor from my unit arguing that "Judith Butler is a lesbian and she tries to impose 'gender ideology' onto children." This despicable comment took place in an academic discussion, and the professor provided links to right-wing media outlets to support her "scientific" argument.

This is, unfortunately, the level of awareness and knowledge of many colleagues I work with. In December 2022, we observed similar attitudes and statements during an academic meeting of a commission appointed by the Academy to prepare and approve the Gender Equality Plan (GEP), a document required by the European Commission of all the scientific institutions that participate in the Commission's grant schemes. This plan remained on paper, unfortunately, and there are no further actions for its implementation. The stalling of this plan demonstrates that while the European Union's measures sound extremely promising and positive, feeding the neoliberal utopian gaze, many of these measures do not indicate real changes and serve only as a compulsory attribute for grant applications. In this context, the future of science in general is endangered, although many consider that there are "protected" fields of science—the natural sciences, for example.

Production of Knowledge and the Rise of "Social Media Scientists"

In classical thought, one of the main purposes of science is to prevent crises and provide reliable information for successful policies and personal development. In times of anti-gender campaigns, not only the social sciences but many other scientific fields are extremely endangered. We are observing a successful discrediting of official scientific journals and associations by "social media scientists," who dictate public discussions and impose their conspiracy narratives. The manipulation of science has been one of the main reasons for the successful development of anti-gender campaigns in Bulgaria. Initially brought to the public by Society and Values, one of the greatest manipulations relating to gender and sexuality involved two pediatric associations in the U.S. The American College of Pediatrics, which is a small religious association, was manipulatively presented as the official American Academy of Pediatrics. Manipulating the name similarities, most far-right media outlets, and even the official media of the Bulgarian Socialist Party—the *Duma* newspaper—presented the anti-trans and anti-LGBTQI+ rhetoric of the College as the position of the Academy, the most renowned pediatric association in the USA. This undoubtedly legitimized the anti-gender campaigns, and this is a manipulation that is still being used in public discussions.

A second major manipulation in science involves the so-called Madrid Declaration, issued in Madrid in March 2018 at an event organized by HazteOir, a conservative religious organization with close ties to the Spanish far-right political party Vox. The so-called declaration repeats the major rhetoric of the anti-gender campaigns; however, in the public discussions, it was presented by the aforementioned media outlets as a declaration issued by the "biggest names" in gender studies on an international level. A simple fact-check of the names included in the declaration demonstrates that none of them is a scientist, and only a few of them have doctorates in theology. The official website of the event is currently unavailable; however, the names can be found in Bulgarian outlets.[1] One of the major voices of this declaration, German Catholic author Gabriele Kuby,[2] was invited to Bulgaria and gave talks on various national media promoting her books against the "global sexual revolution" and "gender ideology." Kuby was presented as one of "the biggest names in science on gender," not only in Germany but on an international level.

These two events of manipulation were met without any criticism by the majority in Bulgaria, and this is how the strategic manipulation of science created an alternative reality. The rhetoric and argumentation are still being used in academic texts and media outlets. Those who, like me, have different opinions and provide scientific data from academic journals are simply declared "paid agents" of George Soros. Although these cases concern the manipulation of science dealing with gender and sexuality, the "social media scientist" puts many other sciences in danger. Usually, these actors do not have any relevant degrees in the fields they pretend to understand; however, they successfully influence the public narratives when it comes to issues of gender, sexuality, COVID-19, climate change, and even history and biology. A team of biologists from the Bulgarian Academy of Sciences has been repeatedly attacked on social media because they mentioned the existence of homosexuality in a biology workbook for sixth graders. Many historians and climate scientists are humiliated, and their expertise is delegitimized, in anti-elitist populist campaigns in different parts of the world.

These events are indicative that the conventional production and dissemination of science are not effective in these new circumstances. A few days ago at a conference, a German colleague was surprised to learn that Gabriele Kuby is a famous author in many countries, stating that she was famous in Germany twenty years ago, however she has been discredited in academia. This made me question whether social scientists pay attention to those outside of their academic bubbles and research interests. Although there is a growing body of literature on anti-gender campaigns, I am afraid that many of our colleagues ignore any backward movements that have the potential to grow under appropriate circumstances, and the Bulgarian case is a convincing example that it's possible. I am also afraid that the exoticization of gender and sexuality studies makes the neoliberal utopian gaze stronger; thus, many social scientists do not pay significant attention to anti-gender processes and manipulation of science, being locked behind the castles of the "high science" they produce and being promised by the neoliberal narrative in many countries that the future is bright and progressive. This is accomplished by governments' introduction of progressive policies, or by wishful-thinking declarations and policies that sound extremely positive but often ignore those who do not read academic journals or have access to them. This ignored group is the audience that exists in the social forums and groups on Facebook seeking salvation for financial or personal problems in the anti-elitist populist promises (Graff and Korolczuk 2022).

The Neoliberal Utopian Gaze Looking at Women

Another very significant dimension of the anti-gender campaigns is the participation of women in this mobilization. It came as a surprise to many of us that some of the main figures in the anti-gender movement are women. Although certain female political leaders, such as Marine Le Pen in France, have been proponents of conservative rhetoric for many years, my neoliberal utopian gaze had not allowed me to consider women as powerful forces in any conservative movements. The anti-gender campaigns in Bulgaria helped me take off my neoliberal glasses and rethink this wrong assumption. The main public figure of Society and Values, Mihaela Dzhorgova, is female; all the female judges in the Constitutional Court decided against the Istanbul Convention. The female leader of the Bulgarian Socialist Party is among the most prominent voices against "gender ideology." What did I miss? What didn't so many of us take into account all these years?

The main political rhetoric regarding gender during the transition of Bulgaria from communism to democracy includes two major discourses. The first one is based on how communism had achieved a great deal of gender equality, and Bulgaria is among the countries with the highest number of women taking high-ranking managerial positions in many sectors. The second discourse is based on European Union values, which promote gender equality and have achieved significant advances. These discourses have projected a mainstream reality that reproduces the mantra of growing and expanding gender equality, where most women are progressive because they have reflected on their unprivileged positions in the past. But this first discourse is false, because the communist regime created the "overburdened woman," who remained the main figure taking care of household chores, and the communist regime did not eradicate certain patriarchal values. The second discourse ignores the reality of those who do not take managerial positions, women who live in poverty, often unable to be financially independent, which creates a culture of learned helplessness. In general, the gender-mainstreaming policies of the EU are imposed mechanically without consideration of regional and cultural realities, with a strong emphasis on cultural feminist perspectives rather than social and economic approaches (Gregor and Grzebalska 2016). This is yet another centralized mechanism for power control, and it bears the potential to ignite further opposition from the masses against the centralized bureaucratic approaches of the EU (Graff 2021; Rawłuszko 2021).

In a study (Darakchi 2019) analyzing a large number of social media comments at the beginning of the anti-gender campaigns, I identified four types of motivation for women to participate in and support the anti-gender campaigns. What is significant is that these patterns of motivation cannot be explained only by economic conditions or only by cultural values, because they include both. In certain cases, it is economic dependence; in others, the reasons are cultural, based on patriarchal values as well as certain modern trends of remasculinization and refeminization promoted by pop culture. I am very concerned that certain left-leaning academic circles completely ignore the cultural values that motivate certain groups of women to participate in and support anti-gender campaigns. While my neoliberal glasses previously did not let me see the whole picture, I believe that specific leftist critical approaches ignoring cultural values would also miss certain motivations.

LGBTQI+ Studies Missing Out on "Ordinary" People

The neoliberal utopian gaze has also missed certain tendencies regarding sexual minorities in policies and academic research. Usually, the development of LGBTQI+ studies within the past two decades has been marked by optimism and conclusions depicting the overwhelming advancement of LGTBQI+ rights and policies, mainly in a Western context. In 2007, Jeffrey Weeks published a book named *The World We Have Won*, and Ghaziani (2011) depicted the "post-gay era," wherein most of the prejudices are erased and nonheterosexual people do not need special places, as they are fully accepted everywhere and do not have to hide their sexual orientation. These positive accounts sound extremely promising, but they only depict certain parts of Western societies. Brown (2012) has argued that homonormativity is explored primarily in cosmopolitan contexts, ignoring contextual attitudes and "ordinary gay lives."

Furthermore, the neoliberal positive account of gay rights and freedom of expression has been strengthened by a capitalist economy and by technology offering goods, services, and access to information that was unavailable twenty years ago. Many governments have adopted progressive legislation, including the LGBTQI+ policies of the European Union, that has been exported to different cultural settings in a process of "homonationalist" strategies (Puar 2018). This creates the illusion in many contexts that the backlash against nonheterosexual people is a dark part of the past, and many organizations and scholars might have seen it this way because they are looking at reality through neoliberal glasses.

Most of the studies on nonheterosexual people in Eastern Europe have been focused on social movements, activists, and political discourses, paying less attention to the lived experiences of nonheterosexual people. This is how we might have missed those who do not engage in gay culture, the gay scene, or activism. In an ongoing study based on sixty-three in-depth interviews with nonheterosexual men in Bulgaria carried out between 2021 and 2022, I have identified a significant portion of respondents who do not recognize gay identity and gay culture. Moreover, many of them support anti-gender movements and use anti-gender rhetoric in their narratives. Distanced from activist networks and gay culture, these respondents have developed "personal communities" that reproduce patriarchal homonormative discourses and oppose the rights of trans and queer people.

Globally, there is a rising phenomenon of people who identify as gay and lesbian and insist on excluding trans and genderqueer people from the

LGBTQI+ movement, often engaging in anti-gender rhetoric. These movements are extreme, to the point where the participation of trans and queer people in the Stonewall riots is discussed as propaganda and a staged event. Such examples are found on Twitter and Instagram under the names "LGB without the T," "Dutch LGB," "LGB," "Gay not Queer," and others. These groups have the potential to grow and create a separatist movement similar to the TERF movement. The social sciences must explore these developments using qualitative methods.

Bulgarian LGBTQI+ movements and activist groups have reacted very ineffectively to the anti-gender campaigns. The liberal mainstream organizations such as GLAS and Single Step do not produce their narratives for mobilization adapted to the local political and cultural climate. Instead, their main strategy has been defensive rhetoric against any attack or discourse targeting them. These defensive strategies often include the neoliberal narrative of human rights and freedom promoted by the European Union. On the other hand, the new left-leaning Bulgarian collectives and groups introduce academic terminology and rhetoric, which remain unfamiliar to many of the participants in social media groups and forums. That is one of the main obstacles preventing these groups from getting more support from nonheterosexual people; being highly educated in Western universities, they often sound more bourgeois than the liberal organizations.

Now What? Why Do We Need a Reconsideration of Knowledge Production and Scientific Solidarity?

Based on the previous examples and cases, in the next few paragraphs I will offer three possible solutions to overcoming this mounting crisis where academic freedom and basic human rights are becoming dangerous and endangered.

First of all, the *distribution of scientific knowledge* must be reconsidered. Due to the high prices of the main publishers in neoliberal academia, scientific journals remain inaccessible for the majority. Furthermore, the development of social media has changed the way people accept information. If we continue to believe the general public will search for information and verify certain claims in academic journals, then we are detached from reality. The anti-gender campaigns in Bulgaria were promoted by emotional and powerful short videos that reached large audiences. Therefore, I believe that the scientific community, especially those dealing with gender and sexuality, should implement a "translation" strategy for their research and basic concepts and target strategic audiences on social media.

This said, a vast sector of the youngest generation is among the biggest victims of the neoliberal utopian gaze. Living in comparatively stable economic conditions and having no reflexive knowledge of the past, many youngsters do not even allow themselves to think that this freedom and prosperity are not to be taken for granted and can be taken away. If we refuse to adapt the tough terminology and explain it in everyday language, we will continue watching how far-right leaders without any degree in social sciences "present and explain" the theories of Judith Butler, Michel Foucault, and other significant names in social sciences to the general audience, translating the manipulative rhetoric of far-right figures such as Ben Shapiro and Matt Walsh to their national languages.

Secondly, the scientific community must realize that the anti-gender campaigns do not affect only gender and sexuality studies, and we must implement *strategies for solidarity, prevention, and intervention* as quickly as possible. In Bulgaria, the anti-gender campaigns created platforms and audiences where scholars from different fields were attacked and discredited. Therefore, each scientific institution needs to evaluate and reconsider its strategies in this new environment and adapt its communication, curricula, and even legal teams for cases of humiliation and discreditation. I believe that the neoliberal utopian gaze fixated on the bright future of gender studies has been and remains a leading approach in many academic environments, either by exoticizing gender and sexuality studies or by fixating on the successful stories, advancements, and policies while ignoring notions of gender and sexuality among under-researched communities and regions. Careful strategic planning will be able to prevent or at least decrease the effects of these movements in academia.

Third, the *scientific associations* also need to reconsider their policies in light of these new realities. During the past few months, I attended three events organized by three different big scientific associations. Two of them did not include any programming on anti-gender campaigns, and my presentation was the only one that merged with topics of social activism in a panel. At the same time, another main sociological event in Europe rejected both papers on anti-gender mobilizations in Bulgaria from my department due to limited spaces. Ironically, the main theme of the sociological event is Uncertainties in Europe, and this might be "prioritization of uncertainties." The preliminary program of that conference became available in August

2023, and there is not a single paper tackling the anti-gender mobilization, and most of the papers are based on quantitative methodology. This raises the question: To what extent do scholars from the field participate in associations' boards, and to what extent do these boards represent the countries of Eastern Europe? Moreover, many of us still need to explain to journal editors and conference organizers what exactly we understand as anti-gender campaigns and mobilizations when we deal with submissions.

Within the last five years, I have attended several events devoted to anti-gender campaigns; however, at this point, we remain a small group of concerned scholars whose work and well-being have been compromised and threatened. I assume that in some cases the lack of panels on the anti-gender mobilization is due to the unfair conditions of these events. For example, for many people working on gender and sexuality part-time, or those whose job status is endangered and who have no access to project funding, the prices of these conferences are impossible to pay. Furthermore, such events often do not have different registration fees for scholars coming from less developed countries who need to pay a sum higher than their salaries for a registration fee and lodging—at least this is the case for Bulgarian scholars. A careful reconsideration of such policies is needed to include anti-gender campaigns as topics covered at major social science events, which will not only empower the scholars dealing with gender and sexuality but also promote awareness of the significance of these developments among scientists from other fields.

One of the major narratives of neoliberal politics is the promise of "never again" when it comes to forces endangering basic human rights and freedoms. This is a promise we were taught to believe, and we lived for many years with this ideal. The past few years have proven this promise to be wrong. Back in 2014, when I was a Fulbright fellow in the U.S., enjoying the positive developments and inspiring stories of my academic bubbles, I could not have imagined that in 2023 the state of Florida would take steps against gender studies, the Supreme Court of the U.S. would overturn *Roe v. Wade*, and Michelangelo's works would be declared "gender ideology." After all, distancing ourselves from the communist past, Bulgarians see the U.S. as the perfect example of democracy and unlimited freedom. Certain aspects of the tyrannic past are being repeated while the neoliberal political discourse turns a blind eye to them and chooses to focus on economic growth and development instead. The scientific community and the institutions must realize this danger and act in time; otherwise, we might witness worse scenarios and loss of human life, especially in the Eastern European context, where many extreme-right leaders call for violence against "gender agents" and "national traitors." This essay based on personal experiences is a call to all those who have not considered the realities outside their academic and personal bubbles. This essay is a reminder that the impossible is becoming possible and that *The Handmaid's Tale* is slowly becoming a reality for many of us.

Shaban Darakchi, Institute of Philosophy and Sociology, Bulgarian Academy of Sciences, holds a PhD in sociology from the Bulgarian Academy of Sciences. His main professional interests are gender, sexuality, ethnicity, and religion in Eastern Europe and Bulgaria. Darakchi is a researcher at the Bulgarian Academy of Sciences and an affiliated scholar at the University of Antwerp. He can be reached at shaban.darakchiev@gmail.com.

Notes

1. See, for example, "17 Contries Rebelled against the Gender Doctrine," *Duma*, March 16, 2018, https://duma.bg/17-strani-vastanaha-sreshtu-dzhendar-doktrinata-n162924?go=news&p=list&categoryId=3.
2. For an example of a lecture by Gabriele Kuby, see Kuby 2018.

Works Cited

Archer, Louise. 2008. "The New Neoliberal Subjects? Young/er Academics' Constructions of Professional Identity." *Journal of Education Policy* 23 (3): 265–85.

Brown, Gavin. 2012. "Homonormativity: A Metropolitan Concept that Denigrates "Ordinary" Gay Lives." *Journal of Homosexuality* 59 (7): 1065–72.

Darakchi, Shaban. 2019. "'The Western Feminists Want to Make Us Gay': Nationalism, Heteronormativity, and Violence against Women in Bulgaria in Times of 'Anti-gender Campaigns," *Sexuality and Culture* 23 (4): 1208–29.

Ghaziani, Amin. 2011. "Post-gay Collective Identity Construction." *Social Problems* 58 (1): 99–125.

Giroux, Henry. 2003. "Utopian Thinking under the Sign of Neoliberalism: Towards a Critical Pedagogy of Educated Hope." *Democracy and Nature* 9 (1): 91–105.

Graff, Agnieszka. 2021. "Anti-gender Mobilization and Right-Wing Populism." In *The Routledge Handbook of Gender in Central-Eastern Europe and Eurasia*, edited by Katalin Fáhián, Janet Elise Johnson, and Mara Lazda, 266–75. London: Routledge.

Graff, Agnieszka, and Elżbieta Korolczuk. 2022. "Anti-gender Campaigns as a Reactionary Response to Neoliberalism." *European Journal of Women's Studies* 29 (1): 150–57.

Gregor, A., and Grzebalska, W. 2016. "Thoughts on the Contested Relationship between Neoliberalism and Feminism." In *Solidarity in Struggle: Feminist Perspectives on Neoliberalism in East-Central Europe*, edited by Eszter Kováts, 11–20. Budapest: Friedrich-Ebert-Stiftung.

Korolczuk, Elżbieta, and Agnieszka Graff. 2018. "Gender as 'Ebola from Brussels': The Anticolonial Frame and the Rise of Illiberal Populism." *Signs: Journal of Women in Culture and Society* 43 (4): 797–821.

Kuby, Gabriele. 2018. "Sex Education: The Sexual Revolution Grabs Our Children." YouTube, February 23, 2018. https://www.youtube.com/watch?v=LxiXHYiAI4E.

Kuhar, Roman, and David Paternotte, eds. 2017. *Anti-gender Campaigns in Europe: Mobilizing against Equality*. London: Rowman & Littlefield.

LaSala, Michael C., David A. Jenkins, Darrell P. Wheeler, and Karen I. Fredriksen-Goldsen. 2008. "LGBT Faculty, Research, and Researchers: Risks and Rewards." *Journal of Gay and Lesbian Social Services* 20 (3): 253–67.

Lovenduski, J. 2022. "Funding Anti-gender Politics in Europe." *Political Quarterly* 93 (3): 530–32.

Puar, Jasbir K. 2018. *Terrorist Assemblages: Homonationalism in Queer Times*. Durham, NC: Duke University Press.

Rawłuszko, M. 2021. "And If the Opponents of Gender Ideology Are Right? Gender Politics, Europeanization, and the Democratic Deficit." *Politics and Gender* 17 (2): 301–23.

Rohde, Achim, and Judit Takács. 2022. "Can Gender Studies Be in Exile? An Introduction." *Intersections: East European Journal of Society and Politics* 8 (4): 1–9.

Weeks, Jeffrey. 2007. *The World We Have Won: The Remaking of Erotic and Intimate Life*. London: Routledge.

From the Courts, to the Streets, to the University: Fighting to Save Gender Studies in Pakistan, 2018–2023

Rabbia Aslam

Abstract: This article traces the recent growing contestation leveled against the discipline of gender studies in Pakistan. In 2020 a petition was filed in Lahore High Court against the teaching of gender studies in higher education institutions across Pakistan that should be seen as part of the national backlash initiated against feminist struggles/movements in Pakistan. Documenting the narratives of five founding heads of WGS departments through in-depth interviews, I have analyzed how WGS has not only historically but also in contemporary times encountered challenges at various levels. In addition to those interviews (primary data), I also relied on secondary sources to unearth those contestations against WGS. It is reflected in this research that WGS has journeyed through different phases, encountering antagonism and resistance, and eventually received acceptance as a field of study in a society like Pakistan, which is highly patriarchal. Though it has gained acceptance over the period, the struggle experienced by the practitioners and scholars of WGS has remained constant. They are labeled as anti-culturalists and anti-religious and stereotyped as "Westerners" toeing the Western philosophy being part of WGS. These allegations are augmented by the arguments around the scope and marketability of WGS reflecting the systemic realities of the neoliberal economic order, where education is valued on its market and commercial basis. Though the Aurat March of 2018, as theorized by feminist scholars, started the fourth wave of women's rights activism in Pakistan, it faced a huge backlash from the state and society alike. Since WGS vehemently supports women and gender rights activism and movements in general, in Pakistan the backlash was also directed against WGS. It is argued and theorized that the growing contestation and backlash to the Aurat March and WGS in Pakistan should be seen in a global context in recent years where anti-gender discourses (coupled with transphobia) are widely shared and disseminated. This article, therefore, situates these challenges faced by WGS within these local and global realities. **Keywords:** court, gender studies, survival of academic discipline, university, street, march

A legal case was launched in 2020 against gender studies university programs in Pakistan, brought by a lawyer named Mirza Adil Mughal to the Lahore High Court of Pakistan. For the last three years, the fate of gender studies as a field of teaching and research—perhaps even more importantly, as the most institutionalized and influential forms of feminism in Pakistan—has hung on the judicial decision-making involved in this case, though the final arbiters of whether gender studies as an academic field taught at Pakistan universities may be those feminists out in the streets who are fighting to get this decision overturned, and who may have won, even by the time this article is published.

Mughal's petition was submitted under Article 199 of the national Constitution of Pakistan (1973). The petition charges gender studies programs with violating the constitution according to Articles 2, 2A, 22, 227, Section 124A, 295, 295A, 298, 337, and Article 230A and C, all of which involve the Council of Islamic Ideology. That council is the highest legal and constitutional body providing legal advice on Islamic issues to the government and national parliament of Pakistan. The petition accuses the field of gender studies of including teachings that are in "nowise unsympathetic" towards, and thereby legitimize and encourage, homosexuality both as an idea and as a practice (Mughal 2020). Given this violation, the petition argues that gender studies—both as a field of teaching and an area of scholarly research—should be eliminated from Pakistan's university system and banned throughout the country in the name and "pursuit of the supreme interest of justice" (Mughal 2020). The petition was written after a period of data-gathering that took place between 2019 and 2020. Much of this data-gathering consisted of harvesting details concerning the nature of women's and gender studies program curricula that could be easily found online, in particular the information posted on the Higher Education Commission website, where all approved curricula, including course outlines, are made publicly available. The petition was filed on October 9, 2020, a time when the Pakistan women's movement was reaching a height of protest, including the massive Aurat marches held annually, starting in 2018, on International Women's Day on March 8, involving public demonstration and rallies throughout the country challenging ideas about women and gender held or promoted by right-wing movements, politicians, and religious clerics in Pakistan. Aurat demonstrators, along with gender studies academics, are often accused of or perceived as overly influenced by Western culture and ideas, particularly concerning the position of women, sexual mores, and the nature of gender, or worse—of betraying Pakistan and Islam and serving as a vehicle by which foreign political agendas are being imposed on Pakistan, destroying its heritage and culture, and bringing it into misalignment with Islamic justice. For the last five years, the country has seemed to be headed in two diametrically opposed directions all at once. On the one hand, in large part because of public protests like the Aurat marches, legislation such as the Transgender Persons (Protection of Rights) Act passed in 2018. The purpose of this law was to protect the fundamental human rights of the Khwajasira (transgender) community of Pakistan. The passage of the law put Pakistan way out in front, globally, on the issue. Yet, a backlash was also created that resulted, earlier this year (May 19, 2023), in a ruling by the Federal Sharia Court that transgender persons could not change or choose their gender markers on their official documents. The court was responding to pressure brought by religious conservatives and right-wing political parties who claim that the bill promotes "homosexuality" and that "anyone can get his or her sex changed," and that these changes would lead to new social evils and allegedly a rise in youth delinquency and, even more vaguely, a breakdown in society (Fatima 2022).

This article clarifies how what has been unfolding in the legislative bodies, in the court systems, and on the street has put the academic field of gender studies at the center of protest against the feminist influence in Pakistan while also providing protection of the field given that same influence. In addition to drawing on news accounts, gazettes, and magazines and the official court records between 2022 and 2023, I conducted five in-depth interviews with founders of the five earliest-established women's and gender studies departments in Pakistan. A major goal of this article is to bring their voices and perspectives to bear on what the purpose of gender studies in Pakistan has been and should be, and what its fate most likely will be.

A Struggle from the Start: Education and Feminist Politics in Pakistani History

State education in Pakistan has always been strictly controlled by the governmental policies to harmonize people divided by languages, cultures, ethnicities, and religious sects, as well as to construct a masculinist nationalist identity as a means of uniting these diverse groups. Education, especially higher education, which has been in large part funded by NGOs working with and through the United Nations, has been vital to the construction of both gender and national subjects and subjectivities in Pakistan and elsewhere in the Global South as well as parts of Europe. Right-wing politics and religious movements are part of the history of Pakistan's universities as well. During the Zia Islamization period (1977–1988), Islamization was a guiding principle in Zia's plan to reform Pakistan. A renewed effort was made to control the entirety of the state educational institutions, including media and education, to promote the mission of General Muhammad Zia-ul-Haq, president of Pakistan from 1978 through 1988. During his time in office, many key draconian anti-women laws were passed such as the Enforcement of Hudood ordinance (1979), a "law of evidence" (requiring two women to testify to equal the testimony of one man), and other laws that were discriminatory toward women. Pakistan historian Perveze Hoodbhoy points out that the 1980s Islamization of education applied to every academic subject—language, geography, history, social studies, and chemistry physics, mathematics, et cetera—and could only be discussed through the narrow lens of religious teachings considered to comprise orthodox Islam (Hoodbhoy 2023). Especially, critical thinking was to be shunned and rooted out of the academy. Academic freedom and intellectual debates at Pakistani universities were thus curtailed and suffered a huge setback during that era. Although the central administration of some state-funded public-sector universities created women's and gender studies programs—mostly with money from, and to satisfy, international aid and development agencies. Still, even those programs were overseen by patriarchal university administrators and were never accepted as a legitimate discipline within the Pakistan academy by many who oppose much of the human rights agenda promoted by the United Nations in general and its initiatives concerning women's rights in particular.

Feminist activism predates the modern university system of Pakistan. Soon after the emergence of Pakistan as an independent state (1947), elite women emerged as public leaders, though they tended to confine their work to be consistent with class expectations that would not put their respectability at risk. The focus of women leaders such as Rana Liaquat Ali khan, Salma Tassaduq Hussain, and other women who hailed from the ruling families of the time, remained fixed on the welfare of the poor (financial assistance, medical care) and the rehabilitation of refugees. To the extent that the efforts were focused specifically on the needs of poor women, they confined themselves to addressing poor women's education, health, and ability to earn an income (Saigol 2021). Such projects were acceptable to their conservative male family members and the patriarchal leaders of their social class. Their concern with the plight of poor women was not at all threatening, because it generally did not address issues of sexism in the ruling classes or as a system that affects all women; nor did they call for a shift in power relations within the family, or for political power to be shared between men and women on the national level. Instead, those feminists were perceived as reinforcing traditional ideas about women as nurturers seeking only to help their less fortunate sisters in ways that conformed to class expectations of the wives of the elites. Apart from charitable activities, some more political women such as Begum Jahanara Shahnawaz and Begum Shaista Ikramullah did focus on enacting a few limited, but nonetheless important, legal reforms to afford women some basic rights within the family, such as the right to registration of marriage and the right to dissolve a marriage (Usman and Saigol 2020, 5). However important as precedents and as providing some limits to the disempowerment all women experienced within the family, these reforms were limited to the family sphere. They did not address women's political rights within society at large and did nothing to challenge the family as the mainstay of patriarchy and the primary structure designed to control women and regulate women's sexual conduct. So long as the emphasis was on welfare and social issues—such as dowry, child marriages, polygamy, and purdah—women advocates at the time did not face severe backlash. To be sure, they were subjected to accusations of adherence to a Western agenda, simply for speaking out and taking on public roles alone. The very elite class of women who shunned the practice of purdah for themselves were seen as undermining patriarchal power and were subjected to invective by individual men and the religious lobby. But, insofar as their agendas were seen either as personal rebellion or in terms of the "uplift and betterment" of poor women, the backlash was not intense and remained confined to the religious clerics. During this period (1970s), women's rights advocates worked in cooperation and collaboration with the state, and the relationship was one of mutual accommodation.

The feminist activism spearheaded by the Women's Action Forum (WAF) in the decade of the 1980s was far more confrontational. It challenged the state's attempts to reconstitute and reorder social, economic, and political structures in line with a facile ideology of Islamization articulated by a regime in search of legitimacy by embracing women's rights at least nominally to satisfy international aid organizations. Feminist activists, mainly belong to the WAF umbrella group, lobbied for an end to discriminatory laws and measures against women. Beginning in the early 1990s, WAF activists fought relentlessly for a secular ethos in the interest of justice and equality (Zia 2022). They were opposed by retrogressive religious patriarchies comprising both men and women at every step. Nonetheless, the struggle for a democratic and secular state by WAF resisted all attempts at silencing, suppressing, and forcing women into compliance by a merciless state (Khan and Aslam 2021). Despite the danger and repressive tactics waged by the state against them, WAF's activism remained focused on the state and the public sphere. In a reversal of the previous feminist work by elites, they neglected the power men wielded within the family as beyond the reach of the secular state. Despite a strong feminist consciousness regarding state power, WAF did not openly challenge men's rights within the family—the very sphere where the rebellious and potentially dangerous body of woman is controlled, sexuality strictly regulated, and patriarchy perpetually produced and reproduced (Khan and Aslam 2021, 10). The main reasons for a lack of focus on the private sphere—with its insidious agenda of hiding, concealing, denying, and controlling women's bodies and sexuality—include the quick pace at which the state was enacting discriminatory laws that were necessary to resist. But the presence in WAF of a large number of conservatives and traditional women who did not want to question the sanctity of the family was also a factor. As Aisha Jalal has significantly noted, relying extensively on family support for sustenance and security in the absence of state structures often makes even activist women hesitant to undermine the only system that they rely on for survival. The patriarchal bargain requires subservience in the domestic sphere in return for support and security (Jalal 1991, 230).

Other democratic movements with implications for women and feminism emerged in Pakistan in the 1980s at the provincial level. Sindhiani Tahreek is based on groups of rural women who were gathered at Sindh.[1] This group has focused on the public sphere of politics and economics to explain the impact of feudalism in Sindh. The main demands of Sindhiani revolved around the return of democracy and maximum provincial autonomy based on principles of federalism (Khan and Saigol 2004). Patriarchal power over women was challenged, especially in the form of violence against women in the name of honor and its manifestation in regressive religious practices, but the body and sexuality—as produced by masculine and statist discourse—remained a jealously guarded, sacred terrain that was not to be touched. As a rural women's movement, Sindhiani was not in a position to challenge the mainstay of local and powerful patriarchies. While WAF and Sindhiani Tahreek mark the second wave of feminism in the 1980s, which confronted and challenged the state, the third wave of the 1990s constituted a diffuse array of practices that some activists do not consider a part of the feminist movement, mainly on account of donor-driven practices and technical instead of political agendas. The nongovernmental organizations that proliferated in the 1980s and 1990s may not have constituted a movement in the narrow sense of the term; nevertheless, a great deal of activist and academic work was produced during this period. In a sense, this period may be regarded as one of theory and reflection in that the funding available enabled a vast amount of feminist literature to be produced and disseminated, concurrent with a relative decline in street activism.

More recently, Pakistan's feminist movement and rights-based activism on behalf of women seemed on the ascent. In the past six years, the annual Aurat March (Women's March) signifies a milestone in the culture of feminist protest, although the organizers of the march have faced serious violent threats ahead of the rallies, and a tense impasse has followed a series of encounters between sexual and religious politics. On one hand, a democratic set of governing practices have emerged, which has been a positive development in Pakistan. On the other hand, in the absence of a visible dictator against whom resistance could be directed, feminists have lost a natural target for their efforts, leaving them with little else but an inchoate sense that legislation governing rights in the public sphere is never going to address or influence power relations between men and women exerted with the family. While publicly, women's rights have gained ground, sexuality and gender identity has been left marooned within a family setting out of reach of the state.

It's Not Just Pakistan: Global Anti-gender Sentiment, Transphobia, and Trans Rights

In recent years, right-wing discourses have targeted gender studies, feminism, and LGBT+ rights in many countries on every continent. Just as in Pakistan, authoritarian governments throughout the world have adopted "anti-gender" and "anti-genderism" rhetoric, accusing their targets of "gender ideology" or "genderism," even. For instance, in 2018 the president of Hungary, Viktor Orbán, banned gender studies at colleges and stated that people are born either male or female (Kent 2018). Another example of global anti-gender sentiment can be found in the United States, in a new state law passed in Florida banning discussions of gender that do not reflect a belief in its essential biological binary nature as well as discussions of nonnormative sexual identities and "critical race theory" or histories of the United States that center slavery or racist institutions (Bernstein 2023). Gender studies as a field is particularly vulnerable, since it is perceived as threatening the core belief systems of cultures, both Western and non-Western. The term adopted by "anti-gender" studies groups, "gender ideology," assumes that gender studies and queer, trans, and feminist movements produce an ideology that poses a threat to the majority of the population, while heterosexuality and a stable gender binary are seen as nonideological and natural expressions of what it means to be human and civilized (Kuhar and Paternotte 2018, 19). The landscape of gender-bashing is complex. Religious and nationalist agents play a part, alongside religious, conservative, and far-right sectors of the public opposing gay marriage, feminism, and women's rights.

While there is a strong public discourse in India that views transphobia and homophobia as themselves the result of foreign influences, as remnants of the British colonial legacy, such a discourse is largely absent in Pakistan, where transphobia and homophobia are widely viewed and touted as essential to the teachings of Islam (Rafiq and Mugloo 2023). This has made it more difficult for Pakistani feminists and queer activists to point to pre-Islamic traditions, or even heterodox traditions within Islam, for their individual rights interpretations as a way to counter anti-genderism discourses. Transphobia has deep roots in Pakistan. The British colonial officers saw transgender people as kidnappers and castrators of children and criminalized them in 1897, which kicked off their subsequent persecution and nonacceptance, although both Islam and Hinduism accommodated transgender people. In the Islamic branch Sufism, gender is understood as an identity form that is fluid, and transgender people are accepted within the practice of Islamic Sufism as embodying the essence of God. But this perspective is not widely accepted and taught in Pakistan, and does not play a strong role in Pakistani education and histories, as it does in India.

On May 19, 2023, the Federal Shariat Court of Islamabad ruled that Sections 2f, 3, and 7 of the Transgender Persons (Protection of Rights) Act—all of which relate to the right to establish one's gender identity on official documents—do not conform with its interpretation of Islamic principles. The court ceased, with immediate effect, the sections deemed "un-Islamic" (Amnesty International 2023). Transgender activists immediately filed an appeal of the ruling (Associated Press 2023). In most of the cases, Islamists and political conservatives have used arguments based on religious and cultural mores, but the LGBT+ activists and human rights defenders have used different positions to argue against these allegations, which are framed within the paradigm of democracy and secularism, but not in every case of struggle. However, the ideological stances of various human rights and transgender activists are incongruent, which makes it challenging to place oneself into a rigid framework of gender identification and identification by other intersecting identities.

In 2023, the trans community challenged the Federal Shariat Court Decision in the Supreme Court of Pakistan (SC). In the petition, it was requested that the SC rule that legislation enacted by duly elected officials represent the Ijma (consensus) of the community and be entitled to a presumption of validity that cannot be overruled by the Federal Shariat Court absent a manifest violation of explicit Islamic prohibitions as outlined in the Holy Quran and Sunnah (Malik 2023). It refers to the fact that the Federal Shariat Court cannot revoke a decision without having given explicit explanation about violation of Islamic principles. This case is also connected to explosive rumors erupting in social and print media in September that an ex-politician's son had married a man, though he has denied this, claiming explicitly that "I am not married" (*Pakistan Observer* 2023).

A religious party (Jamiat Ulema-e-Islam, or simply "ally of government") in Pakistan in September 2022 filed a petition against the Transgender Protection Act of 2018, a law that protects the rights of transgender people. The members and supporters of this party asserted that the legislation would act as a gateway for allowing same-sex marriage (Janjua 2022). The petition shows that due to limited orientation toward the gender-variant and gender-diverse community, reductionism is happening via categorization (division into fixed identities) and the labeling of trans people into a state-defined identity through legislation. This reductionism simplifies something that requires nuance and recognition of the complexity in the way that some Pakistanis understand their own gender identity and sexuality, and of how the rights of women are caught up in those complexities, and to some extent it is truly complicated for the progressive nations in the West as well. With often overlapping but sometimes competing arguments on gender as a concept, it reaffirms the importance of assuming and maintaining a stable sex/gender alignment, by demonizing secular attacks on the traditional family as misguided identity politics that will end up destroying "proper" national identities (Tudoor 2021, 238).

Meanwhile, gender studies as a discipline in Pakistan, as elsewhere, has turned inward to consider gender as much as sexuality as a constructed identity that should be subject only to the individual's personal direction. A tipping point seemed to have been reached in 2018. That was when the discipline of gender studies began to be perceived very differently than in the past. As long as it seemed focused on a limited set of public rights—rights that few women could take advantage of—the study of women and gender only drew fire from the most conservative religious sectors of Pakistan. But when the discipline became perceived as advocating a nonbinary, nonessentialist idea about gender identity and sexuality, it became deeply threatening to a social system that relied on a clear and unmuddied distinction between males who ruled and determined sexual relationships and the division of labor within the family versus females who obeyed, served, and were subjected to sex as dictated by the men of the family. Criticism of feminists for insisting on women's political rights in the public sphere was redirected at gender studies scholars and practitioners for challenging the gender relations at the individual and family level. In fact, gender studies practitioners and scholars at the university were collapsing the two spheres, both public and private, and had become, unlike any feminists before them, deeply threatening on both counts.

Origins and the Contemporary State of the Field of Women's and Gender Studies in Pakistan

Women's and gender studies as an academic field within universities was introduced in 1989 under Benazir Bhutto's premiership as a top-tier trial project funded by the Dutch government through the Federal Ministry of Education (Zubair 2016, 95). That year, the university issued a letter to the planning and development divisions of the major universities of Pakistan to establish a women's studies "center." These centers were not of the same format or considered on par with traditional disciplinary departments, nor did they have the same funding streams. They remained tied to foreign aid. Nonetheless, the result was that women's and gender studies programs were established at five major leading public-sector universities in Pakistan, including Quaid-i-Azam University (QAU) in Islamabad, the University of Karachi, the University of Punjab in Lahore, the University of Peshawar, and the University of Baluchistan in Quetta. The Centre at QAU had already been established under the Centre of Excellence Act of Parliament of 1976.

The Centre is an autonomous entity working through its Board of Governors and chaired by the sitting vice chancellor of QAU and funded by the government through the Higher Education Commission of Pakistan. The Centre of Excellence in Women's Studies was renamed as CEGS at Quaid-i-Azam University Islamabad by the Government of Pakistan and Ministry of Education through a notification issued in 2004 (Khan 2021, 171).²

Two years prior, on April 8, 2002, the Ministry of Education held a meeting regarding the possibility of converting women's studies centers into regular academic departments. Aftab, a former director and a founder of a women's studies center, confirmed that this was in response to a new IMF condition placed on aid to Pakistan, that gender studies needed to be put on a more permanent footing in the university (Aftab 2022).³ Though gender studies remained ghettoized and walled off from the traditional disciplines of the university, this was largely accomplished by 2009 due to the efforts of individual leaders of gender studies centers who fought to keep the pressure on university administrations. "I had to fight for each step," the former director of gender studies at the University of Islamabad explained,

> It was a lonely kind of struggle and others benefited from my struggle. But I had an advantage because I was based in Islamabad. I was able to lobby the Ministry to ensure gender studies departments were established under the proper legal structure. Each government would make promises to regularize it, but I finally succeeded ... and we got it done. (Bari 2023)

In 2009, the government of Pakistan issued a letter to five universities directing the integration of women's studies as departments in their structures. Four universities, in the cities of Peshawar, Lahore, Baluchistan, and Karachi, complied. Only Quaid-i-Azam University did not integrate the gender studies as a department like other social sciences. Beyond the issue of labeling these programs "centers" or "departments," the name of the field of study came to the fore. Unlike in other South Asian countries, there was no deeply ideological shift signaled in the change from "women's" to "gender" studies. At the time, one of the founders of a gender studies department reports, the shift was perceived as keeping up with global trends and a desire to avoid some messy bureaucratic conundrums, as Bari explained further:

> [The] planning commission wanted to transfer this women's studies centre to the women's university. He assumed "women's studies" taught home economics, home décor, and home management, so it made more sense to

house the department within the women's university. Luckily, I convinced them that what the students will be studying is linked to gender power relations, that the program will help students to see and understand the role of gender in society. To avoid having to explain this over and over again, I decided to change the name to gender studies and that was really to keep it safe from being ghettoized by any goof of the ministry again in near future. (Bari 2023)

Bari was able to place the new Department of Gender Studies on less precarious institutional footing by putting "gender" and the study of gender itself at the center and making this explicit. In hindsight, this may seem ironic, considering it is precisely the critical study of the nature of gender that has drawn such political backlash to these programs.

As of this writing in 2023, there are only a few women's studies departments, and a couple of those have the telling name of "women's, gender, and development studies," indicating that the funding streams supporting these programs and the influences on them still come from outside Pakistan. Even when termed "gender equality studies," the implementation, integration, and institutionalization of gender studies in Pakistan universities has long been part of various regimes' adherence to international gender equality commitments, though it is also true it could not have happened without a strong Pakistani feminist movement that also pushed for this result, especially in the 1990s (Bari 1993). There are currently twenty "women's and gender studies" departments functioning in Pakistan, and a few colleges in Lahore are offering a bachelor's degree in gender studies. Yet, even after institutionalization, it is still experiencing an existential dilemma within main public-sector universities due to a lack of administrative support and recent funding cutbacks due to commercialization of education and corporatism that resemble what has been happening in Europe and the United States for some time. Neoliberal commercialization of education, and banking models—also imposed from the outside—encourage or even compel the underdeveloped world to think about how to make education less objectionable and more marketable. Gender studies is not immune to these pressures that are shared with traditional departments, but in some ways gender studies has an added burden, if only because even when it is not being demonized by political reactionaries, not a lot of people even know what the field is about or what a degree in it might be used for. "Humein is ko har dafa bechana parta hey" (we constantly need to make it sellable), as

Ihsan, another former head and founder of a gender studies department, warns (Ihsan 2022).

The data gathered by me in previous research to examine perceptions towards the discipline of gender studies shows that between 2008 and 2020, only 3.7 percent of students identified gender studies as their first choice for field of study in university application. It is unsettling to see such low interest among young people toward this discipline or perhaps toward how factors such as merit, affirmative action, and broader sociocultural dynamic in Pakistan contribute to certain academic disciplines being perceived as less important or prestigious than others (Aslam 2022). Politically unstable societies and uneven economies are always citing the low number of students and then finding that this is linked to financial resources and revenue generation for the field. This is one of the administrative hurdles for making it visible in the eyes of male chauvinistic leadership of the public-sector universities, which are not separated from the global wave of neoliberalism, corporatism, and commercialization of education. The emergence of right-wing movements across the country to resist politics related to women's rights is also a worrying factor for the discipline and its future, as a feminist academic based in Third World contexts and institutions; the inclusion and recognition of feminism, gender, and women's studies programs and curricula within the mainstream patriarchal academy is always rife with institutional politics. In institutional politics, I've seen male professors make accusations against female gender studies faculty members that they are not "good and obedient" women. In turn, patriarchal forces internal to the university have tried to indoctrinate us on the eve of the Aurat March on campus via faculty portals with messaging around the role of "good Muslim women" aimed at getting us to not join the march. At the same time, outside the premises of the university, right-wing movements use the "Haya March" as a counterprotest planted by the state in the middle of the federal capital city, with the state granting permission for marchers to chant a slogan and sing a song about how "ideal Muslim women should look alike" (also known as the "Modesty March"). When one steps outside the campus, then, one encounters public protests, rallies, and marches in all large metropolitan cities, despite threats of violence from right-wing groups (O'Donnell 2020). Even though the federal government authorized the holding of the Haya March in 2023, they prohibited the organizers of the Aurat March from entering any political venues in Islamabad, including as members of the Press Club.

When we look at the overall setup and institutional structure for reducing gender inequalities, it appears alarming because Pakistan is rated the world's second-worst country in terms of gender parity, and ranks 142 out of 146 countries in the World Economic Forum's Global Gender Gap Index report (Ahmed 2023). Nevertheless, there have been some significant shifts in discourse on women's rights since the 2018 emergence of the annual Aurat Marches to express solidarity with women worldwide (including trans women) and to publicly demand their rights as rightful citizens of the Islamic Republic. Since 2018, women in large numbers have taken over the public sphere of the streets, not only in big cities like Lahore, Karachi, and Islamabad, but with each passing year, their numbers keep rising, including women from all walks of life, different social strata, and from smaller cities and towns, such as Multan, Sukkur, and Hyderabad.

The most debated and controversial elements of these demonstrations have been the posters that individual women have composed. For example, their main slogan, "mera jism meri marzi" (my body, my choice), has taken center stage in the electronic and social media channels and is a matter of intense contestation and debates among politicians, scholars, parliamentarians, so-called intellectuals, writers, artists, and the general masses. The sight of thousands of women's bodies occupying the central public space is disturbing to the collective subconscious of the Pakistani psyche, which has identified the erstwhile Islamization and nationalist discourses of women as the source of either family honor or "shame." Most of the resistance discourse came from right-wing elements like the Jamaat-e-Islami and the right-wing MMA, which saw the slogans as a challenge to the traditional politics that have confined women to the veil and walls and have sought only those notions of feminism which promote their own ideology, such as setting up female universities or increasing participation in female-led dars (congregations) and religious gatherings. The fusing of politics and religion and its impact on women is too frequently examined from an exclusively political science perspective centered on state power dynamics. The interface of religion, politics, and gender illustrates the impossibility of separating out the realms of the social from the political, the public from the private, for everyday life is not neatly demarcated into self-contained spaces but flows freely, affecting different dimensions simultaneously. In practice, the conceptual distinctions between the political and the cultural, social, or economic spheres blur. Importantly, a vigorous cultural agenda prescribing everyday norms is a hallmark of all politico-religious projects, in which gender-normative regulations are most visible as dress codes, women's seclusion, and restricted activities (Shaheed 2010, 851).

Religion was always conjoined to politics in Pakistan, a state created for Indian Muslims. Islam's metamorphosis from the religious identity of the majority population to the privileged reference point for the state and society was not inevitable; however, shortsighted attempts to harness the emotive appeal of religion (to quell political oppositions or justify democratic measures) by secular actors, by actors in the civil and political spheres, and by the military establishment legitimized religion as a political coinage and paved the way for politico-religious forces to assert discursive hegemony. The mostly politically motivated usage of Islam peaked under General Zia-ul-Haq (1977–88), whose Islamization policies both negated state promises of equality for female and non-Muslim citizens and encouraged society's most bigoted sections. For too long, Women's Action Forum and other groups have fought against the discriminatory zina (adultery) laws and laws regarding honor crimes, under the strategic legal pretense that the victim is always and permanently innocent or framed, as if they never actually violate the Islamic laws prohibiting adultery and fornication (Saigol 2021, 26). Even when they have acknowledged that some women willingly transgress sexual norms, they have not conceded the strategic response for the larger demand for sexual freedoms. The privatization of sexual autonomy has now become an internalized logic within women's rights activism (Zia 2022, 14). In addition to capitalism, religion is an important factor in understanding the asymmetry of gender in public and private spaces in Pakistan. Therefore, capitalism cannot be regarded as the only cause of perpetuating gendered inequalities, as is argued by different scholars. Also, various Pakistani scholars have observed that the social implications of the state religious discourse are far more compelling than the juridical ones. This has led to various groups and collectives to act as enforcers of religious mores, such as conservative ulema and extremist groups. However, women no longer accept these constraints silently, as evidenced by the aforementioned public protest movement, first called Women's March and then Aurat March (Zubair 2022, 324).[4]

Conservative and right-wing groups in Pakistan are often known to invoke a famous saying: the proper place of woman is in her "chadar aur chardiwari" (veiled and within the four walls of her home). Those who took part in the march last year faced intense backlash, especially online. Some said they received death and rape threats afterwards. While religious and right-wing groups have predictably said the march goes against Islam, even moderate factions have taken issue with what the marchers themselves acknowledge is a provocative approach (Asher 2020). It's also contributed to the voices saying the movement is too Western in its ideals. The march, the legislation, and the legal challenges are a lot more intense, because this is also connected with global politics of women's rights and human rights of gendered and sexual minorities.

Legal Battles against Gender Studies as a Field
In the Lahore High Court in 2020, a petition was directed toward the Ministry of Federal Education and Professional Training, the government of Pakistan, and the chair of the Higher Education Commission of Pakistan.[5] The writ petition falls under article 199 of the Constitution of the Islamic Republic of Pakistan 1973. It states:

> The petitioner is a law-abiding citizen of Islamic republic of Pakistan and a constitutional observer, a financial economist, and data scientist, who has studied philosophy, history, and jurisprudence extensively. (Mughal 2020)

Under the heading of "ground petitioner," the report further states:

> Things are contended as to whether they are right or wrong. The Islamic injunction on there only being two genders, male and female, is squarely branded as illegitimate and "oppressive" and is styled as fact of the problem called "patriarchy" according to women's and gender studies. The solution to patriarchy, we are told in gender studies, is dissolving gender into many innumerable genders of large spectrum through "exploring sexuality" by actively experimenting thereon, and the instrument for that is homosexuality. Gender and women's studies, as it is taught and indoctrinated today, delegitimizes every traditional institution like family, marriage, private property, religion, and the state. (Mughal 2020, 5)

Following that petition, the Lahore High Court of Pakistan petitioned the Higher Education Commission of Pakistan for an evaluation report on gender studies as a subject and the gender studies curriculum offered in universities. Academics are frequently questioned about our subject matter and occasionally decide against taking a position on national and international discussions about LGBTQ rights. In the same vein, due to pressures, it is presumed that marches and protests for International Women's Day are outside the realm of the classroom; thus, ideally, we shouldn't participate in them.

The Higher Education Commission constituted a committee for responding to the petition. They secretly contacted a few individuals working as faculty in gender studies departments and asked them to submit written responses to justify the scope and need of this program to be continued in the universities. In its short report, the committee mentioned that gender studies has already been adopted in the context of Islamic values, tradition, and culture, as indicated in various course titles and content, and it is done without provoking homosexuality among students. The Higher Education Commission laid out its argument to prove that gender studies—if reinterpreted apart from the way it has been taught, as a nonessentialist nonbinary—is not in contradiction to the sociocultural values of the country. But, perhaps unsurprisingly in a country that has a full history of repressive regimes regarding issues of women and other marginalized sections of society, the committee that laid down these justifications was formed secretly; most of the universities' gender studies departments were not consulted, even for something so important as a submission to the high court of Pakistan. As an academic field, WGS has the capacity, and survival strategies, to cope with these diverse dynamics of political, cultural, religious, and economic forces; its praxes of resistance include the soft image-building of the field through organizing different seminars and conferences related to gender issues at the campus level and taking the lead on the occasions of national and international women's days. Forming alliances within the university is another key strategy for survival, mostly practiced by the head of the women's and gender studies program. One of the former directors of such a program said, "I usually went to the academic council meetings without having any agenda, just to show support in order to get support in our difficult times" (Malik 2022). This is an example of how a lobby with other key persons in management can help get our priorities accomplished in a timely manner—for example, new courses, schemes of study, and research approvals. Although the praxis of resistance is very complex and layered, because lobbying and networking with the top management of the university is still unlikely to shatter certain myths and misconceptions regarding gender studies as an academic field, its utility (market scope) and acceptance, and the content of the courses, are still questioned with the suspicion that we are teaching sexuality studies. Gender studies as a field has a shortage of human resources trained in gender-sensitive matters;

limited knowledge and a limited vision toward a gender-just society is one of the reasons there's a lack of experts in the field. Most importantly, stuck societies like ours are not very keen to have paradigm shifts in the sociocultural setup. We adopted the Western sciences and social sciences proudly, but when it comes to the teaching of radical subjects such as feminist studies, sexuality studies, and women's and gender studies—certain fields are dangerous to the social order and existing status quo.

The COVID-19 pandemic has created new, unanticipated challenges. Practitioners of the field feel more unsafe, politically, now that universities have shifted to a hybrid mode of learning, which often involves recording lectures and online discussions. Teaching faculty feel that now they must be careful while everything is being recorded in the classrooms. These pressures affect our lives, scholarship, work, teaching, career, institutions, and political organizing, particularly those that are a sign of or hold consequences for the health and survival of the discipline of feminist, gender, and women's studies. Although content and foundational texts are taught from a local context here as part of a few courses—such as on the status of women, women's movements, and gender-based violence—there is no theoretical text produced in Pakistan as a starting point for conceptualizing gender as a category of analysis. Even though educated middle-class women have worked hard to defend and advance human rights in Pakistan, the way the state approaches gender at a structural level is quite problematic. Further, a few metropolitan universities—for example, Karachi and Lahore—have a strong student base and are offering bachelor's and PhD programs in the morning and in the evening, but there are still questions about the emerging scholarship. It may not reach the standards set in gender studies as a field, because a few of the departments are running like NGOs and consciously are not as rigorous in their scholarship and pedagogy due to repercussions of linking theory and praxis together. Further undermining practitioners', scholars', and students' ability to maintain scholarly standards are the ongoing ways that they are treated only as the liberal face of universities. Between neoliberalism and fear of reprisals, many hesitate to link theory and praxis together or maintain connections with feminist movements, on and off campus. The majority of gender studies practitioners are coping with everyday struggles of hierarchies, administrative leadership, and market utility of the field. For example, one of the practitioners I interviewed explained how in her tenure process, she "experienced that each time in our academic meeting they mentioned how you justify your existence because you have a smaller number of students. We cannot do promotion of the staff and faculty due to so few students" (Khan 2022). It becomes worse when, in Pakistan, religion intersects with education and sees the field of women's and gender studies as promoting a "Western agenda" that's harmful to a traditional society like Pakistan.

Conclusion

A right-wing reaction to women and gender studies has been gaining momentum worldwide over the last few years, and we in Pakistan have been experiencing this as well. Transphobia and anti-gender sentiment are also growing rapidly worldwide, and in Pakistan the reaction against trans rights becomes more and more pronounced. The two are closely linked. Islamists and political conservatives use anti-trans sentiment and hysteria to attack gender studies, claiming the field promotes homosexuality while undermining the traditional institution of the family and religion. The Aurat March and the controversy around it are also linked with the discipline of gender studies as practiced at the university, even though the Aurat March takes place on the streets. Rightly or wrongly, gender studies supports women defining freedom for themselves, and that freedom is usually linked to control over their right to their body and sexuality. At the same time, in the other direction, feminist resistance as fought in the street politics and in the courts is also affecting the teaching of the discipline. It is not only true that gender studies radicalizes students, but students and feminist activists radicalize what we can imagine and what we mean by the study of gender. Such controversies and activism and legal backlash also have the reverse effect. Many academics do not want to be associated with political controversy; they do not want to be at the forefront of political repression in Pakistan. They want to save their careers and their programs by keeping a low profile. Yet, it is the feminists in the streets and fighting for gender studies in the courts that might save the discipline in Pakistan. In turn, Pakistan's future may depend on those same gender studies scholars' ability to enact a transformation of their society from within the university.

Rabbia Aslam has taught at the Centre of Excellence in Gender Studies at the Quaid-i-Azam University in Islamabad, Pakistan, since 2010. Aslam has a PhD in sociology, with research focusing on understanding the challenges and opportunities related to offering gender studies as an academic discipline at universities in Pakistan. Aslam has been a visiting fellow at International Institute of Social Studies. She can be reached at rabbia@qau.edu.pk.

Notes

1. Sindhiani is derived from the Sindhi, which is one of the provinces of Pakistan.
2. An official letter in 2004 was issued to five departments to rename them as Gender and Women's Studies.
3. That interview was a part of my PhD data-collection process, which is related to my topic "Gender Studies as Academic Field in Pakistan: Issues, Challenges, and Prospects."
4. The Urdu word "aurat" literally means "woman" and is derived from the Arabic word "aurat," meaning a thing that is covered or is meant to be covered or hidden from the public eye.
5. In response to the writ petition filed in the Hon'ble Lahore High Court, the title was *Evaluation Report on Subject and Curriculum of Gender Studies Offered in Universities*.

Works Cited

Aftab, Tahera. 2022. Interview. Conducted by Rabbia Aslam. March 15, 2022.

Ahmed, Amin. 2023. "Pakistan Ranks 142 out of 146 Countries in WEF's Global Gender Gap Report." *DAWN*, June 21, 2023. www.dawn.com/news/1760949.

Amnesty International. 2023. "Pakistan: Revocation of Rights of Transgender and Gender-Diverse People Must Be Stopped." May 19, 2023. www.amnesty.org/en/latest/news/2023/05/pakistan-revocation-of-rights-of-transgender-and-gender-diverse-people-must-be-stopped.

Asher, Saira. 2020. "Aurat March: Pakistani Women Face Violent Threats ahead of Rally." *BBC News Asia*, March 7, 2020. http://bbc.com/news/world-asia-51748152.

Aslam, Rabbia. 2022. "Global Development and Social Justice." *Bliss*, April 22, 2022. https://bliss8543.wpcomstaging.com/2022/04/28/gender-studies-is-yet-to-make-its-mark-among-university-students-in-pakistan-findings-froma-sst.

Associated Press. 2023. "Pakistani Transgender Activists to Appeal Shariah Court Ruling against Law Aimed at Protecting Them." May 20, 2023. https://apnews.com/article/pakistan-transgender-courts-b1674911f47712782e8947ef273382ba.

Bari, Farzana. 1993. "Saving Women's Studies in Pakistan." *The News*, September 21, 1993.

———. 2023. Interview. Conducted by Rabbia Aslam. July 10, 2023.

Bernstein, Sharon. 2023. "Florida Bill Would Ban Gender Studies Majors, Diversity Programs at Universities." *Reuters*, February 25, 2023. https://www.reuters.com/world/us/florida-bill-would-ban-gender-studies-majors-diversity-programs-universities-2023-02-25/.

Fatima, Benish. 2022. "Reviewing the Transgender Person Act Is Not about Religion, but about Politics." *Express Tribune,* November 13, 2022. http://tribune.com.pk/article/97644/reviewing-the-transgender-persons-act-is-not-about-religion-but-about-politics.

Hoodbhoy, Pervez. 2023. *Pakistan: Origins, Identity and Future.* Abingdon: Routledge.

Ihsan, Fatima. 2022. Interview. Conducted by Rabbia Aslam. April 10, 2022.

Jalal, Ayesha. 1991. "The Convenience of Subservience: Women and the State in Pakistan." In *Women, Islam and the State,* edited by Deniz Kandiyoti, 77–114. London: Palgrave Macmillan.

Janjua, Haroon. 2022. "Trans Rights in Focus amid Pakistan Legal Battle." *DW,* September 25, 2022. http://dw.com/en/Pakistan-transgender-rights-in-focus-amid-religious-complaints/a-63220427.

Kent, Lauren. 2018. "Hungary's PM Bans Gender Study at Colleges Saying 'People Are Born Either Male or Female.'" *CNN,* October 19, 2018. https://edition.cnn.com/2018/10/19/europe/hungary-bans-gender-study-at-colleges-trnd/index.html.

Khan, Anoosh. 2021. Interview. Conducted by Rabbia Aslam. March 10, 2021.

Khan, Nighat Said, and Rubina Saigol. 2004. "Sindhiani Tehreek: Rural Women's Movement in Sindh." In *Up Against the State: Military Rule and Women's Resistance,* edited by Nighat Said Khan, 192–208. Lahore: ASR Publications.

Khan, Safra, and Rabbia Aslam. 2021. "From Antagonism to Acknowledgment: Development of Gender and Women Studies as Academic Discipline in Pakistan." *Progressive Research Journal of Art and Humanities* 3 (1): 171–85.

Kuhar, Roman, and David Paternotte. 2018. "Disentangling and Locating the 'Global Right': Anti-gender Campaigns." *Politics and Governance* 6 (3): 6–19. https://doi.org/10.17645/pag.v6i3.1557.

Malik, Ranna. 2022. Interview. Conducted by Rabbia Aslam. June 10, 2022.

Mughal, Ahmed Adil Mirza. 2020. "In the Lahore High Court." Reported in Petitions, September 10, 2020.

O'Donnell, Lynne. 2020. "Pakistan Broaches 'Hijab Day' for International Women's Day." *Foreign Policy,* March 7, 2022. https://foreignpolicy.com/2022/03/08/Pakistan-women-rights-gender-equality-aurat.

Pakistan Observer. 2023. "Ali Sethi's Rumoured Gay Marriage with Salman Toor Has Everyone Talking." November 12, 2023. https://pakobserver.net/ali-sethis-rumoured-gay-marriage-with-salman-toor-has-everyone-talking/.

Rafiq, Shefali, and Mugloo Saqib. 2023. "'They Thought I Was a Curse': The Struggle of India's Trans Community." *Open Democracy*, April 7, 2023. https://www.opendemocracy.net/en/5050/india-transgender-discrimination-health-gender-affirmation-surgery/.

Saigol, Rubina. 2021. "The Women's Action Forum, Pakistan: Ideology and Functioning." In *Reinterrogating Civil Society in South Asia*, edited by Rubya Mehdi and Amit Prakash Peter, 1–26. Abingdon: Routledge.

Shaheed, Farida. 2010. "Contested Identities: Gendered Politics, Gendered Religion in Pakistan." *Third World Quarterly* 31 (6): 851–67.

Tudoor, Alyosxa. 2021. "Decolonizing Trans/Gender Studies? Teaching Gender, Race, and Sexuality in Times of the Rise of Global Rights." *Trans Studies Quarterly* 8 (2): 238–56.

Usman, Nida, and Rubina Saigol. 2020. *Contradictions and Ambiguities of Feminism in Pakistan: Exploring the Fourth Wave*. Islamabad: Friedrich Ebert Stiftung.

Zia, Afiya. 2022. "Feminists as Cultural 'Assassinators of Pakistan.'" *Journal of International Women's Studies* 24 (2): 1–14.

Zubair, Shrin. 2022. "Mera Jism Meri Marzi: Framing the Contestations for Women Rights in Pakistan." In *Global Contestations of Gender Rights*, edited by Alexandr Scheela, Julia Roth, and Heidemarie Winkel, 307–25. Bielefeld: Bielefeld University Press.

Contesting Post-truth Chaos through Interdisciplinary Heterotopias

Jeanette McVicker

Abstract: Recent populist rhetoric and politics seek to undermine existing democratic institutions and efforts to make them more inclusive. Connecting new feminist scholarship that confronts the multidisciplinary implications of post-truth populist politics and discourse, especially for higher education, with exemplary heterotopic feminist responses to pandemonia over the past century, this essay considers how previous tactics might be recast to disturb and provoke the existing status quo, creating new strategies for countering contemporary anti-democratic practices. **Keywords:** populism, spatial theory, institutional transformation, coalition-building, outsiders, killjoys, textuality

This essay explores the tension between two key claims: (1) that U.S. academic interdisciplinary programs, especially those focused around intersectionality, anti-racism, social and environmental justice, and climate change (e.g., WGSS, ethnic studies, environmental studies), are particularly vulnerable in the current political and media climate dominated by a "post-truth" ethos that is generating pandemonium within and outside the university; and (2) that such programs, as interdisciplines, have greater resilience to withstand this threat the more they embrace their inherent heterotopic—critical, contingent—potentialities. Heterotopias offer spaces for rethinking, rehearsing, and even suspending or reversing conditions of reality, or "the way things are." Although never fully predictable in their outcomes, heterotopias, defined more extensively below, encourage possibilities for developing creative, mobile strategies and coalition-building: neither permanent nor static, they act as a counter to idealized universalisms—or utopias.

WSQ: Women's Studies Quarterly 52: 1 & 2 (Spring/Summer 2024) © 2024 by Jeanette McVicker. All rights reserved.

Having witnessed and critiqued neoliberal assaults on women's, gender, and ethnic studies in the U.S. in the 1990s that share a common thread with contemporary attacks, I am both anxious in noting the differences inflecting the present post-truth chaos and optimistic in contemplating the vibrant scholarly interventions in response. Connecting new feminist scholarship that confronts the multidisciplinary implications of post-truth politics and discourse with exemplary heterotopic feminist responses to pandemonia over the past century, this essay considers how previous tactics might be recast to disturb and provoke the existing status quo, creating new strategies for countering contemporary pandemonium.[1]

The term "post-truth" gained prominence in 2016, particularly in the U.S. and U.K., to describe the strains of populism informing Donald Trump's presidential election and the Brexit campaign to leave the European Union, and the political disorder and chaos that began to ravage democratic discourse. But the effects of this chaos were visible globally prior to that year, and they accelerated during the upheaval of the COVID-19 pandemic, the 2020 anti-racist and decolonial protests following the Minneapolis police murder of George Floyd, and the January 6, 2021, insurrection on the U.S. Capitol.[2] I am a U.S.-based academic located within a large state university system who teaches across English, journalism, and women's, gender, and ethnic studies, and as such, a significant part of my pedagogy addresses how the politics of language shape literary, cultural, and media texts' production and reception, and through them, constructions of subjectivity and citizenship. "Post-truth" threatens all the fields in which I work and the community (including online) spaces through which I seek to strengthen democratic and social justice initiatives. Feminist scholars (and others) across disciplines are already deeply engaged with the impact of this reality on our pedagogies, methodologies, and institutional participation, in important and exciting ways, some of which I discuss below.

Defining Post-truth Heterotopias

Oxford Dictionary's editors offer this definition for their 2016 "word of the year": "Post-truth—adjective; relating to or denoting circumstances in which objective facts are less influential in shaping public opinion than appeals to emotion and personal belief." They further state: "The compound word *post-truth* exemplifies an expansion in the meaning of the prefix *post-* that has become increasingly prominent in recent years. Rather than simply referring to the time after a specified situation or event—as in *post-war* or *post-match*—the prefix in *post-truth* has a meaning more like 'belonging to a time in which the specified concept has become unimportant or irrelevant.'"

The idea that truth may still exist, but that it has lost its relevance for a large segment of the population, is explored in historical depth by philosopher Lee McIntyre in his book *Post-truth* (2018); his usage also indicates how quickly the term has shifted grammatically from adjective to noun. There may have been an "uptick" in the prominence of this post-truth in 2016 (thanks to Brexit and Trump), McIntyre states, "but the phenomenon itself has deep roots that go back thousands of years, to the evolution of cognitive irrationalities, that are shared by liberals and conservatives alike" (14). He observes that "post-truth amounts to a form of ideological supremacy, whereby its practitioners are trying to compel someone to believe in something whether there is good evidence for it or not. And this is a recipe for political domination" (McIntyre 2018, 13). Tracing the various forms of such political domination is crucial for understanding how and by whom knowledge is constructed, affirmed, and made available for both learning and social participation.

Among the many scholarly efforts to articulate how we arrived at this moment, two recent collections of feminist responses to post-truth stand out as timely critical interventions, especially pertinent for feminist educators. *Gender in an Era of Post-truth Populism: Pedagogies, Challenges, and Strategies* succinctly engages with multiple forms of populist assaults around the globe and through social media. The editors introduce the impact as follows:

> Described by some as a "thin-centered ideology," post-truth populism purposefully manufactures divisions that rest on notions of a struggle of "the people" against a supposed corrupt elite, including feminists and other social justice activists, intellectuals, and mainstream political parties and the media. Lacking a clear policy agenda, post-truth populism largely functions through "narrative antagonism" and relies on conservative appeals to individualism and personal belief, manipulating feelings of "political vertigo" and causing "retreats into tribal epistemologies." Through such post-truth populist manoeuvers, entrenched resentments against an imagined Other are mobilized with powerful and dangerous effects. (Burke et al. 2022, 2–3)

"Feminist Takes on Post-truth," a special issue of *Philosophy and Social Criticism*, offers the following definition and outlines the stakes for democracy as the editors see it:

> By "post-truth," we refer to a variety of discourses and practices that subvert the sense that we share a common world. Because post-truth undermines the norms and conditions that make possible shared political practices and institutions, post-truth politics is fundamentally anti-democratic. The most common response to post-truth has, however, come from those who call for reinstating truth and rationality, with special emphasis on returning to the facts and fact-checking. From a feminist perspective, this approach is worrisome as it risks idealizing the connection between democracy and truth, disowning the tensions within and between them, and suppressing contestation *tout court*. (Koekoek and Zakin 2023, 125)

These collections featuring globally situated contributors provide vital resources for clarifying the myriad operations of post-truth across various political, cultural, and media landscapes and suggesting strategies to counteract their insidious effects, particularly in educational settings. I'm especially grateful for Koekoek and Zakin's caution regarding our often instinctive attempts to use "facts and fact-checking," logic, and a tendency to default to an idealized liberal conception of democracy in response to the lies, disinformation, and appropriation of feminist and minoritized groups' conceptual vocabulary (e.g., "woke") for reactionary aims.[3] If we are engaged in a struggle to redefine reality, we must also see this pandemonium as offering opportunities for changing reality in ways that, as they observe, maintain contestation.

Loosely defined by Michel Foucault in the mid-1960s, heterotopia is an alternative temporal/spatial site (or "emplacement") that occurs within "real" time/space: his initial examples included cemeteries, libraries, museums, mirrors, and ships as well as asylums, prisons, and refugee camps.[4] More importantly, Foucault theorized heterotopias as sites generally activated by some sense of exclusion, difference, or crisis, in contrast with utopias—smooth, ordered spaces that don't actually exist in reality. He further distinguished between utopia and heterotopia: "utopias are emplacements having no real place," while heterotopias are "connected to all the other emplacements, but in such a way that they suspend, neutralize, or reverse the set of relations that are designated, reflected, or represented by them" (Foucault [1967] 1998, 178). Heterotopias manifest, in "real" space, a potential, or temporary, enactment of what the nonreal utopia can only fantasize.

Discussing heterotopias as part of literary modernism, Andrew Thacker (2009) cautions that "Foucault's conception of power as a set of relations rather than an object one could possess suggests that heterotopias cannot be labeled as inherently sites of resistance. Heterotopias are not sites of absolute freedom or places where marginal groups always resist power" (29). In other words, heterotopic spaces signify not the "arrival" of a new static, stable reality but provide a temporal, spatial, or textual pause or location, through which thinking "otherwise" can proliferate possibilities for inhabiting shared realities, for being with others differently, for imagining alternative arrangements of power. Bonnie Honig (2021) takes this caution into account as she appropriates the term for feminist activism (invoking Bernice Johnson Reagon's 1983 "Coalition Politics"): "Heterotopias are 'fugitive spaces' where dissenters or minoritized peoples learn what they want, practice how to be otherwise, and reimagine what the world might be" (70).

Heterotopias and Institutional Practices

U.S. academic feminism has, arguably, always existed in an uneasy relationship with utopian, universalist models fueled by liberal humanism (e.g., "global sisterhood") even as it challenged the hegemonic truth-claims structuring Western imperialism, science, and philosophy. Within the potentially destabilizing space of the modern university, interdisciplinary programs have created remarkably vibrant heterotopias generating compelling theoretical approaches such as intersectional, transnational feminism and critical race theory, and pedagogies that inspire students to think not just critically but expansively about the worlds they wish to inhabit, and to practice skills and collaborative strategies for bringing about those new realities (e.g., experiential and service learning, community engagement projects, developing skills illustrating a feminist ethics of care). All of this is at stake in today's post-truth disorder, which exacerbates the weakening of institutional support for interdisciplinary programs, faculty positions, scholarship, and pedagogy already underway through neoliberal austerity budgeting, which often masks administrative unease regarding interdisciplinary programs' unsettling of disciplinary boundaries of knowledge production and practice. Outright attacks on such curricula, such as the Florida state government's aggressive takeover of the board of trustees and ouster of the president of the New College in early 2023, seek to criminalize and outlaw such spaces for thinking, together with the transformative scholarly work they generate.[5]

Those of us teaching in U.S. feminist academic programs recognize that the current assaults on gender, sexuality, and ethnic studies take a page from an earlier moment of pandemonium: the 1990s neoliberal attacks on higher education and "tenured radicals," especially previous efforts to dismantle women's, gender, and ethnic studies programs. For example, so-called anti-tax groups (such as Change-NY) partnered with conservative university administrators and activist trustees in seeking to use the corporate language of taxpayer accountability and fiscal efficiency to challenge the "value" of interdisciplinary courses—especially in women's and ethnic studies—and general education curricula in state universities, informed by what I called a "politics of 'excellence'" in a 2002 essay tracing these efforts. One such report in 1996, attacking the State University of New York system, was titled "SUNY's Core Curricula: The Failure to Set Consistent and High Academic Standards."[6] It erroneously claimed that a majority of the system's sixty-four campuses "had succumbed to 'multiculturalism'"—specifically, that students were "'force[d] to take courses that often have an ideological or political bent ... Instead of a balanced treatment of different cultures, these campuses offer politicized courses that focus on grievances of different groups, whether based on sex, race, or class'" (McVicker 2002, 237).

Standardization at that time meant "undermining the potential of transdisciplinarity and pluralism represented by programs such as Women's Studies, as well as making the curriculum serviceable to the corporate sector by increasing the technologization of learning" (McVicker 2002, 237). The use of "standards" to signal value, or lack thereof, today replaces "multiculturalism" with "wokeness": pandemonium returns with increased virulence. I further noted at that time:

> The pervasiveness of the rhetoric of "excellence" in [these] initiatives is symptomatic of the becoming with which Women's Studies must now reckon. Transdisciplinary Women's Studies programs of the future will need to develop "new analyses of how gender works in the dynamic of globalization and the countermeasures of new nationalisms, and ethnic and racial fundamentalisms" (Grewel and Kaplan 1994, 19) if they are to be relevant, critical and oppositional practices within the transnational corporate university. (McVicker 2002, 234)

The Florida assaults on education, from the "Stop W.O.K.E. Act" to rejection in 2023 of a new Advanced Placement course (i.e., courses through which advanced U.S. high school students may earn college credit prior to graduation) in African American Studies mimic such rhetoric by suggesting the course "significantly lacks educational value" (Mazzei and Hartocollis 2023), adopting the depoliticized language of "value" to mask political hostility to critical Black and intersectional feminist and queer scholarship. While feminist educators may despair over the recent surge of state legislative initiatives to reject such courses, to ban specific scholarly approaches, and to police and even dismantle gender- and ethnic-focused interdisciplinary programs (often together with broader institutional Diversity, Equity and Inclusion [DEI] initiatives they helped usher in), it is vital that we also recognize how the anger generated by such authoritarian tactics is spurring creative realignments and coalitions across professional academic organizations. The June 2021 "Joint Statement on Legislative Efforts to Restrict Education about Racism in American History" sponsored by the American Historical Association and cosigned by 155 such organizations, including the National Women's Studies Association (NWSA), offers a strategic example. Multidisciplinary coalitions and practices can build resilience to such challenges by calling out the history behind the empty rhetoric of "value" and "excellence" and historicizing other post-truth terminology, such as "color blindness" (evident in the U.S. Supreme Court's June 2023 rejection of the use of affirmative action in higher education), that currently dominate headlines and institutional agendas. Strengthening heterotopic spaces such as interdisciplinary programs and departments, and developing nonhierarchical administrative structures, can potentially provide more than an antidote to post-truth disorder; these strategies can help us reimagine the university itself at a moment when the old model is undergoing rapid transformation, in ways that feminist and other multidisciplinary scholars have advocated for decades.[7] The vital scholarly work on post-truth poses strategic questions while offering tentative responses for the difficult challenges that lie ahead.

Wrestling with the post-truth moment in terms of feminist education, Sondra Hale questions "whether or not it is counter-productive in this era to see the notion of 'truth' as fragmented, ambivalent and negotiable," citing recent criticism of "left" (including feminist) challenges to universalist truths at the heart of Western imperialism, patriarchy, white supremacy, et cetera: "I am simply trying to make the point that the universalism of 'truth' and the validity of the concept of 'post-truth,' when brought into focus, are on shaky ground, but arguably not only for the reasons we have been led to believe" (Hale 2022, 80). She asks whether we "have the tools, methods, and critical pedagogical strategies" to navigate this current pandemonium;

provocatively, she further questions: "In the end, are we overlooking the possibility that this populist challenge to prevalent, established and mainly Western/white/male hegemonic knowledge production espoused in our educational institutions and elsewhere may be a decolonizing and democratizing process at work?" (Hale 2022, 80–81).

Post-truth attacks are especially threatening when one takes into consideration, as Raewyn Connell (2022) does, that "the classical concept of ideology ... adopted by many feminist scholars, which supposed a pre-existing interest that was expressed by the ideological framework, no longer applies. If that is correct, a critical response needs to go further than the unmasking of interests that classical ideology-critiques attempted. The only effective response is constitutive, the *making* of knowledge in other and more adequate forms" (68; her emphasis). She reminds us that "in this element of knowledge work, encounters with the world are transformed into concepts and understanding, and made available for learning, use, and new investigation" (72). And the communal labor of such knowledge work must expand, Connell asserts: "Democratic knowledge movements exist, and are important, for example, in environmental action. A legitimate goal of education is to expand the citizen workforce capable of critique and knowledge-making"; she advocates broader utilization of the feminist work taking place in the Global South as a critical resource for this expansion (75).

Together with most of the contributors to these recent scholarly interventions, Koekoek and Zakin (2023) ask, "In such circumstances, what would a pragmatic contestation, one that takes seriously the reality of collapsing realities, look like?" (131).

Literary and Textual Heterotopias as Post-truth Sites of Resistance

In the preface to *The Order of Things* ([1966] 1973), Foucault observed that "heterotopias (such as those to be found so often in [Jorge Luis] Borges) desiccate speech, stop words in their tracks, contest the very possibility of grammar at its source" (xviii). Opening up the concept to the site of the literary text intriguingly complicates the spaces within which heterotopias might exist within reality, challenging the supposed closure of formal linguistic structures (including grammar and syntax) while also meshing the material with the metaphorical. Contemporary scholars have productively drawn on this form of heterotopia, including Lesley Higgins and Marie-Christine Leps (2022), who consider Foucault's work, together with fiction by Virginia

Woolf and Michael Ondaatje, as comprising a new genre, which they name "heterotopic world fiction," that thinks "beyond biopolitics."[8] "Our book focuses on textual elaboration because that is where thought experiments occur," they write (6).

Deepening our commitment to the heterotopic aspect of interdisciplinarity, I suggest, is one strategy for countering this particular post-truth chaotic moment; toward that end, reengaging with the way feminist writers have utilized heterotopias in the past to confront pandemonium provides not only inspiration but strategies ready for redeployment to address contemporary circumstances. Literary and textual heterotopias can inspire readers to think and imagine in ways that engage critically with this post-truth moment; in the process, the humanities become relevant allies to interdisciplinary programs as collaborative sites of strategic rethinking. In his spatial analysis of literary modernism, Andrew Thacker (2009) asserts, "The concept of heterotopia [thus] represents a fluid sense of social space and the processes to which space is subject . . . It is, therefore, a concept which connects material and metaphorical spaces in the literary text in new and illuminating ways" (29). Furthering his observation, I suggest that the spaces within the literary text can also extend well beyond it, to impact the spaces of readers, and vice versa, becoming a way of generating collaborative reading and thinking "otherwise."

For example, Virginia Woolf's *Three Guineas*, a book-length essay written in response to the pandemonium of the Spanish Civil War, offers surprising currency for our post-truth occasion. Woolf constructs a textual heterotopia that connects the brutality of fascism and authoritarianism—not only in Germany, Italy, and Spain, but also in her native England—with the "tyrannies and servilities" of the British patriarchal home (Woolf [1938] 2006, 168). Controversial at the time and denigrated by her closest friends as too shrill, Woolf indicted the educational system that by and large excluded women and cultivated young men into the vested institutional capitalist interests that led to war, linking it to women's exclusion from the professions, where their participation might challenge the hierarchical power structure. Women should refuse to join the procession of educated, professional men, Woolf's narrator asserts, instead forming a dispersed "Outsiders' Society" to reorder social values and break the stranglehold forged by the institutions that structure daily life—the church, the government, the universities—through power, money, and violence at home and abroad (126). Connecting photographs sent by the Spanish government depicting "dead bodies and ruined houses" (14), which are described but not reproduced in her text, with photographs she did include—of contemporary Englishmen in positions of power wearing full institutional regalia (e.g., the archbishop of Canterbury, the chancellor of Cambridge)—Woolf combines word and image to level a devastating critique of Western civilization while refusing the move of propaganda, a key form for the subversion of truth in her day. Woolf's narrator invites the reader into the fraught spaces of devastation to mourn civilians targeted in a totalitarian war, but not to succumb to propagandistic emotion; rather she calls on "educated men's daughters" to work independently, as collaborative outsiders, to change the conditions of everyday Western life that inspire people to value greed and promote it through violence.

Woolf's "Outsiders' Society" offers a vision of heterotopic collectivity to imagine a world (however limited its class and racial horizon may be) in which education's links to capitalist accumulation and competition—and thus to war-making abroad, as well as violence cloistered within the patriarchal home—are broken, not in some utopian future but in the present reality. Woolf's heterotopic resistance echoes across subsequent decades to inspire—or rather, to conspire with—contemporary theorists who are likewise angry and who equally refuse to normalize oppression, from Audre Lorde to Sara Ahmed and Bonnie Honig (among so many others). Outsiders are angry ("Hatred is the fury of those who do not share our goals, and its object is death and destruction. Anger is a grief of distortions between peers, and its object is change" [Lorde (1984) 1993, 129]); outsiders are killjoys; outsiders refuse to pretend that pandemonium is an acceptable status quo. Their collective, multi-sited rewriting of the discursive systems that maintain white supremacy, patriarchy, capitalism, and violence—including unmasking heteronormative, homogeneous feminism's complicity with such systems ("if feminism is a bubble, we need the bubble to burst" [Ahmed 2017, 259])—creates generative and contestatory heterotopic spaces through which language is reinvented to address the interlocking oppressions of their day; but also, and especially, they offer rhetorical and theoretical strategies that can renew our thinking and determination to change contemporary post-truth reality.

Audre Lorde's compelling articulation of the ways in which anger—"loaded with information and energy" (Lorde [1984] 1993, 127)—can be strategic in its truth-telling function is vital for us to reread in today's post-truth moment. By calling out the universalist utopianism of white, heteronormative feminists that erased "difference" and disparaged Black women's anger, Lorde utilizes anger to generate a heterotopic space within academic feminism that was necessary at the time for reimagining genuinely feminist, anti-racist coalition-building. Writing from a collective perspective of "sisters, outsiders," Lorde asserts, "We are not here as women examining racism in a political and social vacuum. We operate in the teeth of a system for which racism and sexism are primary, established, and necessary props of profit" (128). Lorde continues: "Any discussion among women about racism must include the recognition and the use of anger. This discussion must be direct and creative because it is crucial. We cannot allow our fear of anger to deflect us nor seduce us into settling for anything less than the hard work of excavating honesty" (128). Such honesty is crucial for sustaining contestation of the status quo and the traditional hierarchies of power it attempts to maintain; in our post-truth moment, Lorde's call for honesty is constitutive for the process of "making knowledge" in new forms, as Raewyn Connell advocates. These newly made spaces of knowledge bridge theorizing and imagination, social media and street protest, the classroom and the conference room, the legislature and the courtroom, drawing on the honesty and the anger manifested by the day-to-day work of living "in the teeth" of oppressive systems.

Like Lorde, Sara Ahmed recognizes the importance of "excavating honesty" in her call for rethinking feminist survival in the midst of pandemonium. The brilliant, mobile (heterotopic) tactic of collaboratively drafting a manifesto—which "not only causes a disturbance, it aims to cause this disturbance" (Ahmed 2017, 252)—introduces the feminist killjoy, harbinger of productive, engaging disruption. "To make something manifest can be enough to cause a disturbance. This intimacy between manifestation and disturbance has implications for how we write a killjoy manifesto," Ahmed asserts. "A killjoy manifesto must be grounded in an account of what exists" (252): it must be truthful, even angry, but most of all, it is located in the present, not gesturing toward some future utopian moment. Ahmed's manifesto actively resists and refuses the sham, constructed memory, history, happiness, and inclusion that are necessary to manufacture the smooth utopian surface of a post-truth reality. The killjoy manifesto calls "sisters, outsiders" to enact heterotopic textual and institutional spaces in "a pragmatic contestation, one that takes seriously the reality of collapsing realities" (Koekoek and Zakin 2023, 131) by suggesting that refusal to participate in the oppressive status quo (like Woolf's narrator's refusal to join the procession of educated men) opens further heterotopic spaces for reimagining a more just world and living within that world in the present: "A [killjoy survival] kit can be a container for activities that are ongoing; projects that are projects insofar as they have yet to be realized" (Ahmed 2017, 249).

Bonnie Honig's (2021) brilliant use of Euripides's *The Bacchae* confronts pandemonium dramatically and strategically. Invoking an ancient tragedy that features frenzied dancing maenads worshipping the "outsider" Dionysus on the slopes of Mt. Cithaeron to suggest creative possibilities for contemporary feminist refusal offers readers a literary heterotopia steeped in political resonance. For these women aren't merely dancing outside the city gates: "Fearlessly, they defy orders and abandon the instruments of work, the loom and shuttle.... They establish a heterotopia where they can practice another way of living" (22). They suckle animals instead of children; they find pleasure in each other's company rather than conforming to their cloistered domestic roles. Honig observes that, "away from patriarchy's sex-gender enclosures, the women experience leisure and pleasure in new, intensified ways that alter their experience of space and time" (7). Ultimately, the women tear to pieces the "animal" who comes spying on them, disguised in women's clothing—but who is actually Pentheus, the king himself (seeking to know the "truth" of what happens in this forbidden heterotopic space). Agave, his mother, leads the destruction, not recognizing her son, thinking in her frenzy that she has the head of a lion—symbolic of kingship—in her bloody hands. As Honig writes,

> women like the bacchants, who rise in rebellion against a king, are remembered as drunk or mad and therefore worthless, even while men's political action in concert is celebrated as its own kind of intoxication and their ensuing deaths or exiles are commemorated as glorious: poignant, tragic, honorable, and worthy.... The bacchants claim glory just like men had done before... but demanding glory they also claim the right to the city, and that is a claim to political power. (103)

Honig reimagines heterotopic spaces (like Cithaeron) as sites of "rehearsal," for learning how to refuse prescribed positions within oppressive hierarchical systems offered as the only spaces available for inhabiting the city (here, Thebes): "The risk of the return to the city is absorption into the city's conflicts and the loss of our bearings. It is against that that we rehearse" (Honig 2021, 103). (Re)claiming political power in the midst of pandemonium means maintaining contestation of the discursive systems that oppress, limit, and erase; it means understanding refusal "as an arc and not an act." The arc of refusal, "not teleological but phenomenological" (Honig 2021, 103), suggests that there are multiple ways of inhabiting the city, of affirming "a plural world" (Koekoek and Zakin 2023), of living "in the teeth" of oppression (Lorde), of refusing to join traditional processions (Woolf).

Honig's deep engagement with ancient Greek tragedy here and elsewhere as a strategic component of her feminist political theorizing creates forms of new knowledge and forges new scholarly connections: this is a heterotopic interdisciplinarity offering creative, powerful articulations of contemporary problems, that is historical but also resists linear narratives of utopian progress. I take Honig's reading of *The Bacchae* as an apt analogy, not only literary and metaphorical but political and rhetorical, for what it means to occupy the often fragile and unstable interdisciplinary, heterotopic spaces of WGSS and ethnic studies programs today, within an institutional setting that is rapidly shifting as a result of its own internal contradictions while also sustaining the assaults of post-truth (and neoliberal) politics. If such programs are akin to our Mt. Cithaeron, we must still return to the volatile institutional version of Thebes and navigate its entanglements.

Pausing Pandemonium

Koekoek and Zakin (2023) outline another way to think through this dilemma: "Our gambit is that effective rejoinders to post-truth can be found in practices that affirm rather than repudiate a plural world. By embracing the rich, textured, contingent, and unexpected sense of reality, we can stay on the side of the fragile and the democratic" (130). Strengthening existing coalitions and providing opportunities for new ones to emerge proliferates possibilities for inhabiting both the institution and democracy differently: for example, redoubling efforts to expand voting rights and hold elected officials accountable, especially for those groups who have the least access to political organizations, and urging media to cover national politics as well as communities, including local government and school board elections, more honestly and equitably (emphasizing "not the odds, but the stakes for democracy," as Jay Rosen has urged [2023]).[9]

Within the university, WGSS and ethnic studies might forge new curricular coalitions with other interdisciplinary programs such as environmental studies, public health and medical humanities, criminal justice and journalism programs, and information sciences, to increase visibility and support for interdisciplinary studies generally but also demonstrate the limits of disciplinary knowledge in addressing social problems requiring complex solutions. Strengthening coalitions with disciplinary teacher-preparation programs—schools and libraries as well as nonprofits dedicated to literacy and free speech, such as PEN America—can combat the current educational pandemonium focused on book-banning and transgender disinformation by groups embracing post-truth such as Moms for Liberty.[10] Renewing our sense of shared investment in, and reimagining the connections between, the institution and the community can in turn reshape pedagogical methods, as Hale suggests, and contribute to making new knowledge, as Connell recommends. Emphasizing the heterotopic connections between curricular aims and co-curricular experiences can help students discover, articulate, and practice their values through strategic coalition-building while recognizing the distortions and disorder running rampant in post-truth politics and social media. Young people are already challenging post-truth pandemonium, as their participation and leadership in the many collaborative movements of the past decade—from #MeToo and #BlackLivesMatter to March for Our Lives; climate activist organizations such as Sunrise Movement; and Indigenous movements for water rights and #LandBack, to name only the most visible in the U.S.—significantly demonstrates. If our programs are to remain relevant to them and to the wider public, we must ensure that our professional investment in institutional stability resists complicity with institutional practices that run counter to our values, maintaining a sense of contestation of the status quo, "embracing the rich, textured, contingent, and unexpected sense of reality" to "stay on the side of the fragile and the democratic" (Koekoek and Zakin 2023).

Confronting post-truth pandemonium presents an immense challenge; as we bear each other's grief collectively, we can find temporary solace in counting small victories along the way. Two personal events that renewed my spirits while I was drafting this essay confirm the importance of heterotopic spaces for thinking and creating in concert:

— A former student, now in medical school, texted me out of the blue in response to Florida's assault on intersectionality and other curricula (used with permission): "This is just commentary because I think you're the only person I know personally who actively reads Woolf and would get this, but my god, 'Three Guineas' feels more and more relevant these days, especially 'on what terms shall we join that procession?' Especially w/ academia/medicine and active exclusion + oppression by complicity."

— My state university colleagues and I received word in March 2023 that the New York State Department of Education had formally approved our proposal for a new, standalone interdisciplinary major in ethnic and gender studies, the latest iteration of a program that has evolved, via a long process of collaborative work across two decades, from a minor in women's studies and various ethnic studies minors. The program launches this fall, though in the midst of substantive budget constraints.

Pandemonium seems to generate its own momentum for daily mayhem, but such pauses, however brief, that acknowledge how past work can usefully inform responses to the present and help transform opportunities for building new coalitions, feel restorative. Heterotopias undermine linear narratives of progress that delude us into complacency; they operate on the necessity of continual critique of the status quo. But the hard work required shouldn't prevent us from celebrating the many moments of change that can ensue from such dynamic thinking and creative action.

Jeanette McVicker is professor of English and coordinator of the Ethnic and Gender Studies program at the State University of New York at Fredonia. She has published extensively on Virginia Woolf, including an essay on Woolfian ethics forthcoming in the selected papers from the 2022 annual Woolf conference and an essay on Woolf, archaeology, and prehistory in *Woolf Studies Annual* 28 (2022). In addition to Woolf and modernism studies, McVicker's recent work has appeared in *boundary 2*, *Postcolonial Studies*, and *Philosophy Today*. She can be reached at mcvicker@fredonia.edu.

Acknowledgments

The author sincerely thanks the anonymous reviewers and the editors for their generous, helpful comments, and my friend and colleague Natalie Gerber for her thoughtful editing suggestions.

Notes

1. Kenway (2022) brilliantly identifies one of the drivers of "post-truth" politics and media as "truth parasites" who "have a corrosive relationship to

truth. They eat away at it, drain it of meaning and of moral integrity. They deplete the broad notion of truth and gain strength from doing so" (24). I cite Woolf (1938) 2006, Lorde (1984) 1993, Ahmed 2017, and Honig 2021 as offering examples of compelling literary or textual heterotopic strategies.
2. See, for example, the European Center on Populist Studies explainer on global forms of post-truth politics, and the Political Studies Association's summary of a 2017 conference detailing its global reach. Attacks on science-based government policies and spokespeople during the COVID-19 pandemic made clear the lethal stakes of post-truth discourse and politics in the arena of public health. Climate denialism is yet another example of the global stakes of post-truth disinformation and attacks on scientific knowledge. The murder of George Floyd, an unarmed Black Minnesota resident, by Minneapolis police, captured on video by Darnella Frazier, a Black teen bystander, inspired massive, multiracial protests across the U.S. and globally despite pandemic lockdowns, fueling a post-truth disinformation backlash. Post-truth disinformation was also at the heart of the January 6, 2021, insurrection, based on the lie that the 2020 U.S. presidential election was fraudulent.
3. "Woke," a term deriving from U.S. Black culture, dates back to the era of legal segregation known as Jim Crow. To "stay woke" meant being alert to social injustice and the dangers that accompanied being Black under legal, systemic racism. The term remains a rallying cry in the era of Black Lives Matter. But the term has been co-opted by right-wing politicians and media, led by Florida Governor Ron DeSantis, whose Republican-majority legislature approved a new law (the Stop Wrongs to Our Kids and Employees Act) in 2022 that severely restricts how schools and workplaces can discuss curricula and issue policy related to race, sex, and gender discrimination. Florida's law has become a model for many other states passing similar legislation, and "anti-woke" has become a prominent buzzword in the 2024 presidential election among Republican candidates, who invariably have difficulty defining exactly what they mean by it.

NWSA's "Statement about the Anti-Woke Agenda and Legislative Actions" (2023) reads in part: "We will never request the master's tools to dismantle his house; instead, we will shape and craft our own tools to burn it down so that something better can be created." A remarkable sentence that overtly invokes Audre Lorde's iconic essay and, at least implicitly, Woolf's *Three Guineas*: "Take this guinea and with it burn the college to the ground. Set fire to the old hypocrisies. Let the light of the burning building scare the nightingales and incarnadine the willows. And let the daughters of educated men dance round the fire and heap armful upon armful of dead

leaves upon the flames. And let their mothers lean from the upper windows and cry, 'let it blaze! Let it blaze! For we have done with this "education!"'" (Woolf [1938] 2006, 45).
4. Foucault articulated the idea of heterotopias in a 1967 lecture to the Architectural Studies Circle, not published until 1984 ("Different Spaces"). He also invoked the concept of textual heterotopias in the preface to *The Order of Things: An Archaeology of the Human Sciences* (orig. 1966). Theorists in fields as diverse as modernism studies, architecture studies, and globalization studies have utilized this concept in intriguing ways in the past decade.
5. See Gecker 2023 on the takeover of New College of Florida, a liberal arts honors college in the state university system, and NWSA's 2022 solidarity statement.
6. SUNY's Core Curricula was a joint project of the conservative National Association of Scholars and the Empire Foundation for Social Research. See especially Spanos 1993 for a more comprehensive analysis of "reform" movements in U.S. education and their roots in Roman imperialism.
7. See, for example, Spanos 1993, Spivak 1993, hooks 1994, Readings 1996, Wiegman 2002, and Zelizer 2011.
8. See Nikolchina 2012, who invokes heterotopia in rethinking the role of the seminar outside the formal university and its relation to the political revolution in the former Czechoslovakia, and Higgins and Leps 2022, who consider "heterotopic world fiction" as a rich interdisciplinary counter to biopolitics.
9. Media theorist and NYU journalism professor Jay Rosen has criticized the "horserace" tendencies of U.S. mainstream news media election coverage for many years. He stated his admonition for the 2024 election on Twitter (March 7, 2023): "That's my shorthand for the organizing principle we most need in journalists covering the 2024 campaign. Not who has what chances of winning, but the consequences for American democracy. Not the odds, but the stakes." See his *PressThink* blog for more extensive commentary (Rosen 2023).
10. PEN America is a century-old nonprofit, nonpartisan organization that advocates for writers, libraries, and access to literacy worldwide. The organization is in the forefront of defending libraries and writers against the post-truth onslaught of recent efforts to ban books, particularly those for adolescents, dealing with race, gender, and sexuality. See PEN America, n.d., for more information. Moms for Liberty is a perfect example of post-truth in action: ostensibly begun as a grassroots organization (in Florida) asserting "parental rights" in the midst of COVID-19 school restrictions, it is funded by national right-wing donors and has been labeled an extremist

group (by the Southern Poverty Law Center) for its affiliations with white supremacist organizations and anti-LGBTQ rhetoric in its efforts to take over school boards and initiate book challenges in schools and public libraries across the U.S.

Works Cited

Ahmed, Sara. 2017. *Living a Feminist Life*. Durham, NC: Duke University Press.

American Historical Association. 2021. "Joint Statement on Legislative Efforts to Restrict Education about Racism in American History." June 2021. https://www.historians.org/divisive-concepts-statement.

Aromeeva, Elena, Mirjam Liebroer, and Darren Lilleker. 2017. "Post-truth: Its Meanings and Implications for Democracy." *Political Studies Association* (blog), July 17, 2017. https://www.psa.ac.uk/psa/news/post-truth-its-meaning-and-implicationsdemocracy.

Burke, Penny Jane, Julia Coffey, Rosalind Gill, and Akane Kanai. 2022. "Troubling Post-truth Populism: Feminist Interventions." In *Gender in an Era of Post-truth Populism: Pedagogies, Challenges and Strategies*, edited by Penny Jane Burke, Julia Coffey, Rosalind Gill, and Akane Kanai, 1–20. New York: Bloomsbury Academic.

Connell, Raewyn. 2022. "Truth, Power, Pedagogy: Feminist Knowledge and Education in a 'Post-truth' Time." In *Gender in an Era of Post-truth Populism: Pedagogies, Challenges and Strategies*, edited by Penny Jane Burke, Julia Coffey, Rosalind Gill, and Akane Kanai, 65–78. New York: Bloomsbury Academic.

European Center for Populism Studies. 2018. "Post-truth Politics." https://www.populismstudies.org/Vocabulary/post-truth-politics/.

Foucault, Michel. (1966) 1973. *The Order of Things: An Archaeology of the Human Sciences*. New York: Vintage.

———. (1967) 1998. "Different Spaces." Translated by Robert Hurley. In *Essential Works of Foucault, 1954–1984*, edited by Paul Rabinow. Vol. 2, *Aesthetics, Method, and Epistemology*, edited by James D. Faubion, 175–85. New York: New Press.

Gecker, Jocelyn. 2023. "A College in Upheaval: War on 'Woke' Sparks Fear in Florida." Associated Press. March 31, 2023. https://apnews.com/article/ron-desantis-new-college-florida-woke-15d61ab52724dc447ba6d03238f7719e.

Grewel, Inderpal, and Caren Kaplan. 1994. *Scattered Hegemonies: Postmodernity and Transnational Feminist Practices*. Minneapolis: University of Minnesota Press.

Hale, Sondra. 2022. "Something Resembling 'Truth': Reflections on Critical Pedagogy in the New 'Post-truth' Landscape." In *Gender in an Era of Post-truth Populism: Pedagogies, Challenges and Strategies*, edited by Penny Jane Burke, Julia Coffey, Rosalind Gill, and Akane Kanai, 79–96. New York: Bloomsbury Academic.

Higgins, Lesley, and Marie-Christine Leps. 2022. *Heterotopic World Fiction: Thinking beyond Biopolitics with Woolf, Foucault, Ondaatje*. Boston, MA: Academic Studies Press.

Honig, Bonnie. 2021. *A Feminist Theory of Refusal*. Cambridge, MA: Harvard University Press.

hooks, bell. 1994. *Teaching to Transgress: Education as the Practice of Freedom*. New York: Routledge.

Kenway, Jane. 2022. "Truth Parasites, Right Wing Fury and the Predicaments of Feminist Expertise." In *Gender in an Era of Post-truth Populism: Pedagogies, Challenges and Strategies*, edited by Penny Jane Burke, Julia Coffey, Rosalind Gill, and Akane Kanai, 21–42. New York: Bloomsbury Academic.

Koekoek, Catherine, and Emily Zakin, eds. 2023. "Feminist Takes on Post-truth." *Philosophy and Social Criticism* 49, no. 2 (February): 125–38. https://journals.sagepub.com/doi/10.1177/01914537231152779#bibr23-01914537231152779.

Lorde, Audre. (1984) 1993. "The Uses of Anger: Women Responding to Racism." In *Sister, Outsider: Essays and Speeches*, 124–33. New York: Quality Paperback Books.

Mazzei, Patricia, and Anemona Hartocollis. 2023. "Florida Rejects AP American Studies Course." *New York Times*, January 19, 2023. https://www.nytimes.com/2023/01/19/us/desantis-florida-ap-african-american-studies.html.

McIntyre, Lee. 2018. *Post-truth*. Cambridge, MA: MIT Press.

McVicker, Jeanette. 2002. "The Politics of 'Excellence.'" In *Women's Studies on Its Own*, edited by Robyn Wiegman, 233–42. Durham, NC: Duke University Press.

National Women's Studies Association. 2022. "Presidential Statement: NWSA Stands with Our Colleagues at New College of Florida." January 2022. https://mailchi.mp/nwsa/nwsa-stands-in-solidarity-with-our-colleagues-at-the-new-college-of-florida.

———. 2022. "Presidential Statement on Threats to the Field in Higher Education and Beyond." March 2022. https://mailchi.mp/nwsa/nwsa-statement-on-threats-to-the-field-in-higher-education-and-beyond.

———. 2023. "Presidential Statement about the Anti-woke Agenda and Legislative Actions." March 2023. https://mailchi.mp/nwsa/nwsa-statement-about-the-anti-woke-agenda-and-legislative-actions.

Nikolchina, Miglena. 2012. *Lost Unicorns of the Velvet Revolutions: Heterotopias of the Seminar*. New York: Fordham University Press.
PEN America. n.d. "About Us." Accessed January 12, 2024. https://pen.org/about-us/.
Readings, Bill. 1996. *The University in Ruins*. Cambridge, MA: Harvard University Press.
Rosen, Jay. 2023. *PressThink* (blog). https://pressthink.org/.
Spanos, William V. 1993. *The End of Education: Toward Posthumanism*. Minneapolis: University of Minnesota Press.
Spivak, Gayatri Chakravorty. 1993. *Outside in the Teaching Machine*. New York: Routledge.
Thacker, Andrew. 2009. *Moving through Modernity: Space and Geography in Modernism*. Manchester: Manchester University Press.
Wiegman, Robyn, ed. 2002. *Women's Studies on Its Own*. Durham, NC: Duke University Press.
Woolf, Virginia. (1938) 2006. *Three Guineas*. Annotated with an introduction by Jane Marcus. Edited by Mark Hussey. New York: Harcourt.
Zelizer, Barbie, ed. 2011. *Making the University Matter*. New York: Routledge.

(Re)purposing, not "Rightsizing": Responding to Recent Attacks on Gender, Women's, and Sexuality Studies in the U.S. Academy

Judy Rohrer

Abstract: No one wants to be "rightsized," particularly not feminists, and especially not feminists in gender, women's, and sexuality studies programs and departments (GWSS). Yet that's one of the multiple threats we are now facing, and it is both internal and external. These attacks on GWSS and our cousins are not new, but both the university administrators and the politicos are taking advantage of the current pandemonium to ramp up their ferocity. As a GWSS director of one of the many programs under threat, what I offer is not a right-eous-resistance-to-right-sizing manifesto but a tentative gesture at possible GWSS (re)purposings. I put these rightsizing threats in context of pandemic-inspired calls for radical transformation rather than returns to normalcy. This is not a nostalgic plea for saving something familiar (perhaps a proper object called GWSS, perhaps ourselves as "what a feminist looks like"), nor the staging of a rescue mission into enemy territory (as if we weren't also complicit and always already on stolen land in the imperial university). Instead, I stretch toward an irreverent killjoy stance while exploring queer and trans joy and futurity, kin-making/revealing, and (re)purposing/redistribution as frameworks that open possibilities for other futures. **Keywords:** neoliberal, austerity, queer, kin, crip, decolonial, futurity

No one wants to be "rightsized," particularly not feminists, and especially not feminists in gender, women's, and sexuality studies (GWSS) programs and departments. We have been railing against the notion that there is a "right size" for at least half a century, long before the term entered the parlance of university bureaucrats as a useful gloss for austerity processes. Yet that's one of the multiple threats we are now facing, and, at least in the United States, the threat is both internal and external. The perception is that GWSS programs and departments have gotten too big for our britches, are taking up too much space and sucking up too many resources, and need to be cut down to size.

Neoliberal university executives want to rightsize us back into the closet (often through the slow death of attrition until we are just a pile of bones in the darkest corner; some of us have already commenced the haunting from the "no there" that is there). Or the rightsizing comes by way of smashing us into a veritable rainbow ghetto with ethnic studies and other troublemaker programs that do not measure up to corporatized metrics—in this way our literal footprint is calibrated to our lack of "productivity" (Tuck 2018, 157). In many cases, we do not produce enough SCH (student credit hours) or majors, given our FTEs (full-time equivalency for faculty), thus making us too expensive to yield a good ROI (return on investment). Right-wing politicians want to "Right-size" us out of existence altogether (as I write, Florida is considering a bill banning gender studies). Our right size, in their eyes, is no size at all. So they Right-eously defund, eliminate, and ban us, our curriculum, our books, and our programs.

Attacks on GWSS and our cousins are not new, but both university administrators and politicians are taking advantage of the current pandemonium to ramp up their ferocity. The current chaos exists on multiple scales, including the COVID-19 pandemic, economic roller coaster, racial justice uprisings and white supremacist backlash, attacks on democracy, and student population demographic shifts, as well as the existential global threats of war and climate catastrophe. For those in the GWSS trenches, I am not telling you anything you do not already know. And this is not a right-eous-resistance-to-rightsizing. It is trying to be a tentative gesture at possible GWSS (re)purposings.

I am answering the call to document and reflect on recent experiences by sharing what I can from my precarious perch as director of a once strong GWSS program that's now struggling to survive. In keeping with that call, I offer more observation and aspiration than analytical argument or specific prescriptions. This is not a nostalgic plea for saving something familiar (perhaps a proper object called GWSS, perhaps ourselves as "what a feminist looks like"), not the staging of a rescue mission into enemy territory (as if we weren't also complicit and always already on stolen land in the imperial university). We are not "perfect just the way we are." I suggest that rather than simply resisting rightsizing, we pause and (re)evaluate ourselves as scholar-activists, and our programs and departments as connected to intersectional social movements.

I begin in this paper with moves toward rightsizing GWSS (cutting or otherwise diminishing faculty, staff, budgets, resources, space, autonomy) and offer a case study from my institution. I put this in the context of pandemic-inspired calls for radical transformation rather than returns to normalcy. I build on this, ending with an exploration of queer and trans joy and futurity, kin-making/revealing, and (re)purposing and redistribution as frameworks that open possibilities for other futures.

There is robust scholarship on the impacts of the neoliberal turn in higher ed on interdisciplinary fields including GWSS (Brown 2015; Ferguson 2012; Melamed 2011; Mitchell 2016). This includes a strong critique of the ways those of us in GWSS have participated in the field's domestication and depoliticization. The COVID-19 pandemic came in the wake of this professionalization, as well as decades of disinvestment in public higher ed, including adjunctification, raising tuition, subsidizing athletics, state legislatures starving public institutions for resources, and eroding foundations of shared governance and tenure. Since 2020, these tactics have increased in quantity, and administrations have undertaken even more draconian measures, like program closures, drastic consolidations, mass layoffs, mergers, and financial exigency.

"Rightsizing" GWSS: Institutional Case Study

I work in one of the nation's many regional universities increasingly losing enrollment while state flagships grow in size and stature (Gardner 2023). When I started in 2018 as director of what was then a Women's and Gender Studies program (now Gender, Women's, and Sexuality Studies), there were 3.5 faculty lines and 2 full-time staff, one of whom ran the equivalent of the university's gender equity or women's center. The skeletal program now has 2.25 faculty and no staff, due to early retirement, resignation, and workload reduction catalyzed by the pandemic, all of which is exacerbated by an already existing institutional financial and leadership crisis. Administration has slow-rolled our staff-replacement requests via delays and by offering hires at far lower rank, qualification, and FTE than required. (Killjoy truth: "doors can be shut by appearing to be open" [Ahmed 2023]). They are now gaslighting us by claiming we are being unreasonable and failing our students by not accepting their positions as offered.

Faculty hires are out of the question given our lack of SCH, corporate sponsorships, or external grants. It does not matter that we offer the only sexuality and queer studies minor in the region and that it is increasingly popular with students (from parents of LGBTQ+ kids, to straight therapists, to all varieties of queer folx). It does not matter that our programming was intentionally intersectional and community-facing. It does not matter that two neighboring states have not only banned abortion but also any classroom discussion of abortion, as well as anti-racism and other "divisive" subjects. It does not matter that the U-Haul full of Proud Boys planning to attack a Pride parade in 2022 was apprehended in a town an hour from our campus. It does not matter that one of the early assaults on Drag Queen Story Hour happened in our city in 2021, or that we responded. Because these things do not register for university leadership, GWSS is not understood as a necessary, valuable resource not just for the university but for the community and region.

Our new university president is imposing an aggressive austerity process labeled "Strategic Resource Allocation (SRA)" to "rightsize" the institution. This particular tool dates back to a book published in 1999 (apparently "innovation" is a buzzword applied just to faculty). We are told SRA "entails a systematic, collaborative, and transparent process to examine the ways our resources are being invested" (Eastern Washington University 2023). We know it requires faculty and staff to form circular firing squads by volunteering for SRA task forces. These task forces are charged with sorting all university units (in equal distributions) into five categories, three of which indicate increasingly dire levels of underperformance. In the end, 20 percent of the university will be labeled as barely passing, and another 40 percent will fail the test. And even if the task forces find ways to mitigate harm, their reports are by design mere recommendations, with the ultimate decision-making power residing in administration and the board of trustees. This, at the same time as we have campus-wide surveys documenting plummeting morale and lack of confidence in leadership.

And it turns out the SRA process is paradigmatic of how the neoliberal university reproduces itself right under our noses. A five-minute Google search revealed that our previous university president, who resigned in 2020 after a faculty vote of no confidence, had failed forward to us after a prior vote of no confidence at a university where she had imposed an SRA process. History repeats.

The SRA process is just one strategy currently being deployed by university presidents and boards looking to further corporatize, justifying the cuts they envision, not just in personnel and programming but, critically, also in faculty governance. A 2021 American Association of University Professors report entitled "COVID-19 and Faculty Governance" shares findings from an investigation of "opportunistic exploitations of catastrophic events" (read: academic disaster capitalism) taken in the wake of the pandemic. In a particularly pertinent passage, it states: "Faculty members at the investigated institutions faced the dilemma of either participating in ad hoc governance processes they knew to be flawed in the hope of shaping their outcomes or refusing on principle to participate at all, thereby allowing administrators and board members to move forward without them" (American Association of University Professors 2021). What's a feminist killjoy to do?

Rightsizing our university means eliminating "redundancies" across academic affairs, student affairs, and administration. Apparently, this entails centralizing "diversity" services, programming, curriculum, and spaces. For example, administration has suggested consolidating (excess) lounge spaces for marginalized students. We seem to have a problem, not of institutional racism and settler colonialism, but of too much diversity in too many institutional spaces and across too many budgets. Who knew?

In an early email touting the SRA process, our president insisted the pinnacle of university pride should be "graduating students with marketable degrees who will power the workforce of our state and region." Then, in an op-ed, she schooled, "strategic resource allocation has long been a norm within business organizations"; pointed to "right-sizing" decisions at Microsoft, Amazon, and Netflix; and declared, "It's time for higher education to take cues from industry visionaries" (McMahan 2023). Regardless of what we feminist killjoys do or don't do, I fear GWSS's days at my institution are numbered.

Current Academic-Activist Context

What is happening to our GWSS program is not an anomaly. I read the higher ed journals, talk to colleagues nationwide, sign the solidarity statements, and attend the National Women's Studies Association conferences. Here is some of what I have heard: We lack control over the narrative about our value; we lack data of all sorts, including that which would demonstrate our value (caveat: some have evidence, but it doesn't fit corporatized rubrics); we are not well organized; Republican state politicians increasingly have us in their crosshairs; staying quiet hasn't saved us; and faculty are exhausted, quiet-quitting, leaving. Administrators are adopting increasingly impoverishing and anti-intellectual methods to create "efficiencies":

hiring "expert" consultants to recommend cuts (see SRA process above); tying program funding to four-year graduation rates; penalizing students with "excess credit hours" outside their degrees; pushing "employability" and "career-ready" pathways (with barely veiled racism and classism), and cutting arts and humanities.

Referencing Audre Lorde, Sara Ahmed warns that "surviving the academy is *'not an academic skill'*" (Ahmed 2021, 301), and Lorgia García Peña says, "We cannot survive academia without accompaniment" (García Peña 2022, 47). This means we have to get over our atomized, egoist selves. We cannot study our way into singular mastery of survival techniques. There is nothing self-evident, nothing straight- (or even queer-)forward, about survival, nor is it a permanent stable state of being. Billy-Ray Belcourt suggests "'survival' itself is an eddying concept" (Belcourt 2020, 132), so we must find and hang on to each other in the eddies, knowing they (and we) are always only temporary. Or, as Lorde famously wrote, we who "love in the doorways coming and going . . . were never meant to survive" (Lorde 1978, 31–32).

Perhaps our response to these threats could be to pause, take stock, listen, look around, and then recalibrate and (re)purpose our disciplinary, programmatic, and individual visions to better contribute to transformative change. We might think of this as refusing rightsizing by (re)orienting ourselves to be in right-relation with our students, communities, and ourselves. We can step (further) into survival eddies, accompaniment, and camaraderie (not institutionally prescribed "civility" or "collegiality," which are part of what Ahmed describes as our "positive duty" [Ahmed 2021, 59–68]). And when necessary, we might root back into our multiple movement genealogies and cause "good trouble" by becoming subversives, co-conspirators, and accomplices within the institution (rather than self-declared liberal "allies" or anointed anemic DEI foot soldiers or officials).

Early in the pandemic, Arundhati Roy asked if we could use the pandemic as a portal—"a gateway between one world and the next" that we might "walk through lightly, with little luggage, ready to imagine another world. And ready to fight for it" (Roy 2020). Mid(?)-pandemic, Leanne Betasamosake Simpson wrote: "I suspect we are encountering, not just a single portal, but a kaleidoscope of portals spanning our most intimate lives, our communities, the broader terrain of struggle" (Maynard and Simpson 2022, 250). After George Floyd's murder, Alicia Garza asked, "Are we going to use this moment to tinker with what is or are we going to use this moment to transform toward what can be?" (African American Policy Forum 2020). Scholar-activists are grappling with these questions, aware of all the injustice revealed and produced in this moment.

As monuments to confederates and colonizers are toppled by the power of the people, decolonial, anti-capitalist, abolitionist narratives and methodologies are taking hold in popular discourse: defunding police, rent strikes, debt cancellation, reparations, free college, universal healthcare. As feminist educators, we can help keep them there. Activists, organizers, and advocates are using emergent technologies to collaborate and globalize social movements and campaigns. They are connecting not just across time zones and territories, but also increasingly intergenerationally and intersectionally.

As feminist educators, we can lift up examples of transformative work being done by community organizations and activists. We can remind everyone that backlash is to be expected when the people exercise their power. Our pedagogies and practices can hold space, encourage engagement, and model access, caring, and commitment. An example of this is the September 2022 "Masking and Community Values in Gender and Women's Studies" statement by UC Berkeley's Department of Gender and Women's Studies. The statement begins:

> In light of our campus administration's policy-making masking an individual decision on our campus—we, as a feminist community, want to offer a counter-practice grounded in feminist ethics of care, disability justice, mutual accountability, and the notion of collective access. We believe that health is more than an individual choice; we understand it as part of a larger ecology of care and responsibility towards each other and to our many communities. (Department of Gender and Women's Studies 2022)

The statement ends with a request for masking in departmental spaces and classrooms, as well as avoiding those spaces if COVID-positive or recently exposed. These precautions are known to be effective when infection rates are high, which they were in the fall of 2022. Following the UCB model and the mantra "we keep us safe," when institutions refuse to adopt and maintain public health protocols, we need to be ready to step in.

Garza and others are clear about who has been doing the ongoing work of keeping us safe and getting us all free—women and QTBIPOC activists. Moving in the direction of radical transformation, not tinkering with the status quo, necessarily means centering those most impacted and finding ways to support them, to be in right-relation. It means (re)grounding ourselves in a feminist, anti-racist, decolonial analysis and praxis. That will look different depending on our context, but some guiding frames might include: (1) queer and trans joy and futurity, (2) kin-making/revealing, and (3) (re)purposing and/or redistribution (or stealing back).

Queer and Trans Joy and Futurity

> My concern is not with being included in Native Studies—as if being included was all that we wanted—but with epistemologies that build worlds that can't hold all of us.
> —Billy-Ray Belcourt, "Can the Other of Native Studies Speak?"

We are witnessing a horrifying assault on queer and trans lives, particularly youth, particularly BIPOC: escalations of state, interpersonal, and organized violence; criminalizing and stigmatizing of trans healthcare; athletic bans; hateful rhetoric; political scapegoating; model anti-LGBTQ legislation; and censorship. GWSS can educate and advocate—galvanizing opposition to all these anti-queer and anti-trans attacks. This is happening, but not enough, and in some spaces we have allowed people claiming feminism to undercut queer and trans lives. This is not always as extreme as trans-exclusionary radical feminist (TERF) or Christian right attacks shielded behind distorted notions of "free speech." Cisgenderism has also shown up in the post-*Dobbs* resistance to using "pregnant people" terminology in fights for reproductive justice.

I know I have become comfortable in my advocacy for all-gender bathrooms, ally trainings, LGBTQ housing options, normalization of gender pronouns, personal identification as an old-school genderqueer lesbian in classrooms and committees, and other now quotidian queerings. While these institutional interventions may help create more base-level queer and trans inclusion ("as if being included was all that we wanted"), they are not sufficient to the necessary embrace of queer and trans joy and futurity.

And we need to attend to our curriculum. We need "to ask about the silences even if we do not yet know how to fill them. To notice the absences and the omission" (García Peña 2022, 90). I have allowed the queer disabled scholars on a syllabus to all be white. In the epigraph above, Belcourt is speaking about Native studies, but adherence to limited epistemological frames too small to "hold all of us" is a cross-disciplinary problem. Too often, trans tragedy and death (usually in the form of violence against trans women of color) enters my classroom way before trans joy and proceeds to occupy far too much space, blocking possibility not just for joy, but for the queer-trans futurity it generates.

Documenting damage and raising awareness are often based in unexamined theories of change that rely on colonial logics, because they locate "power and control outside of communities and require them to appeal to the logics of the state to get piecemeal gains" (Tuck 2018, 158). This critique dovetails with the way centering damage, deficit, harm, lack, risk, and victimization can lead to trauma and inspiration porn in the classroom and in our scholarship: "Queers who ride the advantageous waves of whiteness slide smoothly into the depths of the normative" (Belcourt 2020, 55). I have ridden that wave, delighted by my singularly fabulous skill, without considering what generated the wave or contemplating its course into "the depths of the normative." Regardless of institutional disincentive and our own desires toward (hegemonic or risk-free) radicalism, can we find ways to make structural space, beyond incremental and sporadic inclusion, for more queer and trans joy?

Scaling up, it is not an intersectional fail that caused Florida Governor Ron DeSantis, in his tirade against the proposed AP Black History course, to rant: "What's one of the lessons about? Queer theory. Now, who would say that an important part of Black history is queer theory? That is somebody pushing an agenda on our kids" (Bennett and Cuevas 2023). It is not just that "our kids" here are clearly not queer, and only occasionally Black. Rather, the right's "agenda" is adamantly anti-intersectional by design, because intersectional analysis produces knowledge about how power works to maintain systems of oppression. Kimberlé Crenshaw continuously emphasizes how intersectionality helps us think about identities and their relationships to power: "The better we understand how identities and power work together from one context to another, the less likely our movements for change are to fracture" (Crenshaw 2015).

Many who catalyzed mid-century struggles for Black liberation lived queer lives: Bayard Rustin, Lorraine Hansberry, James Baldwin, Langston Hughes, Pauli Murray, and more. DeSantis and the right do not want "our kids" to know this history, to say their names. And the Black freedom struggles these luminaries helped ignite inspired others. Roderick Ferguson, one of the queer Black scholars excised from the revised AP course curriculum, responds: "with large and notable contributions from Black LGBTQ+ people, Black freedom movements and the writings of progressive Black intellectuals have been major inspirations for many liberation struggles and cultural shifts" (Ferguson 2023). He cites Toni Morrison's metaphor of language as a midwife to illuminate how these attacks are intended to interrupt Black futurity, and all its relations known and yet to come. The attacks are meant to foreclose the possible futures opened by the language, histories, and politics of "Black power," "Black is Beautiful," "Power to the People," "Stay woke," "Black Lives Matter." Ferguson states, "Efforts by DeSantis and the College Board are designed to get rid of the midwife, prevent new types of knowledge, people, frameworks" (African American Policy Forum 2023).

Ferguson's book *The Reorder of Things: The University and Its Pedagogies of Minority Difference* was central to building the critique, referenced earlier, of the neoliberal erosion of higher ed and the way it has played out in the interdisciplines (Ferguson 2012). He and others are sounding the alarm bells and asking us to step up to stop the disavowals of CRT, to interrupt the "social reproduction of cowardice" (African American Policy Forum 2023). They remind us, an attack on one is an attack on all. I started this section with the recent assaults on queer and trans lives and am ending with the attack on Black studies, CRT, and intersectionality to emphasize my desire to be bolder in celebrating queer-trans joy so that I and we might participate in the midwifery of audacious, luminous futures. We want to be in the (birthing) room(s) where it happens.

Kin-Making/Revealing

> *Might I suggest you don't fuck with my sis*
> —Beyoncé, "Cozy," *Renaissance*

Beyoncé's album *Renaissance* bridges queer and trans joy and futurity, and kin-making/revealing, in its brilliant homage to Ballroom culture, ethics, and artistry. It is a reminder that Indigenous, Black, queer, and crip scholars, activists, and artists have been modeling practices for making and revealing kin for generations. These practices challenge narrow biological heteronormative notions of kin and suggest we interrogate ways our curriculum and programming reproduce reproductive futurity. These practices also ask that we recognize kin in our other-than-human relations. Those recognitions take us far beyond sensationalized cyborgs or stale obligatory land acknowledgments. They require understanding that "affiliative practices cannot be restricted to the reach of the 'human,' recognizing the queer possibilities of animacy and intimacy with other presences and entities" (Kafer 2019, 7).

Kin-making runs counter to institutionalized DEI practices in its refusal to perform representational window dressing. It disallows our categorization into neat identity boxes by messing up assumed boundaries, including anthropocentric exclusions of "animacy and intimacy with other presences and entities." Kim TallBear proposes "*making kin* as an alternative approach to liberal multiculturalism, for righting relations gone bad" (TallBear 2019, 37). Those "relations gone bad" include our abuse and disregard for the environment and other-than-human beings. TallBear instructs, "Recognizing possibilities of other kinds of intimacies—not focused on biological reproduction and making population, but caretaking precious kin that come to us in diverse ways—is an important step to unsettling settler sex and family" (TallBear 2018, 154).

In this way, kin-making can put us at odds with university administrators who cannot figure out how all these lives (and liveliness) can matter if they can't classify and count them. When we refuse to confine ourselves to tidy DEI grids or perform our assigned difference, we become unruly discontents—complainers instinctively knowing "survival can be a complaint" (Ahmed 2021, 301). We recognize that noncompliance with compulsory diversity performance and tokenism is necessary because "neoliberal aims of multiculturalism are an infrared example of dispossession through representation" (Patel 2021, 53).

Besides the ways this pursuit makes us disloyal daughters to the university, recognizing kin is hard, often uncomfortable, work. Alison Kafer asks, "How long does it take to foreclose on possibilities, to refuse connection, to deny relation? How do my failures to imagine others as crip restrict the coalitions to come?" (Kafer 2021, 416). We worry about appropriation, controlling the representational narrative, our ability to separate ourselves from less worthy others through claims to innocence. Kafer challenges us to think about how these fears and desires get in the way of kin-making/revealing.

Students have taught me about kin-making. They have demonstrated that, "like justice, kin is an assembling sort of word . . . Ancestors as well as contemporaries turn out to be a bumptious lot: kin are unfamiliar (outside what we thought was family or gens), uncanny, haunting, active" (Haraway 2018, 94). I have had white students in Kentucky willing to research their slave-holding ancestry and share it in class and with their families. When teaching in Texas after Obama's 2008 election, a Black student told a white student who was expressing thinly veiled anti-Obama racism, "Don't worry, he's got you." A Seneca student at Syracuse University expressed grief and anger at the loss of ten thousand acres of Allegany Territory, and therefore relations, to the flooding caused by the Army Corp's construction of the Kinzua Dam in the 1960s.

At the 2022 National Women's Studies Association conference, during a Pacific Islander panel where the room was continuously addressed as "relatives," Kirisitina (Kiri) Sailiata modeled and instructed: "We don't make relatives. We are revealed as relatives through our stories." The idea of being revealed as relatives is generative, if not always comfortable because of the violences it can surface. Susan Burch's study of the "Canton Asylum for Insane Indians" honors the way families, communities, tribes, and relatives remember those who were ensnared by Canton: "remembering nourishes relations, sometimes creating new ties, stories and futures. Ancestors past and emerging remember one another" (Burch 2021, 20). Burch describes this remembering as nonlinear, enabling kin-making/revealing in storied temporal eddies.

Refusal, Redistribution, Rematriation, (Re)purposing

Within the colonizing university also exists a decolonizing education.
—la paperson, "A Third University Is Possible"

Interdisciplinary scholar-activists have long recognized the university as colonial, dispossessing, and oppressive across all vectors of subjugation. They have developed various strategies of survival that include refusal, redistribution, rematriation, and (re)purposing. Since Stefano Harney and Fred Moten published *The Undercommons: Fugitive Planning and Black Study* in 2013, the idea that "one can only sneak into the university and steal what one can" (Harney and Moten 2013, 26) has grown legs, appearing in multiple spaces in and beyond the interdisciplines. The university is increasingly characterized as criminal, igniting strategies for stealing back what has been taken. The Undercommoning Collective writes: "The university has always been a thief, stealing people's labor, time and energy" (Undercommoning Collective 2016). Partly as cover for its thievery, the university presents itself as an altruistic part of "the commons," offering gifts contributing to the public good.

In *No Study without Struggle,* Leigh Patel describes how the university operates through a gift economy that positions students from nondominant backgrounds as "only minimally worthy of the beneficence of the university" and therefore burdened with a "complicated mix of emotional and material debt" (Patel 2021, 40). Students of color at elite universities have articulated this to me as feeling like they are walking around campus with "Scholarship Student" tattooed on their foreheads: "Gift economies are a colonial structure that imagines some people as worthy only through the benevolence of people with higher status" (Patel 2021, 40). Consider the recent SCOTUS decisions against affirmative action and student debt forgiveness.

Patel and others have analyzed how the gift economy of the university organizes many of its functions, including service learning, internships, community engagement, experiential learning, alternative spring breaks, programs like Teach for America, and "diversity" or "minority" hires. Through these programs, many of which attach to GWSS, the institution positions itself as public-serving and -facing, benevolent, even "munificent" (Patel 2021, 136). Patel, building on the history of freedom schools and the work of Black studies scholars including Harney and Moten, suggests a decoupling of learning from dominant schooling by calling for "fugitive learning in a settler society."

Indigenous studies scholars insist that in addition to people's labor, time, and energy, land is literally foundational to the settler-colonial university and the engine upon which it runs: "Land accumulation as institutional capital is likely the defining trait of the competitive, modern-day research university... yet land is least likely to be discussed in any critical treatment of it" (la paperson 2017, 25). The research behind the Land Grab Universities digital resource demonstrates the need to get beyond understandings of land theft as simply tied to the footprint of university campuses (Lee et al. 2020). It exposes contemporary property expansion and revenue generation from the dispossession of millions of acres of Indigenous lands.

Further, and this ties back to kin-making, we are challenged to recognize land, the living world ("land, air, water, plants and animals and Indigenous peoples"), as the biopolitical target of settler colonialism (la paperson 2017, 14). This necessarily means recognizing "everywhere land resists and refuses" (la paperson 2017, 21), including all the ways it refuses the academic industrial complex. This is why academic appropriation of decolonization as a metaphor for anything progressive, rather than the specific rematriation of Indigenous land and life, is yet another form of dispossession.

Instead of responding to "rightsizing" threats by ramping up defensive territorialization and posturing for recognition as essential to institutional DEI rhetorics, we in GWSS might consider tactics for redistributing and/or (re)purposing power and resources. As a program director, I am so often asked to quantify outcomes, to enumerate "deliverables," that I find myself more focused on student capture than stretching toward "fugitive learning."

There are various models for refusing and/or (re)purposing the university, for finding and growing the decolonial education that exists within, just beyond, or underneath it. Many are unpublished, forged in DMs, whispers, and collective struggle. Others include being an accomplice, co-conspirator, thief, and someone who provides accompaniment. *A Third University Is Possible* offers another, the scyborg as technology, assemblage, or collective (a queer turn pluralizing "cyborg") (la paperson 2017, xiii). Evocative language describes the scyborg as the "decolonial ghost in the colonial machine"; the "agentive body within the institutional machinery"; the "reorganizer"; that which "subverts," "rewires"; that which is "never a completely loyal colonialist and can often be caught in the basement library, building the third world university" (la paperson 2017). These are all nonindividualized postures or assemblages beyond expected, and therefore ineffective, resistance. They demonstrate why we need collectives that center joyful futurities, that remember, and dream, possibility. In "Biting the University That Feeds Us," Eve Tuck writes:

> I have begun to keep a list of theories of change in my cellphone so I can remember something more meaningful than raising awareness. Something more material than raising consciousness. Something more to the touch than visibility. My list of compelling theories of change: haunting, billboards, visitations, Maroon societies, decolonization, revenge, mattering. (Tuck 2018, 166)

I love Tuck's list and am adding to it those suggested in this article: trans joy and futurity; kin-making/revealing; and refusal, redistribution, rematriation, (re)purposing. I am thinking hard about what it means to "sneak into the university and steal what one can." And about ways to facilitate this for other others—those who were never meant to inhabit the institution, those who are "*in* but not *of* the university"—not as an act of charity, but accompaniment for collective survival.

There are so many questions. How might this inform how my program recalibrates itself regarding the hires we have been begging for, bashing our heads against Ahmed's institutional brick wall? Are there ways to rewire my institution's Strategic Resource Allocation process toward a strategic resource *re*allocation process? How might we in GWSS stop demanding resources for "trauma-informed pedagogy" and "cultural competency training," both of which turn structural violence into individualized pain, mastery, or both (Kelley 2016)? How might we refuse the nonperformatives of administrative DEI culture (Ahmed 2012) and turn more energies to creative reallocation of resources and power, including our own?

For those like me who are advantaged by white privilege and settler colonialism, this means unlearning the characteristics of white supremacy culture that fuel higher ed, including liberal postures of white innocence and benevolence. It means stepping aside, stepping back, interrupting operations that reproduce the academic status quo, including producing more myselves. It means cultivating the ability to "daydream about the underbelly of maps, about that which congregates just below the threshold of visibility" (Belcourt 2020, 72). To stretch into the potential of this moment, I know I need to "move at the speed of trust" (BlackSpace 2020) with colleagues, students, comrades, dissidents, subversives, and accomplices, forming "intellectual communities held together by principle and love" (Kelley 2016).

We are not tinkering. We are "ready to imagine another world. And ready to fight for it." Some of us are gathering across time zones and territories in Zoom rooms on institutional accounts (or less traceable, more secure platforms), conspiring and aspiring to assemble a scyborg, a "decolonial rider within the circuitry of colonizing machines" (la paperson 2017, xxv).

Judy Rohrer (she/her) is a theorist with research interests in a number of interdisciplinary fields: feminist studies, queer studies, Indigenous studies, settler colonial studies, critical race theory, and disability studies. She is currently director of Gender, Women's and Sexuality Studies at Eastern Washington University. Rohrer has published in a number of scholarly journals and has three books: *Staking Claim: Settler Colonialism and Racialization in Hawai'i* (University of Arizona Press, 2016); *Queering the Biopolitics of Citizenship in the Age of Obama* (Palgrave MacMillan, 2014); and *Haoles in Hawai'i* (University of Hawai'i Press, 2010). She can be reached at judy.rohrer@ewu.edu.

Works Cited

African American Policy Forum. 2020. "Under the Blacklight: The Fire This Time." YouTube, last modified June 3, 2020. https://www.youtube.com/live/KQr6j7MoH2I.

———. 2023. "Whitewashing Black Studies: The Fight for African American Studies in the Era of Racial Backlash." YouTube, last modified February 8, 2023. https://www.youtube.com/live/S1VUldeuO0A.

Ahmed, Sara. 2012. *On Being Included: Racism and Diversity in Institutional Life.* Durham, NC: Duke University Press.

———. 2021. *Complaint!* Durham, NC: Duke University Press.

———. 2023. "Feminist Killjoys at Work." Virtual public lecture presented in Zoom webinar at Utah State University, Center for Gender and Intersectional Studies, February 22, 2023.

American Association of University Professors. 2021. *Special Report: COVID-19 and Academic Governance.* https://www.aaup.org/file/Special-Report_COVID-19-and-Academic-Governance.pdf.

Belcourt, Billy-Ray. 2016. "Can the Other of Native Studies Speak?" *Decolonization: Indigeneity, Education, and Society* (blog), February 1, 2016. https://decolonization.wordpress.com/2016/02/01/can-the-other-of-native-studies-speak/.

———. 2020. *A History of My Brief Body.* Columbus, OH: Two Dollar Radio.

Bennett, Geoff, and Karina Cuevas. 2023. "College Board Releases African American Studies Course Framework after DeSantis Criticism." *PBS News Hour*, February 1, 2023. https://www.pbs.org/newshour/show/college-board-releases-african-american-studies-course-framework-after-desantis-criticism.

Beyoncé. 2022. *Renaissance.* Parkwood Entertainment / Columbia.

BlackSpace. 2020. "BlackSpace Manifesto." Californians for the Arts, last modified June 11, 2020. https://www.californiansforthearts.org/antiracism-edit/2020/6/11/blackspace-manifesto.

Brown, Wendy. 2015. *Undoing the Demos: Neoliberalism's Stealth Revolution.* 1st ed. New York: Zone Books.

Burch, Susan. 2021. *Committed: Remembering Native Kinship in and beyond Institutions.* Chapel Hill: University of North Carolina Press.

Crenshaw, Kimberlé. 2015. "Why Intersectionality Can't Wait." *Washington Post*, September 24, 2015.

Department of Gender and Women's Studies. 2022. "Covid Safety: Masking and Community Values in Gender and Women's Studies." Last modified September 2022. https://gws.berkeley.edu/about/covid-safety/.

Eastern Washington University. 2023. "Strategic Resource Allocation." Accessed February 20, 2023. https://inside.ewu.edu/sra/.

Ferguson, Roderick A. 2012. *The Reorder of Things: The University and Its Pedagogies of Minority Difference.* Minneapolis: University of Minnesota Press.

———. 2023. "Fear of a Black Studies Planet." *Chronicle of Higher Education*, January 30, 2023.

García Peña, Lorgia. 2022. *Community as Rebellion: A Syllabus for Surviving Academia as a Woman of Color*. Chicago, IL: Haymarket Books.

Gardner, Lee. 2023. "Flagships Prosper, while Regionals Suffer: Competition Is Getting Fierce, and the Gap Is Widening." *Chronicle of Higher Education*, February 13, 2023.

Haraway, Donna. 2018. "Making Kin in the Chthulucene: Reproducing Multispecies Justice." In *Making Kin Not Population*, edited by Adele E. Clarke and Donna Jeanne Haraway, 67–100. Chicago, IL: Prickly Paradigm Press.

Harney, Stefano, and Fred Moten. 2013. *The Undercommons: Fugitive Planning and Black Study*. Wivenhoe: Automedia.

Kafer, Alison. 2019. "Crip Kin, Manifesting." *Catalyst: Feminism, Theory, Technoscience* 5 (1):1–37.

———. 2021. "After Crip, Crip Afters." *South Atlantic Quarterly* 120 (2): 415–34.

Kelley, Robin D. G. 2016. "Black Study, Black Struggle." *Boston Review*, March 1, 2016.

la paperson. 2017. *A Third University Is Possible*. Minneapolis: University of Minnesota Press.

Lee, Robert, Tristan Ahtone, and Margaret Pearce. 2020. "Land-Grab Universities." *HighCountry News*, accessed February 17, 2023. https://www.landgrabu.org/.

Lorde, Audre. 1978. *The Black Unicorn: Poems*. 1st ed. New York: Norton.

Maynard, Robyn, and Leanne Betasamosake Simpson. 2022. *Rehearsals for Living: The Abolitionist Papers Series*. Chicago, IL: Haymarket Books.

McMahan, Shari. 2023. "Intensive Resource Allocation Process at EWU Will Narrow Focus to True Needs of Students." *Spokesman-Review*, February 12, 2023.

Melamed, Jodi. 2011. *Represent and Destroy: Rationalizing Violence in the New Racial Capitalism*. Minneapolis: University of Minnesota Press.

Mitchell, Nick. 2016. "The Fantasy and Fate of Ethnic Studies in an Age of Uprisings: An Interview with Nick Mitchell." By Zach Schwartz-Weinstein. *Undercommoning*, July 13, 2016. https://undercommoning.org/nick-mitchell-interview/.

Patel, Leigh. 2021. *No Study without Struggle: Confronting Settler Colonialism in Higher Education*. Boston, MA: Beacon Press.

Political Research Associates. 2023. "Organizing for the Year Ahead: Countering Anti-LGBTQ Persecution and Violence in 2023." Vimeo, last modified February 1, 2023. https://vimeo.com/794938844.

Roy, Arundhati. 2020. "The Pandemic Is a Portal." YouTube, April 11, 2020. https://youtu.be/7hgQFaeaeo0?si=jyUOLWzjYl5OETjS.
TallBear, Kim. 2018. "Making Love and Relations beyond Settler Sex and Family." In *Making Kin Not Population*, edited by Adele E. Clarke and Donna Haraway, 145–64. Chicago, IL: Prickly Paradigm Press.
———. 2019. "Caretaking Relations, Not American Dreaming." *Kalfou* 6 (1): 24–41.
Tuck, Eve. 2018. "Biting the University that Feeds Us." In *Dissident Knowledge in Higher Education*, edited by James McNinch and Marc Spooner, 149–67. Regina, Saskatchewan: University of Regina Press.
Undercommoning Collective. 2016. "Undercommoning within, against and beyond the University-as-Such." *ROAR Magazine*, June 5, 2016.

Rage-ography: Rigor, Anti-wokeness, and Technoviolence

Amy E. Slaton and Donna Riley

Abstract: Feminist studies scholars and those in related critical studies traditions have long encountered resistance arising from STEM disciplines and capitalist logics on our campuses and in the wider public discourse. The struggles to establish and preserve feminist studies and ethnic studies programs over the past five decades remind us that the present pandemonium has historical roots that can be traced, not only to identify patterns instructive for us in this moment, but also for a visceral resonance that buoys us in this time and place. We recognize our own outrage at injustice even as we feel the rage directed at feminist studies scholars from sites of elite power, sustained through false dualisms of left and right, minority and majority, woke and anti-woke, STEM and non-STEM. This piece explores the preservation of elite power through the examination of institutions and epistemics at the heart of contemporary wage capitalism: the world of engineering education and practice, and critical resistance within that world. We analyze (ostensibly nonidentitarian) projects such as technoscientific teaching, research, and production. We choose to analyze episodes from the "before times" that reveal a sustained pattern of misogyny, white supremacy, heterosexism, and ableism pervading society and the academy prior to current enactments of that kind. In so doing, we follow an emergent line of inquiry, tracing emotion as well as argument: these dynamics are now, and have long been, fraught with rage. It is the systematic, historically robust, and selective acceptance and denial of rage that we want to explore here as a foundational feature of the present pandemonium, common to feminist studies academic contexts and to engineering, as well as interactions between the two. **Keywords:** rage, feminism, STEM, engineering, anti-wokeness, technoviolence

> The gender studies program at Middlebury came under attack from pundits who characterized its courses as being "categorically insane" after the disruption of a March 2017 talk by Charles Murray, a writer best known for his controversial work linking intelligence and race. Though the talk wasn't about gender studies, Moss said supporters of Murray looked to the gender studies department "to discredit Middlebury and particularly to discredit the side that was against Murray."
> —Elizabeth Redden, "Global Attack on Gender Studies,"
> *Inside Higher Ed*, December 4, 2018

Introduction

A pervasive trope in centrist U.S. media and cultural analysis today holds that the nation is "polarized": ideologically divided and incapable of productive exchange across that divide, let alone of civility. However, the above excerpt—relating to just one of countless similar incidents around the country in recent years, reflects more deep-seated and long-term dynamics than mere societal polarization. Whether we consider Murray's resurrection of debunked nineteenth-century eugenics (Devlin et al. 1997), or the tired tendency to pathologize female resistance (Ramas 1980), we can recognize persistent power relations going back decades and longer.

Thinking with the methods of the discipline of history and with approaches modeled by critical race, feminist, queer, crip, and engineering studies, we suggest that it is only through a highly selective logic bent on conserving the social relations of capitalism as we know them that observers can posit the current social landscape as newly fraught. Arbiters of what shall count as democratic functionality in the United States strategically deploy a taxonomy of particular distinctions and symmetries between "left" and "right," between "minority" and "majority" communities, between "woke" and "anti-woke" dispositions that together preserve fundamentally violent and unjust social structures. These dualistic characterizations, even or especially when claiming to capture a "balanced" outlook, thus reproduce the dehumanizing anti-Black, misogynistic, and other ruthless designs of capital. Women's, gender, and feminist studies programs—and indeed so many related critical studies programs addressing racism, ableism, heterosexism, transphobia, and more—must contend with these dynamics in their continued struggle for survival in today's capitalist-minded universities, which are ever glorifying STEM fields and propping up false disciplinary dichotomies.

In this essay, we want to explore these efforts at conserving elite power.

We examine institutions and epistemics at the heart of contemporary wage capitalism to do so: the world of engineering education and practice, and critical resistance within that world. We deliberately analyze incidents in this sector of the academy that so often appears to have no intersection with feminist studies, ethnic studies, and related disciplines, that is, spaces of innocence-making (ostensibly nonidentitarian) projects such as technoscientific teaching, research, and production. And we deliberately choose to analyze episodes from the "before times" that reveal a sustained pattern of misogyny, white supremacy, heterosexism, and ableism pervading society and the academy prior to current enactments of that kind. In so doing, we follow an emergent line of inquiry, tracing emotion as well as argument: these dynamics are now, and have long been, fraught with rage.

Feminist studies scholars and those in related critical studies traditions have encountered resistance arising from STEM disciplines and capitalist logics on our campuses for decades. Flashpoints have emerged from time to time as feminist scholarship touches elite power—for example, in Irigaray's (1985) critique of fluid mechanics, or in physicist Alan Sokal's embarrassingly misguided attack on *Social Text* (Sokal and Bricmont 1997). The struggles to establish and preserve feminist and ethnic studies programs over the past five decades remind us that the present pandemonium has historical roots that can be traced, not only to identify patterns instructive for us in this moment, but also to tap a visceral resonance that buoys us in this time and place.

For anyone remotely concerned with the flows of power in society, it is hard to avoid the findings that rage is historical and that history is never without rage. It's not only that we must understand rage as Janus-faced, historically empowering both the oppressor and the oppressed, sometimes simultaneously, and thus recognize rage as a pervasive sociability. In addition, we can come to see that the impossibility and disavowal of rage have also historically consolidated power and enabled violence. It is a case of this doubling—the systematic, historically robust, and selective acceptance and denial of rage—that we want to explore here as a foundational feature of the present pandemonium, common to feminist studies contexts and to engineering, as well as interactions between the two.

We are prompted to look back toward the antecedents of the present pandemonium in part because so many minoritized and marginalized communities see no watershed of any kind in social relations of recent years: no uptick in loathing and discrimination for minoritized people but only continuities with long historic injustices. Taking up a critique of capitalism refined in recent feminist analyses of neoliberal trends (Funk 2013), we can track how it is that an idealized universe of ostensibly value-neutral, meritocratic contribution and reward (that is, learning and earning in engineering fields) is made to appear in majority constructions the default mode of U.S. society, with moments of conflict and violence cast as mere aberrations. We also address the impossibility of explicitly addressing the rage, loathing, fear, pleasure, and other affective experiences pervading places of engineering, and the violence inhering in such elisions. We test, too, the potential of humanities-derived and, in particular, historical analytics from feminist studies and related fields to challenge engineering's self-confirming epistemic of objectivity, an epistemic that has historically both disguised and fueled the rage of engineers.

The authors of this piece, Donna and Amy, write as educators and as critical analysts (and in Donna's case, a practitioner) of engineering in the United States. Both of us have experienced online targeting based on our critical scholarship in recent years (Riley 2019). From these positions, we want to explore engineering as a field designed first to elide the rage that enacts violence in industrial capitalism and in military, nationalist, and colonial projects, and then to suppress the rage that accompanies subjects' experiences of that violence (Abdel-Malek 1981; Mohanty 2003). In the worlds of engineering learning, research, and work, as in other U.S. cultural sectors, the aggression of the dominant is greeted as righteous, an expression of high standards, fortitude, and meritocratic sensibilities. Meanwhile, the anger of the minoritized is ill-mannered and unprofessional, it is grievance, it is feminine or queer, and with its messy self-indulgence belongs in ... the humanities (Letts and Fifield 2019).

Historians have just lately begun to analyze how the notion of "the technological" comes into being alongside deeply violent and unjust social relations, alongside the enraged cruelty of the dominant, and, vitally, alongside the enraged resistance of the subordinated (e.g., Alder 1997; Gomez 2018; Mukerji 2009; Mukharji 2018). This is the emerging approach we take up here. We are particularly concerned with the obfuscating notion that rage is ever adequately explained as an expression of individual feelings, as something occurring apart from power relations and social structures. We see the historical marginalization of and derision towards feminist scholarly or pedagogical projects as consonant with a characterization of such projects as grounded in inappropriate sentiment and behavior on women's part. Thus, too, are women reproduced as a distinct and meaningfully lesser taxonomic category alongside men. This paper lays out some possibilities for framing such analysis, both attending to and problematizing the individual technological actor as such—as a gendered, capacitated, knowable body.

We do so in the form of a "rage-ography": a rage-centered life history of a queer, female-identifying engineer (Donna) who has been on the receiving end of much rage, and often experienced her own enragement.[1] This of course isn't the only way to interrogate power, and rage, in the history of engineering, but it is a potent approach, because it keeps two proven taxonomic instruments of power (ascribed gender and sexuality), and the multiple instrumentalities of rage, in view at all times. There will be places where the making of "non-rage" is what we have to follow if we are to understand the operations of engineering in U.S. society: the denial, repression, or renaming of rage in the interests of maintaining power, or alternatively, in the interests of personal safety and survival. Non-rage is in many ways a specialty of engineering, an epistemic enterprise closely identified with objectivity, empiricism, and productivity in Western capitalist cultures.

Feminist science studies scholars have for several decades alerted us to the violent premises of Western scientific knowledge and institutions, and Afro-futurism has carried this project to wider racial and colonial critiques.[2] But still, "applied" knowledge, routine design, construction, standardized production, and other quotidian activities seemingly "downstream" from science (and frequently clear across campus from sites of critical studies)— loosely grouped by many observers under the umbrella "engineering"—have received less attention.

Where will writing this rage-ography take us? It is possible that engineering will not survive our storytelling with its reputation intact. It is also possible that Donna's reputation will be remade, for worse or better depending on the audience. And why would Amy's reputation, in a humanities field but affiliated with a "STEM" institution, not also change for worse or better as she associates herself with this topic, unpalatable to some of her colleagues but virtuous to others? We cannot know where the questions raised by a rage-ography will lead, critically. But, as feminist queer crip scholar Alison Kafer articulates, nor should we want to know the impacts of this writing: redistributive projects depend on committing ourselves to indeterminacy and relationality (Kafer 2013). It is in this space that we can explore the meaning of the present-day pandemonium. We ultimately seek *not* to redeem engineering by admitting feminizing or feminist forces into its confines but to test the possibility that engineering may cease to exist should it ever give up its masculinist, racist, classist, ableist techniques. That said, rage and rage-centered narratives cannot promise generativity without risking becoming self-consoling. We resist that determinist temptation and frankly offer the following three episodes as a new experience of the relations of engineering, feminism, and the academy... started, and possibly ended, in rage.

Three Episodes

Good engineers solve problems. Donna's education and career over several decades has involved raging against the reduced, the cut and dried, the simple and elegant solutions that description implies. She has been asked to find answers, characterize uncertainties, and bring knowledge into the service of environmental and material alteration. Instead, sometimes, seeing the unjust nature of such alterations (owing to feminist studies and related critical disciplines), she has railed against the empirically knowable world and against the clean, hard, fast solution (Hacker 1989). Donna has been asked just to be grittier, just to lean in, just to wait and the dinosaurs will retire. We see alternatives as raging against invisibility and bodily erasure in engineering. The following accounts of three points in Donna's career follow the rage of others and Donna's own rage in this landscape of power exerted and possible empowerment.

Two brief notes on format and style: Sequential stories are only arbitrarily made so through efforts of selection. We cannot pretend that we are not imposing directionality and causality in our very choice to narrate, whether biographically or otherwise. Historicized accounts of people, or places, or things necessarily rely on preselected meanings and significances, and a disposition of empiricism is no escape route (Gomez 2018; Trouillot 1995). So we come to understand that we are writing this piece from an endpoint that looks back from 2023 onto previous moments in Donna's life, and onto a world we are choosing to call "engineering." Donna is a credentialed engineer, tenured full professor, and university administrator: a status that both allows for and alters any chronicle of earlier experiences. The making of any chronicle requires that we conceptualize the present as a result, as a defiance, as an accident, et cetera. We try to reflect here on that unavoidable condition of choice-making in history writing, to better understand why we see rage in the central way that we do.

Second, the episodic accounts below are offered in the first person, centering Donna's understanding of what happened in each, but composed by both Donna and Amy together. At the same time, there is nothing exceptional about these experiences; in fact, these stories are worth telling because there are so many others that can (or, given the vulnerability of their subjects, cannot) be told. And while Donna as an individual is often alone in absorbing another's rage in the moment, or in her experience of rage, the rage she experiences is often directed at a class of people, and thus her response wells up from the collective. Meanwhile, working as a tenured professor in the humanities—a place that still (sometimes) credits the role of subjectivity, affect, and political orientation among its practitioners— Amy is often exempted from the precise sort of professional scrutiny that Donna has faced. While still marked by stigmatizing ascriptions of gender and life stage, her professional risks are lesser. While both authors are white and neither is visibly disabled, Amy's security is greater than Donna's in this precise sense. These differences, and the questions they make possible, inform the writing of this piece. Thus (we hope) our rage-ography of Donna (not a "biography" or "autobiography") keeps the enactments of STEM and the humanities as distinct realms in our sights—keeps the borders between technical and historical heuristics, and between self and other, in the crosshairs.

Enraging Context

We each have recently worked at a STEM-focused institution, one public, one private, with leadership that circulates certain narratives about the innately positive functions of engineering in society. The futurity that engineering learning ostensibly promises to students, and the field's supposed redemptive power for society at large, dominate official communications even as these schools are actively "reorganizing" scholars in the humanities and social sciences, including those in feminist studies, ethnic studies, and related disciplines with the capacity to critique STEM.

Surely, a primary function of writing this rage-ography is to assure that our experience is finally recorded *as* rage, and not as "attitude" or, equally dismissive in this context, as "politics." Like countless women being angry in public who have come before us, we are easily labeled through such rubrics as not merely causing a disruption, but as both inappropriately disturbed in the moment, and to our lasting detriment, as unprofessional. Perhaps especially in engineering but in all disciplinary contexts, our rage can be seen from within our disciplines as a sign of poor impulse control, or worse. We know this because of the rage-filled mockery known as the "grievance studies" hoax (Phipps 2018), which seeks to silence the developing epistemics and ontologies rooted in the authority of our experience, along with our emergent understandings of rage, its promises and perils. We desire a willingness to move towards the incoherence of rage, to stand with disorder, with indeterminacy: such willingness constitutes the real confrontation with the violent ordering, the cruel precision, the ostensible "realism" of engineering.

Episode 1: Coeducation

In the fall of my (Donna's) first year as an engineering student, fourteen women were shot and killed at the University of Montreal, by a shooter raging against feminists (Chalouh and Malette 1991). Piecing together accounts, the shooter reportedly screamed, "You're women, you're going to be engineers. You're all a bunch of fucking feminists. I hate feminists" (Chalouh and Malette 1991; Viner 2000). My peers at the time insisted he was just a madman, not a misogynist. They insisted this was a random act of violence. Two months later, someone slipped a slab of raw meat into my coat pocket that hung on a wall hook while I was eating lunch in the dining hall. It had a note on it that read, "This is what you mean to me." I was walking back to my room, late for lab, when I discovered this cold item in my pocket. I threw it on my bed, too shocked to recognize what it was, and returned hours later to a blood-stained comforter and reported it to the campus police.

Rage is, historically, a weapon designed to kill women—it lives as a weaponized, mechanized masculinity. With further brutality towards the nonmasculine, and towards the mentally ill (a point to which we return below), "madness" is often deployed not just to veil hateful sociabilities like those of the shooter or whomever put the meat in my pocket but also to cover up cultural commitments towards hate. The shooter's ostensible "craziness" is a sheet that covers the weapon itself so that it cannot be seen for what it is. Rage in this incarnation cannot be interrogated for its origins or impacts.

The violent threat communicated through that piece of meat should have been obvious, but my speaking out about it brought only scrutiny to me—what had I done to make myself a target, wasn't I making too much out of this, wasn't it just a joke and I humorless? My roommate, a legacy student, told me I should be grateful that Princeton, a formerly all-male institution, admitted women at all. When I sought therapy for this incident, the therapist immediately made the connection to the dead women at Montreal. My response was to fly into a rage and terminate therapy. There was no other place for my rage in engineering, and so I left what I could with the therapist and carried the rest with me.

The only acceptable strategy I could perceive at that point was the pathway hailed nowadays in our institutions as grit—to be stronger, just keep your head down, do your work, and show them. Grit demands silence, the suppression of rage. These are perpetual expectations of the educationally and occupationally successful in the United States, but they are especially celebrated in STEM sectors where reflection and self-care are felt to be anathema to empirical focus and technological accomplishment (Slaton et al. 2019; González Stokas 2015). So my rage then was redirected inward with every perceived slip, every failure to demonstrate certainty and achievement. Eventually, about a year later, it spilled out onto the pages of my journal in an incoherent rage poem, through which I realized that coeducation at Princeton was a farce. It acted and reenacted emotional, physical, and structural violence, demonstrating to women students that we didn't actually belong.

This experience illustrates how inclusion is not equivalent to equity, let alone security or love, and very likely impedes those outcomes. Impulses toward diversity easily preserve the most profound cruelties productive of, and predicated on, constructions of human difference in American culture. In STEM fields, ideas of individual prowess and meritocracy play a particularly flagrant role in covering the hostility faced by minoritized people. Critical scholars of diversity have started to help us see that the very concept of meritocracy naturalizes the lowered educational attainments of many individuals: every classroom must have a "worst" student, not everyone "needs" to go to college (Secules et al. 2018; Slaton, in preparation; Taylor 2018). As if appropriate phenotype and recognizable forms of intelligence were not enough to enact the historical stratifications of American society, to preserve patterns of dominance, this first episode helps us see that fortitude and suffering are also required attributes for success, contributing to stratified social structures and to violence. I was meant to tough it out, walk it off, bring all blame for all the subsequent fear and discomfort onto myself. But crucially, those were not fundamentally conditions for *my* success in an Ivy League engineering school. They were and remain conditions for the success of those whose security and comfort have historically been fueled by contempt for me and other women—fueled, that is, by rage.

I have witnessed colleagues in critical social science disciplines, as they were pressured to remain neutral in the face of student activism on campus, rather than experience it as a site of engagement—or enragement—at campus injustice. The expectation that we should temper our rage, channel it somewhere more convenient, is both fodder for those who would attack feminist studies from outside, and a tool to protect institutional power from the inconvenient truths critical scholarship produces.

Episode 2: Mentors and the Conservatism of Care

With this second episode, we delineate the ways in which female identification has historically pervaded the Euro-American university as a problem for the institution. As I began my faculty career, I participated in a peer-mentoring group of female engineering faculty members. At each convening, we invited one or two senior mentors who could help us navigate pre-tenure challenges. We followed conventional wisdom that female success in academia depends upon this mentoring; if we could be more like these exceptional women, following their patterns, disciplining ourselves to their playbooks, we too could be successful.

One of our mentors in this program was Denice Denton, then dean of engineering at the University of Washington. She shared her story of being literally locked out of her lab as an assistant professor at the University of Wisconsin–Madison in the late 1980s; she had to take her fight, with the backing of high-powered sex-discrimination lawyers, to the highest levels of the university to address this injustice (University of Wisconsin–Madison Oral History Project 2009). She counseled us to express rage at injustice, as she had seen suppressed rage harm some female colleagues' health. She mentioned her female partner to us, and in that disclosure, I found my first out queer role model in engineering. Then in 2006, one year into her term as chancellor of the University of California at Santa Cruz, where Denton was subjected to homophobic and misogynistic "venom" in both public media and personal email, she died from suicide, jumping from the rooftop of the Paramount apartments in San Francisco (Kapp 2007).

Most colleagues delimit their understanding of Denton's death and its meaning with terms of "mental health problems," citing her long-term struggles with depression. While I am of course not able to come to any reliable or definitive explanation of another's suicide, I nonetheless don't accept that prevailing explanation as a complete and full accounting of her life and its meaning. When I was targeted by social media trolls over my administrative appointment at Purdue (Riley 2019), a friend of Denton took me aside and asked me to reach out if I needed to. That expression of care also cannot be reduced simply or cleanly to positivity. What can rage and its complexities offer us in making meaning of Denton's life and death? What does the mental health label or box serve to cover or foreclose? How might "care" and "support" need interrogation? What might being (scrutinized for being) queer, or being locked out of the lab, have to do with this?

First, why are explanations that might reveal power relations unthinkable in our conversations about suicide, and how do our limited understandings or constructions of mental health render power invisible and unthinkable? What stories are we unable to tell? If my rage regarding the anti-woman, anti-queer conditions of Denton's professional life in engineering is allowed to ground my understanding of these social relations, one result is that Denton's infirmity is analytically decentered. This is not to say that her suffering and need for support in the face of depression are in any way minimized; rather, they are de-medicalized, their existence rejected as a natural or sufficient explanation for her experiences, even for her suicide. We do not want to replace a pathologizing model of her mental illness with a social one that turns our attention to environmental factors; while social models allow us to see structural inequities that the medical model hides, they nonetheless tend to preserve existing definitions of ability and health. Instead, we might adopt a post-social model of infirmity or disability in which our very notions of normalcy and infirmity come into question (Clare 2017; Kafer 2013). We could thus take up Denton's understanding that suppressing rage was unhealthy and expressing rage—allowing for social disorder—healthy. We could admit the conditions in which rage emerged for her, and her understanding of those conditions, as well as institutional responses to them that she encountered, as determinative of what counted as "health" and "illness" in her life, and thus badly in need of interrogation.

What happens to sympathy in such a pivot to a more indeterminate framing of suicide? We believe that sympathy, and love, are actually more fully possible in such thinking (Harrison 1985; la paperson 2017, 92). This inquiring position radically reframes our understanding of how individuals and cultures interact, an interaction that often brings about suffering for many nondominant, "different" individuals. We propose this reframing as a way of bringing disability and the history of professional credibility into conversation with one another and with the specific tendencies of engineering to elide affect, personal suffering, and weakness through stigma (Taylor 2018). This takes us far from a simple understanding of Denton's suicide as symptom of pathology.

Second, regarding mentoring and other forms of care, those who came to understand Denton's death as a final, tragic symptom of an illness were likely sympathetic to her situation. But the liberality and generosity of sympathy enable us to easily preserve our beliefs in human difference and its meanings through regimes of tolerance, welcome, or care. All of these dispositions can enact disablement, condescension, and confinement, including in institutional contexts, through, say, the characterization of marginalized communities as "underserved" rather than as habitually subject to violence (the latter characterization could, after all, seem to justify rage among the marginalized). The conciliatory impulses of centrist liberal leadership, in the U.S. university at least, thus poorly defend against the brutal misogyny of the right (Slaton, in preparation).

Similarly, mentorship, designed as tutelage and guidance, can forestall distress and suffering for mentees in the short term. But like much in the realm of education, mentorship reproduces social positions and institutional commitments; it reifies existing distributions of resources. While mentorship can constitute a gesture of support, can it radically disrupt social relations, and prevent larger and longer patterns of suffering or oppression? What if Denton's mentorship was a mentorship in rage, an ordered tutelage in possible disorders?

The questioning of good intentions, of orderly progress, that we outline with this episode demands a new and rage-centered kind of analysis not yet well described in educational or diversity theory. We don't have the expertise to strategize such an analysis here with real care. Yet we know that feminist studies, ethnic studies, disability studies, and queer studies at their best are productive sites for these questions. And I am comfortable saying that in my early career, expressions of rage would not have constituted the opposite of care, the opposite of support or guidance for those customarily marginalized or oppressed in engineering spaces: they might have empowered exactly those outcomes (Harrison 1985).

Episode 3: Rigor, the Assassin's Tool

Throughout my career as a faculty member, I have witnessed numerous assassinations of faculty candidacies in search committees. Tactical, surgical strikes, using rigor as a weapon, to take people out—most frequently women of color. The white male colleague who said, "I am closer to this woman's research area than any of you and believe me when I say this work isn't rigorous," and she went from shortlisted to DOA. This is the cold steely rage of gaslighting and grit, perfected. The application from a graduate student at an HBCU met with the sneering pronouncement "I've never even heard of that school." The intervention "It's a historically black university" seems only to be read as justification for low rating. HR resurrects her CV in its review of finalists and tells us we overlooked a qualified candidate. The faculty member grudgingly agrees to interview her but only to placate HR. She had already been eliminated, clean and fast, with no accountability. The stories told about candidates behind closed doors to characterize their inadequacy are accepted uncritically. This is the making of whiteness, fueled by the rage of white people, and fueling the rage of its objects.

In deciding on the recipient of a student award honoring work furthering the advancement of women in engineering, I once nominated a woman of color who fostered the advancement of other women of color who went on to assume leadership positions in a national professional society. A colleague snapped, "This award is for women." This clarified nothing, until I realized she meant *white women*. My mouth gaped. Regaining composure, I patiently explained how this student met the award criteria. It was to no avail, because her eligibility had already been categorically questioned.

Even now, these incidents feel simultaneously unlikely and inevitable, impossible and unavoidable. That the faculty colleagues described here would likely be considered "blue-state liberals," abhorring white supremacist violence in, say, Charlottesville or on January 6, belies simple narratives of polarization, of "woke" and "anti-woke." In the face of this messiness, I wonder not only what to do with my rage (that is, how to formulate what might constitute a constructive response to cruelty), but also how it can come to be that I occupy these rooms, appalled at what strikes me as retrograde bigoted cruelty, alongside those who either do not notice or who perpetrate the cruelty. How does a single institution, or discipline, sustain both sensibilities? Any earnest study of gender, class, sexuality, education, and engineering—any thinking on so-called diversity—must try to address that apparent conundrum, because power can never be best understood as anomalous.

My rage in these moments can draw on no explanatory templates that yet exist inside the episteme that comprises engineering. STEM arenas cast individual merit as a series of contributions that are singular in nature, knowable through systems of graded mastery, standardized tests, patents, and resumes, and as Caitlyn Allen (2001) makes clear, through aspirants' willingness to avoid critiquing these wages of science achievement. Rage is at best incidental to my being an engineer, at worst, corrupting and disqualifying. But more deeply destructive, perhaps, is the fact that to my institution and discipline, the existence of my rage is not worth explaining, my desire to understand it irrelevant and worse, evidence of my poor judgment. My rage renders me ineligible to determine the relevance of my sensibilities: only the expert can reflect on expertise (Riley 2017; Secules et al. 2018).

How could a new history of engineering focus on that confounding duality? As one starting point, historians of racial formation and of universities offer powerful explanations of the masking, self-confirmations, and colonialities that constitute "First World" institutions: those universities and related entities that house "cutting-edge" research operations, professional education systems, and other projects of importance to global capital while at the same time producing massive student debt. In this schema (which assuredly accounts for the design and operations of American engineering schools), as described by critical ethnic studies theorist la paperson, the "second university," motivated by liberal and humanistic critique of such inequitable structures, challenges the complacencies of the first university.

Yet that utopic, liberal second university is still a place engaged in perpetuating "the material conditions of higher education—fees, degrees, expertise" and the appropriation of land, rather than in rematriating land or in offering "a school-to-community pipeline, not a community-to-school pipeline" (la paperson 2017, 42). la paperson posits a "third university," one whose mission is decolonization, but which is not, we take it, consoling. This university is multi-scale (personal, community, sectoral), with not-yet-known, and changing, institutional formats. It is one that is strategic (charging fees and granting degrees, perhaps) but not romantic; there are no assuredly desirable outcomes from its operations, but rather its functions and impacts are contingent and changing. It is one where rage happens. It is not necessarily one where engineering survives, or engineering professors find employment.

Conclusions

In her attempts at writing a new and indeterminate history of engineering education that decenters the self-consolations of welcome, Amy has previously challenged the idea that seeking inclusion for those minoritized in STEM can enact democratic goals. Instead, she suggests, engineering and difference come into being together. That which white people do is engineering, that which people of color do is something else; only in exceptional cases is the body of color, the queer body, the disabled body a figure of achievement (Slaton 2010). Thinking about that ontological condition, of engineering and difference coming into being together, through writing Donna's rage-ography has highlighted the functions of rage in the ontology. For dominant actors, rage is a powerful instrument of making categories: white or not, male or not, heterosexual or not, abled or not. For subordinated people, through rage one can illuminate the operations of difference-making to which one is subject. We see rage in this latter way as accountability (Harrison 1985). We would like to include our rage in that characterization, too, thus expanding the definition of incisive historical inquiry to acknowledge its affective features and possibly challenge the very analytic dichotomy between cognition and affect in conceptions of rigorous inquiry in all fields. That dichotomization is itself an instrument of power, challenges to which would constitute political intervention. In STEM arenas, the insistence that cognition proceeds apart from affect currently masks the rage of the dominant as a driver of empirical findings on, say, race or sexuality, or (less studied) in the production of materials, machines, and infrastructures. Also hidden—in humanities, social science, and STEM fields alike—is its role in producing standards of investigative rigor that enact violence (Fifield and Letts 2019, 10–11; Riley 2014, 2017).

For feminist studies and other critical disciplines under attack in the present pandemonium, it is crucial to note that both change and continuity configure the landscape of feminist experience in 2023 in the academy, in terms of both pedagogy and programming on one hand and regarding the daily sociabilities of university life on the other. The political influence of the far right that has been mounting since Trump's first candidacy has brought into being new policy instruments to silence unrest, to murder and incarcerate members of subordinated communities, and to dismantle educational programming that explicates the experiences of women, people of color, queer communities, and other marginalized folk. But none of these twenty-first-century conditions are entirely novel or based on new majority ideas about difference, superiority, and entitlement. As we have tried to show, some of the sturdiest cultural enterprises of Euro-American history—the knowledge and practices of engineering—are foundational to their enactment.

To bring change and continuity to light, we must strive to think the unthinkable: to confront rage, we must turn to scenarios that our culture has rendered fantastic even as they have happened . . . a highly credentialed lawyer being told to "prove" that she encountered a pubic hair on a Coke can; a male U.S. Supreme Court nominee in a congressional hearing sarcastically asking a congressperson if she likes beer; a young woman in a prestigious STEM doctoral program facing repeated verbal threats of sexual assault at the lab bench.[3] We need then to see engineering *not* as a place where rage is prohibited: Donna's experiences from her first days as an engineering student onward render that depiction impossible. Rather, looking much more carefully and critically, we understand engineering in the United States as a set of spaces where rage is not merely present but actually *produced*, as a modality ready to hand for dominant actors and (albeit expressed differentially) for those they subjugate. It is a modality justified and unjustified for different actors of different genders, sexualities, races, bodies, and professional credentials. The very features that make engineering known to us as such—its empiricism, its universality, its futurity, its utility, its naturalized masculinity and whiteness—serve as "anti-rage" instrumentalities when the rage is brewing in the bodies of the un-masculine and un-white, where engineering cannot authentically be rooted (Hundle 2019; Slaton 2010).

It is with this historicization of social relations that contemporary regimes of terror might become clear as such, rather than as departures from some less terrifying cultural norms. Ferguson's (2012) accounts of the founding of ethnic and racial studies units in U.S. universities following the 1980s, and subsequent appropriation and resistance by diverse groups of stakeholders, corrects any impulse we have towards declensionist narratives: we in no sense believe that rage and radical reframings of rigor face insurmountable obstacles. We are thus eager to read and write more rage-ographies. Importantly, these must include rage-ographies of those enraged by perceived challenges to their own security, those devoted to the naturalization of white, male, cis, heterosexual, abled bodies in engineering classrooms and workplaces, and those presently targeting feminist studies and other critical disciplines. Engineering is not just an instrumentality of sorting, minoritization, and elimination but also an instrumentality of threat—and here is where studies of rage in engineering might augment studies of rage in politics, military histories, colonialization, industrialization, or rage in art, sex, and spirituality. The ways in which engineering promises to know and manipulate the world bring about inevitable and selected futures, empirical and mechanical and there to intimidate even before the wall is built... even before the resumes are read, received, or requested. Science assuredly enacts versions of these futures (Edelman 2004), but the inevitability that comprises engineering itself—a field made up of solutions that give birth to problems, of objects that give birth to need—demand specific interrogation (Anderson 2006; Medina 2018; Slaton, in preparation).

What futures might alternatively be portended in engineering by accounting for rage? We can't pretend to predict how rage-as-accountability might manifest, but we might begin by risking putting parts of ourselves into conversation that we previously have not. In the engineering education community, emerging scholars have placed "unpalatable bodies" and "unimaginable passions/loves" at our buttoned-down and distinctly non-rage-y conference (Chua and Smith 2019; Cieminski 2019). This work reveals how much we routinely hide from ourselves and each other.

With constructive avowals of rage, we might come to a place where we can name violence and conflict. This would be not just liberating but disordering—a queering. If we show up as authentic and whole selves, with rage and sex and pain and pleasure—these are multiple disorderings that engineering cannot tolerate. What happens then is no happy ending; it is grief. It is no reconciliation, no continuous improvement, no incremental consolation, no redemption. Rage must take its course.

Amy E. Slaton is professor emerita of history at Drexel University. Her current book project is "All Good People: Difference, Diversity and the Invention of Opportunity." She can be reached at slatonae@drexel.edu.

Donna Riley is Jim and Ellen King Dean of Engineering and Computing and professor in the Gerald May Department of Civil, Construction, and Environmental Engineering at the University of New Mexico. She can be reached at riley1@unm.edu.

Notes

1. This rage-ography is surely owing in some way to Daly's *Gyn/ecology* (1978), written in what she termed the tradition of hag-ography: "Hags may rage and roar, but they do not titter" (17). "Rage" is increasingly finding a foothold as a heuristic for both the formulation of critique via academic scholarship and for enactments as protest or resistance, including through questioning how those commitments have come to be seen as separate from

one another (Kaplan et al. 2021). That purported separation itself is now seen by feminist theorists to be a technique of state and capitalist violence.
2. Feminist science studies, following Haraway's foundational calls (1988), has extended its attention across a wide range of scientific settings, but engineering remains little examined from these perspectives; interrogations of technical activity taking place at the margins of both science and engineering disciplines crucially begin this work (Foster 2017; Giordano 2014). At this writing, Afro-futurism intersects increasingly with STS (Benjamin 2017; Nelson 2002).
3. The last example here is from an anonymized personal account; see also Clancy et al. 2014 on gendered experiences, sexual harassment, and sexual assault in science workspaces.

Works Cited

Abdel-Malek, Anouar. 1981. *Social Dialectics: Nation and Revolution*. Albany: State University of New York Press.

Alder, Ken. 1997. *Engineering the Revolution: Arms and Enlightenment in France, 1763–1815*. Princeton, NJ: Princeton University Press.

Allen, Caitlyn. 2001. "What Do You Do Over There Anyway? Tales of an Academic Dual Citizen." In *Feminist Science Studies: A New Generation*, edited by Maralee Mayberry, Banu Subramaniam, and Lisa H. Weasel, 22–29. New York: Routledge.

Anderson, Warwick. 2006. *Colonial Pathologies: American Tropical Medicine, Race and Hygiene in the Philippines*. Durham, NC: Duke University Press.

Benjamin, Ruha. 2017. "But . . . There Are New Suns!" *Palimpsest* 6 (2): 103–5.

Chalouh, Marie, and Louise Malette, eds. 1991. *The Montreal Massacre*. Charlottetown, PEI: Ragweed Press.

Chua, Mel, and Ian Smith. 2019. "Alternate-University ASEE: An Engineering Education Conference Session from a World Where the Majority of Engineers Are Deaf." ASEE Annual Conference, June 16–19, Tampa, FL.

Cieminski, Mitch. 2019. "Queer(y)-ing Technical Practice: Queer Experiences in Student Theater Production at a Technical University." ASEE Annual Conference, June 16–19, Tampa, FL.

Clancy, Kathryn B. H., Robin G. Nelson, Julienne N. Rutherford, and Katie Hind. 2014. "Survey of Academic Field Experiences (SAFE): Trainees Report Harassment and Assault." *PLoS One* 9 (7): 102172. https://doi.org/10.1371/journal.pone.0102172.

Clare, Eli. 2017. *Brilliant Imperfection*. Durham, NC: Duke University Press.

Daly, Mary. 1978. *Gyn/ecology: The MetaEthics of Radical Feminism.* Boston, MA: Beacon Press.
Devlin, Bernie, Stephen E. Fienberg, Daniel P. Resnick, and Kathryn Roeder, eds. 1997. *Intelligence, Genes, and Success: Scientists Respond to* The Bell Curve. New York: Springer.
Edelman, Lee. 2004. *No Future: Queer Theory and the Death Drive.* Durham, NC: Duke University Press.
Ferguson, Roderick. 2012. *The Reorder of Things: The University and Its Pedagogies of Minority Difference.* Minneapolis: University of Minnesota Press.
Fifield, Steven and Will Letts. 2019. "Prolegomenon: Queer Theories and STEM Education." In *STEM of Desire: Queer Theories and Science Education,* edited by Will Letts and Steve Fifield, 3–40. Leiden: Brill/Sense.
Foster, Ellen. 2017. "Making Cultures: Politics of Inclusion, Accessibility, and Empowerment at the Margins of the Maker Movement." PhD dissertation, Rensselaer Polytechnic Institute.
Funk, Nanette. 2013. "Contra Fraser on Feminism and Neoliberalism." *Hypatia* 28 (1): 179–86.
Giordano, Sara. 2014. "Scientific Reforms, Feminist Interventions, and the Politics of Knowing: An Auto-ethnography of a Feminist Neuroscientist." *Hypatia* 29 (4): 755–62.
Gomez, Pablo F. 2018. "Caribbean Stones and the Creation of Early-Modern Worlds." *History and Technology* 34 (1): 11–20.
González Stokas, Ariana. 2014. "A Genealogy of Grit: Education in the Gilded Age." *Educational Theory* 65 (5): 513–528.
Hacker, Sally. 1989. *Pleasure, Power, and Technology.* London: Unwin Hyman.
Haraway, Donna. 1988. "Situated Knowledges: The Science Question in Feminism and the Privilege of Partial Perspective." *Feminist Studies* 14 (3): 575–99.
Harrison, Beverly W. 1985. "The Power of Anger in the Work of Love." In *Making the Connections: Essays in Feminist Social Ethics,* edited by Carol Robb, 3–21. Boston, MA: Beacon Press.
Hundle, Anneeth Kaur. 2019. "Decolonializing Diversity: The Transnational Politics of Minority Racial Difference." *Public Culture* 31 (2): 289–322.
Irigaray, Luce. 1985. "The 'Mechanics' of Fluids." In *This Sex Which Is Not One,* translated by Catherine Porter with Carolyn Burk, 106–18. Ithaca, NY: Cornell University Press.
Kafer, Alison. 2013. *Feminist Queer Crip.* Bloomington: Indiana University Press.
Kaplan, Carla, Sarah Haley, and Durba Mitra. 2021. "Introduction." In "Outraged/Enraged: The Rage Special Issue," special issue, *Signs* 46 (4): 785–800.

Kapp, Diana. 2007. "The Scandal, the Scapegoats, and the Suicide." *San Francisco Magazine*, March 2007. Archived March 29, 2010. https://web.archive.org/web/20100329015926/http://www.sanfranmag.com/story/scandal-scapegoats-and-suicide.

la paperson. 2017. *A Third University Is Possible*. Minneapolis: University of Minnesota Press.

Letts, Will, and Steve Fifield, eds. 2019. *STEM of Desire: Queer Theories and Science Education*. Leiden: Brill/Sense.

Medina, Eden. 2018. "Forensic Identification in the Aftermath of Human Rights Crimes in Chile: A Decentered Computer History." *Technology and Culture* 59 (4S): S100–S133.

Mohanty, Chandra Talpade. 2003. *Feminism without Borders: Decolonizing Theory, Practicing Solidarity*. Durham, NC: Duke University Press.

Mukerji, Chandra. 2009. *Impossible Engineering: Technology and Territoriality on the Canal Du Midi*. Princeton, NJ: Princeton University Press.

Mukharji, Projit. 2018. "Occulted Materialities." *History and Technology* 34 (1): 31–40.

Nelson, Alondra, ed. 2002. *Afrofuturism*. Durham, NC: Duke University Press.

Phipps, Allison. 2018. "What the 'Grievance Studies' Hoax Is Really About." *Times Higher Education*, October 4, 2018. https://www.timeshighereducation.com/opinion/what-grievance studies-hoax-really-about.

Ramas, Maria. 1980. "Freud's Dora, Dora's Hysteria: The Negation of a Woman's Rebellion." *Feminist Studies* 6 (3): 472–510.

Riley, Donna M. 2014. "What's Wrong with Evidence? Epistemological Roots and Pedagogical Implications of 'Evidence-Based Practice' in STEM Education." ASEE Annual Conference, June 15–18, Indianapolis, IN.

———. 2017. "Rigor/Us: Building Boundaries and Disciplining Diversity with Standards of Merit." *Engineering Studies* 9 (2): 1–17.

———. 2019. "Pipelines, Persistence, and Perfidy: Institutional Unknowing and Betrayal Trauma in Engineering." *Feminist Formations* 31 (1): 1–19.

Secules, Stephen, Ayush Gupta, Andrew Elby, and Chandra Turpen. 2018. "Zooming Out from the Struggling Individual Student: An Account of the Cultural Construction of Engineering Ability in an Undergraduate Programming Class." *Journal of Engineering Education* 107 (1): 56–86.

Slaton, Amy E. 2010. *Race, Rigor and Selectivity in U.S. Engineering: The History of an Occupational Color Line*. Cambridge, MA: Harvard University Press.

———. In preparation. "All Good People: Difference, Diversity and the Invention of Opportunity."

Slaton, Amy E., Erin Cech, and Donna Riley. 2019. "Yearning, Learning and

Earning." In *STEM of Desire: Queer Theories and Science Education*, edited by Will Letts and Steve Fifield, 319–40. Leiden: Brill/Sense.

Sokal, Alan, and Jean Bricmont. 1997. *Fashionable Nonsense*. New York: Picador.

Taylor, Ashley. 2018. "Knowledge Citizens? Intellectual Disability and the Production of Social Meanings within Education Research." *Harvard Educational Review* 88 (1): 1–26.

Trouillot, Michel-Rolph. 1995. *Silencing the Past: Power and the Production of History*. Boston, MA: Beacon Press.

University of Wisconsin–Madison Oral History Project. 2009. "Oral History #644–Denice Denton." https://wiseli.wisc.edu/wp-content/uploads/sites/662/2018/11/oralhistory_transcript.pdf.

Viner, Katharine. 2000. "Hand-to-Brand Combat: A Profile of Naomi Klein." *The Guardian*, September 23, 2000. http://www.guardian.co.uk/weekend/story/0,3605,371824,00.html.

SECTION IV. BOOK REVIEWS

Jennifer Pinck's paintings reflect a turn from a trailblazing career in the design and construction industry to her current journey as an artist. Observing and interpreting the natural landscape, buildings, shadows, light, and color are integral to her process. Pinck draws on decades of experience converting two-dimensional plans into three-dimensional structures. The same attention to detail she brought to her storied career now informs her practice as a painter. In her painting studio in Gloucester, Massachusetts, she has now immersed herself in creating art and exploring mediums and compositions. In her professional career, she was the first woman to obtain a full Boston Builder's License (1986), worked on the tallest cast-in-place skyscraper in New England, and had lead roles on both of New England's megaprojects, first as construction manager on the Deer Island Treatment Plant and then as mitigation director on the Big Dig. She delivered over $6 billion worth of projects through her former company, Pinck & Co., a project management firm serving nonprofit, public sector, and institutional clients. She can be reached at jenpinck@gmail.com.

Jennifer Pinck, *Leaving*, 2022. Oil on canvas.

Jennifer Pinck, *Suitcase Showcase—On the Move*, 2022. Oil on panel.

Review of *Voices That Matter* by Marlene Schäfers

Özgün Basmaz

Marlene Schäfers's *Voices That Matter: Kurdish Women at the Limits of Representation in Contemporary Turkey*, Chicago, IL: University of Chicago Press, 2022

The portrayal of Kurdish women as powerless victims has long been prevalent in the cultural and official nationalist narratives in Turkey. The Turkish state has strategically capitalized on these representations to stigmatize the Kurdish culture as backward and oppressive and to characterize Kurdish men as brutal, tyrannical, and prone to violence while advancing nationalist agendas and justifying ongoing military interventions in Kurdish populated regions. It is worth noting that even scholarly works, despite their intent to provide intersectional analysis of Kurdish women's experiences addressing both gender and ethnic identities, have sometimes inadvertently perpetuated this image of Kurdish women primarily as "the oppressed."

In recent years, Kurdish women, particularly those involved in the YPJ (Yekîneyên Parastina Jin / women's protection units), have garnered significant recognition in Western academia and media. This increased visibility, especially since the lifting of the siege of Kobane in Syrian Kurdistan in 2015, has spotlighted Kurdish women combatants who actively participated alongside their male counterparts and U.S. forces in the fight against ISIS. Indeed, their active participation in traditionally male-dominated spheres of politics and the military has been celebrated not only for subverting the stereotype of Kurdish women. They were also acknowledged for opening new possibilities for subaltern agencies, political empowerment, and revolutionary practices among women, in their resistance against prevailing familial and societal expectations, along with oppressive imperial and patriarchal systems.

However, the images of Kurdish women are often relegated to two extremes: either as silent, oppressed victims or as revolutionary freedom fighters. Within these portrayals, their experiences are often oversimplified and essentialized, with little to no consideration given to their diversity in terms of location, class, ethnicity, sexuality, and politics. It has also obscured our understanding of the intricate effects of both local and global conditions on their lives, shaped by globalization, neoliberal policies, imperialism, and various cultural and political dynamics.

Marlene Schäfers's *Voices That Matter: Kurdish Women at the Limits of Representation in Contemporary Turkey* provides readers with a comprehensive and nuanced understanding of the diversity and complexity of Kurdish women's lives and experiences. This meticulously crafted ethnography delves into the profound world of women dengbêjs, Kurdish folk singer–storytellers who recite nonfictional stories, Kurdish legends and fables, and laments in long, wailing overtone singing. *Voices That Matter* offers a powerful account of their stories and their ongoing struggle for "voice" in contemporary Turkey. It emerges as a profound and thought-provoking contribution to the ongoing dialogue about voices, agency, and empowerment of the subaltern.

The book skillfully connects the experiences, desires, and aspirations of women dengbêjs to the intricate conditions shaped by the complex interplay of patriarchy, capitalism, nationalism, and imperialism. It conducts a thorough analysis of the historical legacies, political significance, communal effects, and personal aspirations of women dengbêjs, all the while shedding light on how their experiences were shaped by the music market's dynamics and patriarchal and imperial disciplinary mechanisms at the backdrop of an ongoing situation marked by political conflict and state violence. By scrutinizing and challenging the prevalent assumption in feminist thought that inherently links voice—having a voice, raising one's voice—with liberation, empowerment, and agency, Schäfers encourages readers to reassess the limits and meanings of agency.

The book is organized into five chapters alongside an introduction and conclusion. Through a comprehensive examination of the textual, poetic, and melodic qualities of the kilam genre, a fusion of singing and narration, chapter 1 provides an account of how women dengbêjs performing kilam evoke visceral emotions, making listeners tremble, shiver, or even shed tears. Schäfers explores the transformative, cathartic, healing, and provocative role of women dengbêjs who, through the artful stylization of their voice and narratives, convert individual pain and suffering into a communal experience. The writer contends that women dengbêjs undertake a vital social and political function. However, rather than interpreting these performances solely through the lens of subaltern agency, she draws attention to the fact that the voice can be detached from its human bearer—whether that bearer gives voice to the sufferings and longings of others or serves as a mere performer of an already constructed text. With careful attention to such matters, Schäfers encourages readers to consider a more nuanced understanding of the relationship between voice and agency.

Chapter 2 further explores how the dengbêjs' performances can contribute to our understanding of the complex and diverse workings of agency within the context of the modern mass media and sound technologies, such as cassette tapes, radio, tape recorders, and social media. Contesting the assumption that technology dilutes the emotional impact of such performances, the writer raises thought-provoking questions about how technology intersects with voice and agency to generate unique and novel forms of intimacy and immediacy between individual and collective subjectivity. Drawing from the ethnographic accounts of women, Schäfers illustrates how tape cassettes, tape recorders, and social media facilitate the transmission and exchange of these highly emotional and gendered kilam performances, connecting them with a broader community. She combines this analysis with the historic role that Radio Yerevan, the Kurdish broadcasting service of Public Radio of Armenia, has had on Kurds living in Turkey during lengthy periods of surveillance and censorship. Schäfers highlights how voice, even detached from its human source, emerges as a powerful social and political tool of preserving and disseminating cultural heritage and a sense of national identity that has endured decades of denial.

In chapter 3, the book delves even deeper into the rich ethnographic accounts provided by women dengbêjs. Focusing on the intricate interplay between the performer's voice, their self, and others' sorrow, it explores the relationship between the collective and individual. Here, the writer argues that the voices of dengbêjs become a site where self and other converges as the performers empathetically relate to the other women's experience of pain and embody the emotional pain of fellow women through their voice. In this nuanced perspective, dengbêjs' voices cease to be mere representations of the performers themselves, or a singular representation of all Kurdish women. Instead, they emerge as an expression of the collective suffering that many Kurdish women have endured. Departing from the conventional framing of the voice as a vehicle for self-representation, Schäfers offers a fresh interpretation of women dengbêjs' voices as a fusion of diverse individual subjectivities and genre conventions, in the formation of a collective narrative. To add another layer of complexity to the intricate relationship between the collective and individual, Schäfers explores how women dengbêjs aspire to leverage these performances for social recognition and financial stability. She also clarifies these performances' utility for asserting Kurdish women's indelible contribution to the formation and preservation of the Kurdish cultural heritage. Their struggle, however, is fraught with challenges, as they confront censure, shaming, and violence from the restrictive patriarchal traditions within both Kurdish culture and the state. Chapter 4 further delves into the multifaceted struggles faced by these performers as they boldly navigate their roles, claiming their authorship and voices as Kurdish women within the complex context of cultural, societal, and political forces, along with the profound impacts of modern mass media and the neoliberal dynamics of the music industry.

Schäfers's incisive examination of contemporary paradigms that exalt the concept of the voice as symbols of empowerment and agency culminates in the fifth chapter and its concluding remarks. She astutely argues that while the politics of representation and the emphasis on amplifying voices may initially seem empowering to marginalized communities, an unwavering ideological fixation on the voice can inadvertently exacerbate the very marginalization it seeks to address. Drawing on a series of compelling examples, primarily focusing on the experiences of women dengbêjs participating in events organized by Kurdish political parties and ostensibly progressive Turkish and European NGOs, Schäfers illuminates how these voices can be co-opted, stripped of their inherent cultural significance, depoliticized, and manipulated to serve different political agendas and interests. In the end, Schäfers makes a persuasive case for the importance of acknowledging the multifaceted nature of the voice. She contends that valorizing the voice without a comprehensive appreciation of its personal, communal, cultural, and political contexts can lead to personal disillusionment and the creation of hierarchical distinctions among voices, wherein some are deemed valuable and useful, while others are rendered insignificant, radical, and perilous.

One notable aspect of the book is its extensive reliance on theoretical frameworks. While this lends depth and academic rigor to the narrative, there are moments when the theoretical discussions overshadow the clarity of the author's core argument. This may pose a challenge even for readers well-versed in the subject matter. However, Schäfers skillfully draws from a diverse array of disciplines and theories of gender, the subaltern, nationalism, imperialism, affect, music, and critical discourse analysis. This interdisciplinary approach not only enriches the book's content but also makes it essential reading for those interested in Kurdish studies as well as gender, postcolonial, and race studies.

Voices That Matter is an assiduously crafted exploration of the complexities and potentials inherent in "the voice" through the lens of the experiences and challenges of Kurdish women dengbêjs in the precarious sociopolitical, cultural, and economic landscape of Turkey. In doing so, the book makes a significant and thought-provoking contribution to the ongoing debates concerning the voices, agency, and empowerment of the subaltern.

Originally from Turkey, **Özgün Basmaz** is pursuing a PhD in American studies at Purdue University. Currently she is completing her dissertation, "Hollywood/Holivut: American Cinema in the Making of Transnational World," and teaching courses for the Women's, Gender, and Sexuality Studies Program at Purdue University. She graduated from the Department of English Language and Literature at Boğaziçi University in 2003. She received her MA in intercultural Anglophone studies from Bayreuth University in Germany in 2006 and then went to the U.S. to receive her second MA in history at the University of Akron. She can be reached at obasmaz@purdue.edu.

Korea's #MeToo Movement and the New Feminist Generation

Haeseong Park

Hawon Jung's *Flowers of Fire: The Inside Story of South Korea's Feminist Movement and What It Means for Women's Rights Worldwide*, Dallas: BenBella Books, 2023

Although there are some scholarly works in English on Korean women and feminism, little has been published about the extraordinary developments of recent years. Journalist Hawon Jung has written in a clear and compassionate tone about what she has personally witnessed on the ground. Jung has done this not only to introduce Korean feminist movements to English audiences but also to advocate for Korean women in the hope that the Korean feminist movement will continue to move forward in the face of the current backlash.

The book starts with the Korean #MeToo movement in 2018, followed by a very brief historiography of Korean women's movements and a new wave of Korean feminist movements. Jung posits that misogynistic online culture in Korea sparked fourth-wave feminism in 2015. This grassroots movement utilized the internet and social media and then took to the streets in 2016. The book discusses major gender issues and women's movements in Korea in roughly chronological order. This approach effectively explains how Korean millennial feminists paved the way for the Korean #MeToo movement to explode, in contrast to nearby countries such as China and Japan, and for Korean feminists to have the momentum to push their work forward. Moreover, the chapter structure provides a clear roadmap of what this new generation of Korean feminists has achieved: from bringing men's sexual misconduct to justice, through fighting against digital sex crimes and defying sexist beauty standards, to winning abortion rights in 2019. Beyond the recent successes of Korean feminists, Jung acknowledges their "divisions and missteps" (7) and the backlash of widespread anti-feminism, especially among young men and in an increasingly conservative political atmosphere. Nonetheless, Jung concludes the book by assuring readers that Korean women, armed with their newfound language and experience of solidarity, will persist in making progress.

An important strength of this book is the use of in-depth interviews that convey the reality of everyday life in Korea and that support the author's arguments. Jung often concludes her chapters, and in fact the book itself, with the words of interviewees to substantiate her own opinions. Furthermore, the personal stories told by the interviewees, sometimes feminist activists and sometimes victims of sexual violence, help readers to establish empathy with the interviewees' journeys to find their voice and solidarity out of pain and shame. The wealth of interviews and Jung's firsthand experience and interaction with feminist activists and victims give this book an almost primary-source quality. The personal accounts are given a broader significance through the use of statistics and public reports.

The author is effective in showing how Korean women have broken their silence, but the book lacks the voice of men, particularly anti-feminist men. These counter-voices could provide the readers with a more holistic yet deeper understanding of Korean women's circumstances. In addition, Jung, who is critical of the essentialism of Korean radical feminists, does not question how other Korean feminists define the category of women. Jung also fails to pay attention to class and diversity issues among women in Korea, such as migrant women workers and foreign wives, even though some of her interviews raise these issues. For instance, Jung introduces a working-class woman who educated herself in feminism, which she described as "an unaffordable luxury . . . a posh, abstract, and meaningless concept that belonged to a different world—the world of well-educated, middle-class people" (142–43). This may be because Jung, coming from a journalism background, intends to present contemporary Korean feminism as it is: second-wave content that overlooks differences between women and women in the fourth-wave medium of digital communication.

In this book, Hawon Jung stands with women activists and victims of sexual violence to present their wounds, anger, courage, and resistance. She allows the subjects of her research to speak in their own words, from their own perspectives. She makes no attempt to impose any theoretical discourse. Because this book presents such a vivid portrait of women's lives in contemporary South Korea, it is well suited for college courses in both Asian studies and women's studies. The examples Jung offers should generate lively discussion and allow the Korean case to help bridge the gap between theory and reality.

Haeseong Park is a member of the Community Faculty at Metropolitan State University. She has published several journal articles and book chapters on Korean women, post-/colonialism, and Christianity. She can be reached at haeseong.park@metrostate.edu.

On Connecting Dots and Keeping Your Eyes on the Power

Georgie Malone

Laura Bates's *Fix the System, Not the Women* (2nd ed.), London, UK: Simon & Schuster, 2023

Fix the System, Not the Women is a rallying cry to reject, without reserve, the ideological linchpin of patriarchy that it is not the misogyny baked into our core institutions that is responsible for gender inequality, but rather women themselves. Whether it is a woman's choice to wear a short dress and get drunk on a Friday night, or her failure to stand up for herself and "just demand" that pay raise, there is always some reason to blame women for the harm that comes their way. Laura Bates's book thoroughly unmasks this discourse to reveal its sinister function: by blaming the women, the system gets let off the hook.

Despite a long history of feminist critique of structural misogyny, Bates is unfortunately not faced with an easy task, writing for a popular audience, when it comes to convincing readers that there is still a thing called patriarchy, alive and well today, that systematically harms women. Nevertheless, she has proven herself more than up to the task. Bates's great strength is in having lifted the enemy out from the theoretical jargon and thrown light on precisely what *systemic* misogyny is, and how it operates today, in such an abundantly clear and accessible manner. She takes in turn many of our core social institutions in the U.K.—schools and universities, policing, the criminal justice system, traditional politics, and the media—and reveals each to be systematically misogynist, using a straightforward formula: an institution is guilty if it displays gender pay and staffing gaps, high numbers of sexist incidents, weak or nonexistent policies to tackle those incidents, and a harmful gendered impact in its institutional output (92). This "test" for institutional sexism is clearly called for in our current political moment, since we must constantly withstand cries of "not all men," showing a persistent, if not perhaps willful, misunderstanding of the meaning of systemic misogyny. Unsurprisingly, one will notice that nowhere in this test is it required that all the men within a given institution are hateful bigots. Once equipped with her test, Bates proceeds to present clear and compelling evidence that, when measured against these criteria, all the above-mentioned institutions in the U.K. are systematically misogynist. Another strength of her analysis is its attention to the intersectional dimensions at play, always bringing out the ways in which this systematic misogyny intersects with other oppressive systems, most strikingly, systematic racism. By the end of the book, she has robustly secured her conclusion that what urgently needs fixing is the system, not the women in it, and resolutely shifts the burden of proof onto anyone who would argue otherwise.

The main source of the book's impressiveness, however, is not just in its presentation of a compelling case for systemic change but in its critique of the ideology that obscures the need for this very change: this is the logic of "fix the women." Bates artfully deconstructs this logic to show how it infects the way male violence is treated at every level, with the result of mystifying the systemic nature of the problem. Bates begins by showing how this ideology is learned early. She demonstrates how schools teach more than just curricula but also the rules of the social game, supplying a "very effective form of 'education'" in sexist norms, including, crucially, the norm that women are responsible for preventing and responding to male violence (25). Examples she draws upon include testimony from women teachers who are expected to withstand daily low-level sexual harassment from teenage boys, and several cases in which school-age girls have been expected to dress differently so as not to provoke harassment from fellow students or male teachers. This allows us to see that expecting women to change is a feature of the system, not a bug. When people in power say the women must change, they are not making bumbling errors of judgment, they are enacting one of the most critical pieces of the patriarchal puzzle that defends against any serious challenge to the status quo. "Fix the women" is what undermines the groundswell for principled, collective women's resistance. "Fix the women" is what normalizes and justifies the violence, rape, and murder. "Fix the women" must be rejected because it is part of the very violence itself.

Despite the book's strength in this regard, when read as a work of *critique*, I'm called to think about how Bates's work is situated in relation to a broader tradition of critical social theory, including especially black radical and black feminist traditions, and I can't help but wonder whether she has adequately discharged the responsibility she bears towards forerunners in these traditions. There are, of course, many ways to change a system and, in her survey of positive proposals, Bates displays a marked tendency to stay quiet about the radicalism towards which her critique naturally leads. Despite allusions to the interrelatedness of patriarchy and capitalism, for example, Bates does not suggest that fixing the system could mean overthrowing the capitalist economic order. Similarly, though she discusses the intersection between patriarchy and historical colonialism, she fails to consider the relationship between gender, race, exploitation, and ongoing neocolonialist projects in her discussion of "global misogyny" (149). For example, when she writes that "there is no country on earth in which systemic gender inequality has been left in the past. And what underpins this inequality is the same in the U.K. as it is in South Africa, India, Canada, or Russia," she omits the role of imperialist regimes in importing repressive and hierarchical gender systems in other parts of the world or in stoking existing divisions (151).

Bates's most glaring omission in this regard is, in my opinion, her failure to draw a line from her critique of policing to police and prison abolitionism. Fully two chapters in *Fix the System* are dedicated to charting institutional sexism, and its intersection with institutional racism, within the U.K. police and criminal justice system. Yet, despite its rich history and relative popularity, abolition is never mentioned as a plausible direction forward. This does a disservice to those scholars who have long argued that abolition is the only answer to these problems. Given the obvious connection, I cannot imagine the omission was not a choice and, presuming as much, there are two ways one might interpret it. On the one hand, Bates is writing for a popular audience that may be new to the kinds of ideas she is presenting. She may thus be wary of forwarding ideas perceived to be *too* radical and, therefore, liable to scare tentative new readers away. By keeping these readers on board, she may argue, she stands to open more minds to her cause. While I do not deny the merit of such pragmatics, there is also a question of responsibility here. By not taking the step to suggest that abolitionist or anti-capitalist solutions should be on the table (in fact, not even mentioning that they *are* undeniably on the table, let alone whether they *should* be), Bates risks giving readers the impression that such ideas, and those who put them forward, are beyond the pale, worthy of marginalization to the fringes of political thought to which they're usually cast. Bates had an opportunity here to push back and explicitly link up her brilliantly clear and accessible analysis with these radical traditions of thought. Unfortunately, it was not one she saw fit to make more use of.

There are two central refrains to which Bates repeatedly refers us: *join the dots* and *keep your eye on where the power is*. The fact is that the power runs deeper, and the dots create much more complex networks, than even Bates gives away in her book. When one keeps one's eyes on power, one cannot fail to ignore the concerns of abolitionists, anti-capitalists, and decolonial scholars and activists. The theme of the present issue of *Women's Studies Quarterly* is "Pandemonium," and *Fix the System* certainly evokes the pandemonium that characterizes much recent feminist struggle in the U.K. Bates thematizes at length the tragic case of Sarah Everard's murder by London Metropolitan Police Officer Wayne Couzens in the spring of 2021. She is right to pay close attention to this moment, because it was a critical one for women in the U.K. We took to the streets enraged, and it was clear to me that the energy at those protests demonstrated that frustration was running deeper, that different causes were being linked up, and that a more radical consciousness was being refined, led especially by groups like Sisters Uncut who unequivocally oppose state violence in all its forms. *Defund* and *abolish* could be read across many of the placards that were held around New Scotland Yard, and great solidarity was displayed across feminist and anti-racist struggle. Pandemonium prevails today, too, as the U.K. sees mass strike waves across the public sector opposing the devastation of our vital public services and the creep of privatization. Here, too, is an opportunity to connect our struggles and build greater solidarity. In a moment like this, it is vital we heed Bates's call and continue to join more dots than perhaps even she is willing to, and to make sure we have our eyes on where the power is, so that we can come together to collectively oppose its misuse.

Georgie Malone is a PhD student in philosophy at the Graduate Center, CUNY. Her research sits primarily within Marxist and feminist political philosophy and critical theory, with particular focus on ideology, pornography and sexuality, and transformative politics. She can be reached at gmalone@gradcenter.cuny.edu.

Disrupting Disciplinary Norms and Advocating for Feminist Solidarity through Coalition Building, Healing Justice Lineages, and Collective Care

Kimberly Williams Brown

Liza Taylor's *Feminism in Coalition: Thinking with U.S. Women of Color Feminism*, Durham: Duke University Press, 2022

Cara Page and Erica Woodland's *Healing Justice Lineages: Dreaming at the Crossroads of Liberation, Collective Care, and Safety*, Berkeley: North Atlantic Books, 2023

Marquis Bey controversially says that anybody can be Black. By that, he means that there is a particular politics that makes one radical that usually has little to do with the skin in which a person is born. Race, of course, matters. We know this because nations have been disseminated in the name of racism, and racial capital hierarchies run the world and have material consequences we observe. But, more importantly, to undo racial capitalism, Bey calls us, as do Liza Taylor, Cara Page, and Erica Woodland, the authors of the texts under review, to understand how racial identity is an approximation to politics that must always be mitigated by a radical consciousness of lineage, history, and collectivity. To be abolitionist in one's politics means more than just addressing the prison industrial complex (PIC). It means understanding that the PIC is one cog in the machine of systems that incarcerate, immobilize, and make sick those of us sitting at the margins. These thematic connections cut across both texts.

Methodologically, both texts combine textual analysis with interviews, conference presentations, and personal experiences. Both texts, especially *Healing Justice Lineages*, call for the reader to engage all her senses and her entire being. To heal is to understand the source of pain and trauma and to work to address that source by creating a plan for unlearning unhealthy coping mechanisms and relearning healthy ones, including understanding how the oppressive systems we were born into may be abolished. In *Healing Justice Lineages: Dreaming at the Crossroads of Liberation, Collective Care, and Safety*, Cara Page and Erica Woodland take us on a journey to deeply understanding the collective healing lineages that have always existed in Black, Indigenous, and People of Color communities and from which healing-justice practitioners have pulled. In *Feminism in Coalition: Thinking with U.S. Women of Color Feminism*, Liza Taylor hopes to heal a discipline rife with discursive understanding of coalition as ontological unfixedness. Political theory, she argues, has exclusively relied on a Marxist orientation that insists on a single axis for analysis of oppression—class. Taylor's work is to introduce to political theorists the work of women of color feminists, who, since the formation of the union and the twin evils of slavery and settler colonialism, have called us to understanding multi-issue coalitions as essential to practical moves of justice to upend oppression. Taylor deftly points to Rosa Luxemburg, whose interpretation of historical materialism disavows the rigidity of Lenin's interpretation and therefore articulates a more fluid and unpredictable sensing of class rooted in the experience of lived struggle. Both texts do the work of healing lineages, although only one text is named as such. Both texts draw on the commitments of lived experiences in Queer and Trans Black, Indigenous, and People of Color communities that sustain us through struggle, resistance, and a willingness to work across differences.

If *Feminism in Coalition* is the theoretical underpinning for a call to action for collective strategies of freedom, then *Healing Justice Lineages* is the praxis that makes the theoretical foundation come alive. *Feminism in Coalition* disputes the "crisis" of post-Marxist left-oriented politics asserting that coalition necessitates an anti-capitalist orientation and a material understanding of what it means to build justice movements across difference. *Healing Justice Lineages* is a call to action to those who want to build long-term infrastructure for collective care and safety outside of carceral strategies. Page and Woodland reinforce this by saying that the book is also a call to action for those who can never have liberation without collective strategies to transform trauma, which is intergenerational, collective, and historical (7).

Taylor, arguing in chapter 1 of *Feminism in Coalition* against Laclau and Mouffe in their text *Hegemony and Socialist Strategy* (1985), disputes the claim that "the movements of the 1960s had exploded the Marxist notion that *class* is the primary marker of forms of social injustice" (7). She takes issue with Laclau and Mouffe's, Judith Butler's, and Jasbir Puar's work that mark all identity categories as forever unstable or unfixed due to ongoing discursive production. The book spends much of the first chapter situating Lenin's and Laclau and Mouffe's orientation in dialectic materialism. Laclau and Mouffe, she argues, inaccurately name a crisis of Marxism as the backdrop to contemporary theories of progressive coalition politics. She says, for example,

> The disjuncture between what coalition activists report in the trenches and what many mainstream political theorists theorize about in academic writing troubles me, and not just because of the charge that it widens the theory-practice divide (which, indeed, it does) and thus delegitimates political theory as a vocation. My concerns run deeper. Dominant strands of contemporary political theory (including, among others, those shaped by post structuralist influences), I fear, are stymied by this growing dissonance, leaving them ill-prepared to conceive of effective intersectional collective responses in a Trump United States. (7)

This paragraph makes clear that political theorists are not "on the ground" in their analysis of the politics of coalition-building. Taylor suggests that political theorists, over time, have become devoid of the ability to be intersectional and collective in their attempt to theorize the current political climate.

Chapter 2 moves more fluidly into a discussion of women of color feminists, who deeply understand the politics of struggle as an organizing analytic toward coalition and against power systems. In this chapter, Taylor invokes Bernice Johnson Reagon, Barbara Smith, the Combahee River Collective, Audre Lorde, and Chandra Talpade Mohanty as feminists in a lineage of writers, thinkers, and activists who articulate what Taylor names as a politico-ethical coalition politics. Coalition must be born in struggle "and must be shaped by a shared and actively chosen political commitment to undermine interlocking oppressive forces" (100). These women of color feminists, she argues, understand that the personal nature of struggle in intimate "home" spaces does not reduce the power of difference.

Chapter 3, titled "Coalition from the Inside Out: Struggling toward Coalitional Identity and Developing a Coalitional Consciousness with Lorde, Anzaldúa, Sandoval, and Pratt," speaks to the importance of developing a consciousness that allows coalitional possibilities. Critiquing Butler, Puar, and others, Taylor demonstrates that their dismissal of women of color feminists is a shallow reading and understanding of coalitional politics. In the middle of the chapter, under a section called "Coalitional Consciousness: Rethinking Epistemological Undecidability," Taylor summarizes the chapter with the following quote: "U.S. third world feminists must recognize that our learned sensitivity to the mobile webs of power is a skill that, once developed, can become a sophisticated form of oppositional consciousness" (129). She ends the chapter with a discussion of Minnie Bruce Pratt's autobiography, a nonlinear account of a white woman's struggle toward coalitional identity and developing coalitional consciousness.

By way of Cynthia Burack's work, chapter 4 theorizes about coalition scholarship as it thinks with *This Bridge Called My Back*. Burack's book *Healing Identities: Black Feminist Thought and the Politics of Groups* is the text that Taylor thinks alongside that is most closely aligned with *Healing Justice Lineages*. This important connection is productive for understanding the role of healing justice as part of coalitional spaces and as part of coming into coalitional consciousness. Although not named specifically, Taylor might agree that a book about healing justice lineages is genealogically kin to her own work tracing and introducing the lineage of Black feminist politics in relation to political theory that has largely dismissed or ignored this lineage. One might say Taylor is attempting to heal a discipline. Comparing *Bridge* to other texts calling for collectivity but falling short of coalitional politics and writing, Taylor makes the argument that *Bridge* and other coalitional texts, such as those by the Sangtin Writers, are politico-ethical coalitional texts.

Chapter 5 departs methodologically and periodically from the first four chapters, as we are invited to think about the coalitional reverberations of the 2017 Women's March on Washington. This chapter attempts to ground the previous textual analysis through the case study of the Women's March by not positioning it as a perfect example of coalition but pointing out that it is the imperfection of the struggle and the missteps of the organizing that clue us in to the fact of an imperfect politico-ethico movement described as the single largest coordinated protest in U.S. history and one of the largest in the world. Taylor effectively argues that the success of the Women's March was its intersectional grounding, its dogged commitment to politics as demonstrated through the removal of anti-choice protesters as sponsors of the march, the movement away from identitarian women's issues to a political feminist stance, and the invitation from women of color to white women to be more intersectional in their politics. Brilliantly, she critiques and names the ontological entrapment involved in calling the march a "women's march," about which the organizers struggled to be precise in their language and commitments.

Pulling from feminists engaged in intersectional work, Taylor brilliantly ends the text with quotes about why coalitional politics are necessary if we are to be effective at changing systems of oppression. In particular, Taylor's calling her field, political theory, to task by admonishing them in the last lines of the book, as she has throughout the text, to be thoughtful about who they cite because citation matters, was the most effective way to end a book tracing the lineage of coalitional building. Political theorists have much work to do to take seriously this text calling them to action about how they understand coalitional politics.

In *Healing Justice Lineages: Dreaming at the Crossroads of Liberation, Collective Care, and Safety*, Page and Woodland take us on a journey engaging our senses and calling us to read not only intellectually but also spiritually. Healing justice as memory work is rooted in the philosophy of liberatory harm reduction that resists the individual consumerist practices of self-care and embraces the coalitional possibilities that require doctors, social workers, legislative policymakers, healers, and organizers to make room for the fact that their ideas of bodies, safety, and health leave out many people in community spaces. The healing justice framework is not merely a response to political, racial, and health forces but a reconfiguration of what it means to be in collectivity and accountable to generational structural harm.

The book is divided into four sections, called "Past: Reckoning with Roots and Lineage," "Origins of Healing Justice," "Alchemy: Theory + Praxis," and "Political + Spiritual Imperatives for the Future." In the first section, Page and Woodland call us to reckon with the past by saying that "forgetting is a tool of white supremacy. It keeps us from building upon prior strategies led by our ancestors and elders" (34). To demonstrate this, they trace the roots of organizations such as the Black Panther Party, the Young Lords, and American Indian organizations that have been steeped in mutual aid, harm reduction, and healing justice work in their communities for centuries.

A beautiful playlist of healing justice songs appears between sections 1 and 2. In section 2, "Origins of Healing Justice," Page and Woodland use water and fire as metaphors for effectively articulating to readers the methods of the southern Kindred Collective as they unroot the histories of transatlantic slavery and colonialism that created histories of trauma in the south. The Kindred Collective began its work at political tables, organizing campaigns in Georgia for migrant justice and racial justice and against Islamophobia with local partners. They did this while also advocating for a greater political role of healers and nurses capable of integrating care and wellness inside movement spaces in response to interrupting the complicity of healthcare systems with police and other criminal justice. Kindred's definition of healing justice is "how we cast into movements our traditions, tools, and strategies to keep our folks in the long struggle for justice. Healing justice must be integral to building liberation and strategies to heal and transform generational trauma and conjure traditions of caring for one another" (130). This attention to generational trauma and a communal and collective response to healing justice is representative of this section and the text at large.

In the third section, "Alchemy: Theory + Praxis," the authors center political frameworks emphasizing that healing justice takes place in geographical, place-based communities and are therefore in right-relationships with people. The authors provide a helpful timeline from 2000 to 2021 of the sites of practice for healing justice. Francisca Porchas Coronado's chapter is a refreshing transnational take on healing justice in New Mexico, as she centers the experiences of Indigenous Mexican knowledge through elders to support a healing justice framework. The chapter introduces us to various healing justice communities across the U.S. by region.

The fourth and final section, "Political + Spiritual Imperatives for the Future," begins with an invocation for healing the land and thinking with BIPOC communities disproportionately affected by the triple violent forces of colonialism, slavery, and climate change. Speaking with environmental justice, land sovereignty, and climate justice movements and advocates, the authors use poetic excerpts from interlocutors in these movements to not only understand the urgency of the moment but also to alert us to the work that is being done on behalf of the earth by these activists. These activists remind us that our coalitions and activism will be intersectional as we heal ourselves and our physical communities. The end of the text reminds us that the medical industrial complex is a prison industrial complex disguised as a place for care. As a result, we must lean heavily into abolitionist practices that ground us deeply into genuinely practiced spiritual lives. We are called to understand how all the parts of our lives and all the places we occupy are interconnected through oppression, but more importantly how this interconnectedness might be abolished and a new path forward realized.

Both books are a call to action. Both ask us to understand queer and trans BIPOC lineages in complex ways and to lean deeply into what they teach us. What we learn from them will transform disciplines, ourselves, and our planet. What I wish both texts did more of was provide a transnational account of coalitional lineages and healing justice lineages. While a transnational frame was not the focus of either text, writing about lineages requires being clear about the impact of international, global, transnational scholars, practitioners, and elders to our understanding of healing justice and coalition politics in the U.S.

Kimberly Williams Brown is the cofounder and director of the Intergroup Dialogue Collective, a nonprofit that uses intergroup dialogue praxis to engage in critical conversations about race and racism in schools and communities. She is an assistant professor at Vassar College in education, Africana studies, and women's studies. She holds a PhD and a certificate of advanced study from Syracuse University in cultural foundations of education and women and gender studies. She can be reached at kwilliamsbrown@vassar.edu.

Works Cited

Bey, Marquis. 2017. "The Trans*-ness of Blackness and the Blackness of Trans*-ness." *TSQ: Transgender Studies Quarterly* 4 (2): 275–295.

Review of *Sexual Misconduct in Academia*, edited by Erin Pritchard and Delyth Edwards

Samantha Seybold

Erin Pritchard and Delyth Edwards (ed.)'s *Sexual Misconduct in Academia: Informing an Ethics of Care in the University*, New York: Routledge, 2023

You cannot read the book that I'm reviewing.

Routledge published *Sexual Misconduct in Academia: Informing an Ethics of Care in the University* in March 2023. It then pulled the book in early September in response to an alleged defamation suit threat, leaving little trace of the volume's existence aside from a few broken links lingering on the interwebs.

This book's story compels me to depart from the standard book review formula. My review is part summary, seeking to answer the pressing question that arises: What voices, and what message, has Routledge censored? My review is also part consciousness-raising, seeking to counter the threatening twin narratives of reasonableness and mundanity poised to justify Routledge's censorship. Let's dive in.

This volume is powerful and piercing, elevating a chorus of voices that document and deconstruct the pervasiveness of sexual assault experienced by early-career researchers and staff in higher education. Pritchard and Edwards emphasize that mainstream conceptions of sexual violence in the university are often narrowly construed as something perpetrated against students. This marginalizes and even erases the coercion, exploitation, and humiliation that women and nonbinary researchers face while navigating the starkly patriarchal corridors of the academy. *Sexual Misconduct in Academia* sets these experiences front and center.

Pritchard and Edwards frame the book's project along two core "intentions": an ethics of care and a pedagogical practice (7). As a moral framework, care ethics delineates the responsibilities of moral agents in relational terms. It is thus fundamentally "grounded in the importance of voice" (7), in the dual radical practices of bringing firsthand experiences with oppression and violence into the light, and truly listening to these voices. Here the normative theory intersects with pedagogical practice, articulating teaching as a practice contextualized by historical patterns of inequality and exclusion. To fail to exercise curiosity and self-reflexivity is to fail to truly commit to the pursuit of knowledge.

The twenty-three authors in this collection meet these aims with a compelling combination of striking vulnerability and critical rigor. Over the volume's eleven chapters, they expose the many interlocking facets of academic patriarchy and how the deployment of sexual violence reinforces this system. Author Poppy Gerrard-Abbott memorably characterizes gender-based violence as an "enablement jigsaw" (64). This violence constitutes the latitude and nonanswerability this system affords to those whom Sarah Ahmed calls the "important men," the well-connected, predominantly white and upper-class scholars who occupy, run, and ultimately dominate academic spaces. Gender-based violence simultaneously maintains this arrangement by keeping women survivors in a constant state of precarity and thus deterred from (even unable to) speak out against the abuse.

Breaking this silence is at once a radical act of resistance and a radical outpouring of care. The authors expose the individual and collective trauma that seeps from academic spaces; the level of honesty and vulnerability on display here is a profound challenge to the forces conspiring to keep us both silent and tolerant toward gender-based violence. Together, the authors' honest revelations extend a mighty reassurance to survivors everywhere: *you are not alone* (221). No other four words are quite so powerful when it comes to breaking the stifling silence that keeps the patriarchy's coercive mechanisms well-oiled and churning along.

In short, this book is essential for anyone who is committed to ensuring that the university is a safe and vibrant space for every person in it.

These are the voices and the message offered by this book, the voices and message that Routledge silenced. This book's fate is of urgent concern, not only to feminists seeking to expose and dismantle the mechanisms, often violent, that keep patriarchal oppression in motion, but also to those who are dedicated to the goods of free expression and academic freedom.

According to Routledge, the book's non/existence hinges on its last chapter, chapter 12, coauthored by Lieselotte Viaene, Catarina Laranjeiro, and Miye Nadya Tom. In their chapter, the authors recount the harrowing enablement jigsaw surrounding an anonymous "Star Professor" in their graduate program. The Star Professor manipulated and sexually abused a number of young women researchers during his tenure in the program.

Following the book's publication, a Brazilian state deputy identified herself as one of the survivors described in chapter 12. The Brazilian news agency Agência Pública noted that the state deputy is one in "a series of allegations of sexual harassment" made by female former students against the Star Professor (Correia 2023).

Meanwhile, Routledge took action as well. It unilaterally removed chapter 12 from the book in response to a cease-and-desist letter that it allegedly received from a lawyer representing the Star Professor. In the letter, the Star Professor identified himself as the researcher described in the chapter and threatened to sue the publisher for defamation. When Pritchard and Edwards turned down the request to remove chapter 12, Routledge pulled the book in its entirety.

Successful defamation suits must prove (among other things) that the publisher of the allegedly defamatory statement made a false statement of fact and did so with "actual malice" (*PBS* 2023). This means that the burden of proof is on the Star Professor to show that the statements in chapter 12 are truly false. Let's not pretend that the legal system listens to or protects sexual assault survivors, but Routledge's decision seems astonishingly premature. No one should be silenced solely on the grounds that what they have experienced has the *possibility* to damage someone else's reputation. But Routledge leveraged the Star Professor's legal threat to cover up the abuse recounted in chapter 12.

In doing so, Routledge affirms the wild degree of power held by men like the Star Professor. Realize that the arm of a global publishing company with £556 million in revenue during 2020 backed down in response to one man's allegations that an anonymized chapter describes him. How much more vulnerable were the early-career researchers whom he targeted during his tenure? Let it sink in.

This book's disappearance is a microcosm of what its twenty-three authors recount in its chapters: manufactured, enforced, coercive silence. The silence is deafening. Yet instances like these are a powerful reminder that the silence is not *inevitable*. As both the book and its demise painfully illustrate, the silence is strategically, violently, and forcefully manufactured.

We must also notice that though this system is resilient and well resourced, it is also profoundly fragile. Something as simple as honesty shakes it to its core, hence the frantic efforts to suppress the change that this book catalyzes.

So, my invitation to you, dear reader: Be an agent of care in the space where you find yourself. Claw away at this monstrous, and monstrously fragile, structure of cruelty by speaking truth. Disrupt it by seeing what is meant to be invisible or erased. Talk about, in a shout or a whisper as you are able, what is meant to fall into the cracks. Stand close beside those whom this cruel system means to isolate and break. Your presence is care. Your resistance is care. Your willful knowing is a lifeline for those who are struggling to survive this manufactured silence.

As a survivor of institutionalized coercion, I cannot begin to say how much it meant to me to hear someone say, "I know, and I care." She saw me. The survivor in your circle may not even realize how crushing the weight of that secret is until you step in to help them carry it. I can promise you, you make a difference.

Lastly, to the survivors, which are so many of us: I hope you catch a glimpse of yourself being seen on the pages of this book. I hope the authors' vulnerability gives you the permission to be vulnerable, even just with yourself. Most of all, I hope that their fearless honesty refreshes and strengthens you. See the cracks in this ugly, fragile superstructure. It cannot contain the light.

Samantha Seybold is a visiting assistant professor of philosophy at Knox College in Galesburg, Illinois. She graduated in 2023 from Purdue University with a PhD in philosophy. Her research interests are in applied ethics, social epistemology, and feminist philosophy. She can be reached at saseybold@knox.edu.

Works Cited

Correia, Mariama. 2023. "Brazilian State Deputy Says She Was Sexually Assaulted by Boaventura de Sousa Santos." *Agência Pública*, April 14, 2023. https://apublica.org/2023/04/brazilian-state-deputy-says-she-was-sexually-assaulted-by-boaventura-de-sousa-santos/.

PBS. 2023. "PBS Standards: Defamation." https://www.pbs.org/standards/media-law-101/defamation/.

Telling Our Story: Making Sense of the Pandemic

Anurekha Chari Wagh

Melanie Heath, Akosua K. Darkwah, Josephine Beoku-Betts, and Bandana Purkayastha (eds.)'s *Global Feminist Autoethnographies during COVID-19: Displacements and Disruptions*, London: Routledge, 2022

Nanjala Nyabola's *Strange and Difficult Times: Notes on Global Pandemic*, London: Hurst, 2022

Both the books under review here (*Global Feminist Autoethnographies during COVID-19* and *Strange and Difficult Times*) are important contributions to the study of the pandemic and its impact on our diverse and intersecting worlds. These two books engage, in multiple intersecting yet distinct ways, the concern raised by Boisseau and Ernstberger in their call for papers for this special issue of *Women's Studies Quarterly* on "Pandemonium." They state that this issue "creates space for feminist studies practitioners to consider the tumultuous circumstances we find ourselves in, to document and reflect on recent experiences, and to draw conclusions about the current state—and possible future—of our field." This appeal is reflected in the writing of Nyabola (2022, xi–xii), who states in the foreword to *Strange and Difficult Times*, "a book about pandemic should not just be about the crises, it should illuminate what the crises meant and what the crises could mean . . . a dirge for everything we lost and a sonnet for everything good we learnt about ourselves." Or, as Purkayastha and colleagures, while introducing *Global Feminist Autoethnographies*, write, "in this collection of essays written by people in or connected to academia, we reflect on our personal experiences through ethnographies on ourselves to unpack and understand changing social conditions during this pandemic" (1).

This review is divided into three sections. The first section will highlight the issues raised by the book *Global Feminist Autoethnographies during COVID-19*. The second section examines the issues, arguments and experiences shared in the book *Strange and Difficult Times*. The third section builds on the threads that bind the two books together through their stories of making sense of the pandemic and the worlds they live, breathe, and create their lives in.

WSQ: Women's Studies Quarterly 52: 1 & 2 (Spring/Summer 2024) © 2024 by Anurekha Chari Wagh. All rights reserved.

Looking Back on a Tumultuous Time

The book *Global Feminist Autoethnographies* covers various issues experienced by diverse scholars in different global academic locations during COVID-19. In the introduction, Purkayastha and colleagues state "that the book of autoethnographies is a record, an act of bearing witness to experiences during this pandemic in the second decade of the twenty-first century" (1). Interestingly, the editors link the experiences of dealing with the pandemic through the "node—academia—to record the disruptions, displacements and distresses." The book is divided into three parts addressing each of these issues in the context of pandemic and academia using the collaborative autoethnographic method.

The first part, titled "Disruptions: Seismic Work and Life Shifts," contains seven papers and a short introduction by Akosua K. Darkwah, highlighting how the pandemic disrupted the world of productive and reproductive work and shifted the notion of academic space. In particular, the papers raise the issue of how the pandemic impacted minority, low-income, and first-generation learners, pushing them into more precarious situations. The experience of tenured and nontenured academics, particularly in the context of disproportionate care responsibilities, is also addressed. Papers also examine how academic educational institutions could not address the needs of diverse student populations. The impact of the pandemic in the context of the eroding of public institutions, amplifying the already marginalized lives of the vulnerable groups within the academic space, is examined. This section also addresses the uncertainties of the university lives of faculty members in relation to teaching methods, particularly the technological challenge of teaching using online methods, the reduction in research grants, and the decrease of administrative support, which shifted the way one engaged with teaching and research. This section, while highlighting feminist principles of care work, emphasizes the negotiations with paid and care work in the same spatial settings, engaging with disruptions in lives by their situated precarities. As Darkwah states, the papers use "intersectional perspectives in understanding the differential costs of the pandemic as well as the differences in the ability of faculty to successfully navigate the disruptions caused by the pandemic" (2022, 22).

Part 2, titled "Distress: Personal Trauma and Institutionalised Inequalities," with an introduction by Melanie Heath, has eight papers engaging with broad issues of (1) how social location impacts experiences of physical and mental health, and (2) the effect of intersecting inequalities on heightened distress for those with various connections to academia (Heath 2022, 115). This part addresses the challenges of (1) dealing with trauma, isolation, and severe illness during the pandemic; (2) the idea of "intensive mothering" during the pandemic, which impacted academics' mental health; (3) the economic precarity of being a student and the risk of being an essential worker during the pandemic; (4) the pandemic impacting people of color in distinct ways, intensifying the trauma of racial injustices and prejudices; and (5) the experience of microaggressions in everyday lives escalating the pain of being both hyper-invisible and hyper-visible during the COVID-19 pandemic as an Asian American. This part engages with the intersecting ways inequalities and injustices heightened and deepened distress during the pandemic.

The third part, titled "Displacements: Transnational Realities and Splintered Lives," with an introduction by Josephine Beoku-Betts, has seven papers highlighting "how the lives of transnational students and faculty were displaced and their strategies of coping and broadening understandings of family, community and belonging" (Beoku-Betts 2022, 214). This section addresses multiple intersecting issues, such as (1) experiences of isolation, trauma, and exclusion as an Asian migrant academic worker identifying as queer and transnational; (2) the debilitating consequences for families living in transnational contexts, which was exacerbated during the pandemic; (3) the need to recognize the multiple intersecting locations of transnational communities, particularly the disrupted lives of families and vulnerable minoritized communities; (4) how these transnational contexts created further marginalization for graduate students; (5) how sensitive and timely planned societal interventions by the state helped to curb the impact of the pandemic to the minimum; and (6) how privilege and marginality intersect with each other, framing different experiences of displacements, isolation, and powerlessness. Additionally, each of the papers engages with the coping strategies used by the authors to deal with anxiety, trauma, fear, and pain intensified during the pandemic, and to build solidarity across geographical and social boundaries. Strategies include engaging with humanitarian and social justice initiatives, increased reliance on digital technology for online feminist activism, curating new strategies for strengthening transnational research practices, and advocating for increased sensitivity for cross-cultural recognition among feminists, queer communities of all races, and migrant communities.

The Stories We Tell Ourselves about Who We Are

The book *Strange and Difficult Times: Notes on a Global Pandemic*, by Nanjala Nyabola, is a collection of twenty essays divided into three intersecting themes: "Life," "Death," and "Normal." The essays use an autobiographical method that links individual experiences to the social, political, and economic macrostructural realities. Right at the start, Nanjala Nyabola articulates her position as a Black African woman located in Nairobi. The twenty essays highlight how the experience of a pandemic is closely linked to how the state organizes, deals with, and records the impact and strategies used by it; and how the global experience of the pandemic could be analyzed through the lens of lockdown, reiterating how divided and differentiated the world was. The book highlights how communities navigated through the pandemic and examines the inadequacies of the given concepts, which do not match the contemporary lived realities of the diverse citizens of the country.

The overarching frame that binds the essays together is the process of "othering" Africa, which escalated during the pandemic in multiple ways, particularly in how Africa was branded as dangerous. As Nyabola states succinctly, "the hollowness of the promises about the whole world being 'in this together' became truly evident when the entire African continent was branded with a scarlet letter of contagion by several countries, notably in Europe, although COVID-19 was far more widespread there ... being black and African was enough for baseless fears of contagion" (x), prompting her to ask a larger question of how to hold on to the idea of global solidarity, when powerful countries found it convenient and appropriate to leave behind more than two-thirds of the world in their quest of finding a way forward (xiii). Such documentation and telling of the story from this marginal location is crucial toward making sense of the pandemic; as Nyabola states, "As an African, I know what it is to exist on the periphery of people's imagination, to be one of the many whose histories are not deemed worth recording or retelling" (xv). This book by Nanjala Nyabola is a political comment on the institutionalization of unequal worlds. She argues that we need to stake a claim on redefining the importance of stories to be told, shared, and documented from marginalized locations, thereby facilitating the process of "centering the margins." In this context, she critiques the idea of dividing the world into "West" and "East," as a political project geared to sideline Africa. According to her, the discounting of Africa is reflected in the way that "in the direst moments Africa found itself completely abandoned, treated as fundamentally disposable by both sides" (xiv).

The first thematic section, "Life," has nine essays, engaging in multiple ways with how the state facilitates documenting knowledge and legitimizing existing ruling regimes, increasing the marginality and stigma of existing vulnerable populations. The author raises pertinent issues, which include the problem of racially profiling Chinese people, the geopolitics of vaccine production and distribution, and how lockdown impacted vulnerable communities (single families, migrant workers, individuals in informal settlements) and nations (Africa) differently, thereby highlighting how unequal and divided our world is. Nyabola writes that the lockdown "intensified the injustices many in our societies were already living with ... lockdowns were not equal things" (27). This structural violence intensified as states legitimized extreme violence against civilians by ensuring law and order.

Furthering the argument, Nyabola raises the issue of the high incidence of police brutality regarding mask usage during the pandemic. Nyabola links it with the historical context of HIV/AIDS and its associated stigma. She writes, "The shape and form of mask usage is contoured by underlying dynamics that preceded the pandemic." Additionally, Nyabola also highlights the importance of recording and documenting the role played by local communities in dealing with the pandemic, particularly in the context of erosion of press freedom. Nyabola writes, "flawed and partial accounts of pandemics that understate the agency of affected communities and overstate the contribution of foreign interventions can have consequences long after the emergency period passes" (53).

This book problematizes the category "world," arguing that it refers to "the people that we think matter," impacting all major policy decisions and access to resources. Nyabola writes, "African countries spent the better part of 2021 begging for medicine and being told in no unsubtle terms that the survival of the West specifically, but wealthier countries in general, was more important than working together to survive the pandemic.... 'Vaccinate the world' turned out to be 'Vaccinate "the world"'" (2022, 66). Such an attitude had one silver lining, that was consolidation of regional solidarity as African countries rallied for each other. Here Nyabola lauds the efforts of Africa Centres for Disease Control and Prevention, which saved the continent, as they recognized that they had better chances of survival together than in waiting for "the world" to intervene.

The second thematic section, titled "Death," contains six essays engaging with the art of questioning. The author demands interrogating the global regimes of power, as this would expose the double standards of providing healthcare, specifically in procuring and distributing vaccines. The author painfully and indignantly raises the question, "Who was worth keeping alive?" (98). Through her incisive writings, she highlights how, globally, during the pandemic, people with disabilities, the elderly, minorities, and poor people were treated as expendable.

The book's third theme has six essays that engage with the idea of "normal" in discussions around the post-pandemic world. The author raises thought-provoking questions concerning the politics of vaccination, particularly government policies regarding access and control over vaccines. The author further highlights the complexity of being privileged in pandemic times and argues that the pandemic tested the limits of the experience of privilege, especially the maintenance of steady income and relative safety. The pandemic has been a catalyst for accelerating inequalities, particularly with millions worldwide losing their employment. Such a loss is devastating, causing increased stress and anxiety and reducing access to healthcare, education, clean water, and decent food.

By raising complex questions about the vaccination war, the author exposes how limited the idea of global solidarity is. COVID-19 and then Omicron exposed how "racism, ableism, nationalism, and classism became a roadblock in nurturing global solidarity." Nyabola writes, "The decision to turn vaccines into a commercial product to be distributed at the maximum price to those who can pay the most has not just cost the U.S. and Europe, it has cost the world. It set the global vaccination project back by months, allowing the disease to foster and mutate and the emergency period to drag on indefinitely" (2022, 130). Such instances address pharmaceutical companies and powerful governments' complicity in sustaining their hegemony. Further, Nyabola urges us not to ignore those who survived COVID-19 and calls for research to comprehend the long-term effects of COVID on physical and mental health.

Significantly, Nyabola has addressed the issue of processing grief to survive in this post-pandemic world and how one deals with the experience of death, loss, uncertainty, fear, and the feeling of betrayal by the systems that are supposed to be in place to protect us. The author nudges us to rethink the idea of "normal" and how we frame it. She argues, "Normal was never particularly kind for too many of us: shouldn't this be an opportunity to reset our relationship with these inequalities?" (133). The question is, do we have the answer? Writing this review in 2023, one recalls the horrific images of bodies being buried and/or cremated during the pandemic and the overwhelming sense of fear that overshadowed the feeling of loss. It feels as if we have not learned anything of value from the pandemic experience. Life is back to "normal," and this normalized life has become increasingly violent, polarized, intolerant, and divided, which is not only frightening and scary but also unfortunate.

Nyabola concludes her book by embracing her "anger." She argues that it is necessary and righteous to have "rage" in times of increased inequality and institutionalization of unfair treatment. For her, the notion of "normal" is flawed and fragmented and without anger, it is not possible to rebuild a "normal" world because to build an equal normal world, one has to "listen" to the stories shared from invisibilized, marginalized, and vulnerable groups, communities, and nations. The critical question is whether the world is ready to listen.

In Conversation with Each Other

Reading these two books together is an enriching experience. In distinct ways, the books address the fragility of the idea of solidarity and the tenaciousness of communities, but also the silences and invisibility of vulnerable groups and communities, the flawed nature of established analytical constructs, the bullying of powerful nations, the realization that this world is increasingly unequal, divided, and differentiated, the belligerence of conglomerates, the loss of trust in neighbors, colleagues, and communities, and the failure of the state to protect its citizens.

Specifically, both books addressed the following:

First, the layered intersectional meaning of displacements, disruptions, and distress experienced differently through our specific locations and positions within communities, nation-states, and global regimes, creating distinctive challenges to our everyday lives.

Second, the importance of recording and documenting their experience and telling their stories to be put on record. By sharing their multiple intersecting stories, the books highlight the shifting trajectories of who belongs to the institution: academia or the nation-state.

Third, the changing social conditions at the local and global structural levels that are perceived in different intersecting spatial locations, either in academia (Purkayastha et al.) and/or as a citizen (Nyabola).

Fourth, the "politics of inclusions," where the inclusionary policies of the state for vulnerable and marginalized groups and communities do not address the structural embedded inequalities based on race, class, caste, gender, sexuality, disability, religion, and region.

Lastly, both books raise significant methodological questions. *Global Feminist Autoethnographies* engages with collective autoethnography as a praxis of solidarity and collective care during the pandemic (Desai et al. 2022, 88–89). *Strange and Difficult Times* raises a core methodological question addressing the politics of knowledge production when engaging with archival documents. According to Nyabola, one has to "read these archival documents in the context within which they were produced.... We have to consider not just what the text says, but also what it does not say and why" (9). For example, in the context of the pandemic, she argues how death and funeral announcements could become a crucial research tool in documenting the experience of the community. It also raises the limited viability of established analytical categories. She refers to "Africa," which represents a geographical construct but does not precisely present the diversity and complexity of being the second largest continent.

The two books have made significant contributions toward making sense of the pandemic. They would interest policymakers, social scientists, teachers, researchers, journalists, and anyone interested in the stories of a pandemic that reflects despair, anxiety, and fear but also resilience, solidarity, and hope.

Anurekha Chari Wagh is a professor in the Department of Sociology at the University of Hyderabad, Hyderabad. She specializes in the areas of gender and citizenship rights, agrarian issues, microfinance, development, teaching and learning, and feminist pedagogy. Her PhD is from Savitribai Phule Pune University in Pune, India, and she was awarded a UGC CV Raman Fellowship (2014–2015) for her postdoctoral research at the University of Connecticut in the United States. She can be reached at anurekha@uohyd.ac.in.

Review of *The Gendered Face of COVID-19 in the Global South* by Jean Grugel, Matt Barlow, Tallulah Lines, Maria Eugenia Giraudo, and Jessica Omukuti

Melissa J. Buehler

Jean Grugel, Matt Barlow, Tallulah Lines, Maria Eugenia Giraudo, and Jessica Omukuti's
The Gendered Face of COVID-19 in the Global South: The Development, Gender and Health Nexus,
Bristol: Bristol University Press, 2022

The Gendered Face of COVID-19 in the Global South: The Development, Gender and Health Nexus opens with a quote by Isabel Allende: "Women are disempowered constantly, and if there is a crisis of any kind—occupation, war, pandemic—the first people who suffer are women." This quote captures the heavy weight of the research undertaken by Jean Grugel, Matt Barlow, Tallulah Lines, Maria Eugenia Giraudo, and Jessica Omukuti to provide a real-time analysis of the COVID-19 pandemic response. The scholars argue that not only was this pandemic a fast-moving public health crisis, but it was also compounded by a devastating human development crisis that threatened to undermine progress made under the United Nation Sustainable Development Goals. Key to understanding the magnitude of and response to this crisis was situating gender firmly within a public health matrix dominated by state capacity failures, global governance shortcomings, economic recession, and resource scarcity. Women and girls disproportionately suffered due to policies that further limited access to healthcare and educational services, exacerbated economic conditions, and increased exposure to domestic violence. Simply put, regional and global policy advocates exchanged the safety and security of women and girls to contain the disease (and potential economic) fallout of the pandemic. Three years later, we are just now starting to understand the ramifications of these policies.

The central driving question of the book focuses on the intersectionality of gender, development, and crisis to improve policy outcomes for women in a post-COVID-19 world. Feminist political economy (FPE) offers an alternative to contemporary economic theory that fails to address the discriminatory nature of socioeconomic and political systems in the current globalized era. By exposing "the permeability and flow between the so-called 'public' and 'private' domains, between the apparently separate worlds of policy, politics and the economy, and the world of family and relationships," FPE interrogates pervasive myths regarding women's vulnerability and choices (38). The very policies designed to protect families and the economy were in fact biased towards men, who already occupied a privileged position of power. To counter the blatant disregard of gender, FPE scholars advocate for integrative and equitable policy development that can potentially be used in future public health crisis. It is in the areas of gender-based violence and social reproduction that FPE distinguishes itself as an important theoretical lens for transcending the divide between the public and private arenas. In challenging this division, the scholars ponder whether a feminist response to COVID-19 is (or was) possible, one that advances equitable and transparent policies and can be used to "build back better for girls and women" (159).

Interestingly, the scholars candidly discuss how many of the recommendations are obvious: "None of this is a surprise"; "The worst impacts of COVID-19 could have been avoided by better policy-making" (147). They also admit that policy analysts and scholars discussed the harmful gendered cost of the pandemic and advocated for substantive change that accounted for the lived conditions and experiences of women and girls. While the authors' recommendations may seem to be unsurprising, the importance of this book should not be discounted, for several reasons. First, the text offers extensive examples of how the international COVID-19 response impacted domestic policy implementation and success in South America and sub-Saharan Africa. These examples illustrate the precariousness of lived experiences of women and girls due to the COVID-19 pandemic. Moreover, the text exudes a sense that we are watching the pandemic unfold in real time. Readers are instantly brought back to a not-so-distant time that was wrought with fear and uncertainty as the world attempted to navigate the pandemic. Second, this matter-of-fact approach reminds the reader that sometimes solutions are obvious. Yes, better policymaking could have improved the outcomes for many women and girls, and yes, many national and regional organizations advocated for such policies. This advice was not followed, and there was real and pervasive human suffering that could have been avoided if better (i.e., FPE-focused) policies were implemented. Finally, the scholars remind us that fortitude and resolve are necessary during times of crisis, and oftentimes the most obvious policy decisions may in fact be the most difficult.

The book concludes with an eight-point plan "which would lay the foundations for stronger and more equitable societies that work for all genders, both in times of 'normality' and in times of crisis" (159). For these suggestions to be effective, "open-mindedness, commitment and honest acknowledgement of the failings of the misogynistic and racist systems and structures which control and dominate global social policy" must be confronted (159). The "build back better for women and girls" plan (a nod to President Joe Biden's Build Back Better framework to rebuild the middle class) challenges neoliberal economic policies that have proven to be detrimental to the lives of women and girls in the Global South. The building aspect of this plan acknowledges that in many cases, governmental policies and practices need to be completely reimagined to better prepare for the next potential healthcare crisis. The scholars center the needs and lived experiences of women and girls as the foundation for creating and advancing policies that focus on human security. The plan includes dismantling the public/private divide narrative, challenging supposedly gender-neutral policies, fostering leadership and decision-making opportunities for women, and implementing equitable *and* accessible policies that include monitoring mechanisms. Promotion of transformative, inclusive, and restorative policies will undoubtably improve not only the lived experiences of women and girls, it will also elevate the quality of society as a whole. Again, the scholars admit they are stating the obvious; in doing so, they challenge national, regional, and international leaders and stakeholders to find the courage to actually follow through.

The COVID-19 pandemic truly exemplifies one of the most devastating and far-reaching public health crises the international community has recently faced. To meet the needs of the global society, public policy must transcend national interests and serve human interest instead. This means taking a hard look at the realities women and girls endured during this health crisis and implementing policies that address these deficiencies. Even though this may seem difficult when considering the scope and magnitude of the COVID-19 pandemic, at the most basic and principled level, adopting a feminist political economy lens is necessary to better understand how the pandemic response failed to account for the disproportionate impact on women and girls due to the accumulation of previous health crises' shortcomings. If we hope to better navigate future pandemics, we must learn from our mistakes and face the realities of how ill-designed plans, no matter what the intentions may be, will most likely result in poor outcomes. Readers are reminded that we do know what good policy looks like. We now need to find the courage to actually advocate, advance, implement, and support these policies so we can move one step closer to achieving gender equality.

Melissa J. Buehler is an associate professor of global studies in the School of Global and Cultural Studies at Marian University. She received her PhD in political science with a certificate in women's studies from Purdue University. She continues to actively collaborate with faculty in various disciplines on projects focusing on teaching pedagogy, service learning, civic engagement, and activism. She can be reached at mbuehler@marian.edu.

Cracking Coloniality: The Transformative Journey of Re-existence in Catherine E. Walsh's *Rising Up, Living On*

Omi Salas-SantaCruz

Catherine E. Walsh's *Rising Up, Living On: Re-existences, Sowings, and Decolonial Cracks*, Durham, NC: Duke University Press, 2023

In the landscape of decolonial and critical theory literature, *Rising Up, Living On: Re-existences, Sowing, and Decolonial Cracks* emerges as a profoundly introspective and transformative exploration of what it means to crack open the suffocating layers of coloniality. At its heart, it is an introspective investigation into the concept of "crack-labor" and the endeavor of challenging the persisting structures of coloniality. Offering a multifaceted approach to the intricate workings of colonial matrices of power, Catherine E. Walsh has presented readers with a profound commentary on agency, resistance, and resurgence.

The book's central theme revolves around this idea of "cracking" coloniality—creating fissures in its structures to disrupt and challenge the deeply entrenched system of domination. As Walsh articulates, these cracks are embodied and situated and stand as testaments to acts of resistance, subjectivity, and struggle against hegemonic powers. The beauty of Walsh's approach is how she transcends traditional academic methodologies, advocating for a mode of inquiry grounded in "doing with" rather than "studying about." It is a call to be more intimate with the subject matter, more embedded in the realities being critiqued. This book is a testimony to the enduring legacy of colonialism and the ongoing labor of creating fissures and cracks that forge existences otherwise.

For readers unfamiliar with the nuances of decolonial theory, Walsh offers a short and accessible (re)introduction to the concept of "coloniality" as a conceptual framework. She reminds readers that colonialism is not just a historical event but has left an enduring matrix of power that continues to influence global structures through the coloniality of power, gender, and, as she argues in this book, the coloniality of Nature. The book's structure is deliberate, allowing the reader to journey through various facets of decolonial thought and crack labor. Starting with "Cries and Cracks," Walsh effectively juxtaposes cries of indignation against colonial violence with the need to disrupt systems that perpetuate it actively. She moves to "Asking and Walking," which emphasizes the process of cracking open coloniality, highlighting the importance of narratives—those passed down, those that need unlearning, and those yet to be forged. In this chapter, Walsh delves into the necessity of introspection, unlearning, and relearning. Through contrasting stories told against those that need to be unearthed and understood, she emphasizes the importance of revising earlier interpretations of histories and epistemologies. Walsh juxtaposes emotional testimonies against rigorous intellectual dissections, emphasizing narratives—those inherited, those requiring reevaluation, and those yet to be crafted. The penultimate chapter, "Undoing Nation-State," critically examines nation-states and their inherent binaries, borders, and fixed incorporations that serve as linchpins in maintaining global colonial orders. Her exploration into the nation-state, as both a product and perpetuator of coloniality, is a clarion call for reimagining geopolitical configurations. At the same time, the final chapter, "Sowing Re-existences," provides hope and direction. Walsh speaks to the acts of sowing life amidst death, celebrating the resilience and fortitude of communities continuously resisting colonial impositions and their violence.

While I have briefly delved into the introductory and concluding sections of the book, I have intentionally left the middle chapter untouched for now. It is the book's crown jewel, deserving of dedicated time and reflection. Chapter 3, "Traversing Binaries and Boundaries," is a tour de force in understanding the complex matrices of coloniality that define and confine various identities and subjectivities outside the partitions of binary-based divisions and categorical boundary-oriented thinking, which I have described as binary thinking and have called towards shifting to nonbinary modes of thought as means to challenge and transcend Western-centric categories (Salas-SantaCruz 2023). In this way, Walsh joins Global South and decolonial scholars advocating for a more nuanced, historically informed approach and comprehensive research methodologies that recognize the unique experiences and challenges of people with "embodied entanglements" in postcolonial and settler-colonial contexts.

Delving deeper into this chapter, Walsh shows us the pervasive inclination of imperialist feminists to view gender and systems of oppression through a Eurocentric lens where the foundational ontological aspects of sexual difference remain unchallenged. Patriarchy and gender, she argues, are often understood as universally oppressive systems, yet the specificities of culture, history, and colonial impositions shape these. In essence, throughout the chapter, Walsh offers Indigenous and Abya Yala feminist work on patriarchy's pluriversality and dynamics outside Western domination to remind us of the various conceptualizations of gender(s) and social relations, or at a minimum, to remind us not to assume gender is a universal category.

The most profound aspect of this chapter is Walsh's exploration of the "coloniality of N/nature." Here, the distinction between "nature" (with a lowercase *n*) and "Nature" (with an uppercase *N*) is paramount. The former refers to the Western paradigm, which understands nature as an entity to be controlled and dominated. This biocentric paradigm perpetuates binaries and hierarchies, leading to exploitative relationships with the environment. On the other hand, the "coloniality of Nature" (with an uppercase *N*) embodies the broader project of coloniality. It symbolizes the imposition of a singular worldview that integrates various domains—cultural, ontological, epistemological, existential, territorial, cosmological, and socio-spiritual. This singular paradigm of existence is woven with threads of Western modernity, coloniality, patriarchy, heteronormativity, Christianity, and capitalism. Each of these threads, while distinct, collaborates to construct and justify the global order that has been dominant for centuries.

Walsh expands our understanding of the coloniality of power and gender by adding to the mix, or the colonial matrix of power, the notion of the coloniality of Mother Nature as being the core or nexus of the colonial matrix and the existential rupturing into dualisms and binaries. Walsh argues that "gender and nature" are vital instruments in the reordering, division, domination, and control of existence, life, and the relational social world (136). Taking us through different conceptualizations, perceptions, and cosmogonies of "Nature/nature" across Abya Yala, she makes clear how varying conceptualizations of Nature sustain cultural and ancestral continuance. She discusses various relational and concrete ways of being that defy Western modernity's universalized projects of anthropocentric, masculine, and secular separations of being/nature and other interdependent and complementary modes of existence. Through examining the separation of humans and nature as central to projects of invasion, colonization, and modernity, where nature is to be dominated, Walsh takes us to contemplate and imagine the existence and practices of "gender" dualities, not gender per se, but *otherwise*.

Walsh's book offers invaluable insights into methodologies, especially regarding historical contexts and contemporary categories. Beyond just a critique, the book offers a roadmap for those who seek to incorporate decolonial strategies in research, teaching, and practice. The book encourages a shift from traditional paradigms to more embodied, situated methods of inquiry. Furthermore, it challenges conventional neo-Marxist and colonial frameworks, advocating for a deeper, more embodied understanding of resistance within the deep cracks of coloniality. *Rising Up, Living On* is an invitation to educators and researchers to reconceptualize resistance, not just as opposition but as a multifaceted, dynamic, and deeply rooted embodiment of re-existence. This book is a must-read for scholars and students who wish to traverse the complex terrain of decoloniality with clarity and purpose. For trans(gender) scholars focusing on the Global South and decolonial trans feminist perspectives, Walsh gives a concise and powerful overview of the duality, fluidity, and forms of androgynous wholes existing across Abya Yala, and other Indigenous cosmologies of existence such as the Maya, Zapotec, Yoruba, and Nahua, and more recent insurgent relations across the Global South that continuously engage in sense-making, or crack-making otherwise. The book serves as an urgent plea for scholars, activists, and readers to recognize the nuances of colonial legacies and the imperativeness of adopting decolonized approaches in understanding identities and experiences. By interlacing empirical examples, historical accounts, and contemporary practices, Walsh foregrounds the importance of understanding how colonial legacies intersect with contemporary sociopolitical challenges.

Rising Up, Living On stands as an emblematic testament to the power of decolonial thought and action and stands as a pandemonium space in academic literature, disrupting traditional paradigms and offering an introspective look into the myriad layers of coloniality. By challenging researchers to delve into the complexities of entangled embodiments, subjectivities, and histories, the book acts as a beacon, guiding us through the chaos and urging a more intimate, nuanced approach to understanding people and their narratives. Just as "pandemonium" represents tumult, disruption, and an opportunity for reflection, Walsh's work provides a platform for reimagining and redefining research methodologies, ultimately leading to a richer, more holistic understanding of our entwined global legacies.

Omi Salas-SantaCruz is the inaugural President's Postdoctoral Fellow in Trans Studies at Penn State University in the Department of Women's, Gender, and Sexuality Studies. They earned their PhD in education with a designated emphasis in critical theory and gender, women, and sexuality from the University of California, Berkeley, and a master's degree in sociology from Columbia University. Their research examines questions at the intersections of coloniality, race, Latinidad, the epistemology of trans inclusion, and practices of being. They can be reached at oss5057@psu.edu.

Works Cited

Salas-SantaCruz, Omi. 2023. "Nonbinary Epistemologies: Refusing Colonial Amnesia and Erasure of Jotería and Trans* Latinidades." *WSQ: Women's Studies Quarterly* 51 (3 & 4): 78–93.

Taking Feminism beyond the Academy

Anna Hotter

Carrie N. Baker and Aviva Dove-Viebahn (eds.)'s *Public Feminisms: From Academy to Community*, Ann Arbor, MI: Lever Press, 2023

Philosophy books—even feminist ones—do not usually include calls to action. Perhaps they know their audience (sedentary introverts). Or perhaps they fail to see what *Public Feminisms: From Academy to Community* takes as its guiding principle: that academics should "reach out beyond their classrooms, labs, and libraries to engage a broader public in collaborative and mutually beneficial relationships that can lead to new knowledge and much-needed solutions to the most pressing problems of our day" (Baker and Dove-Viebahn, "Conclusion," 455).

This rallying cry caps the collection's twenty-two essays about feminist praxis by scholars in anthropology, film and media studies, law, English, women and gender studies, and classics. They have all moved "beyond the confines of the ivory tower" to engage civilian communities in academic activism (Guy-Sheftall, "Foreword," xv). I agree with *Public Feminisms*'s editors, Carrie N. Baker and Aviva Dove-Viebahn (professors of American studies and film and media studies, respectively), that scholars have something to learn from the contributors' examples. My philosopher colleagues and I could certainly use a break from the armchair.

But *Public Feminisms* is no tedious how-to guide. It is a collection of vibrant stories by professors and students who have managed to puncture the spatial, epistemic, technological, and economic divide between academia and public life. Part 1 features essays about using "art, media, and public programming" to engage a variety of communities in feminist scholarship. A women's and gender studies professor at Mount Royal University leads walking tours on "Calgary's adult consensual sex industry" for up to twelve visitors (Williams, "From Classroom to Pavement," 57). Two professors at California State campuses host *Las Doctoras*, a podcast about Latinx feminism and motherhood that "make[s] accessible the feminism that we teach as *profesoras* in the university" (Rose and Lemus, "Las Doctoras," 39). An anthropologist creates a live-action role-play event that lets participants engage with the stories of Indigenous women who have experienced intimate partner violence (Eddy, "Day Angela Died," 83–84). *Public Feminisms* upends the dichotomy between serious scholarship and playfulness—feminist work can be creative and dynamic, while tackling difficult topics.

Part 2, "Activism and Public Education," opens with a story about a Take Back the Night march that connects the University of Toledo to its local activist community. Another essay features three undergraduates who analyze the trans-inclusivity of their HWCs (historically women's colleges) using "duoethnographic methods" (Rodriguez Gonzalez et al., "Building Bridges," 177).

I initially misread *Public Feminisms*'s title—I skipped over the second *s* in favor of a sleeker *Feminism*. But the singular would shortchange the eclectic cross-section of disciplines, modes of engagement, localities, cultural contexts, and epistemic standpoints Baker and Dove-Viebahn showcase. "Feminists generally share a belief in equality and justice for women," the editors note, but "they define the term in multiple ways, with different emphases and priorities" (Baker and Dove-Viebahn, "Introduction," 12). *Public Feminisms*'s plural, intersectional scope is not just a methodological virtue. It also makes the collection fun to read.

Part 3 focuses on "public writing and scholarship" and presents Dove-Viebahn's own experience with interviewing women in film for *Ms.* magazine—"an online platform lends itself to an immediacy not possible with print books" (Dove-Viebahn, "A 'Feminist Lens' on Activism and Inclusion in the Film and Television Industry," 251). It also features a women's, gender, and sexuality studies professor at Oregon State University who publishes on her Baptist faith—"My university press books reached audiences of hundreds across several years. A single piece in *Ms.* Magazine ... can reach thousands in just a few days" (Shaw, "Feminism, Faith, and Public Scholarship," 271)—and a Turkish translator collective that makes one of the few international contributions to *Public Feminisms*. The collection's North American bias (which Baker and Dove-Viebahn acknowledge in their introduction) underlines the Turkish writers' central point: amplifying underrepresented voices—through translation and other radical actions—must be an explicit aim of public feminists (Acar et al., "Translation as Feminist Activism").

Part 4 concludes with essays on "feminist pedagogies for community engagement." It is both the collection's most amorphous category (it finally explodes the divide between "academic" and "public" that Baker and Dove-Viebahn had presupposed) and its most actionable one. A California State University professor reports on her senior-level college class Identity, Rhetoric, and Culture, in which students learn "theories on gender, identity, and rhetorical communities" before editing Wikipedia articles on feminist topics (Brandt, "Activist Possibilities of Wikipedia," 351). Another professor teaches a course dedicated to writing and publishing op-eds at venues like *Teen Vogue*, *Ms.*, *Refinery29*, and *Bitch*. Both essays include parts of the course syllabi so readers can easily follow their examples.

Public Feminisms ends with a story about Michigan State University's Community Writing Center, which reckons with its town's racial divide by providing writing services to the broader public. While the university town of Lansing, Michigan, is racially diverse, the "demographics of our university is significantly more majority white," write Sanders, Prevent, and Bauer ("Orienting Public Pedagogues," 428). They propose that this positioning creates "a responsibility to disrupt whiteness" and to "redress structures that do harm to ... colleagues and students of Color"—in their case, through community outreach and courses on Black feminist pedagogy (428). *Public Feminisms* seemingly wants to convince its reader of her own responsibility to disrupt and redress, and to leverage her positioning for action.

The essays certainly have a galvanizing effect. They make you want to launch a utopian feminist zine, or at least overhaul the odd course syllabus. Baker and Dove-Viebahn do not discriminate between the different modes and projects of public feminism. And while this democratic approach serves *Public Feminisms*'s intersectional agenda, it also leaves open important questions. For example, which "communities" should feminist academics target to address "the most pressing problems of our day" (455)? A bell hooks quote in the preface urges us to bring "the meaning of feminist thinking and practice ... to the masses" (vii). The act of "consciousness-raising" hooks imagines transgresses from academic into public life, but also from feminist into nonfeminist ideological spaces. Effective activism must at some point breach hostile territory.

And while Baker and Dove-Viebahn acknowledge that feminists must "reach people across a broad range of communities" and engage them in "uncomfortable and difficult conversations," few of the collection's essays describe interventions in non- or anti-feminist spaces (Baker and

Dove-Viebahn, "Conclusion," 455). The Baptist OSU professor targets conservative religious readers in her public writing. The undergraduates who edit feminist Wikipedia articles confront a broad, diverse audience with equal editing power. But most contributors eschew mass communication: the leader of Calgary's "Booze, Broads & Brothels" tour markets her offerings at "feminist, queer, and other related social justice-oriented community organizations" (Williams, "From Classroom to Pavement," 62). It is hard to imagine the participants of Queer Apocalypse Solutions, an interactive and delightfully strange "art-life project," are not already sympathetic to the feminist cause. Scholars should engage and learn from nonacademic progressive communities, but they should also beware of reproducing the university's intellectual silo outside the college gates.

Of course, it is risky to take feminism to a less sympathetic audience. *Public Feminisms* gestures at the possible pitfalls with a piece by a McGill University lecturer who researches how Canadian universities protect their scholars from online harassment: "There is a cost to doing work in public spheres that disproportionately is paid by marginalized scholars" (Ketchum, "University Media Relations, Public Scholarship, and Online Harassment," 280). Her findings are dire: "the research team found *no information* directly related to the topic of trolling, doxing, or harassment" on Canadian university websites (283). *Public Feminisms*, too, falls short of educating readers on how to steel themselves against anti-feminist backlash. If it aims to be a didactic work, the collection needs to address the fraught realities that prefigure feminist action.

My own discipline—analytic philosophy—often stands removed from public life, but there has been a recent wave of philosophical "trade books" that target a nonacademic audience. What is notable is not just their success but that many of these books discuss feminist issues. Amia Srinivasan's *The Right to Sex* made the Top 10 of the *New York Times* Best Sellers List. Work by Kate Manne, Myisha Cherry, and Carol Hay is finding readers beyond the university. Maybe Baker and Dove-Viebahn are right that in this moment "feminist scholars are perfectly positioned to engage publicly and decisively in politics, culture, and social life" (448). The fact that feminist philosophy books now sit on display tables at Barnes & Noble is certainly heartening. But we are far from the "billboards; ads in magazines; ads on buses, subways, trains" that hooks demands (hooks 2014, 6).

In many ways, *Public Feminisms* dreams big. It reaches out to us from unexpected places with an all-important message of possibility: feminist scholars can (and should) act on the world outside the academy. I wish the collection's imagination explored even murkier territory, further afield from the progressive intellectual spaces many of us inhabit. That is where its rallying cry will eventually lead us.

Anna Hotter is a PhD student in philosophy at the CUNY Graduate Center in New York City. She works in feminist philosophy, philosophy of action, and aesthetics. She can be reached at ahotter@gradcenter.cuny.edu.

Works Cited

hooks, bell. 2014. *Feminism Is for Everybody: Passionate Politics*. 2nd ed. New York: Routledge.

SECTION V. CREATIVE PROSE AND POETRY

Sim Gill is a doctoral student at the Annenberg School for Communication at the University of Pennsylvania. Her research interests concern the mediation of violence against women and girls as well as the negotiations between discourses of representation, affect, and subjectivity that speaks to a broader shaping of a market for women's safety. Before joining Annenberg, Gill worked in the British Civil Service graduate program known as the Fast Stream. She received her BA in politics, philosophy, and economics from the University of Warwick and her MSc at the London School of Economics, where she specialized in media, communications, and development. She can be reached at simron.gill@asc.upenn.edu.

Sim Gill, *isolation*, 2021. Photograph.

This photograph captures Kensington Park Gardens, London, during the third national lockdown in the United Kingdom. On March 23, 2020, the U.K.'s prime minister issued a stark directive: "You must stay at home." Within a mere twenty-four hours, our daily routines and rituals were cast into uncertainty, our usual distractions temporarily vanished, leaving us with existential queries about what lay ahead, the duration of this new reality, and when normalcy might return. For numerous individuals, this marked their first encounter with a paradigm-shifting global event, encompassing remote work and social distancing, as well as upending familiar habitual practices. On reflection, it is important that our narratives surrounding this period respect and reflect a framework that honestly captures the incompleteness and tensions of this *unprecedented* moment.

That Garden of Hope

Bhavika Sicka

Where speech is not a mynah caged;
Where the voice rings free;
Where home is not a village sacked by war;
Where words are conjured from the cauldron of honesty;
Where knowledge arches its long neck toward truth;
Where the mind is shepherded into meadows of curiosity;
Where reason's rivers haven't emptied into the desert of dull rituals—
Into that garden of hope, dear teacher, lead me.

Bhavika Sicka is an emerging poet from India. She holds a BA in English from Delhi University and an MFA in creative writing from Old Dominion University. Her work has been published in *Pleiades*, *Rattle*, *The Fourth River*, *Hunger Mountain*, *Waxwing*, and elsewhere. She can be reached at bsick001@odu.edu.

Crazy Quilt Activism

Elizabeth Gackstetter Nichols

One of my father's most prized possessions is a vest that my mother made him. It uses scraps of ribbon with bits of velvet and satin sewn together in the tradition of a "crazy quilt." Crazy quilts, an innovation of women's ingenuity and artistry, use the beautiful, odd remainders of other projects to create something valuable and unique.

When I look back on the last three years, my brain swirls trying to get a handle on what it has meant to try and "do the work" in pandemonious circumstances. In some ways, I've felt like a pinball, bouncing from one opportunity to another. But really, I'm not sure I like the metaphor of the pinball. Yes, I've felt thrown from one project to another, but not in a way that leaves me disconnected from each. I think the quilt—built of small moments, sewn together and decorated, the end product more than the sum of its parts—is a more apt comparison.

In the fall of 2019, through a series of connections that I don't fully remember, I received a call from the Center for Human Rights and Constitutional Law (CHRCL). The organization was seeking volunteers to travel to U.S. Border Patrol detention centers and monitor the condition of migrant children in those facilities.

You may remember that the condition of these children was dire. News stories filtered out about the deaths, abuse, and neglect of children alone in sterile cells, often torn from their family members. The Trump administration's policy of family separation, and the intentionally cruel treatment of minors, was a human rights crisis, one that ran afoul of the U.S. Supreme Court 1993 *Flores vs. Reno* ruling[1] that mandated "safe and sanitary" conditions for children in Border Patrol custody.

The CHRCL is the agency with the power to monitor the condition of children in detention and then advocate for them, as a class, in court. The center was urgently seeking attorneys, medical professionals, and counselors to join site-visit teams, and Spanish/English interpreters to facilitate communication. I am not an attorney or a health professional. I am not a professionally trained interpreter. I am a professor of Spanish and gender studies at a small midwestern liberal arts college.

I am fluent in both English and Spanish, however, so I immediately volunteered.

The thing about a crazy quilt is that one doesn't go out and buy new fabric. The goal is to use what you have, to not waste any part of precious materials. My mother used scraps left over from her prodigious and skilled dressmaking to make my father's vest. The fabric built from a crazy quilt is "crazy" for its lack of formal planning and design. It follows the path of the resources at hand.

The CHRCL put me on a team of women going to McAllen, Texas, directly on the border with Mexico. We met and were briefed on the goals of the site visit: to speak directly with children in Border Patrol custody to find out how they were being treated and to ask as many as possible to join the class action suit that the CHRCL would bring on their behalf in federal court. We would work twelve hours a day for three days. We would not be allowed to inspect the actual facilities, only ask children questions about them.

Thinking about the experience strains my grasp on the quilt metaphor. There was nothing beautiful or elegant about my first real confrontation with the impenetrable, antagonistic, and terrifying military/prison industrial complex. The guards hulked before us, slabs of black body armor and weaponry, scowling and barking orders. They were a comically exaggerated representation of the patriarchy—bristling with violence to protect themselves from terrified children.

The site would generate a list of children in custody. We would ask to see a specific child on the list, only to find that 75 percent of the time, the child was "unavailable" (no other explanation given). The guards roamed the hall outside of our interview room, spewing anger at our disruption, at the necessity of working with us, of how it was all a "waste of time."

It was so cold in the facilities that our team bought gloves for the second day. They never turned the lights off. The only blankets were the silver "space" blankets that rescuers use to conserve body heat. There were no soft places in the facility. No round edges or welcoming smiles. The two facilities we visited were stark. Cold. Hard. And they stunk like unemptied Porta Potties.

What could possibly offer beauty here?

Looking back, I choose to see beauty and value in the brave women and children who were willing to risk speaking to an unknown white lady. In our collective resistance and resilience, and the fabric of truth that we put together. In the suit the CHRCL filed, and later won, on behalf of the children.[2] And finally, on the connections I made, in crazy-quilt style, with other women working on behalf of migrants and Hispanics in the United States.

In McAllen, I partnered with a fellow faculty member, a law professor qualified to ask the right questions in order to build a case. We worked well together and, once home, immediately volunteered for another trip through the Immigration Justice Program. This time we would visit the detention center in Dilley, Texas, a holding facility for women and children with legitimate asylum claims. Our job would be to help these women prepare the best claim possible.

Deborah and I never got to make that trip—the pandemic gave Customs and Border Patrol the excuse to deny all access to people in detention and helped drive the inhumane and illegal "remain in Mexico" policy that followed. Deborah and I would go on to do our best in working around the system, following the choices at hand. We engaged in a torturous three-way WhatsApp call with a woman stuck in the camps on the Mexican border with her disabled child, doing our best to prepare the most effective asylum claim possible.

We will likely never know if her asylum claim was successful. And of course, it was work on behalf of just one woman. I choose to believe, however, that the support we offered her, and the piece of legal work we created, was valuable. It represented another scrap, another bit of beauty in the quilt.

Moving in another unplanned direction, before the lockdowns, I also had worked to connect my scrap of activism to any group that would listen to me in Missouri. I came home in 2019, desperate to spread the word about how badly children were being treated. I was convinced that if I could just reach the critical mass of "pro-life" women here in the buckle of the Bible Belt, I could maybe move the needle on public opinion. As I learned from attending local protests, the prevailing narrative was that the stories weren't true—and protesters were often challenged with "but have you seen it yourself?" I had. I advocated and agitated and tried to get into as many churches as possible. This was ultimately unsuccessful. It is likely that the women here didn't want to know.

In the tradition of the crazy quilt, the next steps in my pandemic activist journey were unplanned. I was invited to speak to the local League of Women Voters (LOWV), first in person, and then as the pandemic spread, via Zoom. The league was a group deeply interested in this topic and willing to believe. While the league is officially nonpartisan, the national organization had taken a stand on this issue, specifically on family separation and the treatment of children.[3]

Together, far from the border and constrained by COVID measures, there was little we could do. The league, however, did ask if I could help with another national mandate—one that sought to increase voter registration among eligible Latinx[4] voters. Voting and voter suppression are yet another flank in the patriarchal assault on women's rights and human rights in the United States. The LOWV argues that increased voter participation will mean changes to immigration policy. Hispanics account for nearly 15 percent of all eligible voters in the United States (the second largest voting bloc), yet vote in smaller numbers than other groups (Natarajan and Im 2022).

At my home university, I teach a service-learning course for Spanish majors designed to help them learn from and interact with the Hispanic community. This course has often taken the form of translation projects for local agencies seeking to better communicate with their Latino clientele. Moving to a dedicated and ongoing project on voter registration, however, was an attractive possibility and valuable proposition for my students and members of our community.

In 2021, my class began designing a bilingual website dedicated to spread information designed to help eligible citizens register to vote—and then to vote in our region of Southwest Missouri. The website, *Viva the Vote*, provides a breakdown of the registration process, guidance on how voting works, and then a summary of the candidates and issues for each election cycle.

I am proud of this work that my students have done—adding to the quilt and connecting the work in Mexico to the women's groups locally, attaching the beauty of the League of Women Voters to the energy of young activists working to bolster democracy.

In 2022, with many pandemic measures lifted, students began in-person voter registration events as part of Hispanic Heritage month, connecting with new pieces of the quilt at Drury's satellite campus in Monett, Missouri (a campus that is more than 80 percent Hispanic), and with local Latinx groups such as AcompañARTE.

At the AcompañARTE event, students offered bilingual voter information, promoted from the stage by Drury's director of our CAMP Program for migrant students. Yesy (our director and a part-time DJ on the regional Spanish-language station), encouraged attendees to visit the students' table, offering bona fides for the project's work and goals. Perhaps because of this, a woman felt comfortable approaching one of my female-identifying students (Hadley) with a concern. This woman explained the barrier that fear creates for women voting. Those women who are survivors of domestic abuse are on constant guard for their safety, and fear that going to their assigned polling place puts their safety at risk because they could be recognized and targeted. In speaking with this woman, Hadley noted that there are ways for women to use alternate polling places to vote so they do not have to risk running into their abusers, a fact that is not commonly known. This led to a new part of the project for *Viva the Vote*—the creation of materials and information on the website about safe and anonymous places to vote.

As my class reflected on the project at the end of the semester, they had an overwhelming recommendation for the next class—the need to form more connections with more local and regional leaders in the Latino community. They saw how valuable Yesy's imprimatur was—and how important it was to seek and build links with trusted local leaders. My students (Hispanic and non-Hispanic) represent a valuable piece of the quilt, but only a piece. They recommend that the next class seek out and connect with other velvets, silks, and satins.

My favorite novel is Isabel Allende's *La casa de los espíritus* (The House of the Spirits). I read this novel in undergrad, decades ago, and still teach it in university classes. The novel, a multigenerational saga of resistance and resilience in twentieth-century Chile, agrees in many ways with this idea of women's activism and work as a sometimes unplanned, "crazy" quilt of many pieces.

Near the end of the novel, the protagonist, Alba, is released from a torture center run by the fascist Augusto Pinochet. She is dumped in a small square in the capital and taken in by a woman. A regular woman, one of the "stoical, practical women of our country," the kind of woman "who takes in other people's abandoned children, her own poor relatives, and anybody else who needs a mother, a sister, or an aunt; the kind of woman who's the pillar of many other lives." Alba says, "I told her that she had run an enormous risk rescuing me, and she smiled. It was then I understood that the days of Colonel Garcia and all those like him are numbered, because they have not been able to destroy the spirit of these women" (Allende 1993, 394–95).

As a young woman, this passage took my breath away. As a middle-aged woman trying to hold on in the face of pandemonium and still do the work of supporting and fighting for women and children, I hold on to it with hope.

Each of us. Me. My mom. Yesy. Hadley. Deborah and all the others working for women form a piece of a crazy quilt. A beautiful, messy, chaotic piece of art that connects us all with silken threads and offers hope for the future.

Elizabeth Gackstetter Nichols is a professor of Spanish and gender studies. Her research interests are pan-American beauty practices, cosplay, and popular culture. Nichols is the author of a variety of books, articles and chapters in this field and is currently working on a project with the working title *How Frida, Evita, and Carmen Miranda Used Beauty Work to Become Immortal*. She can be reached at enichols@drury.edu.

Notes

1. *Reno v. Flores*, 507 U.S. 292 (1993).
2. *Alvarez-Flores v. Garland*, No. 22-60021 (5th Cir. 2022).
3. For an overview of LOWV's stance, see League of Women Voters, n.d.
4. I use "Latinx" here carefully, aware that many Hispanics in the United States prefer the term "Hispanic" and that others object to the *x* at the end of the word. As a gender scholar, I prefer this term for its gender neutrality. I will, however, use a mix of these terms in this essay in recognition that there is not consensus on preferred terminology.

Works Cited

Allende, Isabel. 1993. *The House of the Spirits*. New York: Bantam.
League of Women Voters. n.d. "Immigration." Accessed December 7, 2023. https://www.lwv.org/other-issues/immigration.
Natarajan, Anusha, and Carolyne Im. 2022. "Key Facts about Hispanic Eligible Voters in 2022." Pew Research Center, October 12, 2022. https://www.pewresearch.org/short-reads/2022/10/12/key-facts-about-hispanic-eligible-voters-in-2022/.

Pandemonium

Debjani Chakravarty

Only your eyes were supposed to see these words
But now I want some sudden strangers
To see this
And lick their lips in lust, disgust, or discomfiture.

This is like stripping
Exhibiting secret skin
Blurred in smoke-filled air
And bits and pieces of hard, slippery, exclamations.

I know this body was yours
But it is mine too, so
Maybe I can wrap it, post-*Roe*, in a pandemoniac mesh
And a waterfall of scars waiting to start conversations.

You were at candlelight vigils for missing women, possibly murdered.
Where the quiet whispery rain extinguished everything
Touching your charcoal eyes and fevered brow
You thought that as an oppressed you couldn't be an oppressor.

I am walking around noisily on this ground covered
With fallen poems, bird-eaten prose, and dry leaves
Wondering how I missed the rainstorm
The red skies
And the revolution that broke this fence I've been
Sitting on.

Debjani Chakravarty is a sociologist and teaches gender studies to earn a living as she tries to make sense of how we got here. A queer feminist academic and artist, she has published some research, some poetry, and some art. She is socially awkward, introverted, and not on Twitter or whatever it's called these days. Debjani has lived and worked in Michigan and Arizona (as well as in some states in India most people in the U.S. are likely not familiar with) and she currently resides in the absolutely stunning and sometimes heartbreaking state of Utah. She can be reached at debjani.chakravarty@asu.edu or debjani.chakravarty@utah.edu.

Rorschach

Karen Morris

Gentlemen, grim Fathers,
Here we are together in the sickroom—
Lord Yama of the Underworld
(controlling the controls),
who but belly dancing Bodhisattvas
could grab him by his cherry-red horns?

Tell us of the hindrances. Which is worse—
Doubt (that fraud masquerading as a poet)?
Greed (villeinage to bullets and bombs)?
Anger (too many rounds, so little time)?
Or torpor (not the same as sloth? Don't bother)?

Could you imagine anything as serpentine
as your pliant daughters? Dancing
through the shopping malls? Leaving
there in body bags? Could you, Mothers,
your moody daughters? Sullen

little bitches. Could they become sick?
Of course—Stupidity's contagious.
Lusty monks in monks' cells mistaken
for sublime merely simulate daughters'
irrepressible desire. Together

in the sickroom, she dares not feign
describing the indescribable.

Karen Morris is the author of *Nothing Happened Last Night* (Finishing Line Press). She received The Gradiva Award for Poetry (NAAP, 2015) for her full-length collection *CAT-ACLYSM and Other Arrangements* (Three Stones Press). Her poems have appeared in numerous journals, including *Women's Quarterly Journal*, *New York Quarterly, Chiron Review, SWWIM Every Day, Writers Resist*, and *Paterson Literary Review*. She is a psychoanalyst in private practice in Montpelier and cofounder and lay transmitted teacher for Two Rivers Zen Community, an online practice community. She can be reached at klmplex108@gmail.com.

Disposable Subjects

Trung M. Nguyen

You woke up one morning and they already fired your therapist who was the only reason that kept you going through such rough time
You woke up the next day and your favorite professor said this would be his last term, that they told him to wrap him and his children up
like a plastic bag
and just leave.
You woke up another day and they said your entire program was going to be disbanded because of the pandemic and financial struggles
Yeah . . .
The pandemic and financial struggles
are the easiest low blow these institutions could use up to answer the public
to answer us
the students
Though we all know the presidents have been living in a mansion, on a fancy street, funded by the school,
The school? I think we meant *us*

Inspired by the school's pride philosophies of leading in social justice causes, you and the other injured comrades congregated
We talked, discussed, came up with a plan to meet with the school's dean
Tired and worn out, confused and scared
nine months deep into the pandemic
we dragged our faces to another Zoom call
The hashtag, the organizing emails, the rationales that we came up with
in the end
none of them worked
against the dean's only reasoning
Not enough student registrations
in other words

We don't make enough money
for the school
We clapped back: "But the program has always been this size for the past ten years, nothing new . . . "
She insisted: "It has been an on-going struggle, not because of the pandemic"
We resisted: "But you are also ending more than twenty other humanities and social change programs"
She deflected: "Those are some difficult decisions from *the P*"
The P
The P later became what we referred to as our common antagonist
knowing how much they earned while our professors were laid off left and right
My dear professor
I could not believe how much I learned from and put trust in a cis straight white male professor
but he did that!
He was kind, understanding, generous, eager to teach and learn
an unexpected feminist for sure
He said he would be fine because of his privileges, and that many marginalized others would suffer worse
but the U.S. institution destroyed his faith in the promises of academia

My favorite professor planned to leave teaching

Next to him, a hundred other professors and health service practitioners were furloughed
in the middle of the pandemic and lockdown
My friends lost access to psychiatric treatments
I lost access to mental health services
in the middle of the pandemic and lockdown
We were naïve to think our small grassroot campaign would touch them
We showed evidence of how such programs have reached hearts and minds
of teachers, learners, immigrants, low-income workers, refugees, activists, and scholars
here, there, and way over there, across the oceans
Not knowing all they care about is capitalistic materiality

A "consulting" firm was hired to chop all programs that do not earn the school enough money
But how do teachers artists immigrants low-income workers refugees earn as much as business media moguls or engineers?
Will colleges become a cashing machine that grinds the corporate path?
Our most recently glass-cliffed president could not answer

Pedagogy of the Oppressed, The Reorder of Things suddenly make so much sense
No solidarity across disciplines . . .
because the institution
who once prided itself in addressing social justice
decided to save its own P

Upset
Disappointed
Enraged
As a queer scholar from the Global South who put trust in the institution just to be discarded, uprooted, disheartened by administrative greed
I conjure June Jordan's *Poetry for the People* when she said poetry is a political act
of telling the truth
This too is my truth.
That we could not save our professors, our medical workers, our socially progressive program

Upset
Disappointed
Enraged
I wrote this poem . . .

Do you hear me?

We might be the last group graduating, but these won't be our last words to air your dirty laundry

Do you hear us?

If the pandemic does not kill us,
then here comes our roar.

Trung M. Nguyen is a poet and PhD student in women, gender, and sexuality studies at Oregon State University. As a transnational and interdisciplinary humanities scholar, artivist, and educator from the Global South, they center their research and practices on feminist queer and trans studies in the third world, particularly Southeast Asia. They can be reached at minhtrungnicolai@gmail.com.

Works Cited

Ferguson, Roderick A. 2012. *The Reorder of Things: The University and Its Pedagogies of Minority Difference*. Minneapolis: University of Minnesota Press.

Freire, Paulo. 1996. *Pedagogy of the Oppressed*. Revised ed. New York: Continuum.

Jordan, June. 1995. "Introduction." In *June Jordan's Poetry for the People: A Revolutionary Blueprint*, edited by Lauren Muller and The Blueprint Collective, 1–20. New York: Routledge.

On Pandemonium's Many Pressures

Jennifer Schneider

A student of indeterminate age enters a university classroom in a state of indeterminate confusion. The room is simultaneously empty and full. The setting is a blend of both stage and rage. Degree being both a goal and a descriptive term. Somewhere in the distance, a rooster crows. Whether the time is closer to dusk or dawn remains unknown. Rosters are stalled indefinitely. Faux-wooden chairs with metal legs stand still. Cool landings boil. Heat rises. Four rows of desks remain unoccupied. An unopened, fully deflated bag of ruffled potato chips (once *Wise*, now stale) rests on the front desk. The air unusually conspired. The clock on the wall ticks, then tocks. Shadows of students from semesters past track. Lines, both No. 2 pencil lead and Bic ballpoint ink, linger in small pockets of air between *Then* and *Now*. *Here* and *There*. Of ages when thought was celebrated and to think allowed. Forms of speech relative. Relatives only partly to blame. The printed word is no longer celebrated. The pursuit of knowledge no longer the same. A neon red sign that once read WELCOME ceases to blink. Is this a trick, the student asks, then scans the fine print on a flimsy sheet of 8.5" x 11" paper. Politics a stage. Cancel culture all the rage. *Dobbs* and Doll share more than initial consonants. Feminists and studies no longer converge. Conspiracies aside. Amidst conflicts, crises, and pressures, kaleidoscopes spiral. Discipline and disciplines denied. It's not a trick, others whisper. It's a war. Now? she asks. Yes. others say. Bodies dismantled. Rights deprived. Refusals to desist. Eyes linger, then focus on an emergency bell to the left of the bulletproof glass. Affronts on all corners. In and of texts on bookshelves and desks. Should I pull it, the girl asks the shadows that whisper and persist. No, it's a silent alarm. Inhale. Exhale. Breathe. Resist.

WSQ: Women's Studies Quarterly 52: 1 & 2 (Spring/Summer 2024) © 2024 by Jennifer Schneider. All rights reserved.

Queries quarrel as instigators claim denial. Questions toil then coil. Ready. Set. Go.

1. Define politics. Define pandemic. Define pandemonium. Which came first?
2. Can the price of (a) discipline be quantified?
3. Do disciplines have life spans? Are life spans designed or resigned?
4. Can wing spans (right) be measured in degrees of damage? Of freedoms left?
5. Does quantity have a quality? Does pressure have a flavor?
6. Do studies have scents? Are studies defined by cents?
7. Define sense. Define (s)cents. Which came first?
8. Describe discipline's primary form of speech.
9. If a discipline whispers in winds of empty halls, does anyone hear?
10. Define silence. Do silent alarms have voices?
11. If a book falls in (or into) an empty classroom, do its words echo?
12. Define enroll. Define enrollments. Which came first?
13. Define privatization. Define privilege. Can either be quantified in degrees of latitude or longitude?
14. When a discipline is under the weather, who holds or offers an umbrella?
15. In the first sentence of the shared passage, does confusion modify the student, the room, or both?

Jennifer Schneider is a community college educator who lives, works, and writes in small spaces throughout Pennsylvania. She served as the 2022 Montgomery County (PA) Poet Laureate. Her most recent collections, *14 (Plus) Reasons Why* (free lines press, 2023), *EVENINGS WALKS: A Collection of Recollections* (Ethel, 2023), and *Months, Moments, & Mileage in the Rearview Mirror: 2022*, (Alien Buddha Press, 2023), are now available. *On (Pantry) Stock & (Kitchen) Timers*, published by Querencia Press, is forthcoming. She can be reached at jschneider@ccp.edu.

Jennifer Pinck, *If You Know, You Know*, 2022. Oil on canvas.

Jennifer Pinck, *Sunset Trip*, 2020. Acrylic on panel.

SECTION VI. ALERTS & PROVOCATIONS

Disaster Capitalism Feeds Where Care Abandons: A Provocation on the Case of U.S. Higher Education after COVID

Tressie McMillan Cottom

The original intent for this provocation was to distill the forces of capitalism's interconnected pandemonia into a descriptive analysis of its fundamental crisis. That is, that our social institutions never intended to reckon with the profound cost of care, and we find ourselves with few mechanisms left to outsource social reproduction. The argument, as I imagined it, would be controlled and precise.

After I accepted the editors' invitation to join this special issue, it became clear that I did not account for the cost of my own care. My own body and mind exist in the thing I work to analyze. I forget. Or, I would rather not know sometimes. Unfortunately, the body not only keeps the score; it also controls the state of play. I survived the pandemic, its ensuing crises, political destabilization, and the quotidian changes of middle-class life only to be felled by one too many meetings. Sick, disoriented, and still working, I am performing as myself even as it is clear that I am not at all myself. The accretion of disasters that led to my dissociation mirrors the disaster capitalism that defines U.S. education, K–20. Controlled precision is too feeble for the pandemonium.

On an idyllic fall day, a graduate student (he would eventually be declared incompetent to stand trial) shot and murdered his graduate studies advisor in a campus building half a mile from my university office. As dozens of law enforcement performed outside our windows, colleagues and students shut themselves in classrooms, basements, and dorms. On television later, I watched students climb from the window of a second-floor classroom building, dropping five hundred feet to the ground to escape. Their movements are calm, unhurried, controlled. A journalist asks one of these students how they managed to keep their heads. She says that they have been doing shooter drills all of their lives. When America's addiction to semiautomatic guns consumed children in schools, we turned a clear-cut solution into an opportunity for disaster capitalism. No gun-control measures. Instead, we created an industry for school shooter drills, curricula, and paranoia. The guns still exist. The crisis is now a market. The market has matured with its victims. The local paper reports on a survey taken after the shooting. The majority of those surveyed want more protocols like those perfected on elementary school children to be implemented on our college campus. Pandemonium, when embodied, can make chaos look rational.

I work at a large public flagship with enviable rankings. Conservative interests have marked such institutions for political takeover. In 2023 the board of trustees that oversees the state's public colleges appointed two Republican political consultants. The board thinks the chancellor is too liberal, the faculty too empowered, and the students too amenable to liberal indoctrination. The board creates a new school for conservative thought on campus. They override faculty governance on a tenure case. They end state-funded endowed professorships for non-STEM faculty. The chancellor leaves. An interim chancellor has no academic experience. It is the same political strategy that remade public higher education in Wisconsin. The same political strategy is being refined in Florida. The same political strategy is being retrofitted for state systems across the country. Pandemonium is pathogenic.

A second live shooter event shuts down the campus a mere two weeks after the shooting that killed a professor. No one dies. Somehow, this lockdown is more traumatic. I was in a faculty lounge for an hour, maybe two. When the all-clear was issued, I walked toward my department building. Colleagues were pouring from where they had locked down. After the first live shooting event of the semester, we had anxiously checked on each other: "How are your kids?" "Is everyone okay?" What will you do now?" This time, our gazes slid by one another. Shoulders tried to shrug but seemed unable to commit. Half-shrugging, eyes averted just shy of each other's faces, we mostly sighed and said, "Well."

Well. It is the one thing no one seemed to be. It is the thing that no one is supposed to be during a strategic breakdown. That is what we have been experiencing and are still experiencing in higher education and our major social institutions. Pandemonium is the absence of *well*.

Things are decidedly unwell. I recently read an essay about why one-time leftists become conservative reactionaries. The essay argues that it is more important to understand how these ideological turncoats come to be than it is to understand why they choose to abandon their beliefs. Kathryn Joyce and Jeff Sharlet describe our sociopolitical moment as the "current clusterfuck of crises so vast and interconnected that they might more simply be called our condition—such portals, from one reality to another, are plentiful" (2023). I wonder if they intentionally use portals to link our moment to its clarifying flashpoint—the COVID-19 pandemic. The metaphor calls to mind an essay by Arundhati Roy in which she likens the COVID-19 global pandemic to a portal—a threshold between one world and a world that could be remade by our responses to the pandemic's many inequities (Roy 2020). Written in April 2020, the essay does not benefit from our current hindsight. We know that we did not step through that portal into a new world. Instead, we did what Saidiya Hartman gestured toward in her notes on the pandemic, also written in 2020. We built a sieve whose "apportionment of risk and the burden of exposure maintains a fidelity to the given distributions of value" (Hartman 2020).

That sieve distributes well-prepared, ambitious students to my traditional university every year, as it has done for over two hundred years. We have kept moving after COVID, as we did during COVID. Our leadership steadfastly maintained a commitment to "normalcy" for the large, open campus as other universities shut down during the height of the pandemic. A moderate chancellor. A conservative board of trustees. A politically volatile climate. A community tarred as liberal. Anxious parents trained to manage their children's academic careers as investment portfolios, afraid of falling behind in status competition. Bond ratings of planned campus building projects. Financial budgets based on enrollment projections, year-over-year. Every college campus in the U.S. filtered its COVID response through the prism of its cumulative vulnerability to decades of rolling crises that had little to do with public health.

So it is this academic semester. So it will be every semester for the foreseeable future as every event is linked to the preceding event that positions an institution for extraction. The extraction will look different based on a variety of factors. But every institution is being sized up by investors, venture capital, donors, and politicians for parts. Crisis becomes a way to stress-test an institution. My academic semester unfolded along a timeline marked by tragedy, planned destruction, and political destabilization. It is remarkable because it is not exceptional in U.S. higher education. Each institutional event is linked to a cumulative crisis. COVID-19 was a biological event. It did not have to become a destabilizing geopolitical crisis. However, the shock doctrine is the market's ontological imperative in this timeline. Using the means perfected on the world's dispossessed, privatizing interests are exploiting disaster for financial and political gain.

COVID-19 could have been a portal, a ledge, a lens, a hole, a detour—any number of metaphors for change. It became an *accelerant*. That is not necessarily about the biological event. That is about the shock doctrine that turned the event into a crisis. Disaster capitalism is a link between the long half-century of neoliberalism's slow hollowing out of public higher education in particular and the political eradication of higher education's social responsibility more generally. You can see it in any number of political events. We like to focus on Florida. There is good reason. Governor Ron DeSantis made anti-intellectualism a political brand. He did not just issue bills that attack tenure, ban diversity, and make it harder for faculty unions to organize in the state. His administration successfully passed those bills. Florida is showy, but it is not a political outlier. As of July 2023, the *Chronicle of Higher Education* reports that Republican lawmakers have proposed forty-nine "anti-diversity" bills across twenty-two states. Only seven have become law so far (another twenty-nine have been stopped), but that has not stopped well-funded conservative groups from declaring victory. Conservative advocates learned from *Roe v. Wade* that every incremental victory is a path toward their legislative goals.

You can also feel how the pandemic shifted disaster capitalism into overdrive. One example is the experience of institutional time. During the pandemic's most intense shutdown period, time slowed down for many (and fatally stopped for millions of others). On campuses, time was transmuted first by one's work role and then by technology. If your work role afforded you the choice to work remotely during pandemic shutdowns, time became a sliding thing. It shifted between other social roles. Those roles were shaped by gender, race, sexuality, class, nationality, ability, and other identities. If your work role made you "essential," your time was turned into fuel for the skeleton institution. Workers maintained the institutional infrastructure—buildings, pipes, computers, toilets, parking lots—so the university could act as a fiduciary. Then, the liminal space of "online classes" introduced a new pandemic time. Mediated by screens, surveilled, and subsumed not to educational goals but to management indices—this time showed what was possible for a university where the chief information officer had more authority over institutional time than the faculty council. When the economy declared the pandemic over, many of us returned to campus. We may have found that institutional life now moves at the speed of disaster capitalism—fast, chaotic, and seemingly out of our control.

People living through archetypal shock doctrine events frequently talk about losing control. Sometimes, it is losing control of their neighborhood schools, their community, their cemeteries, or their "home." Other times, people describe losing control of their body or spirit. Losing their mind. It is an unappreciated aspect of authoritarianism, the impact on one's experience of temporality. And that is what we are experiencing. Authoritarianism is always there, even in liberal democracies. This moment is about how technology turned that authoritarianism into a disaster-seeking machine with computational efficiency.

With COVID's political pact with autocratic ideologues, those powerful technologies are divorced from even the veneer of democratic responsibility. Freed from social responsibility and politically charged with authoritarianism's global resurgence, a techno-financial strain of disaster capitalism is aimed at weakened institutions. Those institutions are bloated with administrative distractions. Faculty and students are also entangled in the surveillance systems of everyday life. There is admirable organizing happening within and around these sites of destruction. I confess that they seem to be moving at a different meter of time than the clock controlled by technological meters that now run the internal mechanisms of capitalism.

That clock is part of why I was ill. When my eye twitch went on for over a week, I finally saw a doctor. Part of my recovery includes new eyeglasses, bifocals. I tested them out by attending a "film school" event affiliated with a local nonprofit. The organization's mission is to provide humanistic higher education that does not prey on people. It first met online, and now it has a physical location, a bar. The classes are short—once a week, three or four weeks long—and they have a pay-what-you-can model. No one will use these classes to get a certificate or a micro-credential or a degree. The instructors have advanced degrees from very elite universities.

This night, we are learning how to watch documentaries. The projector is acting up. Someone shouts for the instructor to take her time. At that moment, I remember that their clocks were not run by pandemonium, controlled by shock, owned by disaster, ticking for extraction.

I do not pretend this program is a solution for societal disaster. It is small. The founders constantly hustle for donations. It is a fragile thing in a privileged bubble. There is still a case making its way to the Supreme Court that would challenge federal financial aid at private universities, and students are being expelled for peacefully protesting genocide at Columbia University. Still, I am reminded that care, community, and learning can happen in all kinds of institutions. Where care is made incidental to institutional well-being, disaster finds a vacuum.

Tressie McMillan Cottom is an associate professor at UNC–Chapel Hill and principal investigator with the Center for Information, Technology, and Public Life. She can be reached at tressie@email.unc.edu.

Works Cited

Hartman, Saidiya. 2020. "The Death Toll." *Los Angeles Review of Books*, April 14, 2020. https://lareviewofbooks.org/article/quarantine-files-thinkers-self-isolation/.

Joyce, Kathryn, and Jeff Sharlet. 2023. "Losing the Plot: The 'Leftists' Who Turn Right." *In These Times*, December 12, 2023. https://inthesetimes.com/article/former-left-right-fascism-capitalism-horseshoe-theory.

Roy, Arundhati. 2020. "The Pandemic Is a Portal." *Financial Times*, April 3, 2020. https://www.ft.com/content/10d8f5e8-74eb-11ea-95fe-fcd274e920ca.